ALSO BY HOLLY GEORGE-WARREN

A Man Called Destruction: The Life and Music of Alex Chilton

Public Cowboy #1: The Life and Times of Gene Autry

The Road to Woodstock (with Michael Lang)

Grateful Dead 365

Punk 365

The Cowgirl Way: Hats Off to America's Women of the West

Cowboy: How Hollywood Invented the Wild West

It's Not Only Rock 'n' Roll (with Jenny Boyd)

John Varvatos: Rock in Fashion (with John Varvatos)

How the West Was Worn:
A History of Western Wear (with Michelle Freedman)

Honky-Tonk Heroes and Hillbilly Angels:
The Pioneers of Country & Western Music

Shake, Rattle & Roll: The Founders of Rock & Roll

The Rolling Stone Book of the Beats (editor)

The Rock & Roll Hall of Fame: The First 25 Years (editor)

Bonnaroo: What, Which, This, That, the Other (editor)

The Rolling Stone Illustrated History of Rock & Roll (coeditor)

Martin Scorsese Presents the Blues: A Musical Journey (coeditor)

The Rolling Stone Encyclopedia of Rock & Roll (coeditor)

Farm Aid: A Song for America (coeditor)

The Rolling Stone Album Guide (coeditor)

Holly Ge[...] [...]nee and the
award-wi[...] [...] York Times
bestseller *The Road to Woodstock* (with Michael Lang) and two biographies,
A Man Called Destruction: The Life and Music of Alex Chilton and *Public
Cowboy No. 1: The Life and Times of Gene Autry*. She has written for numerous
pu[...] [...]tions, including the *New York Times*, *Rolling Stone* and *Entertainment
We[...] [...]*. George-Warren serves on the nominating committee of the Rock
& [...]oll Hall of Fame and teaches at the State University of New York at
N[...]w Paltz. She lives in upstate New York with her husband and son.

Praise for *Janis*

'I'[...] been waiting for the right person to write the definitive biography of
Janis Joplin! All fans should be grateful it's finally here.'
Rosanne Cash, four-time Grammy Award winner

'[...]y far and away the most comprehensive and best-researched Joplin
b[...]graphy. It's an extraordinary life, set to a legendary rock death arc,
[...]ut the triumph of *Janis* is that George-Warren understands that the
evolution of Joplin's artistry is what matters most. Janis blossoms as she
fi[...]ds her voice onstage, and her act becomes something of great beauty.
S[...], too, does George-Warren's book.' **Charles R. Cross, *New York Times*
[...]estselling author of *Room Full of Mirrors: A Biography of Jimi Hendrix***

'A rich, interesting portrayal of Janis. George-Warren has an engaging
[...]riting style, and I was impressed by the breadth of her new interviews
and information.' **Laura Joplin, sister of Janis Joplin**

'Joplin fans, rejoice! Holly George-Warren's biography is a triumph of
p[...]ssionate scholarship, thus making me love Janis – with all her baffling
an[...] brilliant complexity – even more.' **David Ritz, author of *Respect: The
Life of Aretha Franklin***

'[...] athetic and thrilling. Like an investigative reporter, George-Warren
[...] tracked down every detail of Janis's young life and influences, and,
with loving care, she has given us rare insight into this genius musician.'
Kate Pierson, The B-52s

JANIS

HER LIFE AND MUSIC

HOLLY GEORGE-WARREN

**SIMON &
SCHUSTER**

London · New York · Sydney · Toronto · New Delhi

First published in the United States by Simon & Schuster, Inc., 2019
First published in Great Britain by Simon & Schuster UK Ltd, 2019
This edition published in Great Britain by Simon & Schuster UK Ltd, 2020

1 3 5 7 9 10 8 6 4 2

Simon & Schuster UK Ltd
1st Floor
222 Gray's Inn Road
London WC1X 8HB

www.simonandschuster.co.uk
www.simonandschuster.com.au
www.simonandschuster.co.in

Simon & Schuster Australia, Sydney
Simon & Schuster India, New Delhi

A CIP catalogue record for this book is available from the British Library

Paperback ISBN: 978-1-4711-4094-5
eBook ISBN: 978-1-4711-4095-2

Interior design by Paul Dippolito

Printed in the UK by CPI Group (UK) Ltd, Croydon, CR0 4YY

For Robert Burke Warren, my soul mate,
and Jack Warren, my inspiration

CONTENTS

INTRODUCTION

Don't compromise yourself. It's all you've got.
—JANIS JOPLIN

It's a steamy September night in Nashville, and Ruby Boots is tearing it up onstage at the Basement East, thrashing her electric guitar and belting Janis Joplin's "Piece of My Heart." The 2018 edition of the six-day Americanafest, an annual music conference and festival, is honoring albums from 1968, and Big Brother and the Holding Company's breakthrough, *Cheap Thrills*, has made the cut. Boots, born Bex Chilcott in Perth, Australia, fell in love with Janis's music as a kid growing up on the other side of the world, the irresistible, aching soul in Janis's voice undiminished by time, distance, and even mortality. As when Janis herself unleashed this tune fifty years ago, the crowd—wired into its raw but fearless humanity—pushes toward the stage.

At the Americana Honors & Music Awards Show held at the Ryman Auditorium (former home of the Grand Ole Opry), numerous Janis acolytes take the stage: singer-songwriter-activist Rosanne Cash, a Janis fan since her teens, wins the Free Speech in Music Award; Alberta, Canada, native k. d. lang, who went public as a lesbian in the 1980s, gets the Trailblazer Award. Formidable singers Brandi Carlile, Margo Price, and Courtney Marie Andrews—all nominees for various honors—signal Janis's influence in their blazing performances.

Prior to Janis Joplin's all too brief time in the spotlight, these artists would have been hard pressed to find a female role model to compare with the beatnik from Port Arthur, Texas. The mix of confident musicianship, brash sexuality, and natural exuberance, locked together to produce America's first female rock star, changed everything. As such, Janis still holds sway over multiple generations, artists of countless genres, across the gender spectrum. And although her bookishness, sharp intellect, and deep desire for home with the requisite white picket fence were not at the forefront of the identity she crafted for her fans, those parts of her also informed her every move.

The same could be said of her pioneering instincts. While Janis's era is largely considered a time of release from the strictures of the 1950s, rock was, in fact, almost exclusively a boys' club, and Janis suffered appalling sexism, from both the mainstream and counterculture press, and cold, occasionally cruel dismissiveness from industry pros. Yet she blazed on. Through force of will and unprecedented talent, she showed how rock could include unapologetic women musicians, writers, and fans. Feminist Ellen Willis, a *New Yorker* music critic in the 1960s, called Janis "the only sixties culture hero to make visible and public women's experience of the quest for individual liberation." Patti Smith, Blondie's Debbie Harry, Cyndi Lauper, Chrissie Hynde, the B-52's' Kate Pierson, and Heart's Ann and Nancy Wilson are among the artists who experienced Janis firsthand. They began to breathe in the possibility of their own futures. When Stevie Nicks was inducted into the Rock & Roll Hall of Fame in March 2019, she said that playing on a bill with Janis in the 1960s transformed her: "Her connection with the audience was so incredible that I said, 'I want to do what she did.'"

Through her influence and her own enduring work, Janis Joplin remains at the core of our music and culture. As we look back at pivotal moments in 1960s rock history, she is usually there: the Monterey Pop Festival; the vibrant Haight-Ashbury scene in San Francisco; the streets, clubs, and studios of gritty New York City; Woodstock. She's been feted at museum exhibitions and the subject of theater productions and films. Her first solo album, the eclectic, daring departure *I Got Dem Ol' Kozmic Blues Again Mama!*, sounds as fresh today as upon its 1969 release. Her Monterey Pop performance, documented by filmmaker D. A. Pennebaker, still brings wild applause from a new generation of audiences at screenings, and with YouTube views in the millions and counting.

When Janis hit the Monterey stage in June 1967, few outside San Francisco knew her name. "What is this girl all about?" Monterey co-producer Lou Adler wondered. "Where did she come from, looking like that and leading this all-male band?" Offering a clue, Haight-Ashbury impresario Chet Helms introduced her onstage: "Three or four years ago, on one of my perennial hitchhikes across the country, I ran into a chick from Texas by the name of Janis Joplin," he told the unsuspecting crowd. "I heard her sing, and Janis and I hitchhiked to the West Coast. A lot of things have gone down since, but it gives me a lot of pride today to present the finished product: *Big Brother and the Holding Company!*"

Janis's astonishing performance that day would change her life—and the future of popular music. By the time the five-song set ended with her dramatic reinvention of R&B/blues singer Willie Mae Thornton's "Ball and Chain," thousands of mind-blown fans—and hundreds of dazzled journalists—knew her name and fervently spread the news. Her emotion-drenched vocal style took hold upon other developing singers; Led Zeppelin's Robert Plant among them. Young women who saw her onstage at the Avalon Ballroom or Bill Graham's Fillmore venues still recall the experience: It was like she was singing to or for them, telling their stories, feeling their pain, emboldening them, and absolving them of shame. Janis was a walking live nerve capable of surfacing feelings that most people couldn't or wouldn't, and she was willing to endure the toll it took on her.

Janis never compromised her vision. She wasn't afraid to cross boundaries—musical, cultural, and sexual. Openly bisexual in an era when it was illegal, she was not afraid of jail, of judgment. Similarly, when critics and fans expressed umbrage at her audacity to quit her role as "chick singer" in a band that she felt was holding her back, she did it anyway. Just four days before her death on October 4, 1970, she told journalist Howard Smith, "You are only as much as you settle for."

Janis Joplin never settled. The oldest child of a close-knit family, she adored her father, a Bach-loving secret intellectual and a closet atheist in a conservative oil town. Preteen Janis was a rambunctious tomboy who was also cerebral, curious, and a gifted visual artist, which her parents encouraged. When she reached high school, the 1950s were in full swing, and her embrace of the Beat Generation and of progressive racial views alienated her from her community. Janis's first transgressive act was to be a white girl who gained an early sense of the power of the blues, chasing the music in Gulf Coast saloons and on obscure records. She never fully recovered from the intense scorn of her peers, who also ridiculed her appearance, especially after she patterned herself on beatnik girls she'd seen in *Life* magazine.

Seth and Dorothy Joplin doted on their eldest child in many ways but were ultimately put off by her increasing acts of defiance—the same impulses that would eventually bring her fame. Always an attention-hungry rebel, Janis upped her game in adolescence, spurred on by her budding sexuality, her discovery of rock & roll, and alcohol and speed. The wounds inflicted from the clash of wills during those turbulent years in the Joplin home never healed. Much of her life would be colored by the tension of wanting to belong and getting the attention she missed, while knowing that the best way to honor her family's unspoken creed of singularity was to set herself apart. Discovering her outsize voice helped her find a place to fit in and create a new family—of bohemians and musicians, first, in Port Arthur and Beaumont, Texas, and then Austin, and finally San Francisco. She embraced life with a joyous ferocity, though she could never escape a fundamental darkness created by loneliness and a bleak fatalism bequeathed by her father. Choosing alcohol and drugs as painkillers just made everything worse.

A passionate, erudite musician, Janis was born with talent but also worked hard to develop it, though she would often omit this striving toward excellence from her origin story. When you hear outtakes of her in the studio recording what would be her final album, *Pearl*, she's taking the reins, running the show. During a period when women did not produce their own music, she collaborated fully with her notoriously iron-fisted producer, Paul Rothchild. These sessions were a time of artistic blossoming for Janis. Her ideas—along with her extraordinary voice and her simpatico Full Tilt Boogie band—resulted in a masterpiece. After Janis's accidental heroin overdose in 1970 at the age of twenty-seven, the posthumously released *Pearl* would become her most successful and enduring album, with its single "Me and Bobby McGee" the endpiece to a career that started with "Piece of My Heart."

Janis Joplin's distinctive voice sounds as powerful today as it did when introduced on the airwaves in 1967. More so than any of her peers, it cuts through the digital din, the noise of our age, and lands exactly where Janis wanted: deep inside the heart. Since her time, her work and life have inspired so many women to create their own sounds and walk their own uncompromising paths: from Lucinda Williams to Pink, Amy Winehouse to Carolyn Wonderland, Lady Gaga to Brittany Howard, Alicia Keys to Florence Welch, Grace Potter to Elle King, Melissa Etheridge to Kesha. Williams has written a song about her ("Port Arthur"); Pink hoped to play her in a film; Wonderland does a killer version of a 1962 Janis original ("What Good Can Drinkin' Do"); Etheridge helped induct her into the Rock & Roll Hall of Fame in 1995. That night, Etheridge said, "When a soul can look on the world, and see and feel the pain and loneliness, and can reach deep down inside, and find a voice to sing of it, a soul can heal."

Perhaps that remains Janis's greatest gift.

CHAPTER 1

PIONEER STOCK

Don't write what you are doing;
write what you are thinking.

—SETH JOPLIN

Janis Joplin came from a long line of risk takers: seventeenth- and eighteen-century pilgrims, pioneers, preachers, Revolutionary War and Civil War soldiers, sodbusters, cowboys, ranchers, and farmers. Both her father's and mother's families date back to America's early arrivals from England, Scotland, and Sweden, landing in New England and Virginia. Branches of the family survived shipwrecks, kidnapping by Indians in the French and Indian War, and wagon treks across the continent.

"I'm from pioneer stock," Janis would boast to friends who worried about her drinking and drug taking. Perhaps she was thinking of the ancestral great-grandmother whom Janis's sister, Laura, would later describe in her memoir, *Love, Janis*: "a tough pioneer woman, stout of body and strong of heart, whose inner convictions and faith in her husband carried her across the frontier." If Janis looked deeper, she also might have traced her ambition and restless spirit to her forebears.

Her parents met on a blind date. In December 1932, in the midst of the Great Depression, nineteen-year-old college student Dorothy East went out with engineering school dropout Seth Joplin, twenty-two, in their hometown of Amarillo, Texas. Like their hardscrabble ancestors, Dorothy and Seth would stake out unchartered territory: the American middle class, where they hoped to earn a living with their minds rather than their hands, and safely pass on their upwardly mobile aspirations to their children, though in markedly different ways.

Dorothy East, the eldest of four, grew up in the trauma of her parents' troubled marriage, a fraught union begun in tiny Clay Center, on the Nebraska plains. Settling as ranchers in the newly minted state of Oklahoma, Cecil and Laura Hanson East gave birth to Dorothy Bonita on February 13, 1913. But missing her large farming family back in Nebraska, Laura insisted they return to Clay Center, where Cecil started a hog farm in 1920. Disease wiped out his stock and the Easts went bankrupt and moved in with the Hansons, where Laura reimmersed herself in their fundamentalist Christianity. Cecil struck out alone for West Texas boomtown Amarillo and became a real estate agent, a heavy drinker, and a philanderer. The Easts reunited in Amarillo when Dorothy was a high school senior, but the marriage was broken.

Decades later, Dorothy remained haunted by her parents' "horrible verbal abuse" and violent arguments, her enraged mother sometimes attempting to hitchhike back to Nebraska—without Dorothy or her younger siblings, Gerald, Barbara, and Mildred. While Dorothy tended the children, Cecil would drive out, retrieve his wife, and bring her home. Word spread around Amarillo about their marital problems and Cecil's carousing, which shamed Dorothy, who vowed to have a congenial marriage and never invite small-town gossip.

One refuge she sought was music. Dorothy started singing in church as a child, and by all accounts, she had a beautiful voice. In Amarillo, she joined her school's Lyric Club and participated in light-opera musicales. The *Amarillo Globe-News* singled her out in a review of the operetta *Once in a Blue Moon*: "Dorothy East, as the Moon Lady, was worthy of the praise bestowed upon her from all sides during and following her parts. Her aplomb was excellent and outstanding." Dorothy sang at weddings, Lions Club events, and in local musical productions. "I always had the lead," she told her children later. "My lungs were so good and my pitch so true. In that great big auditorium, [I] could hit high notes and low notes [that would reach] the last row. But it didn't affect my ego any. I didn't think I was the best in town or anything." Still, she harbored the desire to sing professionally. Her father encouraged Dorothy's musical pursuits, while her mother, who'd lost most of her hearing during a childhood illness, did not.

After one Lions Club performance in 1931, the local paper noted that "judging from the applause, she was a regular sensation," with Dorothy "being heralded as a second Marion Talley"—the teenage coloratura soprano plucked from Kansas City, Missouri, to join the New York Metropolitan Opera. Eventually "a New York production man," Dorothy recounted, "got me aside and said, 'If you want to go to New York, I can get you in a show with no trouble at all.'" But Laura East discouraged her daughter, advising her, according to Dorothy, to go to "business college because you can learn some skills . . . you need to earn a living." The talent scout admitted that show business was tough and not "your kind of people."

The New York idea tapped into Dorothy's fears of continuing the chaotic cycle of her parents' lives: It would be an itinerant and insecure life, possibly even bringing disrepute. Dorothy wanted more control than that. Using her vocal talent in a traditionally responsible way, she applied for and won a music scholarship to Texas Christian University, as recommended by her pastor.

She was home for Christmas vacation freshman year when she met Seth, the son of Seeb Joplin, a stockyard manager and former cowboy and sheriff who had grown up on a West Texas ranch, the eldest of eleven children. Seeb's grandfather Benjamin Jopling helped build the US Cavalry's original Fort Worth, one of the outposts constructed after the Mexican-American War. Seth's mother, Florence Porter Joplin, ran a boardinghouse on the outskirts of Amarillo. A native Texan like her husband, Seeb, Florence was the youngest daughter of thirteen children whose father, Robert Porter, had been a purchasing agent for the Confederacy. Seeb and Florence's first child was a daughter, Margaret, followed by Seth Ward Joplin, born on May 19, 1910. Margaret attended boarding school, while Seth lived alone in a one-room cabin behind the boardinghouse, away from the roughneck lodgers. A solitary boy, he lived a spare existence, immersing himself in books. He enrolled at Texas A&M College for two years and then transferred to the University of Alabama to study mechanical engineering. With little money and no help from his father, who'd quit school at thirteen, Seth dropped out a few credits shy of graduating and returned to Amarillo. When Dorothy met him, he was living with his parents at the boardinghouse and pumping gas at a service station.

Seth and Dorothy made an arresting couple: he, a handsome young man with thoughtful, deep-set blue eyes; she, an attractive, vivacious, green-eyed college girl. Yet, at the same time, they were opposites: he, a brooding introvert and would-be intellectual who preferred quiet evenings discussing literature and philosophy; she, an outgoing "flapper" who loved playing piano, singing, and dancing all night. Dorothy was devoted to her mother's Christian beliefs; Seth was an avowed atheist. In good times, one could say they complemented each other; in bad, they were, perhaps, destined for discord. They had in common a passion for music, a desire for a better life, a fierce willfulness, and stoicism. They would give all these qualities, except the stoicism, to their daughter.

When Dorothy returned to college, the sweethearts corresponded. In the intimacy of letters, Seth, in a move uncommon for a man of that time and place, expressed a desire to know his girlfriend's inner self. Dorothy recalled with some surprise: "He once wrote me, 'Don't write what you are doing; write what you are thinking.' It took me rather aback because any previous correspondence I had was to parents, who certainly *did* want to know what I was doing." This inquisitiveness about the life of the mind, as well as a talent for expression through correspondence and the written language, would also surface in their eldest child.

After her summer break in 1933, Dorothy opted not to return to school. Perhaps still hoping to become a performer, she helped out at Amarillo radio station KGNC, but she was soon fired for inadvertently cursing into a hot mike: *"I can't figure the damn thing out."* She prospered, however, at a Montgomery Ward store, where her knack for business led to a promotion from temporary summer help to head of the credit department. Well groomed and always fashion conscious, despite limited funds, she designed and sewed her own eye-catching dresses and accessorized her dark bobbed hair with jaunty hats. She poured her creativity into dressmaking, a pastime and talent she'd pursue throughout her life.

Though Seth didn't prefer nights out dancing, he did enjoy alcohol and occasionally smoking cannabis, legal in Texas until 1937. During Prohibition, he taught himself how to make beer and bathtub gin, which he sometimes shared with Dorothy's father, Cecil, to his teetotaling wife Laura's chagrin. As for Dorothy's vices, she took up smoking at a time when cigarettes were marketed to women in advertisements as "torches of freedom."

In 1935 Amarillo, amid the Dust Bowl in the northwestern plains of the Texas Panhandle, had about a 25 percent unemployment rate. A college friend advised Seth that the Texas Company (later renamed Texaco) was hiring in Port Arthur, in the southeast corner of the state. The subtropical city on the Gulf Coast had the world's largest oil refinery network, a sprawling complex crowded with smokestacks spewing fiery chemical plumes into the air. This thriving industry made the Great Depression seem nonexistent. So Seth packed his few belongings and drove nearly seven hundred miles to Port Arthur, where he hated the humidity, mosquitos, and refinery exhaust. But the friend who recommended him had been correct: the growing city and its largest employer, the Texas Company, offered a man like Seth the chance to earn a decent living *and* work indoors. He would, indeed, *do better* than his parents had. Impressed with his intellect and engineering skills, the Texas Company hired Seth as a manager overseeing the construction of metal containers used for shipping petroleum around the world. There is no suggestion that Seth particularly enjoyed or found great satisfaction in his work, yet he certainly did appreciate the security of a management position for a man of his background. And he gained a sense of importance, especially during World War II, when he would receive three draft deferments on account of his expertise at America's sole manufacturer of oil shipping containers. He would work at Texaco for the next forty years.

>–•◦•–<

"Port Arthur is 100 percent oil" is how a 1932 geology book described one of the three towns comprising the Golden Triangle: a man-made canal linked Port Arthur to Beaumont (surrounded by oil fields) and Orange (home to Consolidated Steel). On January 10, 1901, Texas oil was first discovered at Spindletop, four miles south of Beaumont and fifteen miles north of Port Arthur. The legendary oil well "began with a roar, shaking the ground under the derrick, spewing first mud, then rocks, then six tons of four-inch pipe out of the ground, hurling it into the air like soda straws," according to Texas historian Lonn Taylor. "Then a 150-foot plume of oil erupted, and it spouted 100,000 barrels a day for nine days before drillers could cap it. Spindletop marked the beginning of the modern petroleum industry. Texas—and the world—would never be the same."

Port Arthur's origins actually predated the discovery of oil. Five years earlier, it was founded and named by self-made railroad tycoon and visionary Arthur Stilwell, who built the city along his newly constructed rail line that originated in Kansas City. Ninety miles east of Houston and twenty miles from Louisiana, Port Arthur was situated on the shore of Lake Sabine. The eccentric Stilwell wrote later that his "hunches" for choosing the town's location came from mystical "brownies," or "spirit counselors," who whispered to him in his sleep. In 1898 Stilwell financed the arduous completion of the seven-mile canal, modeled on Egypt's Suez Canal, connecting Port Arthur to the Gulf of Mexico. He built a grain elevator and a port, with a British ship transporting to Europe the produce that had traveled by train from the Midwest.

But the next year, Stilwell's Kansas City, Pittsburg and Gulf Railroad Company went bankrupt, and Port Arthur's development fell to John W. Gates, a shrewd Gilded Age entrepreneur who originally helped finance Stilwell, only to then oust him from their partnership. A barbed-wire magnate later bought out by U.S. Steel, Gates's nickname was "Bet-a-

Million"—the result of a prodigious gambling habit. Among the bets that paid off were his financing numerous oil wells near Spindletop, his founding the Texas Company, and his purchasing the Port Arthur Canal and Dock Company. He built a major refinery and public buildings, including St. Mary Hospital and Port Arthur College. Gates remained the town's primary benefactor until his death in 1911.

When Seth arrived nearly twenty-five years later, Port Arthur was bustling with oil refineries, chemical plants, and shipyards, its canal and port busily shipping petroleum. The population had increased to fifty-one thousand, with an influx of refinery workers from across the state and Louisiana, including French-speaking Acadians, or Cajuns, as well as African Americans and Latinos. From 1930 to 1935, East Texas oilfields "had created the state's great family fortunes," Bryan Burrough reported in his history of Texas oil, *The Big Rich*. At the time that Seth became an employee, the Texas Company ("the most brash and aggressive of the companies") had "refocused its operations, deemphasizing exploration in favor of refining and marketing."

Soon after signing on, Seth sent for Dorothy, who quickly found a job, at Port Arthur's Sears-Roebuck in the credit department. The young couple's goal of settling down, raising a family, and rising to the middle class was under way. On October 20, 1936, Seth, twenty-six, and Dorothy, twenty-three, married, with no relatives making the journey east to attend. On nights out, the newlyweds partied at the boisterous roadhouses that dotted Highway 90, across the Sabine River, in Vinton, Louisiana. Years later Dorothy recalled dancing on tabletops at the same clubs where her teenage daughter would herself raise hell.

The Joplins spent the first seven years of their marriage industriously saving money for the future. One June day, six months after the Japanese surprise attack on Pearl Harbor catapulted the United States into World War II, Seth came home from work and told his wife, "Let's do something for posterity," according to Dorothy. Thirty-seven weeks later, Janis Lyn Joplin was born at nine thirty in the morning on January 19, 1943, at St. Mary Hospital. Twenty-one days early, she was eighteen inches long and weighed only five pounds, six ounces, but was healthy.

After her birth, which he didn't attend, the businesslike Seth, thirty-two, personally typed his twenty-nine-year-old wife a wry memorandum: "I wish to tender my congratulations on the anniversary of your successful completion of your production quota for the nine months ending January 19, 1943. I realize that you passed through a period of inflation such as you had never before known—yet, in spite of this, you met your goal by your supreme effort during the early hours of January 19, a good three weeks ahead of schedule."

The new parents cherished their baby, whose every milestone was documented by Seth's camera. Janis would be the center of their world—a spotlight that she'd always crave—for the next six years, until their second child came along. Seth, though by nature a shy man with a dark outlook on life, would treat his firstborn like the son he'd hoped for. Dorothy, who wanted for her daughter the perfect, respectable life she'd never enjoyed as a girl, devoted herself to full-time mothering. She planned to bestow on her child every opportunity to make her a success. And baby Janis's easygoing temperament helped inspire the new parents with a faith that they would succeed.

"She never was cranky or cross or troublesome," Dorothy recounted. Janis began crawling at six months and standing when less than a year old. Her blue eyes would light up when her father came home from work; as a toddler, she began a ritual of meeting him at the front door. After dinner, Seth settled into his easy chair to read a book and listen to Bach and Beethoven, his eyes sometimes welling up from the beauty of it all. He was very different from most Port Arthur dads.

Janis considered her father "a secret intellectual," she said later, describing him as "a book reader, a talker, a thinker. He was very important to me, because he made me think. He's the reason I am like I am." Her independent streak certainly came from Seth, but although she'd rarely admit it, Janis was equally her mother's daughter, absorbing Dorothy's fascination with fashion, her intense desire for control, and, of course, a powerful singing voice that offered a way out of a staid, restrictive life. Although Dorothy had turned that down, Janis would not.

About four years earlier, in 1939, the Joplins had taken a major step toward their goal of a middle-class life. They left their rental downtown on Sixth Street for their first home: a larger, two-bedroom brick house at 4048 Procter (Port Arthur's main street), with enough room for Dorothy's mother and her youngest sister, Mildred, to live with them. The Easts had finally divorced, with Cecil relocating to Kansas City and cutting off communication with his children. "If I'd had a choice about which parent I kept in touch with, it would have been him," Dorothy said later of her freewheeling father. "But . . . he physically and emotionally divorced himself from all of us." Laura and Mildred East stayed with the Joplins for seven years, until Janis was three and the war ended.

Still devoted to her mother's faith, Dorothy joined the evangelical First Christian Church, a branch of their Nebraska denomination. As for Seth, he "hadn't been brought up in a family that was religious," Dorothy said. "That man didn't belong to anything in his life." The Joplins' youngest child, Michael, remembered "Mom asking Pop if he wanted to go to church. He always said no. I asked him why once, and the gist was he didn't believe in God. He believed in spirituality, but not organized [religion]. He didn't like the preaching." Seth stayed home every Sunday, while Dorothy and Janis—and eventually siblings Laura and Michael—went to the service. As with his passions for classical music and literature, Seth did not overtly express his atheism outside the Joplin home. To be an "out" atheist was to risk harsh judgment, even shame, from the deeply devout Port Arthur community. Only those close to him knew and accepted, and even admired, Seth's convictions. Among that small group was his eldest child, Janis.

Nevertheless, at Dorothy's insistence, Janis was baptized at age ten by immersion at the First Christian Church on Procter Street; she would attend services there through junior high. (Thirty years later, Janis's paint-by-number *Jesus Praying at Gethsemane* would be discovered in a church closet.) Like her mother, Janis first sang publicly in the church choir, and Dorothy taught her in Sunday school. Seth did not object to any of it. The dichotomy between her parents' beliefs, and their mutual respect, became young Janis Joplin's normal.

As a child, Janis displayed her father's restless inquisitiveness. "She was always curious about everything," according to Dorothy, and "if she asked a question, I answered it straightforwardly, even if it was embarrassing. She was probably hyperactive, although I didn't know it. I thought she was just intensely interested in what she was doing. I didn't know that was something you [could] attempt to control." On the back of a photo of a visit to Seth's family in Amarillo, where the rambunctious Janis was allowed to run wild, Dorothy noted that Janis had lamented to her parents, "We are going home now. I'll have to be good." In Port Arthur, appearances mattered: Dorothy, increasingly status conscious, wanted a genteel, proper middle-class daughter. She dressed little Janis in home-sewn playsuits and ruffled frocks, sometimes with gloves and a hat, and much later would teach her to expertly wield a needle and thread.

Janis shared her parents' love affair with music. Dorothy purchased a used upright piano and began teaching four-year-old Janis to play and sing. Seth was proud of his wife's talent, and at first encouraged his daughter's efforts. "She started on piano lessons to learn scales and keys," Dorothy recalled. "I found some wonderful books of children's songs so she could learn to sing and I could play the primary note on the piano and she could get the pitch. From my own singing experience, I could help her with the tone and make the sound of a vowel or consonant correctly. She learned to sing folk songs and started singing them when she went to bed at night. It was absolutely enchanting." Dorothy jotted down on a photo of Janis *"sings herself to sleep."*

As the Joplins' dreams of economic security seemed to be coming true, Dorothy suffered a setback. Still in her early thirties, she was found to have a benign tumor on her thyroid gland. During surgery, the doctor irreparably damaged her vocal cords—and destroyed her singing voice. Soon after, Seth, a quiet, distant man who had trouble expressing his feelings, demanded they give away the piano. He claimed that Janis's "banging on the keys" now got on his nerves. "He'd had a hard day at the office, and you can imagine what those scales were like to him," Dorothy tried to explain. "He said, 'We just can't keep the piano.' We didn't fuss or quarrel about it. When one of us had a vehement opinion about something, the other would accede to that opinion. So I got rid of the piano. It broke my heart."

Perhaps suffering anxiety over her mother's hospitalization, followed by the subsequent loss of music in the house, Janis began sleepwalking. One night, Dorothy found her outside on the sidewalk, seemingly looking for something. When she asked, "Where are you going?" Janis kept saying over and over, "I want to go home."

In the coming months, Dorothy suffered two miscarriages before giving birth to their second daughter, Laurel Lee "Laura" Joplin, on March 15, 1949. A colicky baby, Laura cried constantly, demanding much of her mother's attention. Six-year-old Janis learned to fend for herself, or she would seek out her father, who seemed to recognize himself in his daughter and, for a time, always welcomed her company. As if she were his son, she'd accompany him to the barbershop, where, after Seth's haircut, the barber would trim her bangs.

Later that year, the family decided to move to a better neighborhood: "The lady who lived on our left was married to a sailor," Dorothy recalled. "I don't think she knew any normal words in the English language. She cursed worse than anybody I ever heard in my life! I did not want [my children] growing up learning that kind of language." The Joplins took the next step up the class ladder and bought a larger home in Griffing Park, a leafy new subdivision just outside the city limits. They had made it to Port Arthur's version of suburbia.

The white frame house at 3130 Lombardy Drive, quite modest by today's standards, featured a generous yard where Janis played. Seth tended a backyard garden, and Dorothy baked pies made from pecans picked from their trees. Janis immediately found friends among plentiful neighborhood kids, with whom she roughhoused on playground equipment built by Seth, and put on plays and puppet shows in a theater he constructed. Since her infancy, the Joplins had frequently photographed Janis, and now they took pictures of the two sisters, dressed in identical outfits sewn by Dorothy.

Janis would spend Saturdays with her father, visiting the Gates Memorial Public Library, an imposing Greek Revival–style edifice—Seth's own kind of church. "At my house," Janis said proudly, "you got a library card as soon as you could write your name." Like her father, she learned to treasure books and showed an early aptitude for reading, recognized soon after she entered first grade at the nearby Tyrrell Elementary School in the fall of 1949. Her parents had done all they could to ready their firstborn to become a popular and high-achieving student in Port Arthur's well-funded school system.

CHAPTER 2

TOMBOY

I nearly fell out of my chair, I was so excited!
—JANIS JOPLIN

An intuitive child, Janis sensed that Seth Joplin wanted a son, and certainly she knew that her tomboy roughhousing pleased him. Her deep connection with her father, initiated by her greeting him after work each day, continued until the Joplins' third child, their only son, Michael, came along. Janis felt the loss of that intimacy acutely, viscerally, and it fueled both her lifelong neediness and her imagination.

Socially, Dorothy hoped that Janis would model herself after her. She organized a troop of Blue Birds, similar to Girl Scouts, who met regularly at the Joplins' home, where Janis "was outgoing and made strangers welcome," Dorothy recalled. She constantly sought her mother's approval and would always demand more of her attention than her other two children, Dorothy said.

Janis was so book smart and took to school well enough that her first-grade teacher advanced her to second grade halfway through the year. Then, at age seven, she skipped ahead to third grade in the fall of 1950. The advanced placement proved to be a social handicap: Janis was as much as eighteen months younger than some of her classmates, and smaller than most of her friends. Yet her diminutive stature didn't stop her from acting the equal to her older—and larger—playmates, who sometimes forgot how much younger Janis was.

"She enjoyed the physical aspects of playing," said Roger Pryor, a neighbor two years her senior whose family's home abutted the Jop-lins' backyard. "She liked to play with the guys, boys' sports, baseball. She wasn't bashful, and she could argue. She initiated more than she responded: *'Let's do this! Let's play this game!'* She was stubborn but lik-able."

At ages ten and eleven, Janis, still the unabashed tomboy, was unself-conscious and saw no problem in going shirtless like the neighborhood boys during Port Arthur's long, hot, humid summers. "She played out-side without a shirt until she was in the seventh grade," Pryor recalled. "She was slow in physical maturation. Nobody ever said anything about it, but it was strange behavior for a girl."

Some kids considered Roger a bully, but Janis was fearless and always stood up to him. She even challenged him to wrestling matches. "I felt really ill at ease wrestling with a girl," said Pryor, "and here was Janis wanting to wrestle. My parents had told me time and time again, never fight with a girl. She chased after me. If she caught you, she [sat] down on you. I remember her sitting on me, grinning. Janis would just laugh like a triumphant victor."

Janis may have pounded on Roger because she had a crush on him. Also, a part of her was possibly jealous of the friendship he'd developed with her father. Seth "really liked me," Pryor recounted. "He treated me like a son. He would talk to me, spend time with me, make things like slingshots." Her father also encouraged Janis's rambunctiousness, with no thought whatsoever of encouraging her to stay inside and play with her dolls. He built stilts and an oversized seesaw for Roger and Janis.

His most dangerous construction was "the giant stride," a sort of swing with rings attached to ropes fastened to the top of a pole. Grab-bing hold of a ring, the kids ran in a circle until they lifted to "fly," their legs like wings above the ground. Janis got her first thrilling taste of altered consciousness soaring through the air, holding on to the ring for dear life. Pryor, who would often push the more timid children, re-called, "We'd get those kids going so [fast] they were almost straight out [from] the pole, screaming to stop, and we knew they couldn't last, and they just flew off. We did things to hurt people—not to be mean, but more like a contest to see how tough you were. I know several people got their arm broken on that giant stride." Janis was tough and never got hurt, but Seth later dismantled it. When she did eventually break her arm, it was from falling out of a tree.

Seth's closest friend was Don Bowen, a fellow introvert who worked for Gulf Oil, and whose daughter Kristin—"a real pretty, quiet girl, ultrafeminine," according to Pryor—was nearly a year older than Janis but in her grade. Don was "the only other intellectual in town," according to Janis. He and Seth "got together desperately, and they just dug the fact that each other existed." The Bowens and Joplins traveled across town to each other's home at least once a month for dinner, bridge, and, most importantly, to talk freely in ways they could not out in the cultural backwater of Port Arthur. "When we arrived at the Joplins' house," Kristin Bowen recounted, Seth and Don "liked to listen to classical music and discuss books and sometimes politics. When the bridge table came out, we were sent off to play. There would be something new to play with: a pogo stick or stilts. We went in the backyard and climbed trees. Janis tried a lot of things that boys usually did. I noticed, as a real small child, that she wanted to tell us what to do."

Janis became increasingly defiant, testing her parents well before her teenage years. When they attempted to control her, she reacted with no concern for consequences. At age eight, she still sucked her thumb, so to put an end to the habit, Seth forbade any radio time until her thumb no longer went into her mouth. In response, Janis threw a massive temper tantrum—shrieking, kicking, and hyperventilating. Yet even the negative attention she received from such episodes didn't discourage her obstinacy. For Janis, quantity of attention was more important than quality.

With no air-conditioning and the windows open, sound traveled easily between homes. Pryor recalled listening to Janis battle with her parents: "You could hear the arguments, shouting matches in the house. Like, 'Go to your room to do this' and 'No, I'm not! Make me!' She didn't want to be a dutiful child. She was disobedient. . . . [Seth or Dorothy] would call for her to come inside, and it was eight or nine o'clock at night. Janis would just say, '*I'm not coming in. I'm going to play until every-one else goes.*'"

One particular clash of wills haunted Seth Joplin for decades. He and Janis had been in the backyard playing dominos, and when night fell, mosquitos started attacking. They ran for the house, but Janis accidentally dropped the box of dominos, which scattered. He recalled, "I told her she had to pick them up before she could come in," but she refused. "It was probably silly on my part, but I insisted. She and I stayed out there and fought those mosquitos, and she cried for a good thirty minutes until she finally did it. I think that incident might have had something to do with her later life . . . because she was forced to pick up those pieces. [When] she was forced to do something she didn't want to do, she would do unusual things—against the norm."

In high school, this trait would make Janis persona non grata among her classmates. But as a young girl, such behavior helped keep her father's attention focused on her. Janis was rarely ignored. That would have been the worst possible punishment.

As she became more headstrong, Janis also developed a way to calm herself. While in third grade, she began painting and drawing and showed real talent. Putting images on paper or canvas seemed to soothe her. Her teachers and parents soon recognized her gifts. She responded with more output and dedication. "Janis loved to draw horses," Pryor recounted. "She told me more than one time that horses were real hard to draw. . . . As an elementary school kid, she already knew she wanted to be an artist. You could see the artwork all over her bedroom walls."

"Her coordination was superb," according to Dorothy. "You had to show her once, and she could do it. I immediately got her a teacher who put her right into painting. She didn't want watercolors, she wanted oils." Ever the accommodating parents, possibly hoping to make their daughter more compliant, Seth and Dorothy bought her an easel, paints, and brushes. In later life, Janis would downplay, or even deny, her parents' doting nature—their clear appreciation and support for her early talents. Her myth of the perpetually misunderstood child gave journalists a hook for their profiles, but it wasn't the truth.

Kristin Bowen, like Janis, took art lessons at a woman's home on Saturday mornings. Soon the two girls competed as artists. "Not a fierce competition, but sort of," Bowen reflected. "We weren't trying to do the same thing, but it was on the same path. Our parents were trying to get us to develop skills." Dorothy, in particular, pushed Janis to work hard—and stand out as someone special.

>-+-•-◦-◦-+-◄

When Janis was ten and finishing fifth grade, Dorothy gave birth to Michael Ross Joplin on May 25, 1953, a week after Seth turned forty-three. Pryor remembered Seth was elated: "When Mike came along, that was his day at the stock market. He really liked that, a son."

During Dorothy's pregnancy, Janis had upped her misbehavior at school. Several years before, her kindergarten teacher had cited Janis's refusal to "rest quietly." Now her fifth-grade teacher noted she lacked in such areas as "listens to & follows directions; makes good use of time, and practices good sportsmanship." But, again, this teacher confirmed that Janis was "very talented" in art. With such admiration from her teacher, her parents, and friends such as Pryor and friendly rival Kristin Bowen, Janis invested more and more time in drawing and painting—often to the detriment of homework and other school assignments; the "needs improvement" comments on her report card did nothing to dissuade her. This criticism of her behavior may have fueled her drive.

On Saturdays, while Dorothy stayed home with the baby, Seth continued to take Janis, now joined by four-year-old Laura, to the Gates Memorial Library. A student of history and philosophy, Seth oversaw precocious Janis's book selection, which included numerous illustrated art histories and L. Frank Baum's Wizard of Oz series. She used both as inspirations—and in a few short years, Janis's life would parallel Baum's heroine, Dorothy, as she was whisked from her black-and-white world into a psychedelic Oz of sorts, with her own offbeat companions.

Beginning in seventh grade, in the fall of 1954, Janis transferred to Woodrow Wilson Junior High, an impressive brick building near the Gates Library. The transition from her elementary school, which she could walk to from home, was fairly traumatic. A boyish eleven-year-old, Janis initially rode the school bus, where older kids picked on her. Though their teasing was mild compared with the abuses Janis would have to endure in high school, she cried about it at home. Dorothy quickly organized a carpool with neighbors to solve the problem of the bus rides.

Janis's entry into the new social landscape at Woodrow Wilson was eased somewhat by music, as well as art. She was, after all, the daughter of Dorothy East, once a locally acclaimed schoolgirl singer. And Janis, in some ways, early on, followed her mother's path. She sang in the First Christian Church choir and developed a crystalline soprano voice. She immediately joined Woodrow Wilson's ninety-member Girls' Glee Club, where she would remain for three years. She began making new friends, including a girl named Karleen Bennett, a shy brunette who wore cat's-eye glasses and played saxophone in the school band. Both budding cynics, Janis and Karleen bonded over their mutual dislike of gym class, particularly having to change clothes in front of their more endowed peers. Karleen's father ran a plumbing business, and, almost unheard of in Port Arthur, he had converted to Judaism when he married a Jewish woman. To Janis, Karleen's parents must have felt a bit like her own father—outsiders in a world of Christian conformists.

Meanwhile, Dorothy encouraged her daughter to dress like her classmates, and sewed her school clothes, including the full-circle skirts worn over crinoline petticoats—typical of the era's fashion. Like her mother, Janis was outgoing and determined to make people like her. At the dinner table, Janis's outspokenness and charm were rewarded with Seth's attention and more encouragement to form her own opinions. But her gregariousness did not always sit well with her teachers. They reprimanded her for talking in class, frequently leaving her seat, and failing to finish her homework. Still, she maintained a B average, while her excellence in art won her an Outstanding Achievement award.

Janis celebrated her twelfth birthday in 1955 with a dinner party for a few of her school chums, including Kristin Bowen, who now accompanied her to weekly Arthur Murray dance classes. But rather than learn the fox-trot or the Lindy Hop, Janis wanted to dance to the new kind of music she heard on the radio: rock & roll—named by DJ Alan Freed.

That year, rock & roll broke nationally with Bill Haley and His Comets' "Rock Around the Clock" topping the Hit Parade for three weeks. In March the film *Blackboard Jungle*—a drama about juvenile delinquency—opened with Haley's song as its theme, spurring the record on to national popularity; some excitable teen audiences rioted and tore up theater seats. Other Janis favorites included Little Richard's "Tutti-Frutti" and Fats Domino's "Ain't That a Shame," New Orleans–recorded 45s getting airplay on Beaumont's rhythm and blues station. Elvis Presley, who'd started his career at nearby Shreveport's *Louisiana Hayride* broadcast on KWKH, toured the South constantly and performed at Woodrow Wilson Junior High's auditorium on November 25, 1955. At twelve, Janis was not allowed to attend, but the frenzy around his appearance must have grabbed her attention. She began buying his 45s and spinning her radio dial to catch more of this music that seemed made for her.

Seth Joplin, detesting what he considered the rock & roll "fad" (as did many of his generation), did not like sharing his phonograph with Janis, but he finally relented and occasionally allowed his eldest to play her raucous records. Eventually she'd get her own portable record player for her bedroom.

Janis's Saturday visits to the library with her dad, now including Karleen Bennett, were often followed by a trip to the post office, where Seth would show the girls the "Wanted" posters. Janis and Karleen compared notes on which outlaws they found most attractive. At the library, Seth continued to supervise Janis's reading selections, whereas Karleen chose whatever she pleased—the more risqué the better. At home, she thumbed through the pages, marking any racy sections or curse words to show Janis. The girls became obsessed with "cussing" and even learned sign language so they could curse without anyone knowing. In 1956 Grace Metalious's steamy *Peyton Place* caught their attention, with its back-cover copy: "the big best-seller about small town U.S.A. which has been damned and banned"; its author described as "the young housewife in blue jeans who created America's most controversial novel."

Also that year, Janis saw several influential films with "outsider" themes such as drug addiction, teen rebellion, and premarital sex: *The Man with the Golden Arm* (winning Frank Sinatra an Oscar nomination for his portrayal of a junkie), *Rebel Without a Cause* (James Dean's breakthrough), and Josh Logan's *Picnic* (with William Holden as a charismatic drifter). Dorothy's idea of wholesome entertainment was being usurped, but, consumed with mothering Janis's siblings, she was helpless to stop it. Her husband, meanwhile, was focusing more of his attention on his three-year-old son. Some five years earlier, Seth had first backed away from his daily after-work conversations with Janis when Dorothy scolded him for sharing with his impressionable daughter stories of making homemade beer in college. With perfect timing, rock & roll and novels and movies with "questionable morals" arrived to offer Janis new horizons—a kind of sanctioned subversiveness she could tap into.

That summer, Janis would initiate the process of becoming a full-fledged rebel when she volunteered at a local youth theater. Now a teenager, she looked on while her friends Karleen and Kristin began pairing off with boys, as the less curvaceous, less swan-necked Janis could only long for the amorous attention her peers inspired. At the Port Arthur Little Theatre was a heartthrob named Jim Langdon, a talented trombonist with a dark pompadour. Langdon and his gang, all nearly two years older and a grade ahead of Janis, held sway at the theater, founded by his friend Grant Lyons's mother, a northern transplant. Langdon's affections vacillated between Karleen, Kristin, and other girls, yet it would be Janis with whom he would form a tight yet platonic long-term bond, centered mostly on conversation and music.

At the Little Theatre, Janis, already gaining recognition for her artwork, took on the job of painting sets. To her delight, she was offered a bit part in the play *Sunday Costs Five Pesos*, for which she wore an off-the-shoulder peasant blouse that, along with cosmetics, made her look older. Though she hadn't yet spent much time with Langdon, Lyons, and their friends, she admired their wit, intellect, and daring. Having just graduated from junior high in May, Jim, Grant, and their cohorts climbed to the top of a Port Arthur water tower and painted the slogan "Hi 9" on its side—a feat she envied.

In September, just after starting ninth grade, Janis got her first eyeful of the rock & roll she'd been enjoying on records and the radio. The Joplins bought a television set, still a rarity and status symbol in their neighborhood. On Sunday, the ninth, Janis and her family tuned in to CBS to see the much-publicized Elvis Presley debut on *The Ed Sullivan Show*. His historic, sensual performance riveted Janis: the sultry "Don't Be Cruel," the romantic ballad "Love Me Tender," Little Richard's "Ready Teddy," and her favorite, "Hound Dog." She became so enamored of "Hound Dog," she somehow tracked down the original version: a 1953 R&B hit on the Houston-based Peacock label by Willie Mae "Big Mama" Thornton. How a thirteen-year-old white girl in segregated Port Arthur found the R&B single remains a mystery, but she did. The lyrics in the Presley version refer to an actual dog that "never caught a rabbit." In the original, by contrast, Big Mama calls out a gigolo with fury. Janis took the record to the Bennetts to play for Karleen and her younger brother Herman; she preferred that version to Elvis's, she told them. In a little more than a decade, Janis would catapult to fame with Big Mama Thornton's "Ball and Chain."

>─+─◦─+─<

While in ninth grade, Janis connected with her first boyfriend: Jack Smith, a tall classmate with dark hair who, like her father, enjoyed books and conversation. "We got together over the fact that we both read a lot," said Smith, who recalled that Janis was "bright and cheerful and smart." When Smith, fourteen, and Janis, thirteen, became an item, it was a chaste coupling. "I didn't have the faintest idea what sex was," Smith recounted. Rather than sneak off and neck, they stayed after school to work together on the junior high literary magazine, *Driftwood*. On weekends, their dates included trips to church, amusement parks, and wholesome movies like *The Ten Commandments*.

Smith didn't see much of her rebellious side. He remembered Janis as "delightful and pretty and all the things a young girl of thirteen wants to be, a typical right-up-the-line future sorority girl." Smith gave her a gold necklace with their shared initial, *J*. "If we ever get married," she told him boldly, "all our monogrammed items will be the same." As a member of the Pep Club and the youth service organization Tri Hi Y, Janis hosted social gatherings and at times seemed to be striving toward becoming the thoroughly conventional daughter her mother desired. While her buxom classmates wore torpedo bras, Janis was flat chested and still dressed dutifully in her mother's creations. On a scrapbook page documenting a Tri Hi Y event, Janis sketched a frock with a cinched waist and full skirt and pasted a swatch of gingham, noting, "I wore that dress Mother made me, green and white checks with white trim."

That December 1956, ninth grader Janis sang her first public solo at the church Christmas pageant, which Jack Smith attended. She also performed with some seven dozen other girls at a Glee Club concert. In both, she used the clear soprano that, at the time, she thought was the totality of her voice: a lovely sound, but not as special as her artwork. She still considered herself an artist, not a singer, and would for a few years yet. She also showed aptitude as a writer, encouraged by her favorite teacher, Dorothy Robyn, who found Janis "a very capable student who needs to develop more responsibility." Despite Janis's behavioral issues, Robyn eventually honored her with a merit award certificate for English and journalism: Janis, thrilled by the attention, wrote in her scrapbook, "What a shock! Miss Robyn walks up in the middle of class and casually says, 'Oh, I thought you might like to see this.' I nearly fell out of my chair. I was so excited!" Janis illustrated the moment with a stick figure drawing of herself tumbling to the floor.

Both Janis's artwork and writing were showcased in the 1957 *Driftwood,* with her illustrations on its cover and inside an adorable, illustrated essay, "The Most Unusual Prayer," about her younger brother Michael's attempt to say grace at the Joplin dinner table. That summer, Janis volunteered at the Gates Memorial Library as an assistant in the children's room. She put her artistry to work by expertly drawing large posters featuring the Scarecrow and others from the Oz books who accompany rebellious Dorothy. Janis got her first taste of fame when a *Port Arthur News* reporter interviewed her about the posters. The July 14 article, "Library Job Brings Out Teenager's Versatility," featured a photo of Janis and her Scarecrow drawing, noting that she "was named one of the top artists in the ninth grade" and "outstanding in journalism." Apparently a natural at the sound bite, Janis said she took the job "because it gives me a chance to practice art and at the same time to do something worthwhile for the community."

This recognition, however, could not compensate for the loss of her father's attentiveness. "Pop had always laughed loudly and easily with his kids, until the girls started to become women," Laura Joplin reflected later. "Then he withdrew. Somehow our femininity made it more awkward for him to express his feelings, a task that took effort at any time." Janis cast the blame elsewhere. A decade later, she would recall that her father "used to talk and talk to me, and then he turned right around from that when I was fourteen—maybe he wanted a smart son or something like that."

As for Seth, he would remember a daughter very akin to him, except for her increasing compulsion to publicly flaunt her individuality. Unlike him, she would refuse to keep a low profile. "From about the age of fourteen," he recalled laconically, "Janis was a revolutionary."

CHAPTER 3

THRILL SEEKER

*You shouldn't have to be young until
you're old enough to cope with it.*

—JANIS JOPLIN

Janis always looked back to her fourteenth year as a turning point. In 1970, in interviews and onstage, she would frequently recall that age, usually tinged with bitterness: during a performance of Etta James's feverish "Tell Mama," after singing about finding out "what you need, what you want," she rapped, "I found out when I was fourteen years old, and I've been lookin' ever since." When a journalist asked why she was miserable as a teen, she answered with the provocative "I didn't have any tits at fourteen." While true, this was only part of the story; the part that would get the most attention.

Although she'd begun to seek an edgier pop culture—rock & roll, trashy novels, racy movies—Janis was still invested in being a conventional daughter, with every school activity memorialized in her Thomas Jefferson (TJ) High scrapbook, all carefully hand lettered. As a tenth grader, in the fall of 1957, she joined the TJ High student population of 1,920. She became a member of the Future Teachers of America, worked on *The Yellow Jacket* yearbook, and threw herself into traditional high school pursuits: pep rallies, student elections, and football games. Her mother encouraged her to work hard, achieve, and make friends. "What you wanted was to be popular," her classmate Kristin Bowen explained. "Student council people, football players, and cheerleaders were the ultimate type of people. One of the main goals was *not* to be different. Then you wouldn't be popular."

Popularity depended mostly on looks, and Janis detested hers, particularly since she'd developed acne. She was increasingly insecure about her attractiveness, the beginnings of her lifelong negative self-image. According to Karleen Bennett, Janis particularly hated what she referred to as her "little pig eyes." Janis attempted to improve her appearance by rolling her chin-length hair in large curlers and tinting it red. "She didn't like her hair," Karleen recalled. "She thought her nose was too big, her mouth was too big. She had freckles." Though she and the ninety-eight-pound Karleen were both petite and wore the same size clothes, Janis thought of herself as fat, possibly due to rail-thin Dorothy Joplin's focus on staying slim. With a boyish build, "Janis's waist wasn't small, and this was back in the days of cinch belts, girdles, and eighteen-inch waists," Karleen observed.

Janis and Jack Smith had broken up, and she envied Karleen and Kristin, who had plenty of dates their sophomore year. Janis's only invitation came from a junior named Roger Iverson, who asked her to his induction ceremony for the Order of the DeMolays, a Masonic Youth Order. She commemorated the event by pasting her corsage and other souvenirs into her scrapbook, but it would be their only date.

Yet Janis did not lack for male companionship. She had a new crew of friends who'd become close pals the previous summer. In July 1957, during hurricane season—with two hitting Port Arthur—Janis had returned to the Little Theatre workshop. This time she pushed her way into Jim Langdon's tight-knit clique composed of Grant Lyons, David Moriaty, Randy Tennant, and Adrian Haston. These five young Turks, all rising juniors, fascinated her. Wearing their hair longer than most students' typical flattops or crew cuts, they thirsted for new ideas. At the Little Theatre, Janis began joining their heady conversations, more than holding her own.

The athlete of the group, Lyons, played linebacker for the Thomas Jefferson High Yellow Jackets, lauded locally, like all football teams in Texas. He was the first "Renaissance man" Janis befriended: unlike his teammates, he had "an interest in the arts—visual arts, drama, poetry, writing of all kinds, and music," he recalled about himself and his four best friends. "Our interests were not those of the average Port Arthur high school student our age. We didn't fit into the sea we were swimming in. Janis joined our group, and she was interesting—loud, kinda bossy, and fun."

To budding existentialist Jim Langdon, Janis initially seemed "naïve and shy, a conventional, very straight little girl entering high school. I remember how absolutely shocked and horrified she was—just aghast—when she found out I didn't believe in God. She tried to argue convincingly but wasn't very successful." As the first avowed atheist in her life besides her father, Langdon's views captivated Janis, even as she made a case for her mother's beliefs. Langdon soon discovered that Janis "wanted to grow up a bit and explore who she was. I realized how sharp she was. She gradually became a full-fledged member of our gang and became part of everything we did."

Adrian Haston—like Langdon, the son of a refinery worker—found Janis to be "self-assured and assertive enough to make friends with five guys who were handfuls. That was pretty unusual. She was very bright and talented, but she didn't see it." Dave Moriaty, whose father was a Gulf Oil engineer, owned a sailboat. Janis joined the gang on sailing excursions, but mostly they just drove around, with Langdon or Moriaty behind the wheel. "One night Janis and I drove out to Sarah Jane Road, by a refinery, with the oil flares burning up, a spooky place," Langdon recounted. "We'd just roam around looking for some place to talk." Lyons said they spent their "lives in cars." The main teenage pastime was either "making the Triangle" (motoring between Port Arthur, Beaumont, and Orange) or "doing the drag," cruising Port Arthur's main thoroughfare, Procter Street.

From the beginning, Janis was treated like one of the boys. Though she harbored crushes on them, only one, Randy Tennant, a member of TJ's Slide Rule Club, which Janis would join, asked her out. "It wasn't your conventional date," he recalled. "It was more like two guys getting together and talking about everything, chatter, chatter, chatter. She was good company and could hold up her end of the conversation. She might come up with something interesting or totally off the wall, but she fit in our group."

"I think that summer was pivotal for Janis," said Langdon. "She transitioned very quickly into a different person. We were just a grade ahead of her, but we were a lot further ahead in other areas." Moriaty recalled: "Everybody realized Janis was fun to have around because she raised so much hell. She wouldn't accept her place as a female or an underclassman. She used to call up and demand to go along on our outings. It was unheard of." Janis's questioning of her mother's conformity intensified as she sought knowledge and affirmation from this older iconoclastic group. The former tomboy dove into being the boys' club mascot.

Entertaining them with raucous jokes was one way to get attention, but Lyons recalled Janis sometimes taking charge. "She'd try to make people do what she wanted them to do," he said. "She wanted her own way; she was willful. But God knows she couldn't survive around us very long if she hadn't been. We were a bunch of very pushy people; a lot of strong personalities." Janis saw the outsider boys as her godsend: "They read books and had ideas," she recalled a decade later. "We thought of ourselves as intellectuals." She could easily have been speaking about Seth, whose growing detachment stung less as Janis found her way among younger versions of her father.

When not gallivanting with the guys, engaging in hours of conversation, or cracking them up, Janis maintained her friendship with Karleen Bennett and rising junior Arlene Elster, who attended the local synagogue with Karleen. The daughter of a doctor, Arlene drove her mother's Chevy, with Karleen riding shotgun and Janis in back. They smoked Newports and sang along with the radio blasting. Some drives included stopping by Port Arthur College's tiny radio station, KPAC, to visit classmate volunteers. Elvis still dominated the AM dial that summer of '57 with "Too Much," "All Shook Up," and "(Let Me Be Your) Teddy Bear" in heavy rotation; they saw Elvis on the big screen in *Loving You* at the Port Theater. From Lubbock, Texas, Buddy Holly and the Crickets scored with the R&B–tinged rocker "That'll Be the Day."

Debbie Reynolds was the rare female on the Hit Parade via her strings-drenched "Tammy," from *Tammy and the Bachelor*. To find more diversity, the girls tuned in to Beaumont's R&B station, KOLE, where they got an earful with LaVern Baker's exciting "Jim Dandy" and the amorous "Love Is Strange" by Mickey and Sylvia, as well as Little Richard's "Lucille" and the Coasters' "Young Blood." Other bawdy R&B hits getting play included Etta James's saucy "The Wallflower," better known as "Roll with Me Henry," and Beaumont's own Ivory Joe Hunter's "I Almost Lost My Mind." Sex was all over these songs.

Janis and Karleen eventually got up their nerve to meet KOLE DJ Steve-O the Night Rider. "I remember going up to KOLE a couple times late at night 'cause Janis wanted to," Karleen recounted. "She had this thing about people on the radio, and she wanted to talk to Steve-O because he played rhythm and blues. It was daring to walk into a place where there are older men you don't know and say, 'Hey, you want some coffee? We'll go get some.'" Janis, however, needed to know where the music came from, and, unlike Karleen, she didn't fear risk or confrontation.

>——◦——◦——◦——<

Things were fraught around the Joplin home that fall. In late September 1957, Dorothy had to undergo a hysterectomy, and her relationship with her eldest child began to deteriorate mostly because Janis, emboldened by her summer thick with the rebel boys, became increasingly independent. She was no longer the eager-to-please daughter who just six months earlier had written her mother a birthday invitation: "Dear Mrs. S. W. Joplin, In gratefullness [sic] for being such a wonderful mother for 14 years I would like for you to have dinner with me at Luby's on Saturday the 16th. Janis Lyn Joplin."

Karleen, a frequent visitor at the Joplin home, suspected that "Mrs. Joplin had a hard time bending or being different from how she had grown up," and therefore didn't understand or approve of Janis's new interests. Meanwhile, Seth escaped the family pressures or the recurring darkness of his own mind by disappearing into the garage or the

backyard and drinking alone. Roger Pryor, the son of teetotalers, noticed his neighbor's drinking, including one day when Seth attempted—
unsuccessfully—to walk a tightrope he'd strung up in the backyard.
Usually, though, "when he got loose, he'd just tell old stories," Pryor
recalled. "When he was drinking, he'd smile a lot." For Seth Joplin, as
it would for Janis, alcohol seemed to promise a release into good times
and better feelings, at least in the short term.

For kicks, Janis joined Karleen and Arlene to cruise Port Arthur's
red-light district, crammed with brothels and gambling dens—
establishments that stayed in business thanks to bribes paid to law
enforcement, as well as conservative town leaders who looked the
other way. According to Karleen's brother Herman, "Nearly every boy
in town lost his virginity at Gracie's [brothel]. There was no age limit;
if you had the money at the whorehouse, they didn't care how old
you were."

Such sexual freedom, of course, did not extend to Port Arthur's
teen girls. If word got out that a girl lost her virginity, her reputation
was ruined. Karleen and Janis certainly questioned the hypocrisy: "We
always wondered why it was okay for the boys but wasn't okay for the
girls," Karleen reflected.

One renowned den of iniquity, the Keyhole Klub, was noted not just
for gambling and sex workers but also for serving the best hot dogs in
town. One Saturday, Karleen and Arlene convinced Janis to go inside the
notorious bar and buy them hot dogs while they waited in the Chevy.
When Janis carried out the proof of her gutsy deed, they pranked her
by locking her out of the car. "We wanted to make sure everybody saw
her there," Karleen explained. "She was the first girl I knew to go inside
the Keyhole. We'd make up stupid ideas and then get Janis to do them. I
pushed her into doing things that I wished I could do but couldn't bring
myself to do."

It became clear that Janis "was eager and anxious for our approval
and affection," Karleen admitted, which meant she would put up with
their mean-girl tricks. Other escapades included driving outside town to
a secluded spot, crafting a ruse for Janis to leave the car, and then speed-

ing off without her. Karleen and Arlene always returned to pick her up, but Janis, ever needy and trusting, continued to fall for their pranks. So starved was Janis for their attention, she forgave them for such ill treatment, even as the humiliations mounted.

Once, when she spent the night at the Bennetts' home, "Janis and I got into an argument about whether or not she could sneak out of the house and get back in without my parents knowing," Karleen recalled. She knew Janis's voice could be heard in her parents' bedroom through an air vent, alerting the Bennetts about her plan as the girls discussed it. Fearless, Janis jumped out the window, landing painfully in a bed of rocks and cactus. When she limped back to the front door, Mrs. Bennett was there to scold her, to Karleen's smug delight.

Janis sometimes played a similar role among the rebel boys, becoming "one of our favorite characters," Moriaty reflected. "I hate to think of how we treated her sometimes. She occupied the position of court jester." To Janis, their attention was clearly worth the teasing.

>-+-o-+-<

Janis's thunderbolt moment arrived in the autumn of '57, in the form of Jack Kerouac's *On the Road*. Prior to Kerouac, she was struggling to find her identity: Was she a wannabe "popular" God-fearing girl with curlers in her hair who did the bidding of her boy-crazy female peers? Or the wisecracking, whip-smart, sexless mascot of a loquacious crew of older, self-styled intellectual boys? While both extremes offered opportunities to express herself and feel included, neither would make her feel as free, and as recognized, as the cinematic storytelling of Kerouac.

Every week, Janis read her parents' *Time* magazine with absolute regularity, which is where she discovered a feature about the recently published *On the Road*. Janis immediately borrowed the novel from Jim Langdon. She devoured Kerouac's visceral narrative of Sal Paradise's adventures with reckless Dean Moriarty (inspired by Kerouac's traveling companion and muse, Neal Cassady), whom he described as looking like a young version of the Texas-born singing cowboy Gene Autry. Paradise and Moriarty even passed through the Golden Triangle in *On the Road*'s pages:

"We took a chance on one of the dirt roads, and pretty soon we were crossing the evil old Sabine River that is responsible for all these swamps. With amazement we saw great structures of light ahead of us. 'Texas! It's Texas! Beaumont oil town!' Huge oil tanks and refineries loomed like cities in the oily fragrant air."

Now, driving the Triangle from Port Arthur to Orange to Beaumont with the boys made even more sense to Janis. They, too, could be Kerouac's "sordid hipsters of America, a new beat generation" with their "real straight talk about souls." Sex and drugs and drunkenness and rootlessness—evils that Janis's parents tried to shield her from in her selection of library books lest she suffer the fates they'd seen befall their ancestors. Their warnings and admonishments, however, held none of the power of Kerouac's musical, defiantly antiestablishment prose.

For Janis, *On the Road* was "a revelation," according to Karleen. It would take several years for her to follow Kerouac's lead, traveling from Texas to San Francisco for the first time, but at fourteen, she'd discovered her first kindred spirit in literature, and this would inform everything going forward. Her final break with convention was yet to come, but she began calling herself a beatnik—which she would never stop doing.

Soon after reading *On the Road*, an emboldened Janis connected with her own Sal Paradise: a wrong-side-of-the-tracks TJ High junior named Rooney Paul, who looked like a cross between Elvis and James Dean and lived downtown with his single, working mother. "That was her first love," in Karleen's opinion. "He worked at a drive-in and lived in a rooming house on Procter." Karleen drove her there on several occasions and picked her up an hour later, but the unconsummated relationship fizzled. After Paul quit school in eleventh grade and joined the army, Janis continued to sketch his portrait. In one surviving drawing, he wears a T-shirt, a James Dean–style jacket, and jeans. Apparently, it was Paul who'd done the spurning. "I was very young, and I didn't have any experience in relating to people," Janis later said. "Every time one of my overtures would be refused, it would hurt."

In 1958 Janis, at fifteen, continued going through the motions of a typical Eisenhower-era teen; mementos pasted in her scrapbook at the end of her sophomore year include team-spirit flyers and handbills promoting student council candidates. No hint from these pages of her nascent beatnik identity. Similarly, her first high school annual is cluttered with salutations, advice, and mostly compliments penned by fellow students. Her best friend's inscription, however, takes a different tone, an adolescent hint at irony perhaps, but reading somewhat callous on the page: "Don't believe all the nice things people have been writing about you," Karleen scrawled on the yearbook's back page. "They're not honest. . . . Actually, they're afraid to say you're conceited, young & impressionable!! . . . I realize you know how clever I am, so we won't go into that here. Just keep working & maybe someday you'll be as clever as I am. (Don't hold your breath, till then!)."

Janis's confessional message in Karleen's annual is markedly less caustic and suggests she is confounded by the complicated friendship: "To a good ole egg. I've tried in vain to analyze you, but I can't so I figured—what the hell (heck), stay confused. I wish I could figure you out. Who do you like now—Mickey, Dennis, Jim or David? I hope I will get to know and understand you better next year. Remember me always, SEZ Janis. P.S. Remember—I AM A VIRGIN!"

⊷•◇•⊷

That summer of '58, Janis set out to reinvent herself in the vein of a Kerouac heroine. She got a flattering, very short haircut at the best salon in town. She took up red lipstick and eye makeup, and began visiting a dermatologist for painful acne treatments. She also developed a new laugh, a loud cackle, which she practiced at Karleen Bennett's. "She'd ask, 'Is it annoying enough? Should it be louder?'," Karleen recalled.

In *Time* magazine, Janis read about the scandal of Louisiana's Jerry Lee Lewis, who'd scored the massive hits "Whole Lot of Shakin' Going On" and "Great Balls of Fire" the previous year; his career tanked after the disclosure of his marriage to thirteen-year-old second cousin Myra Gale. The magazine published a letter to the editor condemning Lewis and his teenage fans. Janis was so angered that she wrote her own response to *Time*, defending Lewis, rock & roll, and her generation. Though *Time* didn't publish her letter, she got a sympathetic reply from the news weekly (dated July 28, 1958), which Janis pasted into her scrapbook. She'd later meet the man she championed—with agonizing results.

That summer's watershed came when Janis passed driver's education and got her license—another milestone noted in her scrapbook. Behind the wheel of her father's meticulously kept car, she was no longer a passenger but the master of her destination. "I remember when she backed out of the driveway the first time, alone, and drove out," Seth Joplin recalled. "I watched her. You never saw a bigger smile. She was overwhelmed with the joy of being able to do it alone." Like her beatnik heroes, at last she could cruise the open road. On her first drive, she collected Kristin Bowen, and they conspired to pick up some teenage boys. Kristin reported in her diary: "She let them off except for Billy Brown, [who] sat between us. He was real fresh and sort of cute but loud—biggest flirt I ever saw."

The next evening, rushing home from the Bennetts' house before her curfew, Janis ran a stop sign and crashed into another car, totaling both vehicles; fortunately, she and the other driver were unharmed. After the accident, Seth grounded her. "'How could you be so dumb?' he yelled, in a voice we seldom heard," her sister Laura wrote in her book *Love, Janis*. "It was the biggest problem any of his kids had ever caused, and he seethed in astonishment. . . . Janis was crushed, embarrassed, frustrated, and upset that she had failed so miserably." Once again, she was relegated to the back seat of her friends' cars.

Janis found comfort in records shared that summer by the Little Theatre gang. Langdon collected jazz 78s, and Janis, too, started seeking out new sounds. "In a record store, I found a record by Odetta, and I bought it," she said later of what she called Odetta's folk-blues "ox-driver songs." Born in Alabama and raised in California, Odetta, at thirteen, trained in opera and musical theater before becoming the sole black female folksinger in San Francisco in the mid-1950s. After buying her 1956 solo debut, *Odetta Sings Ballads and Blues*, Janis taught herself to reproduce Odetta's round tones. "I really dug it," she recalled, "and

I played it at a bunch of parties, and everyone liked it. We used to go to all the beaches and . . . sit on the beach . . . and we'd go to this old Coast Guard shack. . . . You'd go all the way to the top, and you'd look out on all this water and marsh, and we used to sit up there and sit around and talk. We were up there one day, and someone said, 'I wish we had a record player,' and I said, 'I can sing.'

"'Come on, Janis, cut it out.'

"I said, 'I can too'. . . So I started singing a real Odetta . . . *ya la la* . . . I came out with this huge voice.

"They said, 'Janis, *you're a singer!*' . . . They told me I had a great voice, and I thought, '*Wow* . . . '"

The moment contained everything Janis had craved for so long: surrounded by a close group of peers and all of them genuinely astonished by her. She could feel it; the music she was singing was rooted in the blues, which spoke to her early sense of loss. She had seen and heard singers who lived an unconventional, road-going life—like Kerouac's heroes—and that road now seemed closer.

"From the very beginning," said Jim Langdon, "when it was nothing more than sitting around a record player on the living room floor or in the back seat with four or five of us, there was never any doubt in my mind that Janis had a world-class voice and that she could do anything she wanted with that voice."

Impacting Janis even more than Odetta was Louisiana-born Huddie Ledbetter: "Grant Lyons told me about somebody called Lead Belly," Janis recounted time and again. "He bought Lead Belly records, which were far-out country blues. I was a soprano, singing in the church choir. I didn't know I had that kind of voice. Then Grant Lyons played a Lead Belly record for me. That started it."

Two decades before Janis heard his music, forty-six-year-old Lead Belly, released after serving a second prison term for slashing a white man's arm, started his career in New York, promoted by Texas-raised folklorist John Lomax. The bluesy songs Lead Belly sang and played on his twelve-string guitar—"Matchbox Blues," "Rock Island Line," "Midnight Special," "Careless Love," "Alberta," and "C.C. Rider" (also called

"Easy Rider")—became some of Janis's favorites. Exploring his music, she eventually learned his topical protest songs, including "Bourgeois Blues": "Them white folks in Washington they know how / To call a colored man a nigger just to see him bow." Janis was six years old when Lead Belly died in December 1949 at age sixty from Lou Gehrig's disease. The following year, his signature song "Irene" became the top pop hit of 1950 as "Goodnight Irene" for folk quartet the Weavers (featuring Pete Seeger). Decades after Janis discovered Lead Belly, Kurt Cobain would cite him as his favorite artist as Nirvana launched into a version of the bluesman's "In the Pines" (also known as "Where Did You Sleep Last Night?") on *MTV Unplugged*.

Janis put her own stamp on songs recorded by Appalachian balladeer Jean Ritchie, known for her pure, mellifluous soprano. "[Janis] had a true chameleon's voice," according to Langdon. "She could sound like Odetta, a black woman with a very deep voice. She could turn around and sing Jean Ritchie's Appalachian songs—this real thin soprano—and it would sound just like Jean Ritchie. She was tremendously versatile, with tremendous range."

According to Grant Lyons, though the boys sang folk and blues songs while driving around, when Janis chimed in, they would, for once, shut up and spotlight her with their rapt, undivided attention. "It was an overwhelming voice," he said. "There was no point in singing along with Janis if she was going to sing like that."

CHAPTER 4

"BEAT WEEDS"

I would never be young again. I'd have to cry all over.

—JANIS JOPLIN

Since childhood, at the Joplin dinner table, Janis's parents had encouraged her to voice her opinions. Now, at TJ High, she spoke out about political and social issues she'd discussed with the rebel boys, at a time when most girls kept quiet. "There wasn't anybody like me in Port Arthur," she told a *Newsweek* reporter nine years later. "It was lonely. All those feelings welling up and no one to talk to. I read. I painted. I didn't hate Negroes."

Not only did she not "hate Negroes," but Janis also stood up for desegregation in an environment particularly hostile to African Americans. During a classroom discussion on integration, Janis was the sole student to argue in favor of black and white students attending school together. This move, combined with her carousing with older boys, her identification with the Beats, and her lashing out at those who ridiculed her, would eventually, by her senior year, cut her off from conventional Port Arthur. She became a pariah in her hometown.

"Everybody was against integration," Karleen Bennett recalled, "or if they were for it, they didn't say anything. Janis did. She got up and started talking about the way she felt about it. You just didn't do that back then. That pretty much resulted in her being picked on for the rest of the time in high school—calling her names like 'nigger lover.'"

Another classmate, Tary Owens, agreed: "It just reached a thing where most of them hated her."

For Janis, segregated Port Arthur, where the black section of town suffered from substandard housing, roads, and education, did not seem much different from neighboring Arkansas, which made national headlines in 1957 when Governor Orval Faubus blocked black students from entering Little Rock Central High School. The year before that, in Mansfield, Texas, a white mob stopped three black students from enrolling in a white school; ignoring a federal court order, Governor R. Allan Shivers sent Texas Rangers to back the segregationists. Defying the 1954 Supreme Court decision *Brown v. Board of Education*, the Texas Legislature passed a 1957 segregation bill delaying integration by nearly a decade. In Vidor, Texas, just outside Port Arthur, the Ku Klux Klan erected a sign warning African Americans (using the offensive slur "niggers") not to be caught inside city limits after sundown. Cross burnings were not uncommon in the area, and carloads of white men sometimes drove through Port Arthur's black neighborhood and, leaning out the windows, assaulted African American pedestrians with two-by-fours—a practice they called "nigger knocking."

>⊷⊶◦⊷⊶⊰

As her junior year began in fall 1958, Janis nonetheless attempted to participate in TJ traditions, even though numerous classmates shunned her. Perhaps with Dorothy's prodding, she tried out for the prestigious Red Hussars Drum and Bugle Corps, a precision drill team that marched at football games and in parades. When she was rejected, she broke down in tears at school. She was accepted into other clubs, though, including the Future Nurses of America, through which she volunteered as a nurse's aid at St. Mary Hospital and learned to give injections. It was a skill she would abuse a few years later. As a prominent member of TJ's Art Club, Janis enthusiastically created bulletin board layouts and posters for the school hallways.

On Saturdays, she spent some rare time with her father. Seth occasionally drove her and her easel to the waterfront to paint "vistas of choppy water, sailboats, fishermen, and diving birds," according to her sister, Laura, who usually accompanied them. As an eleventh grader, Janis still considered herself "an artist" who "had all these ideas and feelings that I'd pick up in books," she reflected later. "My father would talk to me about it." When her greatly admired high school art teacher, Roger Russell, encouraged her to expand her subject matter to the human body, Karleen Bennett posed while Janis sketched her hands and feet. She began studying nudes in her art books; as Janis recalled, she'd "look at these . . . paintings and go, 'Wow!' and I'd try and paint that."

When Dorothy discovered the female nude Janis had painted on the inside of her bedroom closet door, she called Janis a "harlot" in front of Karleen, who recalled checking a dictionary to see what the word meant. It's unclear if Janis's painting was a self-portrait, a friend's body, or from her imagination. After days of arguing with her parents, Janis angrily covered the nude with Jackson Pollock–style paint splashes and eventually painted a seascape over it.

Not surprisingly, Janis began spending as much time as possible away from home. She craved excitement as she drove around with her friends. Karleen and Kristin Bowen often discussed "smooch parties," which Janis, who "didn't get asked to go out on dates," according to Karleen, wanted to experience herself. But when the opportunities occasionally arose, Janis balked. "I remember a couple of guys trying to make it with her at some party, and her trying to come on very tough, very experienced, but actually folding in the clinch," Jim Langdon recalled. "She maybe even cried."

Usually girls went to the drive-in theater only on dates with boys, but Karleen made an exception to go with Janis to *Gigi*, the film musical starring Maurice Chevalier ("Thank Heaven for Little Girls") and Leslie Caron, based on Colette's story of a young Parisian training to become a courtesan. They loved the movie, taking note of the scene in which Gigi learns to make proper drinks for gentlemen friends. The girls later fantasized about being prostitutes, Bennett recalled, "drinking and smoking and having sex all day." Soon after, they asked Karleen's mother, who was laissez-faire compared with Dorothy Joplin, for a cocktail. She mixed them whiskey sours, reasoning that it was better for the girls to try alcohol at home than sneak it elsewhere. "It was the first drink Janis ever had," according to Karleen. "We made her promise she wouldn't tell her parents. We had one drink and thought it was the end of the world—that *this was it!*"

The sense of release provided by spirits clearly resonated within Janis as a way to calm her anxiety, unleash her courage, and dull her fears of judgment from her classmates, her family, and Port Arthur as a whole. Soon she was out drinking beer with the boys. Jim Langdon had joined a dance band that played thirty minutes away at roadhouses along Highway 90, across the Sabine River near Vinton, Louisiana—the same places Janis's parents had frequented before she was born. At one time, from the 1930s to 1953, the strip was crammed with nearly two dozen gambling clubs, bars, and dance halls. A few still thrived in 1959, filled with hard-drinking Cajuns, refinery workers, and underage kids from Texas and Louisiana. The state's largely unenforced drinking age was eighteen, unlike the stricter twenty-one in Texas. Tary Owens, a TJ junior who joined them on outings to see Langdon's band, said, "It started out being once a month, then ended up being almost weekly. We'd go to Buster's first because they had a happy hour with quarter drinks. If you could get up to the bar, they'd sell it to you."

Janis delighted in going across the river to such clubs as Lou Ann's and the Big Oak, downing beers and hearing raucous R&B bands—a real contrast musically to pop radio's Hit Parade fare. Except for New Orleans native Lloyd Price's "Stagger Lee" and Wilbert Harrison's "Kansas City," the dial was packed with teen idols like Paul Anka and Frankie Avalon. On February 3, 1959, two weeks after Janis's sixteenth birthday, a plane crash killed Buddy Holly, the star from Lubbock; J. P. "the Big Bopper" Richardson, a Beaumont DJ who spun black music and wrote "Chantilly Lace"; and seventeen-year-old Ritchie Valens, who scored the hits "Donna" and "La Bamba." In the late fifties, other early rock & rollers were off the radar for less tragic reasons: Elvis got drafted; Little Richard became a preacher; and Jerry Lee Lewis, still unforgiven for marrying his thirteen-year-old cousin, was banned from radio. This vacuum helped create the conditions for an influx of folk music onto the pop charts: the Kingston Trio and others, as well as a thriving underground of roots musicians, including Bob Dylan and Joan Baez, who would influence Janis—and even become her peers.

Despite rock & roll's dip in popularity in '59, the Big Oak and Lou Ann's on Highway 90 continued to rock, albeit with amplified Texas blues, R&B, and the local hybrid later labeled "swamp pop." A low-slung joint with a bar and pool tables, Lou Ann's stage featured Jimmy Reed and other distinctive Texas bluesmen.

The Big Oak, "a large, barnlike place," according to Langdon, "was jammed every weekend, and there'd be fights in the parking lot." It booked primarily local artists, usually white, and always male. A raspy-voiced belter Janis's age, Jerry LaCroix, fronted the Dominos, a raucous R&B combo with a horn section, which he joined at age fourteen. LaCroix, as "Count Jackson," would then form the Counts before joining Beaumont native Edgar Winter in White Trash in the early 1970s (and eventually singing lead for Blood, Sweat and Tears and Rare Earth). The hottest group playing the strip in '59 was the Boogie Kings, which included Dale Gothia, a Port Arthur saxophone player a couple of years older than Janis. Ten years later, the Dominos and the Boogie Kings would inspire Janis's musical direction when she put together her first backing band.

It was an earth-shattering sound shaking the rafters in 1959 Louisiana: "We opened the door, and it was like a freight train coming through that room!" LaCroix recalled of the Boogie Kings, which he later joined. "These guys had five tenor saxophones, a couple of trumpets, a Hammond B-3 organ, and one of those Louisiana drummers. They were playing . . . 'swamp pop music'—Fats Domino, Bobby Charles–style music. There were three lead singers, and all the horn players sang like black chicks in a gospel choir. They had beautiful voices. It was just an incredible band."

The sound and rhythm of these bands unleashed Janis's pent-up energy, no doubt aided by her increasing intake of alcohol. Doing the bump and grind on the grimy, packed dance floor, her adrenaline pumping, she experienced a high that some kids got through sex. Pretty boy Tary Owens, whose family had moved to Texas from Illinois, recalled drunkenly "necking" with Janis in the back seat on the way home.

None of Janis's girlfriends accompanied her across the river to Louisiana's nightspots. Nice girls did not go to Lou Ann's, Buster's, or the Big Oak. But her reputation be damned, Janis thrived in the carload of boys, getting loose, with loud music the backdrop. En route, while popping beers and smoking cigarettes, they tuned in to Beaumont's KJET and heard black DJs like Willie Knighton spin soulful stompers: James Brown and the Famous Flames' early hits "Please, Please, Please" and "Try Me," Ray Charles's "What'd I Say," Jimmy Reed's "I'm Gonna Get My Baby," and Bobby "Blue" Bland's "Farther Up the Road" and "Little Boy Blue." Sometimes they heard local stars such as Clarence "Gatemouth" Brown, born in Vinton and raised in Orange, Texas, a frequent collaborator with Janis's favorite, Big Mama Thornton.

While Janis was pushing boundaries with the boys, Dorothy Joplin attended classes at Port Arthur College to enhance her secretarial skills. With all three children now in school, and requiring extra funds for her elderly mother's nursing care, she needed a job. Dorothy's excellence as a student led the college to hire her to teach typing and then promote her to school registrar. So with both parents now working, Janis began to ignore her curfew. "We stayed out till all hours," according to Grant Lyons. "'Let's go to Louisiana!' My parents gave me a hard time, and I bet a girl's parents would have hit the ceiling if she'd come in at four o'clock in the morning, smelling of beer, especially if she was out with four boys. They couldn't have known where we were going."

As word of Janis's excursions got around school, rumors spread that she was "loose," adding to her already tarnished reputation. Still, according to those who knew her best, Janis had not yet had sex. She didn't go further than playing games of "button poker," a milder form of strip poker, with a few TJ boys. One participant, Mike Howard, recalled Janis losing a game and undoing three buttons on her blouse, exposing her bra to him and another boy. "My friend and I mentioned our button poker with Janis to other friends," Howard confessed, "and I suspect that these little tales degenerated through the high school grapevine until we were buck naked and rolling around in vegetable oil."

Janis's occasional necking, or "ass grabbing," as Grant Lyons called it, at parties or in a back seat with a drunken boy became more fodder for gossip. Yet when Janis dropped by Karleen Bennett's and found her in bed with her boyfriend, she seemed clueless. "She wasn't sure what was going on," Karleen recalled. "She had no idea that we'd had sex. I jumped up, put on some clothes, and went in the living room to talk to her: 'I'm so glad you came in—you stopped me from doing something I shouldn't have done!'" At sixteen, Janis may have drunkenly fooled around with boys, but she was still naïve about the fundamentals of sex, and Karleen didn't divulge what she knew. Like Karleen, her necking partner Tary Owens was convinced that Janis, rather than the "slut" she was rumored to be, would graduate from Thomas Jefferson High a virgin. But the whispers and nasty comments eventually led her to give up any attempt to make her case with her classmates.

By the end of eleventh grade, "she just seemed to want to alienate everybody," Karleen observed. "Before that, she tried to conform. And then one day: 'That's it! You can like me for what I am, or there is nothing I can do about it.'" Her neighbor and former playmate Roger Pryor recalled, "She was hanging out with pseudo-intellectuals, who didn't fit in with other people. They would sit around and intellectualize about things that didn't matter and you couldn't control—really esoteric things about solving the world's problems. They liked being a group that no one wanted to be around . . . cutting her adrift socially from people she had known and liked before." Pryor, content with the status quo, counted himself among the latter: "I remember Janis wanting to sit there and talk. . . . I was busy in the garage, doing something. I made some comment, and she said, 'What's wrong? Don't you want to sit and intellectualize?' I said, 'No, I don't. What's the merit?'"

Though Janis spent most of her time with the rebel boys who were graduating that spring, none of them invited her to the senior prom. She would never forget the pain and loneliness of her exclusion. Still, she'd laugh it off when hanging with the guys, who treated her like one of them, even discussing their attempts to pick up girls. "That's what we talked about all the time," Lyons recalled, "about the problems of getting laid. I assume she wanted to get laid too." He recounted once "having a moment with Janis in somebody's backyard. We were talking, and I felt a very strong tenderness toward her. It wasn't exactly a romantic moment; we weren't necking. Yet it was erotic and poetic, a little soul-charming time." He later wrote a poem, "To J.J.," inspired by the experience.

Janis's 1959 high school annual and scrapbook document how her status had devolved over the year: early on, attendance at the Student Body Congress officers' inaugural ceremony, pep rallies, and clubs, with her picture included in many group shots. A variety of male and female students penned inscriptions in her *Yellow Jacket* yearbook. "Dee Dee" wrote: "When I first heard of you my opinion of you wasn't so good but now I must admit that you are a good kid." Billy McDuffie signed it to "the best hunk 'o junk." One boy thanked her for helping him with his homework.

The most biting comments came, again, from Karleen Bennett, whose commentary was perhaps meant to mock both Janis's own insecurities and those who scorned her, alluding for good measure to Janis's still-intact virginity: "Even if I can't call you all the names everybody else does, I'm thinking them. . . . You know what you are, so I don't have to tell you. . . . Well, I know what you are—even if everybody else thinks you're the opposite. . . . (no, I won't get in the back of anybody's car with you)." Her final lines could well have wounded self-conscious sixteen-year-old Janis: "You have the biggest nose & the littlest beadiest most close-set eyes of anyone in T.J. Funny, your rear end is also the biggest. Too bad the rest of you doesn't match all your shorts and tight skirts!"

Photographs of Janis, many still taken by her father, show a healthy teenage girl with short, wavy brown hair and a developing figure. By then, Janis had reached a height of five foot five and weighed a normal 130 pounds. If Janis found Karleen's jabs hurtful, she doubtless saw them as the price to pay for feeling accepted.

The summer after eleventh grade, Janis worked as a ticket taker at the Port cinema and returned to the Little Theatre, where she again designed sets. The theater had lost its luster, however, since Langdon and the others, preparing for college in the fall, barely participated. As a rite of passage, the guys climbed every water tower in the Golden Triangle, with Janis joining them on some of their daredevil ascents. In the moonlight, they hung out on the beach at the abandoned Coast Guard station, drinking wine and beer. "We'd make a bonfire and sit around on blankets," said Adrian Haston. "The content of the conversation was more serious than it would be for some kids that age." He remembered Janis being preoccupied with "change," probably dreading the upcoming school year without her male companions; their special circle was soon to be broken. Her drinking escalated, exacerbating her depression. Her brother, Michael, remembered as a six-year-old being teased by Janis, who told him, "*I'm drunk! Can't you tell?*"

Loneliness followed the scattering of her friends. Some, including Arlene Elster and Dave Moriaty, went off to the University of Texas at Austin, while others attended nearby Lamar State College of Technology in Beaumont; Karleen Bennett spent her weekends with her new fiancé, and Kristin Bowen retreated from their friendship not long after the two attended a "beatnik party" at which attendees parodied the Beats, dressing in stereotypical berets and black turtlenecks. Janis clearly considered herself the real deal. At school, she wore black or purple tights (rather than the typical bobby socks or hose) with a tight pencil skirt, and on weekends she put on an oversized man's white shirt with Levi's—forbidden at school—and dirty white canvas shoes.

Her senior year, in fall 1959, began at a brand-new building, replacing the thirty-year-old Western deco structure where she'd spent the past two years. A "modern" institutional construction, the new TJ High featured "functional" innovations such as an air-conditioned auditorium, an expansive gymnasium, and an interior courtyard. Its massive Memorial Stadium could hold some fifteen thousand fans of the Yellow Jackets, coached by Clarence "Buckshot" Underwood. Janis would not be among the fans. She had grown to despise team sports and high school jocks and didn't hide her feelings. Her father, she'd been thrilled to learn, had abhorred football as a Texas A&M student—a sacrilege in the Lone Star State. Unlike Janis, however, he was not publicly vocal about it. "He said that attending football games was mandatory there," Karleen Bennett recounted. "So he hid in the closet. . . . He thought football was stupid and a waste of time."

Even though Seth the nonconformist conveyed the value of individualism, both parents urged Janis to try to get along with her classmates. Her father "had much less respect for society's value system than did Mother," Laura Joplin reflected, "but he accepted life and counseled Janis to do the same." Dorothy advised her to sign up for mechanical drawing, but it turned out that girls were not welcome in the traditionally male class, and Janis faced additional taunts and abuse. "I didn't realize I was putting her into a bad emotional setting," Dorothy confessed later. "They began saying she was chasing the boys and that sort of thing. It hurt her terribly."

By senior year, Janis had become "the image of everything the students disliked," according to her friend Tary Owens. One of Janis's tormentors would become the second most famous TJ High graduate. The future head coach of the Dallas Cowboys (and Fox network football sportscaster), Jimmy Johnson was about Janis's age, though a grade behind. The son of an Arkansas-born dairy worker, he'd already lost his front tooth as the Yellow Jackets' star linebacker. He'd learned about Port Arthur's red-light district by age fourteen: "We found a . . . haven for beer drinkers: whorehouses," he wrote in his memoir. "There were eight or nine of them, and they sold beer, and they never questioned our age. . . . The owners wouldn't let us go upstairs, but the parlors were great places for us to hang out and drink beer and . . . look at women who had very few clothes on. They would sit on our laps and kid around with us. The roughnecks and the whores thought we were pretty funny."

Seated in alphabetical order in history class, Janis was stuck at the desk behind Johnson, who, by his own admission, made her life miserable because she "ran with the beatnik crowd." Johnson recalled, "Her crowd was, to say the least, anti-jock. Our crowd was made up of jocks . . . and the cheerleaders and majorettes who hung out with us and wore our letter jackets. Janis looked and acted so weird that when we were around her, mostly in the hallways at school, we would give her a hard time. One of my football teammates nicknamed her 'Beat Weeds.' Beat was for beatnik. . . . '[W]eeds' had a meaning rooted in the jock vernacular of Southeast Texas. Put it this way: in other areas of the country, she might have been known as 'Beat *Bush*,'" he said, referring to her pubic hair.

"Beat Weeds" wasn't the only insult from Johnson and his pals. When Janis walked down the hall, the jocks threw pennies at her and called her "whore" and "slut." Boys whose hands she swatted away when they grabbed her later lied that she'd been an easy lay. If she did date a classmate, he'd try to get her drunk and push her into sex, which she refused. When taunted at school, she'd laugh her loudest cackle, yell nasty retorts, or just toss her head and look away. When caught by a teacher cursing her tormentors, she'd be sent to the principal's office. The star athletes went unpunished. Thirty-three years later, in 1993, Johnson (whose Cowboys had just won the Super Bowl), told *Sports Illustrated* about his former classmate: "Beat Weeds . . . never wore any panties." How Johnson came by this knowledge is unclear.

"People said she was loose, and she did this or that," recalled Patti Skaff, who would replace Karleen as Janis's best friend the following year. "Ten times as many guys as she had ever gone out with said they had slept with her."

Janis's bohemian wardrobe brought her ridicule. Once, Karleen recalled, when Janis was sent home for breaking the dress code, she made a fuss when she returned, screaming up from the courtyard, *"Am I dressed okay now?"* Janis carried her own homemade beatnik version of a school pennant: a tiny felt flag, attached to a stick, with the word *YEA* hand printed on it. "Janis said and did things to see what kind of reactions she'd get," according to Roger Pryor's high school girlfriend, whom he later married, so she became a magnet for abuse. Her days of trying to fit in had ended, and although rejection was the price for presenting her real self, she did it anyway, with increasing conviction. "I didn't have anyone to talk to," Janis said later about her "very unhappy" senior year.

It pained Seth Joplin, himself a lifelong loner, to stand by helplessly while his daughter suffered at the hands of fellow students: "They hated her because she was different," he would tell *Rolling Stone* in 1970.

Dorothy was stricken over Janis's fall from grace at school: she plummeted from being a B student who was well regarded by her teachers to a truant who skipped class, failed tests, and didn't bother to hand in assignments. As the Port Arthur College registrar, Dorothy coached aspiring secretaries who looked nothing like her own daughter and who respected her opinion. Janis rarely listened to her advice, and the years of dutifully wearing her mother's home-sewn outfits were over.

"I remember fights in the house, the screaming," said Michael Joplin. Arguments between Janis and her mother often exploded over Janis's wardrobe, including her filthy white tennis shoes. When the Joplins' housekeeper washed them, as instructed by Dorothy, Janis threw a fit.

As their shouting escalated, Dorothy saw a doctor who prescribed a tranquilizer to help her through the "troubles at home," which, she recounted, "had enough friction in it that I contacted a counselor in Beaumont." Dorothy later told her daughter Laura that she informed the doctor "we were simply losing touch with our oldest daughter, and we'd had a good relationship with her in the past." Seth refused to attend the recommended family counseling with his wife and Janis, saying that therapy "was scatterbrained" and too expensive. Apparently, Seth, who could easily afford the cost, either didn't believe in psychiatry, or perhaps secretly related to his daughter's rebelliousness or worried that his own psyche might come under scrutiny.

Janis did begin seeing a Beaumont psychologist. Years later, in the flush of fame, she'd tell stories to the press about her awful adolescence, including the falsehood that her parents kicked her out of the house. Her family denied this as a tall tale, but perhaps in Janis's mind, the Joplins no longer wanted the person she had become. "Mother would try to get me to be like everybody else," Janis told esteemed jazz critic Nat Hentoff in 1968, "and I never would. She always told me to think before I speak." At her infamous tenth high school reunion, in 1970, she bitterly recalled to a reporter, "Some doctor told my mother that if I

didn't—quote-'straighten up'—unquote—I was going to end up either
in jail or an insane asylum by the time I was twenty-one."

>—+—>—○—<+—<

Janis's artistic achievements remained her sole consolation during senior year, with her winning several art competitions, one of which enabled her to travel to an art event in Houston. Slipping away from the
school group, she sought out the Purple Onion coffeehouse, a shabby
gathering spot for the city's bohemians. During the waning weeks of
1959, Port Arthur had secured its own boho hangout, the tiny Sage
Coffeehouse, opened by Elton Pasea, a Trinidad native and former mer-
chant marine. A close friend of Jim Langdon's, Pasea hung paintings on
the walls, set up chess tables, and played jazz on the hi-fi in the cluttered
storefront. Janis became a regular at the Sage, and Pasea exhibited her
work on the walls. During the Christmas holiday, she reunited with her
old gang, home from college. They celebrated New Year's Eve together
at the Sage, slipping out to their cars to gulp down beer and wine. By
night's end, Janis broke out her best Odetta voice, singing and dancing
on the tabletops.

She had stayed in touch with Langdon, visiting him in Beaumont,
where he attended Lamar Tech and played trombone in various ensembles. "Janis and another girl came up one night to see my Beaumont Symphony concert and came over to my place," he recounted. "I
remember lying on the floor with the lights virtually out, having Miles
Davis's *Kind of Blue* on the record player. Just the three of us. There was
no romantic involvement—just three displaced souls."

A week after Janis's seventeenth birthday, on Friday, January 26, 1960,
she "borrowed" her father's 1953 Willys sedan to "spend the night with
Karleen." She had hatched a plan to see some real jazz musicians—in
New Orleans, some 265 miles away. Langdon jumped at the chance to
accompany her on the four-hour drive; Janis stopped by the Sage and
announced, "I'm going to New Orleans! Anybody wanna come?" Classmate Clyde Wade said, "*You what?* I don't have any money, but I have a
Gulf credit card!" Dale Gothia, of the Boogie Kings, followed them out

the door to the car. "We stopped and bought some beers and headed off to New Orleans!" Wade remembered.

Arriving that evening, they walked the French Quarter, with music wafting from bar after bar. Bourbon Street crawled with people; barkers stood outside clubs, hawking the entertainment—strippers, music, and cheap drinks from to-go windows. In the middle of the night, they stumbled back to the sedan, which Janis wanted to return the next day. A soft rain started falling, and soon it was pouring on Highway 61, making it hard to see the pavement. Barely fourteen miles from New Orleans, in Kenner, Louisiana, the car plowed into the back of a 1959 Chevrolet, which had made a sudden stop. Smoke rose from the radiator.

"Fuck!" Janis screamed. *"My father's gonna kill me!"*

The other driver, Mr. A. E. Gordon, complained of neck pain. The State Police arrived to investigate but didn't issue Janis a ticket due to weather conditions. But when they saw her age—she looked younger than seventeen—they threatened to charge her male companions with a felony, the Mann Act, for transporting a female minor across state lines. Janis had to call Dorothy, who vouched for Langdon and the others and then wired Janis money for a bus ticket home. The cops drove the guys, who had thirteen cents between them, to the city limits, gave them a dollar, and warned, "Don't come back!" The boys stuck out their thumbs.

"I don't know how long we were standing there," Wade recounted, "but here comes this bus driving by, and in it Janis was hanging out the window waving and yelling at us. We looked like hell, and it was hard getting a ride." Eventually the boys hitched part of the way and then called Randy Tennant to pick them up. "When we finally walked into the Sage, everybody knew about the trip," said Wade. "We were treated almost like celebrities."

Janis, on the other hand, faced condemnation at home and at school for leaving town with the young men. Rumors flew that she'd slept with all three. Because so many boys had claimed to have had sex with her, students gleefully believed the gossip. Dorothy's worst fear had come true: Janis's reputation was ruined. "Most of the girls pointing at her and calling her a whore were a lot more sexually active than she was," Tary Owens said. "As a matter of fact, I know that's the case." Janis fought the name-calling by yelling, *"Fuck you!"*

The school guidance counselor accused her of being a bad influence on other students. Janis's truancy and profanity in the hallways increased. In March, the school suspended her, for causes unknown, but most likely for disrespecting school authorities or cursing at her tormentors in the halls. Dorothy met with TJ officials, who inquired why she couldn't make her daughter "be average." Later, Janis mused sadly, "All I was looking for was some kind of personal freedom and other people who felt the same way." For the rest of the semester, she was shunned. Ten years later, Janis would say she'd been a "recluse" as a high school student. One year of anguish and humiliation wiped out any good feelings she'd ever had about her school years; any good memories of friendship in Port Arthur.

With a wan smile, Janis posed—probably in fall 1959—for her senior portrait wearing a cap and gown, which appears in the 1960 *Yellow Jacket*; her copy does not have a single classmate signature or inscription on any of its pages. Though she missed numerous classes, she did manage to graduate with the class of 1960 in May. Some students later swore she staggered drunkenly to the stage to pick up her diploma. Undoubtedly, if she wasn't drunk then, she wasted no time in celebrating her freedom from Thomas Jefferson High.

CHAPTER 5

"18 AND FUCKED UP"

I'm one of those old-fashioned thrill-crazy
kids. . . . I never could see any value or anything
to be sought after . . . except fun.

—JANIS JOPLIN

anis desperately wanted to hit the road like Kerouac, but at seventeen, she was not quite ready, still unsteady in her beatnik persona. Her parents insisted she attend Lamar State College of Technology because of its close location and low cost. Lamar was the school of choice for many TJ grads, with a curriculum focused on training future engineers for the petroleum industry. Janis applied grudgingly, hoping to take as many art classes as possible and to meet like-minded souls. She also knew Beaumont would offer more chances to drink and party, her preferred—and increasingly employed—means of release. And she would be on her own for the first time, her family a half hour away.

Enrolled at Lamar, Janis moved into a two-story brick dormitory for female freshmen. Larger than Port Arthur, and a college town, Beaumont reputedly was more enlightened, but in reality was as conservative and, of course, as rigidly segregated. "You didn't escape Port Arthur by going to Lamar," said David Moriaty, who went to UT-Austin. "There was no dividing line between graduating high school and going across the street to Lamar."

Early on, Janis made friends with a Mexican American girl, Gloria Lloreda, who hailed from Galveston, Texas. They met the day Janis discovered that the school carpentry shop had accidentally ruined one of her paintings with a table saw. "I heard this awful sound," Gloria recalled about Janis's yelling and cursing. "She was so upset! That was my first encounter with Janis." A quiet, sheltered girl from a Catholic family, Gloria admired Janis's spunk, and the two moved into the same suite. "She was so outspoken . . . a liberated female!" Gloria remembered. "We'd go somewhere on campus, and a guy would get smart, and she'd just haul off and use very abusive language. If somebody irritated her, she'd let them know!"

Janis immediately began breaking the dorm's curfew and the school's dress code, which did not surprise fellow TJ alumni who attended Lamar. "There were a lot of girls from Port Arthur in the dorm," Gloria recounted. "They were prim and proper. They told me I shouldn't be friends with Janis because she had a real bad reputation. I said, 'Hey, I like her!' "

Janis found new ways to test limits at Lamar. She, Gloria, and another suitemate, a six-foot-tall freshman named Annette, performed a faux striptease to entice the male residents of the dorm across the courtyard. According to Gloria, "One night, about one o'clock, we turned out all the lights, and we had our swimsuits on under our nightgowns. We flashed the lamp about eight times and put the lamp back [behind us] and did a little striptease. We were very daring with our bathing suits on! We thought they'd never know who it was, but the next day, the guys were coming up to us, saying, 'We enjoyed your strip show!' "

Port Arthur native Patti Skaff was a grade ahead of Janis; she'd attended UT-Austin before flunking out and enrolling at Lamar. They met when the striking brunette posed for Janis's figure-drawing class. Patti, a talented artist from a well-to-do Lebanese American family, loved to party, and soon she and Janis were skipping class and hanging out at bars where IDs weren't checked. "We spent a lot of time getting as drunk as we could," Patti recalled. "We both thought we were outcasts. . . . It was us against the world."

When Janis went on benders with Patti and missed curfew, Gloria and their suitemates covered for her and, if necessary, sneaked her into the room—including hoisting her up to the second-floor balcony along the dorm's outer hallway. "When the monitor would come by, we'd say, 'Oh, she's in the shower,'" Gloria recalled. "Then we'd hear this singing and racket, and [she] was so drunk, [and her friends were] trying to get Janis up to the second story. They couldn't quite get her up there, and she'd fall back down. She eventually made it, [with us] pulling from the top and [them] pushing from the bottom."

Gloria didn't find Janis's new bad habit—shoplifting—so amusing. Perhaps inspired by *On the Road*'s Dean Moriarty and Sal Paradise—or maybe just looking for more thrills—Janis started swiping snacks and clothing. Gloria discovered this during a weekend visit to the Joplins in Port Arthur. "Janis liked to do things to see what she could get away with; to get a little excitement," Gloria surmised. "We went shopping, and when we got back to her house, she took her sweatshirt off, and she had a few things under her shirt: a blouse and a scarf. She did it just for kicks; she didn't need it. I told her, 'Look, when we go out together, no more of this!'" But a few weeks later, at a Beaumont drugstore, while Gloria was paying for mascara, the "guy at the counter asked [Janis] to open her purse," said Gloria. "She did, and she had some stuff in there. He told us to leave and never come back. I just laid into her, and she said, 'I'm so sorry. I won't ever do it again.'" Perhaps she refrained around Gloria, but Janis would shoplift off and on until being arrested in Berkeley, California, for the misdemeanor of petty theft in 1963.

Janis introduced Gloria to her Port Arthur friends, including Patti Skaff, Jim Langdon, and Adrian Haston, and before long, Gloria and Adrian became a couple; they eventually married. At first, "I didn't even think about going with Adrian because I thought Janis liked him," said Gloria, "but she said, 'No, we're just good friends.'" As usual, Janis remained one of the guys, without a boyfriend. She and her college gang, which included other freshmen from Port Arthur—Janis's fellow music fan Tary Owens, her junior high beau Jack Smith, and the well-heeled Philip Carter—became friendly with Beaumont's bohemians. "We sort of merged into a much larger network of people who hung out, talked together, and went to the same parties," Langdon recalled.

The Stopher family was among the most interesting: originally from Thibodaux, Louisiana, Henry (aka Wali, born in 1939) and Tommy (born in 1941) were the eldest of three brothers who grew up in Beaumont with their widowed mother, a pianist and teacher. They lived in a two-story house at 2080 Blanchette Street, with the boys' bedrooms on the second floor. Tommy, a handsome young man with numerous girlfriends (one friend called him a "lothario"), was a driven artist whose work dazzled Janis.

"Tommy was a brilliant man," Henry Stopher said of his brother. "He started sketching, drawing, and painting at about fourteen, and he did that every day. When everybody sat around in a room jawing away, Tommy had a sketchbook and was sketching stuff." The two brothers had traveled in Europe together, and Tommy had studied at the Kansas City Art Institute before returning to Beaumont. Janis wanted Tommy. At a party at the Stophers' one night, he and Janis paired off. "With both of them being artists, the idea was that they were going into the bedroom, and it was going to be some fantastic deal," Henry said. "When they came out, they were both really angry. Apparently, things didn't work out." Nonetheless, months later, when driving through Beaumont with Karleen Bennett, Janis stopped the car next to the Stopher house. "Wanna see the place where I had sex the first time?" she asked Karleen, pointing to a second-floor bedroom window.

After her interlude with Tommy Stopher, Janis no longer held back when guys wanted to have sex with her. She had nothing to lose in terms of reputation, as the Port Arthur coeds in Beaumont still gossiped about her being a slut. According to Patti, her attitude became "If you're gonna damn me anyway, well, I'll just go ahead and do it. Okay, motherfucker, you said I did it, *I'll just go ahead and do it.*"

At the same time, her relationship with Patti deepened, perhaps to the point of Janis being sexually attracted to her. "We didn't ask each other for anything," Patti said. "It was just friendship. We just enjoyed being together." They fantasized about leaving Lamar. "She wanted me to hitchhike to California with her. But I didn't think she and I would get too far together. Neither one of us had a pot to piss in. We'd probably just bog each other down totally." Onstage ten years later, while doing Etta James's "Tell Mama," Janis rapped about being seventeen, "when you get those strange thoughts in your head, and you don't know where they came from, those strange little weirdnesses happening to you, and you don't know what they are." She then segued into the song's lyrics: "You need someone to listen to you, someone to want you, someone to hold you, someone to want you. . . . *Tell mama, baby!*"

Janis was possibly confused by her sexual feelings for Patti, during a time when being queer was a crime in Texas (with sodomy a felony in every state until 1962). Five years later, following a physical exam and blood tests, Janis's doctor diagnosed a possible "hormone imbalance." Janis interpreted this as an explanation for her sexual attraction to both women and men. In a 1965 letter to her male lover, she speculated that this supposed "imbalance" was the reason she was "not really a woman or enough of one or something. . . . Maybe something as simple as a [hormone] pill could have helped out or even changed that part of me I call ME and has been so messed up."

During freshman year, Janis's sexual encounters were with men, including a one-night stand with a former TJ student, Dave McQueen, who now attended Lamar. The son of an ex-con who'd become an oil worker, McQueen, like Patti, graduated from high school a year before Janis. Tary Owens introduced them right before Janis moved to Beaumont, telling McQueen that she was, like them, on the fringes—"clearly one of us." When they met for coffee at a Luby's Cafeteria, McQueen found Janis "out of sight. We were just book reading, rebellious, and hell raising," he recounted, "and we all eventually wanted to go to North Beach," in San Francisco, to join the Beat Generation. One night, in Beaumont, Janis and McQueen had sex in the back seat of his car. "I always thought she was pretty," he recalled, "and we found ourselves sitting next to each other and went from there."

Soon after, Janis introduced him to Patti, and her best friend became McQueen's lover. "She was hurt when Dave and I got together," Patti reflected, possibly not realizing that losing *her*, rather than McQueen, was the source of Janis's pain. All of Janis's close friends paired off, including Jim Langdon, who settled down with Rae Logan, a Lamar student whom he'd marry the next year. Still, the couples included Janis on their outings, with the gang often cutting class to party. One afternoon, Rae and Jim, Gloria and Adrian, and Janis took off for Austin, where they shared a motel room and threw a party that included their UT friends David Moriaty and Randy Tennant. Janis didn't see much of the town, but eighteen months later, a subsequent trip to Austin would change her life.

In Beaumont, Janis's music exploration continued. Jim had become fascinated by Lamar professor and noted folklorist Dr. Francis Abernathy's field recordings and early blues 78s, which he shared with Janis and others. "Jim Langdon rummaged around in the English Department and got into Dr. Abernathy's collection of records," Henry Stopher recalled. "He had a bunch of twenties and thirties blues singers' records, and that's what Langdon took. We all listened to them and were just blown away. I was so locked into my little culture, it took me a long time to even understand the words. But Janis listened over and over and over, and soon she was singing Bessie Smith songs."

Janis sought out more recordings by the Empress of the Blues (1894–1937) and became obsessed with what 1920s writer Carl Van Vechten described as Smith's "cutting her heart open with a knife until it was exposed . . . so that we suffered as she suffered, exposed with a rhythmic ferocity." Already attracted to the "sincerity" of Lead Belly's music, Janis "started reading books on blues, and I kept coming across the name Bessie Smith," she recounted in 1970. "So I wrote away and got a bunch of her records. I just really fell in love with her"—so much so that she exaggerated the number of years she imitated Smith's style: "The first ten years I sang," Janis claimed later, "I sang just like Bessie Smith. I copied her a lot, sang all of her songs." In reality, Janis died ten years after discovering Smith. Just two months before her death, Janis helped buy a headstone for the blues queen's unmarked grave and discussed the possibility of setting up a scholarship fund in her honor. "No one ever hit me so hard," she told Smith biographer Chris Albertson in 1970 as they listened together to a Smith recording at Columbia Records' studios. "Bessie made me want to sing."

>→←◦→←◦→←◦←◦←◦←

Though enthralled with Smith and the blues, Janis still considered herself primarily a painter, not a singer. She gave her paintings to friends, including Langdon, to whom Janis gifted a nude self-portrait in shades of blue, clearly influenced by Amedeo Modigliani (1884–1920). Just as she researched Smith, she read about and romanticized the self-destructive Italian artist's tragic and brief life, marked by alcoholism, drug addiction, and disease. Modigliani, referenced by Kerouac in *On the Road*, was newly celebrated with a 1958 retrospective at New York City's Museum of Modern Art, which Janis read about in *Time*. That same year, the artist's daughter, Jeanne, published *Modigliani: Man and Myth*, featured in the news magazine's December 1 issue. Soon after, the painter's moody, angular portraiture and female nudes began influencing Janis's own developing work. Her parents hung one of her striking, dark-hued male figures on their dining room wall. They praised her portrait of eleven-year-old Laura Joplin. But her family and friends' admiration of her work, and the few sales she'd made via the Sage Coffeehouse, were no longer enough to give her the confidence and attention she needed as a visual artist. Exposed to Tommy Stopher's skillful—and unique—paintings, sculptures, and assemblages, she began to lose faith in her work. The fear that she lacked the singular talent her parents and teachers had identified and promoted must have filled her with dread: Who could she be now?

Rather than work harder at developing her own original vision, Janis drank more than ever. "We'd scrape up money, which nobody ever had, and go down to the Paragon Drive-In and get a gallon of beer for fifty cents, if you brought your own jug," Patti remembered. "We'd all drink it, then we'd throw up. We thought we were having a great time." Janis also occasionally popped diet pills—amphetamines—widely available on campus.

A trip to Houston, ostensibly to hear music at some clubs, ended with Janis's hospitalization. "When I was 17, I went to Houston, took a lot of pills, drank huge quantities of wine, and flipped out," she wrote in a letter five years later. Although she minimized this harrowing episode, writing, "I was sent home, put in the hospital, and I did fine," when she returned to school, she began seeing a psychiatrist *and* a psychologist. Her diagnosis and treatment are unknown, but certainly the speed, combined with her voluminous alcohol consumption, had taken a toll, exacerbating her tendency toward depression. Years later, Janis variously told a doctor and several friends that she'd been treated for alcoholism at seventeen; that she'd undergone insulin shock therapy; and that after a nervous breakdown at college she had been admitted to a Beaumont hospital. None of her claims have been substantiated. When asked in the early seventies about Janis's mental health crisis at seventeen, Dorothy Joplin downplayed it, saying that her problems resulted from her "cutting classes and her conscience . . . bothering her." Whatever the case, by semester's end, Janis had earned a B in English composition but flunked her other classes.

Despite her Houston breakdown, and therapy, she dealt with her academic failures by continuing to drink when she returned to Port Arthur. During winter break, the revelry continued with friends old and new. Philip Carter hosted frequent parties, attended by Janis and Patti, still her major confidante. "Phil's parents were off to the country club on New Year's Eve, so he invited us all over to his house for a party," Patti recounted. "[Janis] and I were goaded into fighting with each other. I don't know why—maybe we were just out of our minds. We were drinking vodka and . . . had this catfight, hair pulling, buttons popping. . . . Janis came bouncing down the stairs with her shirt completely ripped open and her breasts flying, and Philip's mother and father walked in the front door. His mama started screaming. They threw us out immediately." Neither girl would return to Lamar for the spring semester.

>─╼─◉─╾─◄

When Janis turned eighteen in January 1961, she was at loose ends, no longer passionate about painting, not yet emboldened by music, a failed student, confused and depressed. For the first time, she toyed with the idea of becoming a professional singer. After attending a Beaumont community theater rehearsal for a musical comedy called *The Boy Friend*, she confessed to one of its featured vocalists, Lamar student Frances Vincent, "I wanna do what you do!"

Vincent recalled: "She said it passionately—I think she wanted to be the center of attention." Janis later compared singing to painting, saying, "Singing makes you want to come out, whereas painting, I feel, really keeps you inside. When I started singing, it just sort of made you want to talk to people more and go out more."

Janis sang only casually, among friends, but she researched her possible new vocation by visiting Port Arthur's record shop and playing discs in the store's listening booth. "We'd spend hours listening to a stack of records," Patti recalled. "She got into the blind blues singer Reverend Gary Davis and Bessie Smith. That's what we went home with. But she listened to everything: jazz and country but mainly old black blues." Among C&W artists, she particularly liked Hank Williams, and she was fond of Cajun music such as "Jole Blonde," originated by Port Arthur fiddler Harry Choates, later called "the godfather of Cajun music."

When Patti visited the Joplins, they discussed music. Dorothy described her own aspirations as a teenage singer, while Seth sat quietly in his easy chair, with Bach's *The Well-Tempered Clavier* on the hi-fi. Patti's father owned a Webcor reel-to-reel recorder, and at her house, Patti recorded Janis attempting Bessie Smith numbers. But the Skaff family began discouraging their daughter from seeing Janis after Patti's younger brother, Sammy, informed his parents of Janis's bad reputation at TJ. Then Janis and Philip Carter drove to the Skaffs' with a young black man sitting in the back seat. He was just someone they'd picked up hitchhiking, but Patti's father imagined that Janis was aiding his daughter in a secret affair "with a Negro" and flew into a rage. Sammy Skaff appears to have continued to stir up trouble: when he and his best friend, George William "G. W." Bailey (who would become an actor in the TV series *M*A*S*H* and the *Police Academy* movies), saw Janis at a backyard BBQ, they reportedly hassled her, and, as usual, she fought back, yelling and attracting attention. Spotting her ninth-grade beau Jack Smith drinking beer and listening to music, she grabbed him, he recalled, and said, "Be my white knight! Be my white knight!" Smith did just that, shoving Bailey and telling him to leave Janis alone. (Bailey later described the incident as "a wild party going on with a little marijuana. A scuffle broke out, but it really had nothing to do with Janis.") In any case, Jack and Janis reconnected at the party and began spending time together.

The Joplins tried to contain Janis's problems by keeping her away from Michael and Laura, now eight and twelve, respectively. "Their seething hostility greeted Janis's attempts to encourage Michael and me to adopt her ways," Laura wrote later. Undaunted, Janis kept up her outrageous behavior: getting drunk, staying out all night, and seeking thrills and attention. One of her most dangerous pranks involved climbing with some friends to the top span of Port Arthur's Rainbow Bridge, which crossed the Neches River. Perched on a catwalk two hundred feet above the water, one of them threw a beer bottle at a tugboat far below. A motorist spotted the hooligans, but when several squad cars arrived, Janis and company somehow managed to talk their way out of being arrested.

>-+-◊-○-◊+-◄

In March Dorothy insisted that Janis enroll at Port Arthur College, where she could learn keypunching, a marketable skill in 1961. Beginning as a "half-day special student," Janis soon switched to full-time status and actually thrived in the business school setting. An excellent typist, she also got high marks in accounting, marketing, English, and keypunch. Her delighted mother later praised her as "a wonderful typist and a good keypunch operator." In July, with Janis's training complete, Dorothy arranged for her to move in with her sister Mildred in Los Angeles. Now known as Mimi, she resided not far from their other sister, Barbara Irwin, a divorced real estate agent. Janis's dreams of seeing her mythical West Coast were about to come true.

"Since I helped Mildred [in the past], I thought surely she'd be willing to help me in return," Dorothy explained later. "So I asked if Janis could stay with her for a little while and see if she could find a market there for her keypunch skills." Janis, though excited about the trip, told friends she'd been "banished" by her mother so she wouldn't be a bad influence on her siblings. One Saturday in July, Janis boarded a "smelly" Greyhound bus, in Laura's words, with her belongings packed in a brand-new set of luggage purchased by her mother. The nearly 1,700-mile trip, crossing Texas, New Mexico, and Arizona into California, must have given Janis visions of the journeys she'd read about in *On the Road*. And like Sal Paradise, she made friends with a fellow traveler onboard: a young African American man whom she sat next to for most of the journey.

When Mimi and Barbara met her at the bus station, Janis enthusiastically introduced them to her new friend before her aunts whisked her away. Dorothy had told them nothing about their fledgling beatnik niece's interests and talents beyond her skills at keypunch and accounting, but Janis would soon make herself fully known to her aunts.

Mimi lived with her husband, Harry, and fifteen-year-old daughter, Donna, who later recalled being impressed by her cousin's courage to travel alone to California. Their Brentwood home had a shed out back, used primarily by Harry as a painting studio. Janis moved into the space, where they set up a makeshift bed. Her first night there, she stayed up until almost dawn, working on a painting, surprising Mimi in the morning.

With her aunts' help, Janis found work as a keypunch operator at the General Telephone Company's Santa Monica branch. She rode the bus to work Monday through Friday and began saving money to rent her own place. Janis mostly kept to herself but would occasionally bring someone home. One rendezvous Mimi never forgot was when Janis announced that a guy with "perfect hands" would be posing for her portrait of a man playing guitar. She recalled Janis saying, "Don't think I'm crazy about him. I'm not. He's in for a shock when he finds out I just want to paint his hands." Another edifying incident with her unusual niece occurred at a restaurant featuring live music. As the band played the New Orleans classic "When the Saints Go Marching In," Janis kicked off her shoes, leapt from her seat, and sang along in her strong soprano. Until that moment, Mimi had been unaware of Janis's vocal talent.

Eventually Janis's aunt Barbara Irwin found a cheap apartment for her niece, but it soon became clear Janis couldn't handle the responsibility of paying rent. Barbara, whom Dorothy described as "a great deal more witty and humorous" than Mimi, invited Janis to move in with her and her teenage daughter, Jean. Twice divorced, Barbara had "more in common" with Janis, according to Dorothy, and squeezed her into their two-bedroom apartment. A heavy drinker involved with a married broker at the real estate agency, Barbara sometimes included Janis in their daily cocktail hour. Eventually, though, Jean became jealous of the bond Janis formed with her mother, and the atmosphere grew tense. Janis, meanwhile, was eager to check out Venice Beach, the Beat haven next to Santa Monica, and to begin her beatnik life in earnest.

Described as a refuge for "bohemians [who] played new jazz LPs and old blues 78s, drank wine, beat drums, blew kazoos, smoked marijuana, and took Benzedrine to help them stay up and shoot their revelations through the night" by Lawrence Lipton in his 1959 book *The Holy Barbarians*, Venice had passed its peak by the summer of 1961. A sure sign that Venice was passé was *Life* magazine's 1959 feature spotlighting the neighborhood as "Beatsville."

In 1905 Venice's founder, entrepreneur Abbot Kinney, had modeled the area after the canals and architecture of Italy's Venezia, promoting it as the "Coney Island of the West." In the 1950s, with its dilapidated buildings and canals filled in with concrete, Venice became a cheap destination for poets, writers, and jazz musicians. When Janis discovered it in August '61, the area was "known throughout the city as the place to go for an easy score, an easy bust, an easy roll," according to John Arthur Maynard's *Venice West: The Beat Generation in Southern California*. In addition to Beats, "tourists, sun-worshippers, and bodybuilders still crowded the beach by day, but the night belonged to the muggers, the drunks, and the psychopaths."

After a chance meeting with a Venice resident on a city bus, Janis's fascination with the Beat community swelled, and she put the wheels in motion to leave Aunt Barbara's. She saved enough money from her keypunch job to rent a cheap garage apartment at 25½ Brooks Avenue, between Speedway Alley and Pacific Avenue, about a block from the beach.

Alone at last, Janis was ready to experiment. She'd finally found the freedom to explore drink, drugs, and sex with a variety of partners, male and female. Her arrival coincided with the last gasp of the Gas House, a Beat hangout for poets, musicians, and artists since 1959 that constantly battled local ordinances (such as a ban on bongo playing) intended to shut it down. It had become primarily an art gallery with the rare acoustic performance, including some impromptu busking by Janis.

By 1961, most of Venice's notables had fled the scene: Eric Nord, aka Big Daddy, an early Gas House impresario, had returned to North Beach, where he opened the Co-Existence Bagel Shop. Prominent Beat poet Stu Perkoff had sold his Venice West Espresso Café and become a heroin addict. His café, under new ownership, continued to thrive, however, and Janis became a regular there. She began regularly smoking pot and learned the art of rolling joints, later referring to herself at the time as a "grasshead." One of her new friends, a scrawny guy nicknamed Big Richard ("because he wasn't," explained Janis) first turned her on; another gave her Seconal, a barbiturate, or downer, and she soon mixed "reds" with wine for a sloppy buzz.

Her beatnik pals also encouraged her to sing and make art. Though she may have visited the Modigliani exhibition at the Los Angeles County Museum of Art that year, her taste now veered toward the "conceptual." On her apartment wall, she displayed a collage comprised of a rope, a desiccated bone, and dried peas salvaged from a pot of soup. One day Aunt Barbara and her boyfriend dropped by for a visit and were appalled by the apartment's squalor. Eying an old barrel filled with garbage in the center of the living area, Janis's aunt groused, *"You weren't raised to live like this!"* They left, never to return. Although Barbara was herself a bit of a swinger, Janis's lifestyle crossed the line.

"Barbara always wanted things to be right," Seth Joplin said, "and once Janis [got her Venice apartment], Barbara wiped her hands. They just dropped her."

Janis was actually becoming pretty disgusted with Venice too. "I was hanging out with all sorts of big-league junkies," she reflected later, "although I didn't understand it at the time. People kept burning me and stealing from me all the time, and I finally got very unhappy with everything." When she blew off her job at the phone company, she'd earned some $1,300 (the equivalent of $8,000 today) but gradually spent most of her funds.

She hitchhiked alone to San Francisco to finally check out North Beach. When she wrote Jim Langdon about her plans, he and Randy Tennant hitched from Texas to meet her there but were arrested in Wyoming for riding the rails. On her solitary adventure, she found Lawrence Ferlinghetti's City Lights bookstore on Columbus Avenue and hung out at cafés such as the Co-Existence Bagel Shop. Still only eighteen, she had trouble getting into bars where the drinking age was twenty-one but occasionally cajoled someone into buying her a bottle of wine. She crashed in SRO hotels for $8 a night or slept in the park.

Janis's new Beat look came from a North Beach army-navy surplus store: a funky World War II leather bomber jacket, lined with sheepskin, which she usually wore inside out. She gravitated to a Beat hangout on Grant Avenue, the Fox and Hound, and, while smoking a cigar, chatted up the doorman, Dave Archer, who recalled her inquiring about "*sangin'*" inside. Amused by the tomboyish Texan, he got her in, where she sang an a cappella "Silver Threads and Golden Needles," a 1956 C&W recording by Oklahoman Wanda Jackson. She later invited Archer, who was gay, to her shabby hotel room, where they stayed up all night talking and drinking wine.

At one point, Janis hitchhiked with a girl named Sally Lee to LA to retrieve her meager belongings; her new luggage was long gone. Once back in North Beach, Janis's San Francisco stay was short lived; she had just enough cash for a bus ticket home. She was "18 and fucked up," she recalled later in a letter. Her first stop in Texas was at Jim and Rae Langdon's house in Beaumont. "She had on her sheepskin jacket and looked really wild," recalled Rae, then pregnant with their first child. "She had all these crazy ideas. My sister came in and was kinda shocked." Jim, who'd not yet smoked cannabis, urged Janis to share her stash with him and Henry Stopher, who'd stopped by to visit. "Jim was relentless," Stopher recounted. "'I know you have some pot, Janis. We want to smoke it. Come on!' And she was like, 'No, man, there's just enough for me.' But finally she rolled us a skinny little joint."

After a couple of days, she took a taxi home to Lombardy Drive. "I'll never forget her showing up," said Seth Joplin. "We didn't think she was coming. About two days before Christmas, a cab came, and out jumped Janis. She and the cabbie started throwing pasteboard boxes out all over the yard. She had her belongings packed in about ten boxes all tied up neatly with white string. I remember the expression on that cabbie's face. He looked at her and looked at all those boxes and looked at me. It was funny."

Perhaps only a man watching his daughter live undeterred by fear—as he'd wanted to do—could be amused by such a sight. His prodigal child had returned from California to recuperate from pushing her limits, and just like in the parable, her father welcomed her. Thus would begin a pattern of Janis venturing to the West Coast, pushing the limits until exhausted mentally and physically, and then seeking refuge among those who loved her, even as they understood her less and less.

CHAPTER 6

HELL RAISER

*I never seemed to be able to control my feelings, to keep
them down. . . . When you feel that much, you have superhorrible downs. I'd run away, freak out, go crazy. . . .*

—JANIS JOPLIN

Back in Texas, when Janis reunited with her friends, they immediately recognized changes in her: she was more worldly, self-assured. As their crowd's sole pioneer, who'd ventured beyond the Golden Triangle to North Beach, she had picked up the Beat lingo; she cursed more than ever, made casual drug references, and could expertly roll joints. Scraping by on the streets for a while, she'd discovered the emotional intensity of dangerous behavior—perhaps the only behavior that could match her live-wire feelings and the neediness inside her. It was as if she were flying on her dad's backyard giant stride and couldn't bear to get off.

Not long after Janis told her friends about singing publicly in California, Jim Langdon brought her along to his friend Jimmy Simmons's gig in Beaumont on New Year's Eve. The Lamar student performed with a jazz band and invited her onstage to do a song—no one can remember which one. But instead of a soft "girl singer" voice, Janis belted in her bluesy Bessie Smith style. The spotlight ended after one number.

"They wanted a sweet-sounding little thing, for white people," Langdon recounted. "She didn't sound like June Christy—though I think she could have if she wanted to. Jimmy wouldn't let her sing anymore. He didn't like her. She was not what people were used to."

Langdon, unfazed, looked for other opportunities. Among the musicians he knew, Mexican American Ray Solis played piano in several bands at the Big Oak and Lou Ann's. When the pair was hired to develop a jingle for a Nacogdoches bank celebrating its fiftieth anniversary, Langdon suggested that Janis sing it. They recorded audio for the commercial with words based on Woody Guthrie's "This Land Is Your Land." "We put cornball lyrics to it," said Langdon. " 'This bank is your bank, this bank is my bank, from Nacogdoches to the Gulf Coast waters. Fifty years of savings, fifty years of service, this bank belongs to you and me.' Janis sang in a folk style over the band. The bank didn't buy it—but that was her first recording."

Janis escaped Port Arthur to hear music, driving with Tary Owens to Beaumont, where they were among the few whites at black clubs with jazz and R&B bands. Occasionally, they bumped into a pair of albino brothers, Johnny and Edgar Winter, talented Beaumont musicians a few years Janis's junior. In years to come, Janis would reconnect with Johnny Winter in New York, perform together, and commiserate about their neighboring hometowns. Through Langdon, Janis met African American trumpeter George Alexander, a former sideman for "Gatemouth" Brown, who taught music at a local high school and played jazz on weekends. "We were getting into black culture as much as we could," Owens recalled. "We'd go to these little after-hours places in Beaumont and Orange to hear black music." Whites were allowed there—unlike segregated venues in Port Arthur.

Soon after turning nineteen in January 1962, Janis reenrolled at Lamar as a commuter student for the spring semester. Because of her earlier failure there, and as an attempt to rein in her partying, Seth and Dorothy insisted she live at home. Janis looked for alternatives, including an abandoned drive-in movie theater concessions building, which she wanted to fix up. Her parents absolutely forbade it, Janis gave in, settled into her old bedroom, and began attending classes a few days a week. At night, she worked as a waitress, "slinging Schlitz," as she recalled, at a nearby Port Neches bowling alley. After work, around midnight, she'd convene with Patti Skaff, now engaged to Dave McQueen.

Tearing off the hairnet she was required to wear, she'd pick up a six-pack and drive to the Skaff home. "I'd sneak out, and we'd go off to drink beer . . . and just look at the moon," Patti recounted about the pair's rejuvenated bond.

Other nights, Janis met her old pal Jack Smith, also working in Port Neches and whose girlfriend was away at college. They took in music at Port Arthur's Pleasure Pier, and, during segregated concerts by black artists such as Chubby Checker and Jimmy Reed, they listened from the parking lot. Janis railed against her hometown's racial bigotry and was pleased when scandal took down the town's sheriff, after it was revealed he had received $85,000 in bribes from racketeers. The State Justice Department had begun investigating him after the *Beaumont Enterprise* ran articles exposing graft, gambling, and prostitution in Port Arthur; as a result, most of the city's brothels and gambling parlors were shuttered.

One evening, while she and Jack waited at an open drawbridge for a tugboat to pass below, Janis goaded Smith into getting out of the car and stealing a lightbulb from the drawbridge gate. After he drove across the bridge, police pulled him over. At the station house, he was taken into the detention room for questioning while Janis pleaded for his release: "*The lightbulb was burned out! It wasn't any good! Let him go!*" "Janis just ate them alive," Smith recalled. He was released without being charged. On the way home, she cried hysterically, her guilt and remorse the cost of once again pushing limits.

In February Patti and Dave McQueen married and invited Janis and classmate Philip Carter to join them on their honeymoon trip to New Orleans during Mardi Gras. Carter lent his father's car to the venture since the couple "had no money, about ten dollars," Patti recounted. After splitting up and roaming the French Quarter and drinking all day, they planned to reconvene and spend the night in Carter's sedan. When Janis arrived back at the car, the other three, passed out, didn't unlock the doors quickly enough to let her in, and she ran off in a drunken huff. When she returned the next day, Janis nonchalantly informed her friends that she'd picked up a sailor who had a hotel room, "so that she could get some sleep." Janis no longer tolerated rejection from friends, even if unintentional. As a street person in North Beach, she had learned to do what it took to get by and expressed no shame about it.

That spring, on jaunts between Port Arthur and Beaumont, Janis, the girl who'd remained a virgin through high school, was clearly the most sexually adventurous among her crowd. She slept with strangers and with other women—during a time when same-sex relationships in Texas were closeted at best. Jack Smith recalled Janis's conflicted emotions about being attracted to women. At a beach party, explaining to him why she'd disappeared into the back seat of a car with a girl, she said, "Alcohol makes you do funny things." When he drove her home, she asked him, "Does this make me a bad person? How do you feel about me now?" Smith later told writer Alice Echols that he assured Janis "his feelings for her hadn't changed, adding, 'It just seemed perfectly natural for Janis to be so adventuresome.'" When Jim Langdon witnessed Janis's coupling with a Beaumont woman, she was "very open about it. She just did what she felt like doing . . . with anybody."

Janis's feelings for Patti McQueen became obvious one night while Dave worked the night shift as a radio DJ. During a party at the McQueens' basement apartment in Beaumont, Janis and Patti began kissing while everyone looked on. "We were pretty wasted and were talking to each other, and we just looked at each other and embraced and kissed each other," said Patti. "That was just a thing of love right in the middle of a crowded room of people. She and I really did love each other very much." Her husband arrived during their embrace and proceeded to "get drunk as a skunk," recalled Gloria Haston, "and that caused a lot of trouble." An hour later, McQueen angrily hurled a bottle at his wife, who had passed out next to several others on a bed, including Jack Smith. Rather than hit Patti, the bottle smashed into Smith's face, knocking out his front teeth. Crying and again blaming herself for the incident, Janis drove her bloodied friend to the hospital. "We followed her car all the way back to Port Arthur," said Adrian Haston. "She was horrified that that happened."

After laying low for a while, Janis would invariably reconnect with Patti like star-crossed lovers—with often damaging consequences.

"When Patti and Janis got together, it could be poison," Jim Langdon recounted about the nights they all crossed the river to party in Louisiana bars. A particularly rough nightspot was the Shady Rest Motel Lounge, with an alligator-filled pond out back. Janis and Patti "hustled the guys to play pool and buy them beers," Langdon recalled. "The guys thought the girls were coming on to them and they were going to get something out of it. When they found out they were with us, it got very testy."

Following one of their late-night, early-morning Shady Rest excursions, during which the girls pulled their usual tricks with the locals, an infuriated and drunk Dave McQueen squealed out of the gravel parking lot, with the girls, Langdon, Phil Carter, and Jack Smith crammed in his 1955 Oldsmobile. Flying home along Highway 90 at a hundred miles an hour, he suddenly skidded out of control. Some recalled the car overturning; McQueen said he blew two tires and swerved off the road. Miraculously, no one was seriously hurt. Langdon crawled out and limped down the road until he found a phone to call his wife to pick them up. "I finally drew the line and said I'm not going anymore with Janis," Langdon said. After that, Janis and Patti drifted apart; eventually the McQueens moved to Houston.

In Beaumont, Janis met Lamar student Frank Davis, a folk-blues guitarist and singer. Impressed with his musicianship, she picked him up, and the two had a brief affair. "Janis could be adorable and incredibly lovable," according to Davis, "but she would swat you like a cat playing with a mouse to get you angry, even violent, so you'd be at her level of passion."

As Janis saw her friends moving on with their lives, a loneliness began to take hold. To her dismay, Jack Smith had enrolled at West Point and planned a move to New York in June. Just weeks before he left, on a weekend in May, with her family out of town, Janis drove her father's car to Smith's house around midnight. She suggested that instead of their usual jaunt to Louisiana, they go to Austin. He had intrigued her with tales of "the Ghetto," a University of Texas off-campus party house filled with beatniks and musicians. Among them were her old friends David Moriaty, now a third-year engineering student; his roommate Tary Owens, who'd transferred from Lamar to UT; and the Stopher brothers, Tommy and Henry.

At five thirty in the morning, Janis and Jack pulled up to a ramshackle two-story building at 2812½ Nueces Street, on a back alley not far from the university. As they wandered into the warren of apartments, most with their doors wide open, they heard acoustic guitar, banjo, and harmonica. They picked an apartment, walked into its kitchen, and there on top of the refrigerator sat a stocky man with a blond crew cut playing banjo: John Clay, three years older than Janis, was a linguistics major and budding songwriter from West Texas. "We talked and joked," Clay recalled. "She was in a fun mood and could make a whole party come alive. But I didn't know she could sing until the [next] night." While Jack Smith bunked with the Stophers, Janis spent the night with Clay.

The next evening, another Ghetto resident, harmonica player Powell St. John, was jamming in the backyard with guitarist Lanny Wiggins. "We were playing, and Janis just sat down and started to sing," St. John said. "We were flabbergasted! She was incredible. Her vocal talents were fully formed when I met her." Clay, quite judgmental about music, was amazed by her "command of style, great range, and very powerful voice—about as strong as an opera singer's." St. John, a senior majoring in art, was smitten with Janis, who was barefoot and wearing a tight black dress, her hair now hanging down past her shoulders, with bangs framing her pale blue eyes. "That night, she invited me to her bed," said St. John.

Full of excitement about the effect of her singing on such an intriguing group of people, and flush from two sexual flings in forty-eight hours, Janis promised to return to Austin soon. As they pulled out of the driveway heading back to Port Arthur, she turned to Smith with a big grin and said, "Jack, I think I'm going to like it here!"

CHAPTER 7

WALLER CREEK BOY

When I sing, I feel like, oh, when you're first in love.
—JANIS JOPLIN

Austin became Janis's mecca. To convince the Joplins to let her attend the University of Texas as an art major, she pointed to Port Arthur native Robert Rauschenberg, the world famous artist who'd studied at UT in the late 1930s. "She told them, 'I want to be like Rauschenberg,'" Jack Smith recalled, "and Mom and Dad said, 'Fine.'" But as a UT student, Janis did not follow in Rauschenberg's footsteps or even refine her painting skills. Instead, she discovered herself as a singer: gaining an audience, building her confidence, and holding sway as Austin's most mesmerizing blues singer. Yet, while surrounded by a tribe of like-minded bohemians, she continued to push her own emotional extremes, boozing and brawling—and foreshadowing a long pattern of self-sabotage. As she would recall in a letter three years later, "I went to Austin to go to school because I had gotten with some folksingers up there. All I did there was be wild, drank constantly, fucked people, sang, and generally made a name for myself on campus."

Enrolled as a freshman for 1962's summer session, Janis, like all first-year female students, had to live in approved housing. She found, not far from the Ghetto, a women-only boardinghouse whose elderly landlady retired early at night—making curfew breaking a cinch. In June Dorothy drove Janis to Austin, with Laura along to help carry her sister's belongings up to her second-floor room. As soon as they left, Janis walked the ten blocks from her new home at Nineteenth Street and Nueces to 2812½ Nueces. The Ghetto originally served as an army barracks during World War II. In the late 1950s, the owner converted it into apartments, with two on each floor and an additional one-room studio above the adjoining garage. With a shady backyard and secluded location just west of campus, it was a refuge for Austin's bohemians. Ted Klein, a bearded artist and musician who named it "the Ghetto" after renting there in 1959, said, "Virtually all who entered became artists, writers, poets, or musicians—despite their original intentions." Most apartments cost about $40 a month.

At the Ghetto, Janis reconvened with Powell St. John, a sensitive young man from Laredo, Texas. Three years Janis's senior, he had taught himself harmonica as a child, eventually learning the more difficult chromatic harmonica, playing country, folk, and Dixieland. At the Ghetto, he occupied a downstairs apartment where he worked up tunes with Austin native Lanny Wiggins, whose older brother, Ramsey—a Ghetto regular—had introduced him to St. John. In the vein of bluegrass duos such as the Blue Sky Boys, they'd named themselves the Waller Creek Boys after a polluted creek running through the UT campus. "A sad, sad stream," St. John said of Waller Creek. "There was nothing alive in it—it was downstream from the university Chemistry Department, and they dumped their chemicals into the creek. Sometimes the water was bright yellow."

Inspired by Woody Guthrie, the Waller Creek Boys learned their repertoire of Old English balladry and topical tunes from records and songbook collections compiled by Texan John Lomax, the UT folklorist who discovered Lead Belly. Lanny Wiggins, a folk music expert, sang and played guitar and banjo. Neither he nor St. John, though, drew from as deep a well as Janis did. "This nineteen-year-old girl had really done her folk homework," St. John recounted. "She knew rhythm and blues tunes I had never heard. She knew much more about music than we did. Janis was very serious about her art. She had a frivolous side, but she was a very intelligent girl." While a few white college kids, primarily in the Northeast and California, discovered and collected blues records from the twenties and thirties, Janis was the rare *female* blues scholar. St. John and Wiggins invited her to join the Waller Creek Boys—her first-ever band.

Once Janis came on board, the group's repertoire expanded to include R&B and blues, including her beloved Bessie Smith. "With Janis involved, that was the whole," St. John said. "You build a chair with two legs, and it's not stable. Put a third one there, and you can sit." She soon picked up an autoharp, which she'd heard on albums of Jean Ritchie's Appalachian balladry, and taught herself to play.

"I was in a hillbilly band, mostly hanging out," Janis told writer David Dalton in 1970. "Never went anywhere without my autoharp. I was supposed to be going to college, but I just went up there so I could get it on. We used to sing at this place called the Ghetto and just hang out and get drunk a lot, get in big fights, roll in the mud, drink beer, and sing, pick, and sing."

Her brawling was primarily with John Clay, who was angry over Janis's having dumped him for Powell. Clay started drunken arguments that deteriorated into screaming matches with Janis. He later accused her of having "a paranoid personality," and that she "would sense rejection real quick—on the other hand, she'd reject others." Janis, embarrassed by her one-night stand with Clay, a bit of an oddball, had sworn him "to some kind of secrecy, and when he fiendishly said something about it at a party, she almost went nuts," recalled a Ghetto resident. "They had a couple of knock-down, drag-out, roll-down-the-stairs kind of fights." One night, in the Ghetto's backyard, she smashed Clay in the head with a metal sand pail. She joked to another friend that Clay "made love in iambic pentameter." Having endured unkind comments herself, Janis now seemed to vent her insecurities by mistreating the hapless Clay. And the more she drank, the meaner Janis could be.

Regardless of the friction she helped to create, the Ghetto remained "Janis's home away from home," according to Henry Stopher. "One day, when I was attempting to clean the floors, Janis grabbed my mop and said, 'You're doing it all wrong! This is the way you mop a floor!' And she took that thing and scrubbed the floor to perfection."

In addition to playing in the Ghetto's backyard, the Waller Creek Boys had performed the previous spring at a "folk sing" on campus. Held at the student union's Chuckwagon dining hall on Wednesday nights, the hootenanny was the brainchild of Beaumont native Stephanie Chernikowski, a UT student and music fan who had seen Elvis in 1955, around the time he'd played Janis's junior high. Chernikowski's wide circle of college friends included numerous musicians. To hear their music on campus, she rented the Chuckwagon, invited her pals to bring their instruments, and put up posters to spread the word. The folk sing caught on quickly. "It was pretty spontaneous," recalled Chernikowski, who would become an acclaimed music photographer in the 1970s. When she first heard Janis at the Ghetto, "she belted blues like no white girl I'd ever heard. Lanny and Powell kept trying to get her to perform at the folk sing, but she was seriously shy."

Finally, after much prodding, Janis agreed. Sneaking several beers before the Waller Creek Boys took their turn at the mike, she loosened up and belted the blues. Even the most humble of stages seemed to transform her. "Other than her friends at the Ghetto, that was the first time anybody in Austin saw her," according to Chernikowski. With such an attentive audience, Janis's confidence grew. She began to relax in the spotlight and chat amiably between songs, her self-assurance as a performer magnifying with the applause.

As word spread about the Waller Creek Boys' Wednesday-night sets, the folk sing grew packed. Sometimes thirteen acts waited to perform at the Chuckwagon's open mike, but most spectators were there to hear Janis. "She was so charismatic, and her voice was bluesy with a gritty edge," said Chernikowski. "Nobody had seen anything like her before in Texas." Early on, Janis alternated with Wiggins on vocals, and sometimes they sang duets, as on Jesse "Lone Cat" Fuller's "San Francisco Bay Blues." The trio's repertoire included "Stealin', Stealin'," a 1928 number from the Memphis Jug Band, featuring St. John's harmonica, as did "C.C. Rider," which she'd picked up from a Lead Belly record. "Her vocals were just supersharp on Lead Belly," St. John remembered. "She learned a lot of her singing and her approach to style from Lead."

Before an audience, Janis inhabited Bessie Smith numbers such as the gut-wrenching "Black Mountain Blues." She also taught the group Jelly Roll Morton's raunchy "Winin' Boy Blues," a barrelhouse tune about New Orleans pimps and prostitutes. In the Waller Creek Boys' slightly cleaned-up version, Janis took the role of Storyville's "Winin' Boy": "I'm the winin' boy, don't deny my name / Take a look at Sis, she's down on the levee doin' the double twist." She used her alto to scat-sing Ma Rainey's 1930 blues "Leaving This Morning ("Kansas City Blues)." And she employed an emotive vibrato on the blues classic "Careless Love," preferring Lonnie Johnson's obscure 1920s version, she later said, to Lead Belly's better-known rendition. As she came into her own, Janis made more song suggestions and experimented with different keys. A favorite was "St. James Infirmary," which she originally discovered on a 1933 Josh White recording. Her version, said St. John, "was unnerving."

Janis's reputation reached the editors of UT's *Summer Texan* newspaper, who requested an interview. Assistant campus life editor Pat Sharpe met Janis at the Ghetto for a chat. It would be Janis's first newspaper coverage since the Port Arthur paper praised her artwork as a library volunteer in 1957. A "freshman majoring in art . . . who looks like a beatnik," is how Sharpe described Janis, who played Lead Belly records all during the interview. "She Dares to be Different!," published on July 27, 1962, included a photograph of Janis strumming an autoharp, her mouth wide open in song. Unlike most campus coeds (or "bubbleheads," as Ghetto residents called them) with teased beehive dos, Janis "doesn't bother to have her hair set every week," Sharpe noted, "or wear the latest feminine fashion fads." Instead, "she wears Levi's to class because they're more comfortable" and "goes barefooted when she feels like it."

Janis told Sharpe she'd earlier performed in Port Arthur and at Venice's Gas House but claimed to have no musical training. "This lack seems to be an asset," Sharpe wrote, "for Janis sings with a certain spontaneity and gusto that cultivated voices sometimes find difficult to capture. . . . Janis's current ambition is to be a folksinger, though she really prefers blues. . . . She really began to think seriously about singing when she came to the university this year." Nervous during the entire interview, Janis gulped down a pint of vodka afterward rather than her usual beer or wine, according to John Clay. "That's the only time I ever saw her get sloppy drunk."

With her heightened profile, Janis looked for more venues to prove herself as a "folksinger." She booked a few nights at the newly opened Cliché coffeehouse, backed by guitarist Ted Klein, but its audience preferred a soaring soprano such as Joan Baez's to Janis's bluesy alto. Baez, two years older than Janis, had become the face of folk music on college campuses since her 1959 breakthrough at the Newport Folk Festival and subsequent albums on the Vanguard label. Janis admired the folk star, though she sometimes scoffed at her "pretty" voice and Old English and Scots-Irish balladry. "Janis said negative things about Joan Baez from the end of one day to the next," one friend recalled. Yet Janis occasionally broke out her own soprano, à la Jean Ritchie, on mournful Appalachian folk songs such as "The Cuckoo." "She could sing those mountain ballads better than most," according to St. John, who would catch her at the Ghetto sounding like Baez.

At the Chuckwagon, Janis now took center stage like a professional. "I was fascinated by her," recalled Jack Jackson, an accountant at the Texas State Comptroller's Office, and, by his own admission, "as straight as could be." The folk music fan became a regular at the Chuckwagon to hear Janis play autoharp and sing. "I was immediately impressed by her. She was wearing leotards and a funky sweatshirt; her hair was in disarray. But I could tell she was a very unusual person, who was beautiful in the deeper sense of the word. I knew she was a person worth knowing.

"So one night, after the folk sing, I followed her. . . . I lurked along as she took a leisurely saunter up Guadeloupe [Street], stopping here and there at coffeehouses, talking to people on the street. It must have taken her an hour to get to the Ghetto. I was bold as brass and walked right up and introduced myself to her. She remembered me from the folk sing and offered me a drink of wine and was just real nice. Before I knew it, I moved in [with David Moriaty as his roommate]. And Janis was the magnet."

With so many available young men, Janis's polyamorous nature ignited. Her affair with St. John fizzled after a month or so, but they remained close. She "couldn't be with a boyfriend long because she'd have to start fighting," according to John Clay. When her overtures toward Lanny Wiggins were spurned, "she was in a real bad mood because Lanny didn't want to be her boyfriend." Instead, Janis had a fling with Wiggins's brother, Ramsey. "Janis liked to fuck," Ramsey told writer Alice Echols. "She enjoyed it . . . and wasn't insulted by an invitation couched in the most basic terms: 'Hey, Janis, wanna ball?' That alone, her refusal of guilt and shame about fucking, was enough to endear her to me forever."

"Her next boyfriend was a guy named Bill Killeen," Clay recounted. "At the beginning of it, she was sweet as pie, in love." A Massachusetts native, Killeen graduated from Oklahoma State University, where he'd started a humor magazine, *Charlatan*. He moved to Austin in his beat-up 1950 Cadillac hearse to write for the *Texas Ranger*, a satirical monthly humor magazine that mocked UT traditions. Killeen's friend Gilbert Shelton, a brilliant cartoonist, had recently been appointed its editor. Shelton, who'd been inspired to draw by the cartoons in the *New Yorker* while growing up in Houston, returned to the University of Texas in the summer of '62, after having graduated two years earlier. A former *Texas Ranger* cartoonist, he'd been working at a hot rod magazine in New York. Previously a history major, Shelton reenrolled at UT as a freshman in the Art Department and took over the *Texas Ranger*. His first step was to increase the magazine's comic strips, paving the way for a national underground-comics explosion. He collaborated with Killeen as the writer of *Wonder Wart-Hog*—Shelton's most iconic series until his countercultural *Fabulous Furry Freak Brothers*. A pianist and guitarist, Shelton became a regular at the Ghetto, where he would sing old-timey gospel music with Janis. It was at one of the numerous parties he threw at his nearby house that Janis met Killeen.

Bright, articulate, and creative, Killeen was tall and slender with dark hair and eyes, and looked a bit like Janis's old beau Jack Smith. The night they met, he fell immediately for Janis, who was dressed in a black sweater and dark tights. The pair strolled over to the State Capitol grounds, where they watched bats flying around, which Janis found "hilarious," Killeen recalled. "She was not like any girl I'd ever met . . . more like a guy in a lot of ways. She really had a zest for life. She wanted to have fun and didn't want to miss anything. Janis and I slept that night on the Capitol lawn under one of the monuments. We were fooling around, and a Capitol guard kind of halfway threw us out."

Janis began spending nearly every night with Killeen at Shelton's. "We were together all the time," he recalled. By September, another Chuckwagon regular, Win Pratt, a former Princeton University student and son of a UT professor, offered the couple an empty house owned by his father. They set up house there, with Janis occasionally cooking recipes her mother had taught her.

Early on, Killeen learned that Janis had a confounding temperament: overreacting to trivial things but behaving nonchalantly about more serious matters. When she tried to fry a chicken, "she kept getting madder and madder because she knew the chicken wasn't done," he recounted. "Finally, she got up and just slung everything all over the place and said, 'This thing is no goddamned good, and you know it! Let's go out and get something to eat!'" Around the same time, Janis started passing blood—which she tried to ignore. "I remember her going to the bathroom a lot because she was bleeding so considerably," Killeen recalled. "I said, 'What the hell's going on? You need to go to a doctor.' She grudgingly went to the infirmary, and eventually after a month it stopped." It turned out she'd had a miscarriage, which she later blithely reported to former boyfriend Powell St. John, who was in all likelihood the baby's father.

Though Janis enrolled for the fall semester, she spent her time singing and partying, ignoring most of her classwork, including art. "Janis was a pretty good illustrator," according to Killeen, but the tepid response to her paintings, as compared with the acclaim she enjoyed as a singer, led Janis to abandon her former dream. "She told me she found out she'd never be any good," Seth Joplin recalled later. "So she just dropped the whole thing. She wouldn't even try anymore."

She managed to write one article for the *Texas Ranger*, but mainly she partied with Shelton, Killeen, and the magazine staff. The university paid *Ranger* editors a nickel for every issue sold, and following each new publication, the staff threw a party. When not hanging out at the Ghetto, she and Killeen palled around with Shelton and his girlfriend Pat Brown, once traveling together to Nuevo Laredo, Mexico, to check out the border-town bars.

One Saturday afternoon, Janis met Julie Paul, an Austin native and country-and-western fan who liked to drink. Julie spotted the Waller Creek Boys and Janis, toting her autoharp, walking home from Zilker Park after they'd won a Parks Commission talent contest, with Janis singing "This Land Is Your Land." When Julie pulled over her Triumph TR3 convertible and offered a ride, Janis jumped in next to the masculine-looking woman "built like a fullback," according to one friend. The two clicked, and Julie soon took Janis to a beer joint that would expose her singing to a wider audience.

Threadgill's, on North Lamar Boulevard, opened originally as a Gulf gas station in 1933 by Kenneth Threadgill, an amateur yodeler and a fan of Jimmie Rodgers, "the father of country music" whose career started in 1927. After years of pumping gas out front and selling bootleg whiskey from the back door, Threadgill turned his business into a beer joint in 1948. On Wednesday nights, he hosted "singing sessions" featuring local "hillbilly" musicians paid in beer. Threadgill stayed behind the bar, mostly, dispensing pickled pigs feet and cheese and crackers. In 1959 a few UT grad students who loved bluegrass, among them Bill Malone and Stan Alexander, discovered the place and joined the Wednesday-night jams, usually populated by truck drivers, mechanics, and construction workers.

"It was a spontaneous type of thing: we just sat around a big wooden table and took turns singing with each other, trading songs in all kinds of combinations," Malone recalled. "There was no amplification." When Janis and her rowdy crew arrived in the fall of '62, Malone didn't like them at first: "I was about nine years older than Janis," he said, "and in the last stages of my PhD degree. I was prejudiced against them, and

I remember Janis saying, 'He doesn't want us here.'" But as soon as the Waller Creek Boys kicked off with "Stealin', Stealin'," Malone—a country music scholar who would write the seminal *Country Music U.S.A.*—changed his mind. "Her voice was just so distinctive," he recounted. "She sang with such great feeling and power that she couldn't be ignored. Everybody sat up and took notice." Soon Malone was harmonizing with Janis on "Silver Threads and Golden Needles," and she was carving her name into the oak table, alongside other musicians' names.

At Threadgill's, the Waller Creek Boys became more of "a bluegrass band," said St. John, and Janis "always had to do a certain number of mountain tunes, hillbilly, country and western." Among her favorites were vintage numbers by the Maddox Brothers and Rose, who advertised themselves as the "most colorful hillbilly band in the world." On their version of "Philadelphia Lawyer," Rose Maddox's brazen, distinctive vocals particularly inspired Janis's own twangy attack.

Janis found a great mentor in the jovial Kenneth Threadgill, who was about the same age as Seth Joplin. "I remember the first time we went out there to that wonderful place," said Bill Killeen. "Mr. Threadgill practically adopted Janis after he heard her. She was a little shy. . . . There were some English teachers out there singing, and he had all those Jimmie Rodgers [records] on the jukebox. She'd started with the blues stuff and folk. But . . . they were doing all that country stuff; she got right into that too. She did all these old religious things, and [Janis thought] that was a riot."

Threadgill ensured that everyone treated Janis with respect, even when she insisted on singing black music in the segregated bar. "It was a very strange amalgam of people," Janis recalled, "all these old Okies, a bunch of college professors—older cats—into country music intellectually, the first of the folk trend. The young upstarts . . . were into it, too, and that was us. . . . Mr. Threadgill, he surpassed them all! He was old—a great big man with a big belly and white hair combed back on the top of his head. He was back here dishin' out Polish sausages and hard-boiled eggs and Grand Prize and Lone Star . . . and someone would say, '*Mr. Threadgill, Mr. Threadgill, come out and do a tune!*' And he'd say, 'No, I don't think so,' and they'd say, *'Come on, come on!'* and he'd say, 'All right.' He'd close the bar down, and then he'd walk out front, and he'd lay his hands across his big fat belly, which was covered with a bar apron. . . . He'd come out like that and lean his head back and sing, just like a bird, Jimmie Rodgers songs, and he could yodel. *God, he was fantastic!* . . .

"I was the young upstart loudmouthed chick: 'That girl sounds a lot like Rosie Maddox, don't she?' I'd sing Rosie Maddox songs, and I'd sing Woody Guthrie songs, but one time an evening I'd say, 'Can I do one now?' and they'd say, 'Okay, let that lady have a turn,' and I'd say, 'Give me a twelve bar [blues] in E.' I sang blues."

While Threadgill gave Janis the confidence to sing the blues she loved, she also grew close to his wife, Mildred, who, similar to Dorothy Joplin, tried to suggest hair and makeup improvements. "Janis was a character," Mildred recounted. "Cussed like a sailor and usually wore jeans and a coonskin cap. Wore it over the worse mess of hair you ever saw. One day she was sitting at the table, and I came in with my [camera] and told her to fix her hair and I'd take her picture. It was long and tangled—a mess. She didn't want to, but then she combed it, and I said, 'Put on some lipstick.' . . . I talked her into it, and when she saw herself in the mirror, she said she couldn't believe it was her if she didn't know it."

Janis pleased the Threadgills with her plaintive country songs, such as Kitty Wells's 1952 hit "It Wasn't God Who Made Honky Tonk Angels," which she'd introduce as a "hillbilly blues number." Originally an "answer song" to Oklahoman Hank Thompson's "The Wild Side of Life," blaming an unfaithful wife and barfly for wrecking their marriage, Wells's version takes the woman's viewpoint, calling out the husband's own cheating. Janis sang it "in a high, shrill bluegrass kind of sound," said Threadgill. She "could really punch and put over a song. I thought a hell of a lot of Janis. She was just a kid and called me 'Daddy.'"

Janis's following expanded to as many as two hundred fans, including clean-cut college kids, who squeezed into Threadgill's. "Crowds got so big that it was hard to hear," said Bill Malone. "Somebody brought in a little amplification system, and then it became more formal." Eventually Jack Jackson—now a *Texas Ranger* cartoonist using the nom de plume Jaxon—documented the music with a reel-to-reel recorder. "I just took it upon myself to stick the microphone in front of her face," he recalled about capturing the Waller Creek Boys arguing over which key or song to play, with Janis usually the loudest. In addition to country standards, they played a weeper written by Julie Paul, "Empty Pillow on My Bed," which Janis crooned accompanied by mandolin.

Janis, who'd written some poetry as a teen, began composing her own songs. One of the first addressed the hopelessness of chasing the blues with booze. She introduced "What Good Can Drinkin' Do" by saying she "wrote it one night after drinking myself into a stupor." Accompanying herself on autoharp, she wailed it with a fierce vibrato: "I drink all night but the next day I still feel blue / There's a glass on the table they say it's gonna ease all my pain / but I drink it down, and I still feel the same / I start drinkin' on Friday night then I wake up on Sunday, and ain't nothin' right."

Another original, her rhythmic "Daddy, Daddy, Daddy," inspired everyone in the joint to clap along. "She exuded this energy that was so captivating," said Jack Jackson. "She completely dominated the room. It was like, '*Janis is here!*' She was really in command, and a rip-roaring character, wild and woolly, always chortling."

After a couple of months of Threadgill's sets, Jackson recorded a demo tape of Janis at the Ghetto, performing mostly her blues material, either accompanying herself, or backed by St. John, Wiggins, or the accomplished guitarist Minor Wilson—whose stage fright prevented him from gigging. On the recording, Janis sounds mournful and vulnerable, almost broken, on the blues nugget "I'll Drown in My Own Tears," backed by Wilson on guitar. Her spare version is reminiscent of a 1951 track by Kansas City R&B vocalist Lula Reed. Though she enjoyed singing country music at Threadgill's, Janis was still drawn most keenly to the blues, once telling Bill Killeen she wished she were black "because black people had more emotions, more feelings, and more ups and downs than white people." Janis, who knew only a few African

Americans at that point, seemed to be describing herself—and ideas she'd conjured based on the blues music she loved.

Occasionally, Janis ventured to the segregated east section of Austin, where African American clubs such as the Victory Lounge on Eleventh Street featured jazz and R&B. Police often hassled whites who crossed the color barrier. "Once I went over there with Janis," St. John recalled, "and we were standing outside the club. One of our friends, David Martinez, saw Janis's purse lying open on the grass, and there was a little dog turd next to it. So he just flipped it into her purse. Janis saw him doing it and went ballistic. As soon as she raised her voice and started gesticulating, a cop drives up. He saw her wrestling with a Hispanic guy and was going to arrest him. We had to talk him out of it."

>―◆―◦―◆―<

Even with the adulation at Threadgill's, Janis remained restless. At the Ghetto one night, she met twenty-year-old Texan Chet Helms, who'd dropped out of UT to hitchhike around the country. This fascinated her. Janis yearned for that kind of adventure and longed to return to San Francisco.

Inevitably, she and Killeen had begun arguing, with disagreements instigated largely by Janis. Her insecurity ran so deep, it seemed, that she'd push away those close to her before she got hurt. "It was real hard to get along with Janis," he said. "She was always testing." Janis's outspoken fearlessness baffled him: "I remember when people first started talking about LSD, what it did to your brain and all—pretty scary stuff. I said, 'I don't want anything to do with that stuff.' And Janis said, 'Well, I want some right now!'"

Yet for all her bravado, Janis actually feared hallucinogens. She preferred getting wasted to becoming more "aware." In Texas, peyote was legal and available at Hudson's Cactus Gardens outside Austin; several Ghetto residents cooked up the foul-tasting cactus buttons, ingested them, and tripped for hours. But Janis never tried it. With Tommy Stopher and St. John, she once shared a skinny joint someone had mailed her from California. "It was my first joint," St. John recounted. Generally, pot smoking was rare at the Ghetto; residents were petrified about getting busted—and for good reason: the place was under surveillance by the authorities and student narcs. Years later, a list of those targeted as suspected deviants, including Janis, was discovered among the papers of a former police chief, with Ghetto denizens' names listed next to their alleged illegal or immoral activities, including drug dealing, promiscuity, homosexuality, and drug addiction.

The most prevalent drug in Austin at the time was the amphetamine Dexedrine, used by students, including Janis, who mixed it with the occasional Seconal. "Uppers and downers at the same time were something she found fun," said St. John. "She told me one time, 'You go up and then down, and then up and then down!'" She seemed drawn to the chemically induced state that sometimes mirrored her own intense, seesawing emotions.

In November 1962 Janis and Killeen were evicted from their house by Win Pratt's father when he discovered them living there. After moving out, the couple drifted apart. Win, a handsome Golden Gloves boxer, invited Janis to hitchhike with him to Dallas to see Joan Baez, who'd just appeared (wearing jeans and barefoot) on the cover of *Time*. Janis jumped at the chance. Frequently on the Ghetto turntable was Bob Dylan's debut LP, released by Columbia in March: It featured several blues covers, including "House of the Rising Sun," that were among the Waller Creek Boys repertoire, and a couple of originals, one of which, "Song to Woody," was an ode to Woody Guthrie. Janis loved the record.

>─+─◆─○─◆─+─<

As Janis's relationship with Killeen fizzled, her attachment to Julie Paul intensified, and they became lovers. "I didn't put the make on Julie," she told one friend, "she did on me. I'm not queer, but I'm not averse." Conversely, her sometime guitarist Ted Klein recalled Janis announcing she'd decided to become a lesbian. Another Ghetto habitué said that Julie "took care of Janis and treated her like a boy would treat her." The pair's love affair, said St. John, was a "classic romantic relationship," which Janis didn't hide from her friends. "I think Janis was priding herself on having an AC/DC outlook on life," said Jack Jackson. "If she could find a man that made her happy, that was fine. If she could find a woman that made her happy, that was fine too. This was long before people started coming out of the closet."

But Janis's relationship with Julie turned just as tempestuous as her affair with Killeen. She still slept with the occasional guy, and Julie snapped to a friend that her lover "went through men like Kleenex." She was particularly jealous of Travis Rivers, a married student who fooled around with Janis. One night, Julie drunkenly ran through each apartment in the Ghetto, yelling, *"Where is that little bitch?"* Apparently, Janis sneaked out, but Julie, in her intoxicated state, fell down the staircase. Although she wasn't injured, rumors flew that Janis had pushed her. John Clay dispelled them. "Julie was built pretty strong," he said. "She would have torn Janis up if she'd caught her, but Janis did not throw Julie down the stairs—she ran away from her."

Janis invited Julie to Port Arthur one weekend. Her old friends found Julie too possessive and didn't like her. The pair spent much of their time across the river in Louisiana bars. Back in Austin, Janis organized a field trip to the Big Oak, with Tary Owens, Dave Moriaty, Win Pratt, Travis Rivers, Ghetto regular Pepi Plowman, and Johnny Moyer, a trumpet player. At the Big Oak, Janis and Pepi began teasing boys and doing the bump and grind together, just as Janis had with Patti Skaff. As before, her thrill seeking soon yielded disastrous results.

"I was playing pool next door, and someone came running in, saying 'Janis has started a fight!'" Travis Rivers recalled. "I went into the dance hall, and, oh my God, the dance floor was a melee! Janis liked to 'dirty bop'—the dance where you grind your hips into your partner's—and some guy had grabbed Janis's tit, so she slugged him with a beer bottle. The next thing you know, everybody's beating on each other."

"She baited the swamp boys, and the Austin people decided they were going to protect her honor," Moriaty recounted. "They didn't realize there were certain things you don't do over there." Pratt smashed a guy's mouth, knocking out his teeth with his high school ring. One of the locals then broke Johnny Moyer's jaw. The fight escalated into a near

riot in the parking lot, with some denizens getting into cars and trying to run over the brawlers. Finally, the Austinites managed to escape
into their car and sped off. "The poor bastard driving us was convinced
they were chasing us," Rivers recalled. "We got home, but I don't think
Johnny Moyer ever played trumpet again."

Another disaster occurred in December, when late one cold, rainy
night, Janis, Julie Paul, and John Clay crammed into the TR3 to drive to
New Orleans. "In Lake Charles, Louisiana, we were pulled over," Clay
recalled. "You could imagine what we looked like—Janis was wearing her
Buffalo Bill jacket. It turns out the guys who stopped us were immigration
officers, and they suspected us of being illegal Canadian immigrants!"

After they reached New Orleans, Julie and Janis got into a fistfight,
with Julie the victor. Kicked out of the car, which raced off, and with
no money, Janis had to fend for herself. She turned to prostitution just
as she had the last time she visited New Orleans, with the McQueens.
She solicited men looking for a good time, and who were willing to pay
for it, making enough money for a ticket back to Austin. "I got a phone
call from Janis," Rivers recounted. "'Can you come get me at the bus
station?' I picked her up and said, 'What the fuck happened?'" Janis described her latest misadventure, informing him nonchalantly that she'd
earned the money to get home by "turning two tricks." Janis would
later tell friends that during other lean times, she'd tried prostitution
but didn't always have much luck finding johns willing to pay for sex.

＞◆＞─○─◆◇─◄

Her showdowns with Julie Paul were one thing, but it was a cruel campus "joke" that finally broke the bond between Janis and her tribe in
Austin. Each year, the Alpha Phi Omega fraternity sponsored its annual
fund-raiser by holding an Ugliest Man on Campus competition, with
students voting for candidates nominated by various frats for $5 each.
"Normally, they would elect a really ugly, toady linebacker from the UT
football team," according to Travis Rivers. In late fall of 1962, Janis was
anonymously entered as a contestant—her picture gracing posters all
over campus.

Though she laughed it off to some friends, and even convinced one that she had nominated herself, most of those who knew her well, such as St. John, believed she was devastated. "She had already been profoundly hurt over and over," he told filmmaker Amy Berg. "[The contest] crushed her. Saddest thing you ever saw. I had never seen Janis cry. Janis had a very tough exterior, but it really got her; got her bad."

Janis did not "win"—the prize went to Lonnie "the Hunch" Farrell—but Dorothy Joplin later recalled receiving an "anguished letter" from Janis about the ordeal. Travis Rivers posited that her reputation as a lesbian led to the frats' nasty joke; others linked it to their hatred of the Ghetto, whose residents were often at odds with frats and jocks. Whatever the root of the cruelty, the effect was similar to the abuse she'd undergone in Port Arthur. "Finally, I decided Texas wasn't good enough for me," Janis wrote in a 1965 letter. "I wanted to go to California again."

CHAPTER 8

BLUES SINGER

*California . . . you can do what you
want to do, and nobody bugs you.*

—JANIS JOPLIN

"I rarely heard Janis when it didn't raise the hair on the back of my neck and it didn't send chills down my spine," is how Chet Helms described the effect of Janis's singing. In January 1963 the self-described "beatnik on the road" became Janis's savior.

"I couldn't stand Texas anymore," she said. "I was wanting to get the fuck out of there, but I didn't have quite enough nerve to leave by myself." He invited her to hitchhike to San Francisco, where, he assured her, she would "knock 'em out of their socks" with her voice. There, Janis would come to deepen her musical identity and embrace the part of herself that so identified with Bessie Smith, absorbing the great blues singer's depth of feeling and emotional honesty into her own sound.

Before leaving Austin, Janis played a farewell gig with the Waller Creek Boys at Threadgill's on Saturday, January 19, celebrating her twentieth birthday and liberation from college. Skipping final exams, she officially withdrew from her five classes—perhaps as a fallback plan, in case San Francisco didn't work out and she returned to school. On Wednesday, January 23, she and Helms stuck out their thumbs and headed for their first stop: 3510 Avenue D, in Fort Worth.

A year older than Janis, the tall, bespectacled Helms was born to Texans in California; after his father, Chester Leo Helms Sr., died when Chet was nine, the fundamentalist Baptist family settled in Fort Worth. In 1960 he entered UT, where he initially signed on with the Reserve Officers' Training Corps (ROTC) and the Young Republicans. But Helms was soon transformed into a civil rights activist, joining the Students for Direct Action (SDA) and working to integrate Austin's movie theaters and lunch counters. He became a regular at the Ghetto, discovered peyote and pot, and made friends with a bisexual black student who turned him on to Texas-born visionary saxophonist Ornette Coleman and other jazz musicians. After quitting UT—a month before Janis moved to Austin—he traveled between San Francisco, Mexico, and the East Coast. When they connected in December, "Janis started talking about the West Coast," Helms recalled, "and her experiences in Venice. She was very well read in the Beat literature, as was I, and was very attracted to San Francisco." Eager to escape Texas's "repressive environment," Janis was like "so many extraordinary singers, writers, and musicians who came out of Texas," said Helms, because there, the only freedom "you had was what you created for yourself with your imagination and artistic expression."

Their journey's first stop, at his mother's Fort Worth home, did not go well. "I had called and told my mother, 'I'm bringing a friend,' " Helms recounted, and she said, 'Oh, I'll fix dinner!' " But Janis's unkempt, masculine appearance—in Levi's with a half-unbuttoned chambray work shirt and no bra—was a shock "when my mother answered the door," recalled Chet's brother John. "Janis was standing next to Chet, strumming her autoharp and softly humming a tune." Though she "was very sweet and polite with my mother," according to John, she overheard Janis whisper, "Let's go get some beer," which rankled the teetotaling Christian. Her morals were offended further at dinner, when Helms asked if he and Janis could spend the night, explaining, "We're not sleeping together, we're just friends." Her response: "A young unmarried woman can't stay here; what would the neighbors think?" So John drove the travelers to the outskirts of town that same night, to hitchhike west.

Their two were picked up by a series of long-haul truckers. Janis cuddled with Helms—much like Bobby McGee, in the Kris Kristofferson song she would later immortalize. In a couple of days, they reached

Santa Maria, California, Helms's birthplace, where his aunt Ruth lived. She invited the couple to spend the night, and the next day gave them $20 and bought them bus tickets for the 250-mile journey north to San Francisco. Two weeks later, Janis wrote Aunt Ruth a thank-you card with $20 enclosed.

On Monday, January 28, 1963, they arrived in San Francisco, where it's "a lot freer—you can do what you want to do, and nobody bugs you," Janis told a journalist later. She wanted to live like a beatnik and sing the blues. In her mind, the two went hand in hand, and she said, "A lot of artists have one way of art and one way of life, but they're the same for me."

Building an audience of Texas college students had not been so difficult, but San Francisco presented a challenge Janis wasn't sure she could handle. Helms and a musician friend, David Freiberg, with whom the pair crashed, offered to help. Their first stop was Coffee and Confusion, previously the Fox and Hound, on Grant Avenue in North Beach—the same venue where Janis had hung out two years earlier. New owner Sylvia Fennell was "a tough but likable New Yorker . . . whose width, height, and depth were the same measurement," according to Steve Martin, a stand-up comedian there in 1965. The storefront coffeehouse, still manned by doorman Dave Archer, was small and makeshift, with rickety chairs and tables and an old upright piano, its walls decorated with a few abstract paintings that resembled "wilting flowers and chunks of decomposing beef," said habitué John Gilmore, a writer and former Hollywood actor. "It always stank of the iodine and ammonia they used in the mop water."

Helms convinced Sylvia Fennell to add Janis to that night's open-mike hootenanny. The policy was to vet prospective singers, most with "smooth vocals," according to Helms. "Janis stood up onstage, perfectly rigid, and belted four or five riveting country blues songs." Her voice hit patrons like a Molotov cocktail. "Sylvia said, 'Pass the hat! Pass the hat!'" recalled Helms. "She got a standing ovation and about fifty, sixty bucks—a huge amount for two kids who'd just hitchhiked from Texas with no money."

The few female singers then performing at Coffee and Confusion were sopranos who emulated Joan Baez's balladry. Twenty-year-old Janis, by contrast, belted Bessie Smith blues in an earthy alto, delivering somewhat raunchy songs about lowlifes and two-timers. An earlier generation of San Francisco singers, whose styles were more akin to Janis's sound—Odetta and Detroit-born Barbara Dane—rarely performed locally. "People later told me that Janis was a big fan of mine, but I don't recall ever meeting her," said Dane, herself a Smith devotee. "Listening to Bessie Smith seventy-eights, I realized how much her songs defined women in a different way than pop music did. They gave me a lot of strength—those old songs spoke for things I was going through." Janis must also have taken to heart the messages of songs such as "I've Got What It Takes" and "Tain't Nobody's Business If I Do."

Janis soon became a regular performer at Coffee and Confusion. She "looked more like a frumpy girl . . . behind the counter of a hot dog stand than a singer," recounted John Gilmore. "Like a beatnik, yet also country-bumpkin looking. She wore old jeans that had baggy legs but were so tight at the seat and hips the seams were coming apart. Despite the winter chill, she was barefoot." Perched on a stool, with her eyes closed, Janis "sang with a mixture of tones," he wrote later, "from low slurring sounds to almost cries, underplaying the lyrics in a way that hinted—even threatened—suppressed emotion boiling just under the surface, like a riptide beneath a smooth, rolling wave. She did things with her throat and the lyrics like an abstract painter moving pigment on canvas, separating what she was from any obligation to the song. Her voice would crack a little, a sharp tone in the middle of a soft word, as though she had been struck with a sharp pain. It wasn't until the applause erupted and the tension slacked that she opened her eyes."

Just up the street from Coffee and Confusion, the Coffee Gallery at 1353 Grant was a larger place with two rooms, a stage, and a bar, which had hosted readings by Ferlinghetti and other Beats in 1959. By 1963, it attracted more tourists than bona fide Beats, but it retained a cache among up-and-coming folkies. Though Janis was under twenty-one, she got inside with the help of bartender Howard Hesseman, an actor with the Committee, a comedy improv troupe. (Hesseman later starred on the TV sitcoms *WKRP in Cincinnati* and *Head of the Class*.) Again, Janis aced her audition and joined the club's nightly cast of revolving musicians, who hipped her to folk venues across the bridge in Berkeley and also in nearby towns like Palo Alto and San Jose. In Berkeley, on February 21, Janis was arrested for shoplifting—probably a bottle of wine. After taking her mug shot and charging her with a misdemeanor, the police released her, and she hitchhiked back to San Francisco.

Earning just a few dollars from her occasional gigs and panhandling, Janis had no place of her own. She sometimes crashed on the floor at Coffee and Confusion or with people she met at clubs. When she'd first arrived with Helms, they'd spent a few nights together at David Freiberg's, but the pair did not become lovers. "We were quite close, slept in the same bed, and were intimate to a degree," said Helms, "but we never consummated it." Initially, he tried to guide Janis's career and bookings, but she made it clear that she was a free agent. Though they drifted apart, Helms kept track of Janis's efforts, and in three years' time, he'd become a major player in her career.

Janis realized she could improve her sets if she had accompaniment. At the Coffee Gallery one evening, she approached two musicians just after the duo had performed. They hadn't met her or seen her act. "It was the break between sets," recalled Larry Hanks, then a twenty-four-year-old guitarist and baritone singer, "and she said, 'Hey, does anybody play any blues?' We said, 'Sure! We can try!'" With no rehearsal beforehand, Hanks and his partner Roger Perkins joined her onstage that night after watching her play autoharp on "Silver Threads and Golden Needles." "Roger was pretty adept at faking it," said Hanks, "better than me. But between us, we conjured up some plausible accompaniment for things like 'Careless Love.'"

Seated on stools behind her onstage, the duo was dazzled by Janis's vocal power. "Right from the beginning, she would just blast everything out front," Hanks recounted. "There was no restraint. She sang hell-bent for leather all the time." On the Memphis Jug Band's "Stealin',

Stealin'," the two joined in on vocals, their bass and tenor voices blending well with hers. Janis had found her new Waller Creek Boys.

The trio made plans to meet at a Pacific Heights Victorian, where Hanks and Perkins rented rooms. Both Californians—Hanks, from Berkeley; Perkins, from Claremont—they had been gigging together for about six months. "Janis had heard us a few times, so she knew what we did," said Hanks. They taught her the Carter Family spiritual "Gospel Ship," on which Perkins played banjo. The three alternated lead vocals for the verses, with Janis using her Texas twang to sing "I spend my time in prayer and when this ship comes in, I'll leave this world of sin, and I'll go sailing through the air." They harmonized on the chorus, "I'm gonna shout and sing until heaven rings when I'll bid this world good-bye."

"I have to do a Bessie Smith song every time I play," Janis told her new bandmates. Hanks and Perkins didn't know any tunes by Smith or other female blues singers, so Janis taught them Ma Rainey's "Leaving This Morning" and Smith's "Black Mountain Blues." She also sang her twelve-bar blues original "Daddy, Daddy, Daddy." Janis downplayed her own songwriting, though; an avid reader of the folk magazine *Sing Out!*, she'd possibly read Dylan's comments on writing: "The songs are there. They exist all by themselves just waiting for someone to write them down." In the same article, folksinger Gil Turner noted that "Dylan avoids the terms 'write' or 'compose' in connection with his songs." Janis later told a journalist, "Sometimes I write down the words so I don't forget them, but I don't write songs. That's a whole different concept. I just make them up." In "Daddy, Daddy, Daddy," she did her best attempt at a Bessie Smith–style number, using well-trod blues tropes: "Well, I brag 'bout my daddy to all the women that I see . . . / Never say those damn women Lord, they're tryin' to steal my daddy away from me. . . . / Yeah, if your daddy likes walkin', walks five miles a day / No matter what he wants, child, he walks off far way." Before leaving Austin, Janis had written and recorded with Powell St. John a song for Julie Paul, the mournful "So Sad to Be Alone," accompanying herself on autoharp, but there is no evidence that she ever performed it in San Francisco.

After a few rehearsals, the loose-knit trio polished a seven-song set. "The three of us were pretty cooperative," Hanks said, "as far as finding common ground with songs we knew." For their first Coffee Gallery gig, Janis wore a man's oversized white shirt and jeans, her hair now hanging down past her shoulders. The Coffee Gallery held seventy-five people—as compared with Coffee and Confusion's thirty—and the place was packed for their debut, the audience stomping their feet and clapping along to the music. "When singing the songs, she was really *in* them," Hanks recalled. "All the emotional expression was pouring out." Like a pirate, she cackled and joked between numbers, throwing off sparks.

The trio also performed on *Midnight Special,* a long-running Saturday-night live radio program on Berkeley's KPFA. The show's host, Gert Cherito, picked participants from hopefuls who auditioned around ten o'clock. "Nobody was booked; it was a round robin, with a big mike in the center of the circle of artists," Hanks explained. Having made the cut, Janis, wearing her usual half-unbuttoned chambray shirt and jeans, passionately sang "Black Mountain Blues." Hanks then took the lead vocal on Doc Watson's version of "Columbus Stockade Blues," with Janis adding harmonies. She made an impression on the Albin brothers, eighteen-year-old Peter, seated next to her, and his brother, Rodney, a folk impresario who would soon book her for a college music festival. "Janis wasn't wearing a bra," recalled Peter Albin, who admitted to eying her breasts. "She looked like she had been through it. Her face was broken out. She was incredibly loud, singing the blues in a very rough, hard style."

Another Coffee Gallery regular, South Carolinian Billy Roberts, asked if he could join them on some songs. He had already written a future garage-rock classic: "Hey Joe," a hit for the Leaves in 1966, and the first single for Jimi Hendrix the following year. At the Coffee Gallery, Roberts added his acoustic guitar and vocals to the trio's blues covers. "Billy's fingerpicking was very eccentric, strikingly dramatic," Hanks said. "He snapped the strings, took big long pauses, and had a dramatic way of singing." The four meshed well, so they booked a future night where each played a set, joining in with one another on particular songs.

Although the boys drank beer between sets, Janis refrained, instead staying focused and sober throughout the gig. But outside on the sidewalk, it was a different matter: "Afterward, she was either raring for a party—or else she was shy," Hanks said. Usually, Janis would ask, "Who's got some wine?" Other friends, such as John Gilmore, recalled Janis looking around for speed, which she called "dope." "She took a lot of pills," he recalled. "She used speed to rise above her depressions, then booze to control the speed." To counter loneliness, "she was up for whoever wanted to come along," said Hanks. "There was a kind of openness as far as sexuality goes." Though Janis kept things strictly business between herself and Hanks, Perkins, and Roberts, "she seemed interested in other guys pretty fluidly and easily and quickly."

Playing together, the foursome split their meager earnings. To make more money, Janis wanted to learn guitar so she could accompany herself. She managed to save enough to buy her first acoustic at a pawnshop. She asked renowned fingerpicker Tom Hobson for lessons, but after a handful, he encouraged her to focus on her vocals. She learned enough, though, to break out the guitar on a few songs. Her performances impressed several musicians on their way to successful careers, including Herb Pedersen, whose Pine Valley Boys shared a bill with her at Coffee and Confusion. "She did a set where she played a little guitar and autoharp and sang very pretty," he recalled. Chicago native Nick Gravenites "saw her at the Coffee Gallery, playing autoharp and singing really great country blues," on bills with fledgling folkies David Crosby (before he joined the Byrds) and Dino Valenti (a future member of Quicksilver Messenger Service with David Freiberg). Gravenites would later play a major role in Janis's musical life.

Branching out from North Beach, Janis ventured to San Jose's Folk Theater, a small storefront that hosted weekend hoots. Among the musicians she met there was "Jerry" (real name: Jorma) Kaukonen, a student at the University of Santa Clara. "I had recently arrived from New York and saw the sign for a hootenanny," said Kaukonen, whose fingerpicking was inspired by a Janis favorite, Reverend Gary Davis, whom he'd seen in Greenwich Village clubs. "I grabbed my guitar, and in the closet-sized backstage area, I met Janis. We got to talking, and I knew a bunch of the same songs she did. So she asked me to back her up."

Also a fan of Bessie Smith, Kaukonen was floored by Janis's voice. "Janis was [three years] younger than me, but she had this old-spirit sound," he recalled. "It was such a treat to back her up. She channeled Bessie Smith without trying to clone her. What really got to me was her passion." On "Trouble in Mind," an eight-bar blues recorded originally by a host of women—Chippie Hill (in 1929), Victoria Spivey (1936), Dinah Washington (1952), and Nina Simone (1960), among them—Janis used her vibrato to bring to life the song's despairing lines: "I have almost lost my mind / Life ain't worth livin', sometimes I feel like dyin.'" For future gigs, Janis and Kaukonen worked up more numbers, including Jelly Roll Morton's "Winin' Boy Blues," Ma Rainey's "Leaving This Morning," and Bessie Smith's "Nobody Knows You When You're Down and Out."

Around the Bay Area, local bluegrass groups ranged from Berkeley's Pine Valley Boys to Palo Alto's Liberty Hill Aristocrats (comprised of the Albin brothers) and Wildwood Boys, featuring Jerry Garcia on banjo, Robert Hunter on mandolin, and David Nelson on guitar. Janis began meeting the players, some of whose repertoires mirrored that of the Waller Creek Boys. Her next stop, the Top of the Tangent, was a folk club recently opened in Palo Alto by a pair of doctors at Stanford University. The small venue was on the second floor, reached by walking through the Tangent Pizza Parlor. At a Wednesday-night hoot, Janis sang a cappella, again winning more fans, including Garcia, Ron McKernan (nicknamed Pigpen), and Nelson, the future cofounder of New Riders of the Purple Sage.

"She got up onstage and started singing this jug-band song," David Nelson recalled, "and me and Garcia were 'Wow!' It had so much power—just fucking incredible. I thought, *Here's somebody who got into this obscure kind of music and adopted the style*, but then I realized, *She's not adopting it, she* is *it.*"

The Tangent booked Janis for April 5 and 6, sharing a bill with a bluegrass group called the Westport Singers; the club's ad in the *Stanford Daily* newspaper listed her as "Janice Joplin—Great Blues." Bookings there were quite prestigious; two weeks later, the headliner was legendary Delta bluesman Skip James. Janis asked Kaukonen to back her, but on the night of the gig, she didn't show up; he went on without her. "I never found out what happened," Kaukonen said. "But thanks to her, I started getting my own gigs at the Tangent."

To counter the stress and insecurities in building her career as a blues singer—as well as the dark energy that always trailed her—Janis was drinking heavily. Copious amounts of red wine, often swallowed with "purple hearts" (Dexamyl, a dextroamphetamine/amobarbital combo), began interfering with her performances. "She wasn't using hard stuff then," according to John Gilmore, "mostly grass and speed and a little hash when she could get it. But she couldn't or wouldn't operate without her 'dope.'" Gilmore captures well Janis's emotional layers at the time and how she swung between them—a tendency she would never really abandon:

"She could be tough as an alligator," he recounted. "I saw her hit a guy one night at Coffee and Confusion. She was about to hit him again when the dishwasher grabbed her arm to restrain her. It didn't stop her. She threw a punch with her free hand and caught the guy in the stomach, knocking the wind out of him. . . . A tough-talking, pushy, hard-nosed, barroom brawler ready to slug it out, and then suddenly [she'd] grin and laugh and be a pal, which in turn could give way to this sad, delicate person, intimate and feather voiced, neither feminine nor sexy, just vulnerable."

At the Coffee Gallery one night, Janis met another newcomer: nineteen-year-old Linda Gottfried, who'd arrived by bus from Los Angeles. They "clicked right away," according to Gottfried, who appreciated Janis's sardonic humor. "It was almost like I'd found the other half of myself." The two sometimes crashed together in the basement of a friend's house on Sacramento Street, and both popped purple hearts washed down with cheap Red Mountain wine.

Janis cruised both men and women and often frequented the Anxious Asp, a funky bar at 528 Green Street in North Beach. There she noticed a petite African American woman who resembled a cute young boy. With close-cropped hair, large, luminous eyes, and high cheekbones, Jae Whitaker, twenty-five, had moved to San Francisco in 1961 with her white lover, Polly. Eventually the couple split, and Jae moved into a hillside Victorian house with several roommates near the Castro district. One evening at the Anxious Asp, Janis and Whitaker played a game of pool and then wandered over to the jukebox, singing along to Bobby "Blue" Bland. Whitaker recalled originally wanting to be with Janis's companion Linda Gottfried, but "a bisexual friend from Little Rock, Arkansas" told her, " 'Janis is the one you should go for!' " Whitaker recounted. "Janis had apparently talked to him about me, and she was always smiling at me. I think she liked me because I was cute, I didn't come on heavy, and I was kind of androgynous. That night, we all went to my friend Howard Hesseman's house and smoked some grass. Janis and I got to talking and then started kissing, and that's the way it began."

In late spring, Janis moved in with Whitaker and her roommates at 186 States Street, where she at last found some physical stability. It was a large, comfortable house, with steep front steps down to the street. Whitaker had a car, and the two drove to North Beach to play pool or to Marin County for fresh air. On one jaunt to Stinson Beach, they ran out of gas. Janis insisted Whitaker hide in the bushes while she stuck out her thumb to get them a ride. "She thought we wouldn't get picked up because of my skin color," Whitaker recounted. "I said, 'Fuck you! That's prejudice!' " Their argument continued until a car stopped and took them to a gas station. Janis was scarred from her adolescence in Texas, according to Whitaker. "She told me that they were always calling her ugly and a 'nigger lover.' She thought of herself as ugly. I would just hug her and tell her how beautiful she was."

Whitaker encouraged Janis's singing career and suggested she have promotional photos taken. Janis asked for a session with Marjorie Alette, who had photographed her performing at San Jose's Folk Theatre with Kaukonen. Dressed in a baggy sweater and faded jeans, Janis posed with and without her acoustic guitar at Alette's apartment. Whitaker wanted to be included in some shots as well, but Janis begged off. "She felt that if she became a star, having her picture taken with a lesbian would somehow hinder her progress," Whitaker said. Janis still worried about her parents' opinion of her, too, and told her lover that one day she wanted to have kids and "a house with a white picket fence."

"I was Janis's picket fence for a while," Whitaker recounted. "She used to tell me, *'I really, really love you.'* But deep down, I knew we weren't going to be a lifetime couple. She seemed like a lesbian, and she had been with another woman before me, but in some way, she didn't take it seriously. Emotionally, she wanted to please her folks and be the way she was brought up. In her mind, that would make her 'whole.'"

Whitaker insisted that Janis get a job to help with household expenses, though their share of the rent (split four ways) was only $17.50 a month. "I told her, 'I can't support you,' and she said, 'What am I supposed to do?' I said, 'You're smart. You can find something.' So she found a clerical job—and that didn't sit too well with her. It didn't last very long, but she paid her rent."

At Whitaker's house, Janis frequently played Bessie Smith records, listening carefully to her phrasing. "She absolutely loved Bessie Smith and knew so much about her," Whitaker said. "I think she really identified with her. Once she said she felt like she was the reincarnation of Bessie Smith." A brawler, bisexual, and heavy drinker like Janis, the Tennessee-born Smith became Columbia Records's top seller in 1923, and remained a star until the Great Depression. Louis Armstrong said of Smith, "She used to thrill me at all times, the way she could phrase a note with a certain something in her voice no other blues singer could get. She had music in her soul, and felt everything she did. Her sincerity with her music was an inspiration." Smith reshaped others' songs and "charged them with joy and sorrow that appeared to be born of personal experience," wrote Smith's biographer Chris Albertson. Masterfully blending pathos and defiance, lust and despair, making her listeners believe every word she sang—such were the lessons to be learned from Bessie Smith.

Janis also turned Whitaker on to Bob Dylan's debut album. "I'd never heard of him," Whitaker said, "and I asked her, 'Is he an old man? He sounds like he's in his seventies or eighties.' And she said, 'Hell, no! He's only twenty-one!'" In May they drove to the first annual Monterey Folk Festival, where Janis finally got to see Dylan in person. During the weekend-long event, hosted by Barbara Dane, Janis performed a few blues tunes at a Saturday afternoon open-mike competition where judges picked the best up-and-comers. She won and got free tickets for the Saturday-night performances, which included the Wildwood Boys, Greenwich Village's New Lost City Ramblers, Texas bluesman Mance Lipscomb, *and* Bob Dylan. His second album, *The Freewheelin' Bob Dylan*, was a week from release.

Still fairly unknown on the West Coast, Dylan's "Masters of War," "Talkin' John Birch Paranoid Blues," and "A Hard Rain's A-Gonna Fall" reached deaf ears at Monterey. As a surprise guest, Joan Baez appeared onstage, where she urged the noisy, restless audience to "Listen!"—explaining that Dylan was "speaking for me and everyone who wants a better world!" When Baez joined him on a powerful "With God on Our Side," the audience finally paid attention.

The next day, back at the fairgrounds, Janis spotted Dylan walking across the lawn. "Janis goes up to him," Whitaker recounted, "and says, 'Hi, my name is Janis Joplin, and this is my friend Jae.' He said, 'Hi,' and she said, 'I just love you, and I'm going to be famous one day, too.' And he said, '*Yeah—we're all gonna be famous.*'"

CHAPTER 9

METH FREAK AND THE SATURDAY NIGHT SWINDLE

*"Kozmic blues" means no matter what you do, you get
shot down anyway. One day I finally realized it ain't never
gonna be all right—there's always something going wrong.
It's what you wish was that makes
unhappiness—the hole, the vacuum.*

—JANIS JOPLIN

After six months of performing and steadily gaining fans in the Bay Area, Janis began to lose focus. As in Austin, following an initial period of excitement and commitment to singing, she ran into resistance, or, in some cases, thwarted her own chances of breaking out. Then, in the weeks following, her restlessness nearly ate her alive, fueling her drinking and pill popping. When she eventually reached out to her father for help, he gave as best he could, but his own bleak outlook on life would serve as a shattering revelation to Janis: disappointment, suffering, and pain, he told her, would be her constant companions—no matter how hard she tried to escape them.

"I did really great in my singing when I first got there," Janis wrote in a 1965 letter. "People treated me as if I was going to be famous. But it was only a few months til I was drunk all the time and hanging out on Green Street at the Anxious Asp. Sure is a sordid story, isn't it?" Her aborted booking at Top of the Tangent wasn't Janis's only no-show.

Rodney Albin, director of the San Francisco State College Folk Music Festival, hired her to perform at a prestigious daylong concert—listed in the program as "Janet Joplin." But on May 23, 1963, the weekend after she met Bob Dylan at Monterey, she didn't turn up.

Janis had saved enough money to take off for Dylan's stomping grounds in New York City. Later in the fall, she prowled the Village scene, checking out Gerde's Folk City on West Fourth Street, where Dylan had played his Manhattan debut two years earlier. Seeking connection and comfort, she moved on to Port Arthur to spend Christmas with her family, but Texas felt more oppressive than ever, especially after President John F. Kennedy had been assassinated in Dallas on November 22. Janis visited old friends at Jim and Rae Langdon's party in Lafayette, Louisiana, where Jim now worked as a newspaper reporter. Among the Port Arthur crowd, Janis was the only one who'd flown far, far away.

In early 1964, back in San Francisco for her twenty-first birthday, Janis's drinking escalated. Since she and Jae Whitaker had broken up, she was again without a home and drifted from place to place. She partied in North Beach bars with Linda Gottfried and pals such as Jim Fouratt—who soon became a prominent gay activist and helped bring about the decriminalization of homosexuality in San Francisco in 1976. "I'd see Janis at the Coffee Gallery, and afterward we'd go out drinking," said Fouratt. "We didn't have money, so occasionally we'd go to restaurants, eat, go to the bathroom, then leave out the back door without paying." He was drawn to Janis's raucous sense of humor, and the pair spent nights carousing and getting drunk, after which he'd sneak her into his male-only boardinghouse.

Though absent for a while, Janis hadn't been forgotten by club owners or musicians, and her reputation as an extraordinary singer continued to spread. She bought a secondhand Vespa to travel more easily to gigs in Berkeley and all around the Bay Area. According to her California driver's license, issued February 21, 1964, she was living at 1515 Gough Street in Lower Pacific Heights, then a cheap neighborhood of San Francisco. The Cabale, opened by Cambridge folkies Debbie Green and Rolf Cahn (Barbara Dane's former husband) in 1963, was Berkeley's premier coffeehouse. Originally a shoe store, it was long and narrow, with rows of tables and chairs facing the stage. One February evening, Janis showed up early, prior to a later Coffee Gallery booking. Performing at the Cabale that night was Bob Neuwirth, an East Coast musician and painter, soon to become Dylan's aide-de-camp—and, years later, Janis's. Green asked Neuwirth if Janis could do a song before his set.

"She got up and sang a capella and knocked everybody out," Neuwirth recalled. "Then she said, 'I gotta get back to North Beach!' She jumped on her motor scooter, pulled onto San Pablo, and got hit by a car. Everybody ran out to the street. I put my jacket under her head, and then the ambulance took her. She didn't want to go to the hospital—she wanted to get back to San Francisco."

The extent of Janis's injuries—possibly a serious leg wound—and the length of her hospitalization are unknown; she didn't notify her family. But the accident further derailed her. "Record people [had come] in from LA, heard her, and said, 'Oh, she's fabulous,'" remembered her friend Chet Helms, who kept tabs on her career. "One was from RCA, and Janis was on the verge of a big deal that would have transformed her monetarywise and careerwise. Then she had the accident on her Vespa and totaled it and ended up in the hospital. The deal just went away during the course of her recovery."

After Janis recuperated, she traveled with LA native Linda Gottfried to Los Angeles to try her luck at the city's two major folk clubs: Doug Weston's Troubadour and the Ash Grove. Through Gottfried, she met session guitarist Steve Mann, who offered to back her at the Troubadour's open-mike night. Working up a couple of numbers backstage with Janis, Mann was impressed that "she could get her body and soul into that deep-down black blues sound," he said. After the show, "she had no place to go, so I invited her home to stay at my folks' house. She was fun—never a dull moment." Janis sang him some originals, another aspect of her musicianship that fascinated him.

In San Jose, Janis reconnected with Jorma Kaukonen, recently married and finishing college. He'd continued to pursue music, sometimes playing with Steve Mann, and had purchased a Sony reel-to-reel tape recorder. He invited Janis to his Fremont Street home to rehearse a set of songs: "We just fit together," according to Kaukonen. "Janis was great anytime I was around her, because it was always about the music. We both loved it so much." Kaukonen flipped on his recorder to capture their rehearsal, while his Swedish wife, Margareta, seated in the small room, typed a letter to her family. The so-called *Typewriter Tapes*, a bootleg that's circulated for decades, document the musicians, which also included Steve Mann, laughing and enjoying themselves, working on song arrangements and exchanging compliments as the tunes come together. Kidding around, Janis demonstrated an exaggerated soprano "theater voice" and joked about a chiffon dress she planned to wear onstage before a "gold lamé curtain." The tape captured their performances of the Reverend Gary Davis's "Hesitation Blues," Smith's "Nobody Knows You When You're Down and Out," and a Janis original, "Long Black Train Blues," with mournful lyrics such as: "That train start off slowly, my tears keep streamin' down / I cried, 'Oh Lord, why was I left in this godforsaken town?' "

Backed by Kaukonen, Janis was more relaxed than when performing solo. While he showed off his expert fingerpicking, she improvised her vocals. Among the musicians who sometimes joined them was Steve "Richmond" Talbot, an accomplished blues guitarist as well as a brakeman on the Southern Pacific Railroad. When they played Janis's "Mary Jane," many mistakenly thought it a Bessie Smith song. Inspired by 1920s hokum jazz numbers, its lyrics glorify the joys of marijuana: "Well, I have known women that wanted no man / Some that wanted to say / But I never knew what happened in this world / Til I met up with Mary Jane. . . . / Oh, when I'm feelin' lonesome and I'm feelin' blue / There's only one way to change / I walk down the street now lookin' for a man / One that knows my Mary Jane."

Four months after her return, in April 1964, Janis once again left San Francisco, this time with a former girlfriend of Jae Whitaker's named Linda Poole, a supporter of her music. Janis purchased a cheap secondhand Morris Minor and drove the spindly yellow British convertible straight to Austin, swallowing speed along the route. On April 16, self-confident and cheery, Janis performed for the first time in fifteen months at Threadgill's alongside her mentor Mr. Threadgill and the Waller Creek Boys. A friend recorded the set, which included their old repertoire, as well as Hank Thompson's 1960 honky-tonk number "A Six Pack to Go," with Janis tooting a kazoo. The night ended with everyone joining in on a rousing version of the Carter Family's "Will the Circle Be Unbroken."

Then their final destination: New York City, where Janis and Poole crashed at the Lower East Side apartment of bartender-actor Ken Hill, a former San Franciscan. The neighborhood, filled with abandoned buildings and burned-out cars, had plenty of cheap apartments for artists, musicians, and writers, in addition to Ukrainian and Polish immigrants and Puerto Rican families. Muggings and robberies were routine in the area, and drug dealers hung out on street corners. Hill tended bar at the Old Reliable, an Eastern European tavern on Third Street between Avenues B and C, with an Off-Off-Broadway theater in its back room. It became Janis's hangout, as did Slugs' Saloon, a music venue down the block—both of which offered dirt-cheap drinks. Slugs's owner Jerry Schultz booked primarily modern jazz, including Sun Ra, Ornette Coleman, and Sonny Rollins (decades later, the building housed the Nuyorican Poets Café). On off nights, he let Janis accompany herself on guitar to a smattering of people. On Monday, May 25, she performed at Gerde's Folk City, sharing an open mike with accomplished folk guitarist Jerry Silverman.

At Village folk clubs, she noticed guitarists playing louder acoustic twelve-strings, so she bought one and tried to teach herself the more difficult instrument. But the British Invasion's electric rock & roll predominated that summer, blaring from car and apartment windows. The Beatles scored six number ones in 1964, displacing folk music among both tastemakers and music fans.

Janis called her parents from New York to assure them she was working as a keypunch operator and singing in clubs on weekends. Dorothy Joplin, in a sign of support, made and mailed her daughter a costume for her appearances, a blouse embellished with mirrors and orange embroidery and a scarlet-and-white satin cape. Janis gave away the clothes and kept wearing her daily uniform of a black shirt and Levi's. She'd lost weight, because of her frequent speed intake, and she'd lopped off her hair.

During Janis's nearly four months in New York, it's unclear how often she actually worked or performed there. Some who knew her thought she earned a shaky living hustling pool games in neighborhood bars. She spent much of her time drinking at gay bars and popping pills with "a stocky, short-haired butch lesbian" named Adrianne, according to Janice Knoll, whose fourth-floor walk-up on East Second Street between Avenues A and B was one of Janis's crash pads. Janice and her husband, Edward Knoll, like many in the neighborhood, injected speed. In July Janis and Adrianne "announced they wanted to shoot speed," and Janice initiated them. Just months earlier, Ed Sanders, a poet and cofounder of folk-rock anarchist combo the Fugs, had filmed an underground documentary, *Amphetamine Head: A Study of Power in America*; it depicted neighborhood residents hitting up in a shooting gallery near the Knolls' apartment. "Anyone who lived on the Lower East Side and spent much time mixing with the street culture encountered A-heads," Sanders wrote in a 2012 memoir. "They roamed the streets, bistros, and pads shooting, snorting, or gobbling unearthly amounts of amphetamine. . . . In some apartments," he observed, "a hypodermic needle boiling on a gas ring was almost as prevalent as a folk guitar by the bed."

Janis later looked back at the "stifling atmosphere" of her New York summer as part of "my gay period—first Jae, then Linda Poole and I went to NY where I was running around w/faggots and . . . taking deximil [Dexamyl] constantly. I finally escaped that." The impetus to leave New York, she would claim, was to return "to San Francisco for the first time kind of wanting to find an old man and be happy." Later, she would view her Manhattan venture and her return to San Francisco as her going "out into the world with great vigor and need, and every time [getting] really fucked up."

En route to California in late August, Janis stopped in Port Arthur, where she gaily put on a show for her family about her grand time in New York. She picked up her fifteen-year-old sister, Laura, from school band practice and gave her the beat-up acoustic she'd replaced with a twelve-string guitar. "In the front bedroom off the kitchen," Laura wrote later, Janis played and "sang some deep-throated blues and showed me how to barre chord and slide across the frets." During the brief visit, her "analytical" father, said Laura, warned Janis about her rickety convertible's copious oil leak, but she countered with "I love it! It's so great to just drive cross country with my hair in the breeze!" To reassure them, Janis sent two postcards along the way: one from Reno ("unfortunately the Nugget was filled so I slept in the back seat of my car parked in a Royal gas station") and one with an image of the San Francisco–Oakland Bay Bridge, and, printed in big block letters: "Thur. 10:30 A.M. SIGH!"

Upon her return, Janis's pal Dave Archer, from Coffee and Confusion, recommended digs in the nineteenth-century Goodman Building at 1117 Geary Boulevard, in the low-rent Fillmore district. "She soon lived across the hall from me," Archer wrote in a 2002 memoir, "a tiny box with a sleeping loft." Janis took up with Malcolm Waldron, a biker from Detroit, and he moved in for a while.

Back singing at her usual haunts, Janis connected with a popular Dixieland jazz bandleader in Berkeley named Dick Oxtot. A forty-four-year-old multi-instrumentalist and former mailman, he was the rare musician who hired women. Years later, Oxtot recalled that one night while his six-piece outfit was playing the Cabale, "a tough-looking gal roar[ed] up on a motorcycle" with Waldron. After Janis sat in with them, the bandleader was so impressed that he hired her as his new singer. Soon after, he invited her to cut some songs in a Berkeley studio. Though she'd sung into a reel-to-reel recorder several times, the occasion marked Janis's first proper recording session. With a New Orleans–style intro on clarinet, trombone, and cornet, Janis trilled her vibrato on the folk-gospel staple "River Jordan." They also did a jaunty "Walk Right In," a 1929 number by Gus Cannon's Jug Stompers that had become a big hit for the Rooftop Singers in 1963. Janis "sang from her crotch," in the parlance of the folk trio's guitarist Erik Darling, followed by a modulation at the end, hitting the highest notes in her range. Backed by piano and horns, her "Mary Jane" complemented the 1920s selections. She was also "sensational," said Oxtot, on "Black Mountain Blues" and "Careless Love."

Oxtot played the recordings for acclaimed jazz bandleader Turk Murphy to see if he'd like to feature Janis. Murphy dug the sound, and, sight unseen, he told Oxtot to bring her to his next gig so she could join him on a number. Wearing a black cocktail dress provided by Oxtot's wife, Janis sat with the Oxtots right in front of the stage, but Murphy ignored them. During a break, Oxtot approached him to ask when Janis could sing, and Murphy told him, "I can't let her up here! *She's a beatnik!*" Humiliated, Janis quit singing with Oxtot as well.

Soon after, she contacted guitarist Steve Mann to accompany her. She'd moved upstairs into a larger apartment, sharing it with Linda Gottfried, and asked Mann to bring over his reel-to-reel. "I packed up my recorder, with a reel of tape and a microphone, and went over to her place on the bus," Mann recalled. She rolled him joints "from a mayonnaise jar full of weed. I'd smoke one, and I'd be *there*. It was good stuff. But when she sang, she didn't smoke pot." Occasionally swigging from a bottle, Janis "belted out those blues and gave all her energy to the music," he said. "Her voice just poured through me and came out my fingers. We recorded about eight or nine songs, all blues. All the songs were from her repertoire, not mine, but anything Janis sang, I just found her key, and we started in, because it was just the best old down-home blues singing possible. She was really good at taking cues and feeling when it was time for a guitar break. We both knew when the song was going to end, and it all came out great on the tape. She was a pro."

>─◆─○─◆─◁

Since her return from New York, Janis had gone from popping purple hearts to shooting methamphetamine. Much like on the Lower East Side, the drug later known as crystal meth proliferated in the Bay Area.

The previous January, to meet the growing demand, a self-taught chem-ist named Augustus Owsley Stanley III moved from LA to Berkeley and set up a makeshift lab to manufacture the drug before switching to the compound for which the name Owsley would become synonymous: LSD. In North Beach, dealers selling meth hung out at the Hot Dog Palace on Grant Avenue. "We walked right into a speed crowd," Chet Helms said later about the twenty-four-hour greasy spoon, also known as the Amp Palace. "I found Linda [Gottfried] and became a meth freak!" is how Janis put it. "Jesus Fucking Christ!"

In the beginning, "we thought our creativity was growing," Linda Gottfried explained. " 'Wow! We can work all day and all night' . . . Janis was painting, writing songs, studying blues singers' phraseology." Their SRO became a gallery of speed-induced artwork. "Janis and Linda hun-kered down there," Dave Archer recounted, "sitting up in bed day and night for weeks, making hundreds of ink drawings that ended up . . . all over the floor and walls. Their drawings covered the walls, floor, bed, dresser, and window ledge."

Janis's meth-induced euphoric binges fizzled into black depressions, relieved only by the next speed rush. One night, sitting at a bar, she wrote an anguished letter to her father at his office. (Their private cor-respondence no longer exists—Seth destroyed it.) Janis later described having written about "how you guys always told me it was going to get better, and I always thought it was an incline up and that one day it would level off. And you know, motherfucker, it ain't leveling off. I felt God had played a joke on us, and I was pissed off."

Seth Joplin, concocting a business trip, flew to San Francisco to check on his daughter. In anticipation of his arrival, Archer wrote, Janis got her friends to help clean up the "1,800 drawings" cluttering the apartment and disguise her true situation. "The plan was that Linda would help Janis [with a] makeover, from 'Beat chick on major drugs and alcohol' to 'semiprofessional Beat about town,'" Archer explained. "I ran into Janis in the hall one day, dressed for a test run, her hair pinned into something 'semi-stylish,' wearing makeup, plus a nice skirt with sensible flats. I laughed. *Don't laugh, motherfucker!*' But Janis was laughing the hardest. . . . It will always be one of my fondest memories . . . [Janis] standing there in that preposterous getup, with that smirk, and then laughing like a ventriloquist using a witch puppet."

Janis's ruse worked—or her father saw only what he wanted to see: "She was living in a little, old, scuffy apartment," Seth said later, "and seemed to be getting by all right. She wasn't visibly on dope. She was drawing welfare. She just did what she wanted to do"—including zipping up and down the San Francisco hills in her Morris Minor, her dad holding on for dear life. It "sure scared me," he recounted. "She never would slow down; both feet on the floor, one on the accelerator and one on the brake."

Seth couldn't reassure his daughter that things would turn around, and was equally incapable of reacting emotionally to her despair. Instead, he confirmed that she'd discovered what, in his mind, was life's dark truth. He called that truth "the great Saturday Night Swindle": people mistakenly believing that if they work hard all week, they'll get to have fun on the weekend—that there'll be a payoff for the drudgery and hardship of everyday life. But what actually happens is that the reward never materializes; you'll be cheated by life's vicissitudes—the Saturday Night Swindle, in his words—leading to a life filled with disappointment and unhappiness. Seth could only advise Janis to accept this depressing fact intellectually, as he had, and to endure it.

Linda Gottfried remembered Seth's visit. He was "really intelligent, and he talked to her directly, looked her in the eyes." Janis, too, never forgot their Saturday Night Swindle talk: "It's one of the few things I can remember clearly" from that drug-addled time, she told journalist David Dalton five years later.

"It struck me like a fucking lightbulb," Janis recalled. "That's all there was." The realization only made her more "pissed off," fueling her drugging and drinking. She would later give the Swindle her own name: the kozmic blues, which to her "means no matter what you do, you get shot down anyway."

By her twenty-second birthday in January, Janis was a full-blown meth addict, with the time between injections shortening by the day:

"I wanted to smoke dope, take dope, lick dope, suck dope, fuck dope—
anything I could lay my hands on, I wanted to do it. Hey, man, what is
it? I'll try it. How do you do it? Do you suck it? No? Do you swallow it?
I'll swallow it."

Janis continued looking for "an old man" and shagged a succession,
including one of her guitarists, Michael Pritchard, who recalled their
first six days together as "twenty-four hours a day, real intense." She
mooned over Patrick Cassidy, a handsome Beat poet who, it turned
out, had been married to a woman who would later be Janis's closest friend. Linda paired off with Janis's former fling Malcolm Waldron,
while Janis set her sights on one of the Amp Palace's most colorful
habitués: George "the Beast" Howell. A sometime night watchman at
the SRO Hotel Dante, George the Beast was a big man and "kind of
a poet," wrote one North Beach denizen. "He slept where he could
and cultivated acquaintance with the rotters, pimps, poets, and crystal
merchants who congregated after midnight at the Hot Dog Palace." He
looked like a biker, wore an army fatigue jacket and a gold earring—and
had severe mood swings, veering from congenial to violent. "Their relationship was really stormy," Linda Gottfried observed. "He didn't give
her many strokes."

Janis dealt speed to support her increasing habit. Pat Nichols, who
later took the name Sunshine, remembered "a pretty messed up" Janis
"pounding on my door. This is a three-story house, and I'm shouting
down the stairway, 'Who is it?' and she said, 'It's Janis Joplin! I want to
sell you some speed!'" The meth took a mental and physical toll; her
face broke out, and, barely eating, she dwindled to skin and bones.

Janis and Linda Gottfried moved into a cheaper, windowless basement apartment—$25 a month—on Baker Street, where they holed up
and shot meth daily. One night, outside the Anxious Asp, Janis was badly
beaten by bikers, to whom she probably owed money for drugs. She lost
her status at the places she used to perform, and instead became known
as someone who'd ask for an advance, take a break from her set, and
then not return to finish—or not show up at all. At Coffee and Confusion, Sylvia Fennell posted a handwritten sign: "Anyone caught giving

Janis Joplin money before the end of her set will be fired. Any customer who gives her money will be 86ed." Soon her gigs dried up.

When she attempted to join the Mainliners, a band formed by San Francisco State art student George Hunter, he rebuffed her. "She wasn't in real good shape," said Hunter, who'd borrowed one of her jazz LPs. "The term 'speed freak' is pretty accurate in her case. I couldn't see integrating her into my band, because she was such a mess."

Through Janice and Edward Knoll, who'd moved from the East Village to San Francisco, Janis met a man who appeared to be the opposite of those she'd been seeing: suavely handsome, well dressed, and articulate. New Yorker Peter de Blanc called himself an engineer—like Seth Joplin—with a master's degree. He drove a Land Rover and claimed to come from old money. "Peter was this very charismatic person," Linda Gottfried recounted, "a real gentleman. Mr. Smooth Talk." He and Janis became inseparable. "He loved Janis, and she loved him," said Gottfried. "This was a great love affair . . . the first time I ever really saw Janis's heart open." And like Janis, "He was crazy for methedrine."

Janis had nearly stopped singing; de Blanc didn't care for the blues and preferred pretty soprano voices. Her days and nights with Peter mostly revolved around speed and its effects, de Blanc throwing a rubber ball for hours against the apartment wall. Janis weighed less than a hundred pounds, and de Blanc, suffering from delusions, began stashing guns in his car. "He had advanced paranoia and thought he was receiving messages from people on the moon," said Gottfried. De Blanc told Janis he wanted to marry her after they got clean. Hallucinating and delusional, he committed himself to a hospital psych ward.

Chet Helms heard from friends about Janis's condition and stopped by her apartment. "She was emaciated, almost catatonic, just not responding," he recalled. "Janis would change her mind two hundred times before she got to the door. That's like terminal speed." Linda Gottfried planned to join Malcolm Waldron in Hawaii to get clean, and Janis agreed to return to Texas. Her friends raised enough money for a bus ticket home. De Blanc, still suffering from delusions, was hospitalized again. They promised to reunite in Port Arthur once they were both free of their addictions. In May 1965, after a farewell party, Janis boarded a Texas-bound Greyhound.

A few years later, in retelling the story of this San Francisco residency, Janis underplayed how harrowing the end had been, and she elongated the sporadic two and a half years she'd spent there: "I stayed there for five years," she said, "doing what young people do—finding out and changing and hanging out and bumming around, I guess you'd call it. I decided to go back home and straighten out, go back to college, even get married." For the first time in her life, Janis had fully pledged her heart to someone. But her relationship with Peter de Blanc turned out to be the biggest Saturday Night Swindle of all.

CHAPTER 10

TEXAS COED

*It's such a quiet and peaceful existence,
and I'm enjoying it so thoroughly.*

—JANIS JOPLIN

After the long bus ride home to Port Arthur, Janis arrived at Lombardy Drive weighing a skeletal eighty-eight pounds. She collapsed in sixteen-year-old Laura's bedroom and slept for days. As she withdrew from amphetamine addiction, she suffered anxiety, depression, mood swings, and stomach ailments. At twenty-two, she began to assess her past and future. Truly frightened of how close to death she'd come, Janis focused on changing her life, transforming into the "normal" daughter her parents wanted, and giving up the thing that nearly led to her demise: music, and its accompanying lifestyle and intoxicants. Thanks to her engagement to Peter de Blanc, the "white picket fence" seemed attainable; life as a housewife and mother a safe option. She could at last fit in, her inner darkness and turmoil smothered by domesticity. Yet, over the next year in Texas, the shadows returned as she struggled between her love of singing and her desire to please her parents. Though a part of her would always long for the white-picket-fence life, her talent was just too big to be contained by any kind of boundary, even when she was the one trying to impose it.

Janis's appetite gradually returned, and she wolfed down Dorothy Joplin's comforting, familiar dinners. Her stewed vegetables, ham hocks and pinto beans, roast beef, and fried chicken helped nurse Janis back to

health and gain weight. Laura drove her to the Jefferson City Shopping
Center to buy clothing, including underwear—which she didn't own—
and long-sleeved shirts to cover her needle tracks.

At the dinner table, Janis discussed going back to Lamar and her
impending marriage to de Blanc. Over the next five months, she wrote
Peter some seventy letters. Her correspondence functioned like a journal, where she could dissect her feelings, letter by letter, coming to
terms with her past as well as reporting on her new life. Just as Seth
Joplin had once asked Dorothy to write him what she was *thinking*, in
a way her mother was unable to do, Janis put down on paper her in-
nermost thoughts. She clung to her future plans with de Blanc as if to
a life preserver. And with her powerful will, she shut out warning signs
that Peter was not the "knight in shining armor" she'd once asked old
boyfriend Jack Smith to be. When Janis first met de Blanc, her speed-fed
delusions and scattershot thoughts could explain her overlooking his
many faults. Back in Port Arthur, sober and increasingly healthy, Janis
nevertheless desperately still held on to her fantasy. She saw de Blanc as
the one thing that could save her life, while her exceptional voice could
lead only to her destruction.

"I hope you get to leave San Francisco. Wow, everyone should
leave—it's so nice out here in the real world where people are happy
and proud of themselves and good!" began her first letter to de Blanc,
who was still in the Bay Area. Peter did not live in the "real world," nor
was he "good," however. He traveled to Mexico soon after Janis's departure and began an affair with New Yorker Debbie Boutellier, an airline
employee and San Francisco State student. They made plans to move
together to her Manhattan apartment. In San Francisco, Linda Gottfried
met another of de Blanc's lovers, who was several months pregnant and
claimed he was legally married to yet *another* woman in New York, with
whom he had a child. When Gottfried notified Janis, her disclosures
didn't seem to affect Janis's dream of a future with Peter.

"I so want to be with you," Janis wrote him. "I don't mind your . . .
analogy to a cat's 9 lives. I don't mind if you've had 8 wives before me,
then I would get to be what I want—the last and lasting one—the one

you keep. But I could only count 3 or 4, can you verify that there really are 8 please? Wow, then you'd have to take me because I'd be your last chance."

Of course, Janis kept this information from her family and reported only de Blanc's many achievements, as he conveyed them: a genius in electronics, an MA from McGill University in Montreal, Mensa membership, undercover work for the French army during the Algerian war in the late 1950s. He claimed to have dual citizenship and hail from an affluent family in upstate New York. In reality, de Blanc grew up in Niagara Falls, New York, and never attended college. A skilled liar since his teens, he'd married young but deserted his wife and child, assumed someone else's identity, and moved to the West Coast, where he used a variety of aliases, posing as a prosperous deal-making entrepreneur. He knew how to flatter intelligent women, and a former lover told writer Alice Echols, "You could be yourself one hundred percent with him. I know that's how Janis felt. He was very open minded and accepting of who you were."

De Blanc was as charming in correspondence as in person. Desperate for stability and love, Janis let his sentiment wash over her. "I've never read such a nice letter," she once wrote back. "I started crying and saying SIGH. . . . Wow, baby, I hope you mean it!" After receiving another, she replied, "The reason I wanted to write was just to tell you how beautiful your letter was—my first love letter. . . . It was lovely, Peter, and I'm so glad you feel that way—I love you for all time."

De Blanc occasionally telephoned Janis. She would wait by the phone with the kind of desperation she'd had previously for her drug connection. It was as if she'd replaced meth addiction with obsessing over Peter. When they made plans for his first visit to Port Arthur, to prepare him, she described her family in a lengthy, touching letter:

> My mother—Dorothy—worries so and loves her children dearly.
> Republican and Methodist, very sincere, speaks in clichés which she
> really means and is very good to people. (She thinks you have a lovely
> voice and is terribly prepared to like you.)

My father—richer than when I knew him and kind of embarrassed about it—very well read—history his passion—quiet and very excited to have me home because I'm bright and we can talk (about antimatter yet—that impressed him)! I keep telling him how smart you are and how proud I am of you. . . .

My sister—15 [sic] years old—lovely sweet girl (I very magnanimously brought her a makeup bag y'know—show her a few tricks, heh heh. You should see her! 2 drawers of hair rollers—a makeup table w/2 mirrors and 3 shelves of makeup—quite the young lady! I'm taking lessons from her). She's learned to play guitar quite well on a guitar I gave her last year and she sings Joan Baez ballads in a very sweet voice. In fact, tonight she's singing at MYF [Methodist Youth Fellowship] and I'm going to hear her. She thinks quite a bit of me—much more than I thought. My father and I were talking and he said that Laura had said that she didn't think that I was wrong in anything that I have ever done and that made me feel very nice. I keep slipping and calling her "Linda" which she recognizes as a compliment—i.e., she is like a friend to me. We talk about folk music and I talk about you and she's thrilled for me.

My brother—Michael—now about 5' tall! Absolutely huge and grown almost [age twelve]—boyish grinning smile and floppy hair— Levi's and bicycle. Loves me dearly—wants me to live at home and likes to show off and impress me—proud, embarrassed, wants my affection—Wow, he's a nice little boy! I sure do love him. I've always wanted a boy just like Mike—I like him.

Janis enrolled at Lamar, signing up for classes in world history and English literature. She regularly went swimming and golfing, played backyard badminton, and polished card games, such as bridge, with her family. Several of Janis's old friends stopped by to welcome her home. Though Patti and Dave McQueen lived in Houston, Patti drove to Port Arthur for a visit. "She was waiting for this fellow she'd fallen in love with," she remembered. Now married, Philip Carter and his wife, Diane, lived nearby, as did Adrian and Gloria Haston; when classes started in

July at Lamar's Summer II session, Janis carpooled with Adrian, a graduate student. But most of her time was spent at home. She especially enjoyed Sundays alone with her father, listening to Beethoven, while the "three religious Joplins," as Janis referred to them, went to church.

Almost as if she'd assumed a new identity, she wrote her fiancé about who she'd been and the person she was becoming. "Strange, it's such a quiet and peaceful existence and I'm enjoying it so thoroughly. . . . Fun isn't what I want these days. Strange, I never thought I'd ever say that. I'm one of those old-fashioned thrill-crazy kids, you know, or at least I was. I never could see any value or anything to be sought after in anything except fun—and now dig me—I've got better things to do than Fun."

By late July, her love letters, anticipating his long-awaited visit, also detailed her Lamar classes ("reading *Sir Gawain and the Green Knight*— a medieval romance") and academic achievements. Finally, in August de Blanc arrived in Port Arthur, having traveled from New Orleans— where he'd secretly been with Boutellier, his girlfriend. The Joplins found him gracious, polite, and seemingly happy to see Janis. "He was tall and slender with a dignified air," Laura wrote in her memoir, *Love, Janis*. "He had straight blond hair, parted to the side, that kept falling across his face. There was a certain nervous rhythm about his efforts to keep it out of his eyes. He wore a rumpled suit, but exuded a demeanor of calm strength."

Dorothy Joplin wouldn't allow the couple to sleep together. "He looked at Janis, and she at him," Seth recounted, "and Dorothy said, 'I don't care how you look—you're not going to sleep in this house that way.'" Regardless, de Blanc charmed Dorothy and Janis's siblings, and, before departing, he asked Seth for a private discussion in the backyard. "Soon Dad called us back and announced, 'Peter has asked for my daughter's hand in marriage, and I have consented,'" Laura recalled. "Janis jumped up and down, hugging Peter and clutching his steady arm as if it were a tether to reality. The moment excited us all." He planned to return at Christmas with a ring and asked that the family wait until then before announcing their engagement in the local paper.

After receiving what must have been a prearranged call from Boutel-lier in New Orleans, de Blanc claimed he had to leave suddenly due to a death in his family. He explained he'd be staying with his aunt, uncle, and "cousin Debbie" in New York and gave Janis his new address: a brownstone on West Seventy-Fifth Street between Central Park West and Columbus Avenue.

Flying to New York, he continued his performance, writing the Jop-lins "in flight" on Eastern Airlines stationery. Still ingratiating himself, he thanked them profusely for their hospitality and, appealing to Doro-thy, apologized that the "grammer [sic] and sentence construction in this note is ridiculous." Soon after, he shipped her a silver-plated cof-fee service: during his visit, she'd been embarrassed that she couldn't serve coffee properly. He called Janis and asked if her mother would like matching candlestick holders too, and she told him, "No, we only use candles during hurricanes." When she reported the conversation to her mother, Dorothy "whimpered," and Janis dashed off a note to Peter, saying, "If it's not too late, Mother would like those candlestick holders. . . . She curses my pragmatism."

Dorothy started planning the wedding dress she'd make her daugh-ter, while Janis began stitching a "Lone Star" pattern quilt, like one her mother made in the 1930s. "My mother was really charmed by your letter (although I must say she seems very smitten by you anyway)," she reassured de Blanc. "I really have to tell you how much my family liked you. My brother keeps . . . going, 'Gee, I sure would like to have Peter for a brother-in-law,' and Laura peeked up underneath her hair once to say, 'and he has such broad shoulders! Sigh.' Mother thinks you are very polished and have lots of potential—that's a compliment. . . . And even Daddy got up out of his reading chair (!) to come into my room and tell me that it looked like I'd picked a fine young man who could go anywhere he wanted too [sic]—'sure is smart!' And me, well, I still think you're just perfect. . . . I love you. And so does my family."

In the six-page letter, dated August 21, she also related that Linda Gottfried, now married to Malcolm Waldron, had gotten a teach-ing job in Hawaii and that she and Dorothy were sending her "a few reams of advice." Janis described several new "school outfits" she'd bought, accompanied by her sketch of one. After her final exams, she planned to take her siblings to a Houston Astros baseball game, sew new dresses, work on her quilt, have an engagement photo taken, and visit the doctor—"we now suspect an ulcer." Her sense of humor intact, she mused about her trousseau. "Mother has told me that when I get married, she will give me a beautiful crocheted bedspread, which her mother made. So my hope chest is filling. I do have to get one. . . . Do they still make them? Good heavens, are they expensive, big, heavy? Do you know what they are? I think they're an American myth. I'll probably just have to sit all my hopeful belongings over in a corner somewhere."

Anxiety continued to plague Janis, though, and when de Blanc's letters stopped briefly, she called him in New York. Boutellier, who answered, claimed to be "Cousin Debbie" and lied that Peter couldn't write because he'd run out of stationery. Janis sensed the deception, and later, after Debbie answered again, she confronted de Blanc via the U.S. Mail: "When that girl answered, I just felt really wronged. I just wanted you to say Oh wow baby, I love you and of course she's just my cousin, silly . . . but you didn't. You just fucking sat there and acted like you didn't care what I thought or if I felt hurt."

Janis had also clearly realized that no matter how hard she tried to fit in at Lamar Tech (she'd even taken "poise lessons," according to Laura), her classmates still considered her a weirdo—and that she, herself, could never be one of them: "Thought that since I wasn't KING BEATNIK and ATTENTION-SEEKER anymore," she wrote de Blanc, "and I wore dresses and shoes and makeup and acted quietly and . . . look like everyone else. . . . But I'm still just sort of different somehow . . . all those blithering coeds w/their cotton print dresses and blondish fluffy hair and Texas drawls and *Oh now ya'll cum on!*'s just know that I'm not one of them. But then that's fair, I guess—I know they're not one of my kind of people either."

Janis depended on her family more than ever for the attention she needed. "Mother is getting worried about me because I stay home too much," she wrote de Blanc. "She doesn't think I spend enough time with 'people my own age.'" Dorothy bought recorders for the family, perhaps to offer Janis a wholesome musical activity, and the Joplins began nightly practice sessions on the instruments. Dorothy, Janis wrote to de Blanc, was "the most earnest recorder player I've ever seen, stubbornly thudding her foot & peering at the book through her bifocals."

When de Blanc finally called, his ruse of family wealth became more elaborate, with tales of yachting with an uncle and his pending inheritance: "Talking to you about money this evening sort of sobered me up," she wrote him on August 24. "After we hung up I was kind of giddy-panicky—you know, walking around on my tiptoes, wringing my hands and shredding napkins, whining, 'Oh MOAN, money! What'm I gonna do! Whimper. I never even knew anybody that wasn't plain old ordinary. We're too young! I wanted to be able to make meatloaves & stews and save money cleverly on my household budget. Oh why did this have to happen to me? I made such a good poor person. . . . How was I to know? He didn't look rich! Jeez, he was as funky as anyone else. . . .' My family just sat back and snickered incredulously. My mother kept saying, 'Well, Janis you can be happy & have money too. I mean, you don't have to fix tuna casseroles to have a happy marriage.' Mike said, 'Wow, Janis, he's still the same on the inside, he's just better on the outside.' Daddy just put his head in his hands and chuckled, while Laura said, 'Well, if you don't think it'll work, tell him you have a sister'. . . . I finally decided that if you did have money, even though it would put a crimp in my Peter-and-I-struggling-together-uphill-poor-but-happy-anyway plans, you would do something useful with it—like starting your own business again or putting it away for the kids to go to college, or blowing it on a honeymoon in Europe (I kind of liked that one . . .) and it wouldn't really get in our way.

"I mean what I'm trying to say is doing nothing is very detrimental—we both know that only too well, dammit—and I don't want to just live a useless bored life of ignoble ease. . . .

"In fact, your telling me that upset me so much that I had to go out into the backyard and play two swift games of badminton to calm down. . . . Later, Daddy took me aside, placed one hand on my shoulder, looked seriously into my eyes and said, 'Just remember, Janis, we've always done all we could for you.' Then he gazed out the window sternly. Then he turned back around to me w/ his eyes twinkling and giggled back into the living room."

Janis's white-picket-fence fantasy, together with her being straight for the first time in years, led her to become more introspective, dwelling on thoughts and feelings she'd either put into her singing or pushed aside by drinking and drugging. Watching television coverage of the Gemini 5 manned flight orbiting Earth, Janis was transfixed by—and perhaps longed for—the astronauts' freedom to "orbit . . . without its atmosphere & soon to be leaving it altogether," she wrote de Blanc, who claimed interest in working for NASA in Houston. "[W]hich brings to mind your security clearance, what's happening?"

Reporting on his supposed job searches, de Blanc had mentioned needing a security clearance. Dorothy promptly researched technology companies looking for personnel with Peter's "qualifications," and Janis mailed him a list of "firms that are hiring and in dire need of technicians," including Dow Chemical, National Cash Register, IBM, and Texas Instruments.

Meanwhile, Janis, fearful of repercussions from her addiction, got a complete medical exam and wrote her fiancé that "this was sort-of my last showdown w/fuckedupedness—to see if I had really made it out or if it was still hurting me. And I really have made it! Jesus damn, I'm really alright, and ain't nobody gonna make me be ugly again! I am not anemic, there is nothing wrong w/my liver or my blood and no gyn problems that he can see now, although if I have any more problems, he said he would probably give me some hormones. He suspects hormone imbalance because of the fact that I've never gotten pregnant. [She may have not considered her 1962 miscarriage a pregnancy.] Talking about that [hormones] kind-of embarrasses me."

Over the next three months, de Blanc detailed numerous excuses to postpone the marriage, including his illnesses and hospitalization, a new job that did not work out, and lack of funds. For unknown reasons, he even suggested a visit from "Cousin Debbie" to the Joplins on his behalf, but it never materialized. He penned one bizarre note in Russian. Janis wrote increasingly alarmed letters and made near-hysterical phone calls to sort things out. "Heavens," she wrote him, "I don't want to wait two years or anything! I'd like to get married in February or March right after I finish this semester. . . . So please let's try to save money so we can get married. It's nice being engaged & everything, but I think I'm going to like the married part better."

At one point, de Blanc contacted Seth at work, asking for a loan until his delayed "inheritance" came through. Seth apparently sent de Blanc a check to cover supposed medical tests at Beth Israel Medical Center in New York. In a September 11 letter, he apologized to Seth for "taking the liberty of calling you" and, in another note, for the delay in publicly announcing their engagement and for "all the esoteric wordplay." He scrawled in large letters across the bottom of the page: "I Want to Marry Your Daughter—How About It?"

Janis took a full course load at Lamar that fall and concentrated on her studies. She proudly mailed de Blanc a sociology paper, for which she received an A, with the humorous note "I guess having depressing firsthand knowledge of social problems helped. . . . Mother said to call it my application for the position of wife of a Mensa member. Hope you don't think I'm silly sending this."

Her next letter included her engagement photo—in which she appeared elegant and solemn, with a wounded look in her eyes, her hair neatly pulled back from her face and styled into a chignon atop her head. She wrote, "I hope I look pretty enough to show to your family or friends. *Oh phoo*, this is the first time in my history of being an egomaniac that I've felt shy. . . . I'm so fucking insecure—I've got to constantly fret." In the same September 28 letter, she described the kozmic blues: "I've been moaning lately about the pains of growing up. All kinds of pain. My most recent grievance is a very real pain because of a wisdom tooth. My lower jaw is all swollen & everything's a drag. But there seems to be an almost insufferable amount of less literal but just as potent type of pain we (young people) have to go through. Of late, I've been saying how very glad I am to be finally clearing the brink—to be happy & grown-up and able to relax and not ache all the time. God, I would never be young again. I'd have to cry all over. My Father & I were bantering on this subject the other night at dinner. He quoted the old cliché about youth being wasted on the young, and I said in all earnestness, although everyone else laughed, that you shouldn't have to be young until you were old enough to cope with it. But, dig me, I'm a real, live, set-in-my-ways, be-wisdom-toothed adult now! God, at last!"

In October, with de Blanc still remote, Janis at last turned to music. As in the past, singing provided a salve and helped her regain self-confidence. "My guitar playing is growing by leaps & bounds," she wrote him. "I do a really great version of a blues called 'Come Back Baby' in G [a 1955 Ray Charles tune]. I really wail on it. If you can call it wailing when you do it all alone in your bedroom w/your door closed. . . . I've got a high . . . falsetto part in it that is too much! I wish I had fans that thought I was as good as I do. So far, this is my best thing. I'm working on some others & I do them fairly well but I still don't have enough to do a set or anything. Besides, where would I do it? Poor Dad is being driven to distraction by my practicing. Laura's guitar playing doesn't bother him too much. She plays quietly and sings softly. But me! I've got a big thumb pick & I really play! & really sing too. And he sits in the living room feverishly trying to be calm & placid & listen to Bach. Poor thing." On a rare outing together, Janis and her father went to the movie *Ship of Fools*, based on Katherine Anne Porter's despairing 1962 novel, but instead of "good old-fashioned escapism," she wrote de Blanc, it "was very depressing & I identified with absolutely everyone in it."

>⋅⋅⊙⋅⋅<

Janis looked up her former college friend Frances Vincent, a singer who waitressed at Beaumont's Halfway House, a folk music café located in a 1909 bungalow. With Vincent's referral, Janis was offered a gig and began polishing her old repertoire. "The people from the Halfway

House wanted me to work this weekend," she wrote de Blanc, "but I didn't feel I'd had enough rehearsal, so I didn't. Didn't feel like it anyway." Philip Carter suggested she record at the home of his friend Neil, a classical musician with Beaumont's symphony. On October 10 she wrote de Blanc that she'd "been up there about 9 fucking hours doing the damn thing and I only got 3 songs! Gawd, what a drag! Neil didn't really know how to record on his recorder. It was really a hassle. Singing & singing, being nervous, Jesus Christ! I got all weak & shakey for a while, but we finally stopped to eat. Then I felt better but the tape recorder was broken so I just quit. Damn, I'm tired. Well anyway to the tape. Two tunes: 'Come Back Baby' & 'Once I Lived the Life of a Millionaire' [a version of "Nobody Knows You When You're Down and Out"], and one really pretty ballad 'Once I Had a Sweetheart' [a traditional English ballad recorded by Baez]. I hope it's alright & I hope the blues don't scare people. I'll send it as soon as I can. Anyway, it's engraved with the blood from my cheeks so I hope you like it."

Janis continued to reflect on her earlier recklessness, as if trying to convince herself she was now changed and "attempting to look at my life objectively from my new happy vantage point," she wrote de Blanc on October 14. She described her tumultuous periods in Venice, Austin, and San Francisco. Her conclusion:

> *I really seem to have been trying to do myself in. . . . I've been worrying about this quite a bit, but I've decided that there is no chance. . . . I guess whatever I used to hate myself for, I don't anymore. Or maybe I've just grown up. . . . It's not there anymore. . . . After each horrible experience during my recuperative period, I always nurtured the belief that what I had done or just left was really pretty cool . . . But damn, I've never felt so positive about anything not being desirable. I guess I've really changed my mind this time. . . .*
>
> *Every night, I try to go to sleep, my head starts filling w/ past unhappinesses—am I obsessed, and why? Why do I think about all of this shit? . . . I guess we've both managed to plow through a lot of shit. . . . It's been enough to make me nothing short of fanatically determined*

to have it right once, and that's what we're doing, right? . . . I wish we
could be together. I want to be happy so fucking bad.

Night after night, lying in bed awake, her mind churning, Janis managed
to convince herself that her self-destructive tendencies had diminished
and that it was safe for her to return to music. She began channeling
her feelings into lyrics, composing melodies to accompany them on
guitar. One of her new songs fantasized what she'd hoped to attain with
de Blanc: "Come away with me / And we'll build a dream / Things
will seem / Like they never seemed / They could be. . . . No one will
cry alone in their sleep / There'll be no loneliness hidden down deep
/ Just like the Pied Piper / I'll walk through the streets / Gathering all
the happy people I meet / We'll join hands and / Fly through the sky
/ Leaving our troubles / Here to die, all alone." She taught it to Laura,
who loved it and memorized the song. But years later, Janis ridiculed
it as clichéd, telling her sister, "Sing it all you want to, Laura, but don't
tell anyone I wrote that."

"Turtle Blues," on the other hand, presented a more authentic self-
portrait of Janis, hiding away in her shell, "thinking too much." "Turtle
Blues" would appear on 1968's *Cheap Thrills*:

> *I guess I'm just like a turtle*
> *That's hidin' underneath its hardened shell.*
> *Whoa, whoa, oh yeah, like a turtle*
> *Hidin' underneath its hardened shell.*
> *But you know I'm very well protected*
> *I know this goddamn life too well.*

Janis performed before an audience for the first time in nearly a year
at the appropriately named Halfway House. "It was really nice," she
wrote de Blanc. "They have an old blind man named Patty Green playing piano. I might work there this weekend . . . If I do . . . I may sing a
few ballads and back myself. I've gotten quite a bit better on the guitar
and can actually do an adequate job of playing now. I've been learning

some new ballads from Laura and some of her books. You liked that kind of singing, so I'm going to be able to do it. . . . I've been playing all day, and it's really nice. But [folk] scares me more than blues. It might evolve into a weekend gig, too." She then added, lying to him—or to herself: "But it's funny, I'm not all that ambitious anymore. But I'd still like to do it."

In mid-October, de Blanc informed her that he was returning to the hospital to see if a parasite was causing problems with his spleen. Janis implored, "Please have your cousin Debbie write to me. Is there any way she could get me an airplane ticket so I can come up there to see you?" She enclosed Russian tea cakes she'd made—"Mother's favorite recipe"—but warned they were "very fatty, so make sure it's ok to eat them." On October 19 Janis wrote a cheery letter to him at Beth Israel, describing her latest purchases for their future home: "2 sheets & 2 pillowcases—really beautiful linen w/scalloped rim for $15! I know that is . . . ridiculously high but they are simply lovely and will last forever. (Mother said she's never had any linen that nice since she's been married.) . . . You wouldn't believe what I did last night—sat around reading the Sears & Roebuck catalogue making out lists of what I want & what I need & how much they cost, etc. Sigh, I sure am happy." At letter's end, she inquired, "How are you doing in the hospital? How are you reacting to treatment? Do you feel sick? Are your white blood cells dying?"

Shortly after that letter, de Blanc claimed that his psychiatrist, who put him on tranquilizers, told him not to marry until his health improved. The "inheritance" never materialized, nor did a diagnosis for his health problems. To cope, Janis took Librium, a tranquilizer used for panic attacks, and she began seeing a psychiatric social worker, Bernard Giarratano. In one of their first sessions, he recalled, she told him, "I want to be straight . . . like Port Arthur."

Finally, Janis could no longer avoid the truth about de Blanc. She wrote him for the last time on November 11: "It's . . . getting hard for me to believe and understand you!" Her letter explored her anguish and terror, as well as her determination to deal with her fears more clearly, something that her therapist had helped her do.

Dorothy East Joplin doted on her firstborn, Janis Lyn, and strived to give her the perfect childhood, including a brick home on Procter Street, Port Arthur, Texas, 1943.

Seth and Dorothy Joplin made three-year-old Janis the center of their attention, c. 1946.

Janis, c. 1946, was a tomboy who loved to climb trees, and once broke her arm falling from one.

Janis worshipped her father, here holding baby Laura, and inherited his love of books and cynical outlook. Father's Day, 1949.

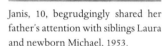

Dorothy loved giving her family the stable middle-class lifestyle she didn't have, which included entertaining a Blue Bird troop she helped organize; Janis, seven, is at far right, practicing a curtsy.

Janis, 10, begrudgingly shared her father's attention with siblings Laura and newborn Michael, 1953.

Seth Joplin constructed outdoor swings like the giant stride for Laura, Michael, and Janis, 13, in their backyard on Lombardy Street, Port Arthur, June 1956.

Janis devoured books and loved to draw and paint. She combined both interests the summer after ninth grade as a volunteer at Gates Memorial Library in Port Arthur, making posters for the children's room. This photo ran with a 1957 Port Arthur News article, the first time Janis appeared in the press.

In their front yard, Dorothy Joplin and her children pose in their Sunday best. Janis would soon forgo church and stay home with her atheist father.

Janis said her father "used to talk and talk to me, and then he turned right around from that when I was fourteen. Maybe he wanted a smart son . . ." At the Joplin home, 1957.

Janis's junior class photo, which appeared in the Thomas Jefferson High yearbook, *The Yellow Jacket*. By the following year, she was a pariah for her progressive views and love of black music.

At 18, Janis took a cross-country bus to Los Angeles and moved from one aunt's home to another's before striking out on her own in a Venice crash pad, beatnik-style. Here she poses with her California cousins, Jean Pitney (*left*) and Donna MacBride (*right*), c. 1961.

Janis first found fans while playing with Austin folkies known as the Waller Creek Boys, featuring fellow University of Texas students Powell St. John (*left*) on harmonica and Lanny Wiggins (*center*) on guitar and banjo, 1962.

Desperate to make it as a blues singer in San Francisco coffeehouses, Janis posed for publicity photos soon after she hitchhiked from Austin in 1963.

Janis asked guitarist Jorma (then Jerry) Kaukonen to accompany her at the Folk Theatre in San Jose, California, the first day they met there backstage. Here, joined by an unidentified harmonica player, Janis wore her street clothes, a man's chambray shirt and dungarees.

Janis stopped in Port Arthur with her newly purchased twelve-string guitar after spending the summer shooting pool and taking speed in New York City, 1964.

Janis in the living room of the Joplin home with her parents and sister, Laura, before driving back to San Francisco, September 1964. When she returned nine months later, she was an 88-pound speed freak.

Janis posed for this 1965 engagement photo in Port Arthur during her recovery from drugs, a period of abstinence and a return to college; marriage to Peter de Blanc, a con man and hustler, was not to be; his betrayal scarred her for life.

Janis and Chet Helms on Pine Street, soon after she returned to San Francisco to join the band he managed, Big Brother and the Holding Company, 1966. Fame was around the corner.

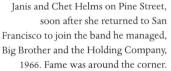

Janis found her tribe in the Family Dog, whose Pine Street members and friends are seen here in 1966; Janis is sixth from right (wearing shades), standing near James Gurley and Peter Albin and surrounded by various members of the Charlatans; on top of the truck are Chet Helms and Sancho (the canine depicted in the Family Dog logo). Sam Andrew stands in front of the truck, and Nancy Gurley (in black) is in the front row at right, holding baby Hongo. Janis sent her family the photo with the note: "These people are all friends of mine! Aren't they amazing?!"

Janis's new family: Sam Andrew, David Getz, a smitten Janis, James Gurley, and Peter Albin in San Francisco, 1966.

After this bucolic photo session at the Dixon Ranch in Woodacre, Marin County, Janis wrote home about the pictures, "They're going to use one on a poster for the Family Dog! Gawd, I'm so excited!"

Janis about to take the stage with Big Brother for one of many free concerts at Golden Gate Park's Panhandle, in Haight-Ashbury, 1966. At her left is guitarist Sam Andrew; at her right is the band's friend Ariel Wilcox, and at the mike is "The Buddha from Muir Beach," who often emceed shows.

Big Brother posed outside their communal home, "Argentina," in rural Lagunitas, in Marin County. The portrait was art-directed by psychedelic graphic artist Victor Moscoco with the image appearing in his poster for the band's gigs at the Matrix. Janis is wearing a favorite blouse made from a recycled tablecloth, 1966.

Janis and her beloved dog, George, a mutt she rescued as a puppy soon after moving from Lagunitas to the Haight. She once called the shepherd mix her "salvation."

Janis loved meeting fans and signing autographs, here after an outdoor concert at McNears Beach, California. "I dig it. FAME, FAME, heh, heh," she wrote her mother.

Big Brother playing around during a photo session at the Palace of Fine Arts, San Francisco. The band members could squabble like siblings but loved one another deeply.

At the Fairmont Hotel, Janis and British director Richard Lester (*A Hard Day's Night, Help!*), who cast Big Brother in his film *Petulia*, starring George C. Scott, Julie Christie, and Richard Chamberlain. In an attempt to capture the San Francisco hippie vibe, the movie also featured the Grateful Dead playing at the Fillmore.

Janis and then-beau Country Joe McDonald; their relationship quickly devolved from giddy love affair to what McDonald described as a pair of "control freaks" with battling egos.

Janis plastered a wall of her new apartment on Lyon Street with the iconic poster shot by Bob Seidemann: "Very dramatic photograph & I look really beautiful!" is how she described it to her parents.

Onstage at the June 1967 Monterey International Pop Festival, Janis broke through with her spectacular performances. Her version of Big Mama Thornton's "Ball and Chain" is a highlight of the documentary on Monterey made by D. A. Pennebaker, who demanded she be in his film.

In her Lyon Street bedroom with George (who accompanied her to Monterey) and her unnamed cat. She referred to her animals as her "family"; they helped stave off a gnawing loneliness.

After Monterey, Janis palled around with Jimi Hendrix, an amateur photographer who filmed her, Sam Andrew (*left*), and the Fugs' Ken Weaver in the Fillmore dressing room. During one Big Brother gig, Hendrix babysat Hongo Gurley.

Big Brother live at the Carousel Ballroom, in San Francisco. Janis had become the focus of the band's performances.

Janis in the living room of her Lyon Street apartment, decorated with posters and photos of Bob Dylan, the Grateful Dead, and herself. Her friend, designer, and confidante, Linda Gravenites, crashed on the daybed.

America's most powerful
rock manager, Albert
Grossman, became like a
second father to Janis. She
hung on his every word, and
he thought her talent was
too great to be in a band like
Big Brother.

"Janis would cackle, she'd
laugh so hard, and was fun
to be with—very vocal, very
outspoken, very funny," Jefferson Airplane vocalist Grace Slick
said of her friend. "There was
none of this pretend demure
shit going on." When the two
women posed for Jim Marshall,
"Janis and I said, 'No matter
how hard he says "smile," we
don't smile.'" The tenacious
Marshall eventually got his way.

Big Brother celebrating
"the big time" at their
massive rehearsal space
they called the Warehouse.
Now managed by Albert
Grossman and signed to
Columbia Records, they
were meeting big success,
and this led to the band
busting up.

Newly minted major-label artists Big Brother pose with Albert Grossman (*far left*) and Columbia Records President Clive Davis at Manhattan restaurant Piraeus, My Love on February 19, 1968. "Signed the contract on the 26th floor of the CBS building, met the president, had a press party, & got drunk," Janis reported to the Joplins. "From all indications, I'm going to become rich & famous. Incredible!"

Big Brother played to rapturous audiences in New York City at the Fillmore East, backed by the Joshua Light Show, 1968.

*I've been fairly adamant about my determination not to get fucked
up again. Well it seems now to have developed into a rather neurotic
tenor. I never relax anymore. . . . I seem to be really mortally afraid
that things won't go right somehow and I'll end up back in that hellish
jungle that I'm obsessed with. . . . The reason I went to that counselor
is because I had suddenly realized that I was building my stability and
progress on sheer terror and that won't work! It's too precarious. I sit
in classes and never do anything wrong, but it's just because I'm so
horribly afraid. I keep talking about "one step back" being the end of
me and everything. . . . From my new slightly objective vantage point,
induced by Librium and a few days easy breathing, I think I was maybe
a little disproportionately afraid of you too. You see, I was really sure
that you were finding yourself unable to cope w/ things and that I
couldn't trust you, that is, put my trust in you. . . . So anyway, this is
it—I'm much calmer now. No longer terrified when I talk to people,
and I'm going to try and get this irrational fear under control.*

It is unclear if de Blanc ever confessed his infidelity or if Janis confronted
him about his double life. But their "engagement" was over. Undoubtedly, Librium kept her emotions in check while her marital fantasy
crumbled around her. Yet de Blanc's betrayal and deceit would have
lasting effects, making it nearly impossible for Janis to trust those who
claimed to love her.

As she grieved, she sharpened her focus on music. She booked another Halfway House gig and visited the Jester, a folk club in Houston
where singer-songwriter Townes Van Zandt played blues and country-
and-western covers as well as dark originals such as "Waiting 'Round
to Die." Janis auditioned there to mixed reviews, according to her old
fling and Jester regular Frank Davis: "She was too damn strong for everybody."

Janis had more success at Houston's Sand Mountain coffeehouse,
opened by middle-aged Corinne Carrick and her son, John, to present
"girls with pretty voices and guys with deep voices," said performer
Don Sanders. Janis auditioned with "Winin' Boy Blues," recalled Sand-

ers, who "didn't know what the hell to make of it. Her face turned red, and she kinda swung back and forth and whacked on her guitar and sang with all her body . . . powerfully crossing the gender line. I didn't think she had a chance in hell of communicating with the audience. . . . She was really wild, although John Carrick liked her a whole lot." Janis passed the audition and got a December booking.

Janis's Thanksgiving weekend show at Beaumont's Halfway House yielded her first rave review: her old friend Jim Langdon, by then a writer for the *Austin Statesman*, caught the performance. In his Night Beat column, he described her California odyssey and called her "the best blues singer in the country." After such humiliation from Peter de Blanc, the accolades meant much to her, rekindling her self-esteem, and were a reminder of how singing could bring a quick, dependable high.

Terrified that Janis would backslide, Dorothy Joplin did not want her to perform. But her daughter could not be stopped, though "she was very anxious about it," Frances Vincent recalled. Driving to Houston in December, Janis left her mother a note with details about the coffeehouse, her traveling companion Frances Vincent, and Corinne Carrick, who was putting her up for the night.

Onstage, Janis wore a black sheath dress and pumps, her hair pulled back conservatively. The coffeehouse was packed, and she "blew them away," according to Vincent. "It was just incredible to see all these people there who were well thought of as folksingers. . . . They were astounded." Among them was singer-songwriter-guitarist Guy Clark, who'd seen her at the Jester and thought she "wasn't making any compromises. . . . [I]t was far out."

Janis visited the Langdons in Austin during the holidays, playing guitar and singing to their two young children next to the Christmas tree. It must have been painful experiencing the life she'd wanted with de Blanc. When she stopped by Threadgill's and other Austin clubs, she discovered that rock & roll now ruled the scene. Even Kenneth Threadgill had formed a band, the Hootenanny Hoots, with Julie Paul on drums. Former Waller Creeker Powell St. John played in the rock group Conqueroo, and Beaumont's Johnny Winter, who'd formed a blues rock trio with a Port Arthur drummer, played the clubs. But Janis continued to focus on the blues and folk songs she'd learned on guitar, including Ida Cox's "Wild Women Don't Have the Blues," which she'd picked up at the Coffee Gallery from George Hunter's bandmate Dan Hicks.

A highlight of Janis's new set was her chilling take on Buffy Sainte-Marie's "Cod'ine." Janis had written her own lyrics to the Native American folksinger's song about codeine addiction, from Sainte-Marie's 1964 debut album. When Janis performed it, she credited Sainte-Marie, but mentioned that she'd changed the words to include these harrowing lines: "On the day I was born, the grim reaper smiled. . . . Cod'ine became the object of my dreams. . . . It's the reason I breathe, it's the reason I walk, the reason I sleep, the reason I talk / Soon my devotion will all be paid / Cod'ine will kill me, that's the bargain that we made." Her gripping delivery assured her audience that she had lived a version of those awful words.

><+>-0-<+>-<

Janis was back at Lamar Tech in January 1966, but once again music had captured her heart. During a weekend visit to Austin, she sang Powell St. John her new song, "Women Is Losers," which "encapsulates Janis's feminist side," said St. John, "connecting to that strong female in her. Janis was smart. It was a gripe about what a bitch it was to be a woman." Janis, he added, "struggled with that a lot." Janis asked St. John to teach her one of his, and he gave her "Bye, Bye Baby." She learned it in time for her debut at Austin's new club on Red River Street, the 11th Door, the first weekend in March. St. John, Tary Owens, and other friends were surprised by Janis's new onstage persona.

"She appeared in a very adult and somber black dress," said St. John's bandmate Bob Brown. "Everything was quite formal, the kind of performance you'd expect for an assembly of college professors. . . . We were proud of her and respectful but incredulous. It was an amazing transformation from the jeans-sweatshirt-brawling-cursing Janis we knew."

Jim Langdon had arranged the gig and booked a photographer

and a local radio station to document the set. The bootlegged recording demonstrates Janis's confidence handling a mixture of blues and
folk covers and originals. Her own "Apple of My Eye," an up-tempo,
modern-sounding blues, was possibly inspired by the Animals' 1964 hit
version of "House of the Rising Sun" or the Stones' cover of Bobby
Womack's "It's All Over Now." Jelly Roll Morton's "2:19" (written by
Mamie Desdunes) was a jazzy blues sung in a sultry alto, while "I Ain't
Got a Worry," which she credited to singer-songwriter Hoyt Axton,
documented, in a yearning soprano, her wistfulness about the Bay Area:
"I'm going back to Frisco / All my friends are there. . . . It's heaven by
the Bay." And the self-penned "Turtle Blues" mimicked the Bessie Smith
songs she loved, with lines such as "I ain't the kind of woman / Who'd
make your life a bed of ease. . . . But if you want to go on drinkin',
honey / Won't you invite me please." During her song introductions,
Janis sounded formal, even scholarly.

Though the show went fairly well, Langdon recalled it was "a mixed
crowd. A lot came expecting to hear something like Joan Baez or [Texas
folk singer] Carolyn Hester. Instead they hear Janis with a couple of
balls the size of cantaloupes. Half the crowd was crazy about her, and
the other half had no idea what to think—like they were hit by a neu-
tron bomb."

The following Sunday, Janis returned to Austin for a high-profile
event Langdon organized at the Methodist Student Center Auditorium
to benefit blind fiddler Teodar Jackson. Janis was the only woman in
the afternoon show, among a half dozen blues and rock acts, including,
notably, a new group, the 13th Floor Elevators, featuring a raggedly
charismatic young singer, Roky Erickson. Janis's set was well received
by the sold-out crowd of four hundred, particularly her encore, "Turtle
Blues," which she introduced as "semiautobiographical."

While she "stole the show," according to Langdon, Roky Erickson's shrieking vocals were an eye-opener for Janis. The teenage singer
showed no restraint when he sang, his raspy howls and yelps delivering surreal lyrics. "That was the electrifying thing about Roky," said
St. John, "that he could hit those notes—the scream of the banshee."

Erickson's emotional, unrestrained sound would inspire Janis's first attempts to be a rock singer.

Her ambition growing and her confidence building, Janis wrote Langdon from Port Arthur, thanking him for his help and asking for more bookings, as well as copies of press clippings and photos from the concert. In just five months since her nervous sets at the Halfway House, she was ready to plunge back into "show bizness." She started a new scrapbook, her first since 1959, and artfully placed on its pages an 11th Door matchbook, a concert handbill, onstage photography, and clippings of her reviews.

During her therapy sessions with Bernard Giarratano, however, she echoed her mother's fears that performing could destroy her. Dorothy wouldn't allow Laura to attend Janis's concerts, even those at alcohol-free coffeehouses. Seeing Janis's joyfulness return, Giarratano encouraged her to play music, and she occasionally took her guitar to sessions. Janis engaged in occasional flings with women and men, which she discussed candidly with the therapist: "She said she enjoyed it," he recalled, "but she would come in terribly disappointed [if] her night's liaison didn't work out so well . . . [saying that] a fifteen-minute lay wasn't worth a damn."

Just after her college semester ended, Janis returned to Austin for a week with Jim Langdon's family. She had earlier written him that she was "seriously contemplating" spending the summer there, though she worried it "would probably be a disaster." She wondered if he could "get me enough work to keep me from starving."

Then, without warning, she learned from a friend that her old beau Travis Rivers, now living in San Francisco, had driven to Austin to find her. As Janis explained in a letter to her friend Linda Gottfried Waldron: "He was bearing word from Chet Helms, who is now a big man in S.F. who throws big dances with great rock & roll bands and Bill Ham does his light shows. Wanted me to come out there and sing with this blues band he has. So I called . . . and he verified it very enthusiastically and also told me if I got freaked out, he'd at least give me a ticket to go home. So I thought I'd just go. . . . Talked to all kinds of people and no one discouraged me!" As excited as she was, however, Janis, chillingly, sensed the danger ahead: "Everyone thought it was a good idea! MOAN. I so wanted to be discouraged!"

But she lied to Waldron about not wanting to leave and being encouraged by her friends to go. Langdon, for one, thought her leaving was a bad idea. "I didn't trust Travis," recalled Jim, who had already booked several upcoming Austin gigs for her. Worrying that Janis could be hurt again, he recommended she hone her craft and rebuild her confidence in Austin before jumping back into the fray in San Francisco. But after Janis and Travis Rivers reunited at a friend's house, they fell into a passionate night of lovemaking. "Travis . . . is kind of a madman but a groove! (Like a less refined Pat Cassidy . . .)," Janis wrote of her longtime crush. "And he's huge and hairy." Langdon recalled her explaining that "she hadn't had a good ball in an awfully long time, and Travis was a good ball!" That was reason enough, she said, to go with him to San Francisco. When she called Helms—"Do you really think I'll make it this time?"—he assured her she would and that speed had vanished from the scene. He neglected to mention his role in the city's LSD-fueled dances.

Rivers, who'd previously met Seth and Dorothy, urged Janis to tell them about her plans, so they drove from Austin to the Golden Triangle. On May 27 she saw her therapist, saying she wanted "to go be what I am," Giarratano recalled. "She was miserable in Port Arthur and had to get out."

While Rivers waited in the car parked on Lombardy Drive, Janis went inside and couldn't bring herself to tell Seth and Dorothy the truth about her plans; instead, she claimed she was returning to the Langdons'. On May 30, nervous and excited, she climbed into a '53 Chevy, toting a duffel bag of clothing, books, and some weed. With Rivers behind the wheel, Janis sat next to another passenger: "a really freaky methadrine [sic] person (terrible and nervous and ugly and omnipresent with lots of dope and points [syringes]," as she described in an unsent letter to Linda Waldron. "I'm really freaked out! Very humorous actually—it's the one thing I wanted to avoid—very uptight about it—finally assured myself

I wouldn't have to be around them, and here he is! God, he's another George the Beast, only not likable!"

As in her letters to Peter de Blanc, Janis now began to mull over her conflicted feelings about relaunching her music career, with a former partner in crime, but one who—like Janis—had gone straight. "I really want to try to do a new rock and roll thing," she wrote Waldron, "and Chet says he already has the set up and really wanted me to sing, says the guys who make up the band have all heard me and think it would be a gas. . . . After all, I say to myself—it's summer—I could call it a summer vacation and go back to school. . . . [I] dig traveling again and have lots of grass and it's really kind of nice. . . . Sure do wish you were around though. Little afraid of the city, wish I had a friend there. . . . Linda, can you imagine the knot this all brings to my stomach! Whew, I am scared to death! *More later.*"

CHAPTER 11

BIG BROTHER'S CHICK SINGER

*Playing is the "mostest" fun there is—feeling things
and really getting into it. That's what it's all about.*

—JANIS JOPLIN

"The San Francisco music scene . . . is first of all the freedom to create here," Janis said, nine months after her arrival. "Musicians ended up here together [with] the complete freedom to do whatever they wanted to [and] came up with their own kind of music." In San Francisco, Janis would expand her vocal style and find validation among a new gang: a close-knit group of iconoclasts who'd been on the forefront of an emerging counterculture. Her adopted musical family, Big Brother and the Holding Company, served to provide Janis stability and opportunity, allowing her to forge a unique artistic identity. While simultaneously propelling them to fame, Janis's voice would become both the key to the struggling band's success and the reason for its eventual demise. Big Brother was doomed to be left behind. But Janis's immersion into the Haight-Ashbury scene would culminate in her finding her voice as a new kind of female singer.

On this, her third journey to San Francisco, Janis's traveling companion did not rush to reach their Emerald City. Much to her delight, Travis Rivers took time to romance Janis along the way. Amorous stops in El Paso, Texas; Juarez, Mexico; and Golden, New Mexico cemented their bond.

"Halfway through New Mexico," Janis claimed the following year, "I [was] conned into being in the rock business by this guy that was such a good ball. I was fucked into being in Big Brother." In her origin myth, she downplays her burning ambition to become a successful singer. But in reality, of course, the con artist in her life had been Peter de Blanc, a harrowing tale of which she rarely spoke. Rivers, on the other hand, drove Janis to her destiny and one of her own making.

On Friday, June 3, 1966, they reached San Francisco, where they connected with Helms, recently married to an aspiring actress. He now wore his hair below his shoulders and had cultivated a full beard. With his wire-rimmed glasses and vintage morning coat, he looked like a character from the Old West. He paid $35 a month for Janis's new home: a room in the run-down Haight-Ashbury district at 1947 Pine Street. When Janis had left in '65, Pine Street was becoming ground zero of the developing counterculture. Helms fell in with the Family Dog House: communal residents of Pine Street named for their love of canines or possibly their scheme to launder drug-dealing profits into Family Dog, a pet cemetery start-up in a vacant lot that never materialized. The Family Dog began hosting themed rock & roll dances, beginning with "A Tribute to Dr. Strange," held at the Longshoreman's Hall on Fisherman's Wharf, where fun-loving seekers took LSD while partying to bands such as Jefferson Airplane and the Charlatans, founded by Janis's friends George Hunter and Dan Hicks. By the summer of '66, the scene had expanded to weekly psychedelic dances at the Fillmore Auditorium and most recently the Avalon Ballroom.

On their second night in San Francisco, Janis and Rivers went to see the Grateful Dead at the Fillmore, an old ballroom located up a rickety staircase in a predominantly black neighborhood. Inside, she joined the swirling bodies, long-haired men and women, dressed in an eclectic mélange of vintage clothing, exotic fabrics, and ethnic garb—"seven different centuries thrown together in one room," according to one initiate.

"The big dances . . . blow your mind!" is how Janis later described them in a letter home. "Fantastic—the clothes and people! Pure sensuousness . . . bombarding the senses . . . astound[ing] you." From the Palo Alto folk scene, Janis knew the Dead's leaders and main vocalists: guitarist Jerry Garcia and Ron "Pigpen" McKernan, who played the organ and blues harp. She instantly tuned into the band's extended blues jams, recognizing "Stealin', Stealin'" and a few other songs. Their loud sonics and the psychedelic light show, projected by Pine Streeter Bill Ham, melding blobs of color onto the band transformed the music into something she'd never experienced. "[It] completely stoned me!" Janis remembered. "*Whew!*" She hadn't been so energized since doing the dirty bop in Louisiana roadhouses or so thrilled by a scene since first encountering Austin's Ghetto.

On Monday morning, June 6, Janis wrote her parents "with a great deal of trepidation" after Jim Langdon informed her that Dorothy had become hysterical when he told her where Janis was. Apologizing for sneaking off to San Francisco, she explained that "Chet Helms, old friend, now is Mr. Big in S.F. Owns 3 big working rock & roll bands with bizarre names like Captain Beefheart & His Magic Band, Big Brother & the Holding Co., etc. . . . seems the whole city [has] gone rock & roll and [he] assured me fame & fortune."

Janis painted a wholesome picture of her road trip west: "camped out at night along the Rio Grande, collected rocks, etc." She tried to downplay her excitement and persuade her parents—and perhaps herself—that she wasn't diving back into a life that had almost killed her. She sounded nonchalant about that afternoon's scheduled first meeting with Big Brother and the Holding Company and joked about the outcome, comparing herself to one of the few female pop stars of the day. "Supposed to rehearse w/ the band this afternoon, after that I guess I'll know whether I want to stay & do that for awhile. Right now my position is ambivalent—I'm glad I came, nice to see the city, a few friends, but I'm not at all sold on the idea of becoming the poor man's Cher."

Evident from the letter is Janis's concern for her parents' feelings—and her worries for herself:

*I just want to tell you that I am trying to keep a level head about everything
& not go overboard w/ enthusiasm. I'm sure you're both convinced my
self-destructive streak has won out again but I'm really trying. I do plan on
coming back to school—unless, I must admit, this turns into a good thing.*

    *Chet is a very important man out here now & he wanted me specifi-
cally, to sing w/ this band. I haven't tried yet, so I can't say what I'm
going to do—so far, I'm safe, well fed, and nothing has been stolen. . . .
I'm awfully sorry to be such a disappointment to you. I understand
your fears at my coming here & must admit I share them, but I really
do think there's an awfully good chance I won't blow it this time.
There's really nothing more I can say now. . . . You can't possibly want
for me to be a winner more than I do.*

That afternoon, only her third full day in the city, Janis met Big Brother
and the Holding Company for the first time at their Henry Street rehearsal space in an old carriage house built for horse-drawn fire trucks.
"It was an organic place," recalled guitarist Sam Houston Andrew
III, who was twenty-four. "People were nursing babies in one corner
and making silk screen prints in another." One of the building's ten-
ants, artist Stanley "Mouse" Miller—who designed psychedelic posters
advertising Family Dog dances and other events with partner Alton
Kelley—hailed from Detroit, as did Big Brother's twenty-six-year-old
guitarist James Gurley. From her folkie days, Janis remembered bassist Peter Albin, twenty-two, who had formed the band in spring 1965
with Andrew, then a grad student at the University of California at
Berkeley. Originally playing together in a massive Victorian boarding
house at 1090 Page Street owned by Albin's uncle Henry, Big Brother
was discovered early on and named by Helms, who charged fifty cents
admission to their Wednesday-night jam sessions. He then introduced
them to Gurley, who'd been working out his odd tunings alone in a
closet. Helms booked the group at clubs and happenings—including
San Francisco's first Trips Festival—and at the Family Dog's Avalon
Ballroom, which he'd opened two months earlier in April. After several
personnel changes, Big Brother completed its lineup in March, settling

on twenty-six-year-old drummer David Getz, a New York–born artist and Fulbright scholar.

As far back as 1963, James Gurley had heard Janis sing at the Coffee Gallery, where "the strength and power of her voice blew my mind"— around the time that Peter Albin first saw her in Berkeley and Palo Alto. Sam Andrew had never experienced Janis firsthand but had heard of her through friends. Only Getz had no prior knowledge of Janis, and the night before her arrival, he dreamed of a gorgeous woman as their new vocalist.

Janis looked more Texas tomboy than glamorous "girl singer." Her hair pulled back, she wore denim cutoffs and a baggy shirt, along with a healthy glow. The guys, on the other hand, looked hip, with longish hair and cool clothes: Gurley, in particular, had the air of a shaman, his light brown locks hanging straight down, and his gaunt face and blue eyes projecting quiet intensity; Peter Albin, with a grown-out pageboy and colorful shirt; and Dave Getz, with an unruly dark mop, traded humorous banter. Tall, lanky Sam Andrew, with his chiseled, handsome face and shaggy hair, exuded a friendly warmth. "When I first met Janis, she was not a stranger to me," he said. "Her accent, her attitudes, even her clothes made her seem like a sister or cousin from my mother's side of the family, who were all from the same part of Texas as Janis."

"I met them all, and you know how it is when you meet someone: you don't even remember what they look like, you're so spaced by what's happening," Janis recounted. "I was in space city, man. I was scared to death. I didn't know how to sing the stuff. I'd never sung with electric music, I'd never sung with drums."

The volume of sound, with the amps cranked up, overwhelmed her at first. "It was as if she had caught hold of a passing freight train barreling through the night and was not sure if she could hold on," according to Sam Andrew. "She always had a firm grip on the pitch, though— never a sharp or flat moment. She sang really fast, and she talked really fast. Janis always had this thing of total insecurity and total power at the same time, and it was really something to be confronted with both of them. You never knew which one to relate to."

As they started playing, she realized the guys were treating her like a bandmate rather than an auditioning hopeful. Big Brother had played dozens of shows over the past six months and built an enthusiastic following. But the musicians aspired to the kind of success the six-piece Jefferson Airplane enjoyed. The first of the new bands to score a major record deal, the Airplane had two lead singers, former folkies Marty Balin and Signe Anderson, and the male-female dynamic worked well. An up-and-coming group, the Great Society, also featured a charismatic female singer, Grace Slick. Big Brother wanted a woman's voice to complement Peter Albin's baritone. They'd auditioned several, but no one clicked—until Janis. She "knocked us out, *instantaneously*," Dave Getz said, and Big Brother welcomed her into the band.

Big Brother's next show was less than a week away: a double bill with the Grateful Dead at the Avalon. They all knew the 1920s blues "Trouble in Mind" and "C.C. Rider," and Janis jumped in on vocals. "At first, she sounded like Bessie Smith on a sped-up seventy-eight," Sam Andrew recalled. "It was very treble . . . very thin, in the upper register, like a tape on fast-forward." With no experience singing over electric guitars and drums, she quickly altered her style and pitched her vocals to soar over the roaring wall of sound, sometimes shrieking like Roky Erickson of Austin's 13th Floor Elevators.

"She seemed so scared," Henry Street resident and scenester Suzy Perry said, "trying to please, wanting so much to belong. I felt so sorry for her." Janis finally loosened up on the gospel song "Down on Me." "I'd heard it before and thought I could sing it, and they did all the chords," she recalled. She secularized "Down on Me," turning it into a sensual, sultry blues. "Janis changed the lyrics, as well as the way she sang it," cutting the religious references, said Sam Andrew. "Janis's voice was right on the money from the first minute she sang with us."

"Still working w/ Big Brother & the Holding Co. & it's really fun!" she wrote the Joplins later that week, on the eve of her Avalon debut. "Four guys in the group—Sam, Peter, Dave, & James. We rehearse every afternoon in a garage that's part of a loft an artist friend of theirs owns & people constantly drop in and listen—everyone seems very taken w/

my singing although I am a little dated. This kind of music is different than I'm used to."

She enclosed an ad for the Avalon gig, clipped from the *San Francisco Chronicle*, and commented on the scene, intending to humor her family: "Oh, I've collected more bizarre names of groups to send—(can you believe these?!) The Grateful Dead, The Love, Jefferson Airplane, Quicksilver Messenger Service, The Leaves, The Grass Roots. . . . Tomorrow night at the [Avalon] dance, some people from Mercury [Records] will be there to hear the Grateful Dead (with a name like that, they have to be good . . .) and Big Brother et al. And I'm going to get to sing! Gosh I'm so excited! We've worked out about 5 or 6 numbers this week—one I really like called 'Down on Me'—an old spiritual—revitalized and slightly bastardized w/ new treatment."

Janis reassured her parents she was safe and living in a respectable place: "a room in a rooming house. Very nice place w/ a kitchen & a living room & even an iron & ironing board. Four other people living here—one schoolteacher, one artist, don't know the rest." She also put a positive spin on her chances of success and on the professionalism of Helms's "corporation," the Family Dog, even though in reality it personified laid-back hippie disorganization. "Chet Helms heads a rock & roll corporation called the Family Dog—replete w/ emblem & answering service. Very fancy. Being my entrepreneur (and mostly having gotten me out here without money—I still have $30 in the bank I'm hoarding), Chet rented me this place for a month. He says if the band & I don't make it, to forget it, & if we do, we'll have plenty of money."

And she told them what they wanted to hear about herself, lying that she was "something of a recluse." She also dangled the hope that she might return to college and assured them she was not taking speed: "I'm still okay—don't worry. Haven't lost or gained any weight & my head's still fine. And am still really thinking of coming back to school, so don't give up on me yet." What Janis didn't write was that college would be a backup plan if she wasn't accepted by the band's hip audience. Dave Getz, who drove her to rehearsals, recalled that she constantly wondered if she was following the right path. "She had a lot of misgivings," he reflected.

But during rehearsals, Janis learned quickly, experimenting with new vocal techniques. Taking another cue from Roky Erickson, she began to let loose banshee wails when Gurley's and Andrew's guitars crescendoed in their improvisational jams. With Peter Albin's baritone taking the lead in most songs, Janis unleashed high-pitched shrieks as accents. On Big Brother's sped-up version of "Land of 1000 Dances," her raspy sound hinted at Wilson Pickett's soulful version, then on its way into the Top 10. From her teenage days cruising Port Arthur with the radio blasting, Janis already knew some of Big Brother's rock & roll repertoire: Little Richard's "Ooh! My Soul" and Shirley and Lee's "Let the Good Times Roll." On a twelve-bar blues, such as Tommy Tucker's "Hi-Heel Sneakers," Janis pushed her voice as far as she could, trying to avoid sounding "dated" like a coffeehouse folkie. Big Brother twisted blues tunes into another sonic realm so that she barely recognized them: on "I Know You Rider," originally a 1927 Blind Lemon Jefferson recording, Janis added call-and-response vocals, while James Gurley—nicknamed "Archfiend of the Universe" for his dark, cacophonous guitar style—played atonal, angular leads. Albin kicked off Howlin' Wolf's "Moanin' at Midnight"; joining in on vocals, Janis added startling yelps. Five days after their first meeting, she was ready for her debut.

The Avalon Ballroom took up the top two floors of a former dance academy on Sutter Street, not far from Janis's former home at the Goodman Building. Before the venue's April '66 opening, Helms had installed fluorescent and strobe lights to accentuate the audience's Day-Glo-painted skin while partiers glided across burnished wooden floors. From the balcony, Bill Ham's amoeba-shaped projections provided the only stage lighting.

On Friday, June 10, "We boys came out and did our insane, free-jazz, speedy clash jam," Sam Andrew recalled of Janis's opening night. Then, after their first few numbers of "freak rock," Janis strolled onstage, taking her place next to Peter Albin, who nonchalantly told the crowd,

"Now we'd like to introduce Janis Joplin." "Nobody had ever heard of fuckin' me," Janis recounted later. "I was just some chick, didn't have any hip clothes or nothing like that. I had on what I was wearing to college. I got onstage and I started singing—*whew!*"

The crowd, already under the influence of the sonic barrage, focused mostly on Gurley's Les Paul guitar. "He played out there," said Bill Ham. With Ham's light show projecting color onto Gurley's skinny physique, his abstract noodlings riveted the stoned audience. But when Janis began to move rhythmically, shaking her tambourine, and belted "Down on Me," the audience was instantly transfixed.

"*What a rush, man! A real, live drug rush!*" Janis recalled vividly of the moment. "All I remember is the sensation—*what a fuckin' gas, man!* The music was *boom, boom, boom,* and the people were all dancing, and the lights, and I was standing up there singing into the microphone and getting it on, and *whew!* I dug it! I said, '*I think I'll stay, boys. . . .*'"

From that night on, Janis's world revolved around Big Brother. She "was fabulous," Helms said of her debut. "The audience concurred; they'd never heard anything like it." Near-daily rehearsals followed, with Janis, having passed "the test," being further integrated into the group. A quick study, she diligently jotted down lyrics, and the band adjusted its approach to make room for the dynamic new vocalist. "We started trying to sing harmonies with Janis, and we added very defined beginnings and endings to our songs," according to Dave Getz. The musicians shortened some of their lengthy improvisations to accommodate her singing, while Janis expanded her vocal palette, veering from high-pitched shrieks, to gospel-inspired testifying, to Bessie Smith blues. Big Brother valued democracy, with each member except Getz taking vocal turns, so that Janis sang lead only on four or five numbers, while adding harmonies to the guys' songs.

Two weeks after her June debut, Big Brother returned to the Avalon for a weekend of gigs—two shows each night. The first of several bookings over the next few months, the evening set the pattern for Janis's new life. Onstage, she grew less inhibited with each appearance. Chet Helms compared her with the performer he'd seen only a short time before in coffeehouses: "Suddenly this person who would stand upright with her fists clenched was all over the stage. Roky Erickson had modeled himself after the screaming style of Little Richard, and Janis's initial stage presence came from Roky, and ultimately Little Richard. It was a very different Janis."

She had transformed herself from self-conscious folk-blues singer to emotive, sensual performer. Soon her impassioned vocals drew audiences to the lip of the stage. "I couldn't stay still," Janis explained later. "I had never danced when I sang; just the old sit-and-pluck blues thing. But there I was moving and jumping. I couldn't hear, so I sang louder and louder. You have to sing loud and move loud with all that in back of you." Peter Albin continued as front man, making arch or absurd comments. Janis would lean over and banter, *"What are you talking about?"* as she played tambourine.

The eight-hundred-capacity Avalon filled with Big Brother fans and the curious at $2 each. "The whole environment was the show," said Helms. The crowd was "as key an element of the performance as the musicians themselves." On the low, unlit stage, the band blended with listeners, which leant a casual intimacy that helped Janis feel comfortable. "There was this sense you were part of the audience," Getz said, "and the vibe of the audience and the energy they gave you and that you gave the audience was an interactive thing. Everybody got a high." Janis had found her tribe—and herself. "When I sing, I feel, oh, like when you're first in love," she'd tell a journalist the following year. "Like when you're first touching somebody. Chills, things slipping all over me. It was so sensual, so vibrant, loud, crazy!"

Fellow musicians were duly impressed by Janis's talent. Though the stage had no monitor speakers to aim the sound back at the performers, she managed usually to stay on key—a rarity for most local singers—and yet be heard over the band's roaring guitars. Her old friend Jorma Kaukonen, now the lead guitarist of Jefferson Airplane, brought bandmate Jack Casady to check out Janis.

"The first time I heard her sing," recalled the bassist, "she was just fantastic—one of the few white singers who could sing the blues well.

She hit that Bessie Smith genre right on the money, hit it solid." Casady, a rabid record collector, would eventually give Janis the R&B song that would take her to the Top Ten.

>–+◆–०–◆+◄

Janis soon began forming a personal bond with her bandmates. Albin, married with a young daughter, was a bit standoffish, but she became close to Dave Getz and the others. "We made out in the back seat of my car, three or four times," Getz recounted. "I thought maybe we'd have something, but she didn't want to get involved with me sexually. At one point, she said, 'No, I can't do this. I've gotta go.'"

She and Travis Rivers were still "sweethearts," according to Rivers, but they were drifting apart. Living on Pine Street, where she used to buy drugs, Janis worried about crossing paths with speed freaks and dealers. "She was very afraid of drugs," Getz recalled. "She said, 'I don't ever want to see anybody shooting drugs.'" Then one night, when she discovered Rivers and a friend hitting up in their room, she freaked out. Apologizing, Travis claimed they were injecting mescaline, not speed, but Janis was furious. "She was easily bruised," Rivers said. "I had hurt her feelings once before, and I had to hold her in the air over my head with her arms facing away from me so she wouldn't hurt me. She was screaming. I never forgave myself for it."

Trying to win her back, he proposed marriage the next day, but she turned him down. Certainly thoughts of Peter de Blanc's betrayal and false promises were still fresh. "She said, 'I'm about to become incredibly famous and will have access to any boy I want,'" Rivers recalled, "'and I want to take advantage of it.'" In the four years he'd known Janis, he had experienced her "two sides," he explained. "A perfectly sweet, wonderful, well-bred, lace-curtain girl"—the Janis that craved the white picket fence. Her other side, the rowdy, cackling "West Texas cowgirl/sailor persona—which she presented when she was unsure of how she was going to be accepted. That was the side she used onstage."

Rivers moved out of their tiny room—with a bed, sink, and not much else—and slept in a closet down the hall near the communal bathroom. Janis began to socialize with the band, and at one point, when she and Getz stopped by the Anxious Asp, she ran into her former lover, Jae Whitaker.

"She was a very cute, foxy, little black chick," Getz recalled. "We were playing pool with her, and when we left, Janis told me, '*That chick*, she does something to me. We had a thing together way back, and she really turns me on.' Janis wasn't doing it to shock me; she was just out there with it." Though a worldly artist from New York, who'd studied at the San Francisco Art Institute, Getz admitted to being "really unfamiliar with that whole possibility. I didn't know what to make of it."

Janis soon made peace with her old flame, and Jae would bring her new girlfriend to Big Brother shows. However, Janis was again abruptly confronted with her past when a letter arrived from de Blanc, who'd somehow gotten her address. Writing from Rochester, New York, he chastised her for quitting school and returning to San Francisco: "Are you really a go-go girl now, have you converted to a role of diddley bop?" Feigning concern about "the real Janis," he questioned her "preservation instincts, self-control." She saved that and other de Blanc letters, though it's unclear if she wrote back or ever saw him again.

Among her bandmates, Janis was attracted to Sam Andrew, a bookworm and former grad student in linguistics, but she was particularly drawn to the aloof and spacey Jim Gurley. The Detroit native had been an itinerant musician after briefly serving as a "human hood ornament" in his father's daredevil driving act during which the car, with James secured to the hood, sped through a wheel of fire. Gurley's wife, Nancy, a former teacher and also from Detroit, was a vivid and constant presence around the band, as was their baby boy, Hongo. The Gurleys had lived among the Huichol Indians in Mexico in the early sixties, and Nancy shared the esoterica she'd picked up there and through her study of the occult. Described by Albin as "the original earth mother," Nancy was as talkative and outgoing as her husband was quiet and introspective. While he'd spend hours trying to replicate the sound of John Coltrane's saxophone on his guitar and execute John Lee Hooker blues riffs, Nancy crafted God's-eye symbols from colorful yarn. A mystical totem signifying the power of "seeing and understanding the unseeable and the unknowable," the God's eye became Big Brother's band symbol. Nancy and Peter Albin's wife, Cindy, made large, multicolored God's eyes that adorned their amplifiers. Nancy's style—long peasant dresses worn with strands of hand-strung beads—greatly affected Janis's nascent look, and she began wearing necklaces Nancy gave her.

The first weekend in July, Nancy didn't join the band on a trip to Monterey, where Big Brother headlined a two-day "Independence Dance" at the very fairgrounds where Janis had met Bob Dylan in 1963. This time Joan Baez was in the audience. Janis, having grown more confident onstage, gyrated and swayed while the guys jammed. Albin, who reported he "didn't dance much," was put off when she "tried to be sexual" toward her bandmates, particularly when she "put the make on me." He recalled, "She said, 'Let's dance,' and did all the rubby-dubby stuff."

Apparently James Gurley felt differently, and that night, he and Janis slipped away and had sex. The attraction deepened, and he moved into Janis's room on Pine Street, with Gurley explaining later that they "were in love." The tryst lasted for a couple of weeks until Nancy barged in one morning while they lounged in bed and demanded her husband return home. An open-minded bohemian who grew up in a wealthy home and earned her master's in literature, Nancy believed in free love, but she had her limits. James moved back in, and, surprisingly, Nancy and Janis's friendship flourished even while Janis continued to carry a torch for the intriguing guitarist.

Big Brother was booked for a few out-of-town gigs, beginning with the Red Dog Saloon, in Virginia City, Nevada, where the Charlatans had kicked off the rock & roll-revival-meets-LSD-taking counterculture during the summer of '65. While Janis had been recuperating in Port Arthur, she heard from friends about the 1859 mining town that had been invaded by the Family Dog and their pals. It became the testing ground for the Haight-Ashbury scene, with Bill Ham projecting the first light shows while the Charlatans—art students and musicians wearing Old West garb—played rock & roll at the nineteenth-century saloon, with most participants tripping on mushrooms or acid. The Red Dog's handbills, drawn by Alton Kelley, set off a demand for unique art-nouveau-gone-amok posters advertising Avalon and Fillmore shows. Janis started her own collection, grabbing phantasmagoric posters from walls and lampposts in the Haight to decorate her room.

When Big Brother arrived in Virginia City for a weekend of shows, Janis must have laughed at the irony of escaping Texas only to be surrounded at the Red Dog by would-be cowboys decked out in hats, chaps, and gun belts—some with real firearms—and women dressed as dance-hall girls. In three years' time, the music industry trade magazine *Cash Box* would anoint Janis the Rock & Roll Calamity Jane.

Big Brother also flew to Vancouver, British Columbia, to play Canada's first Trips Festival. When no one met them at the airport, the near penniless band members had to schlep their equipment and hitchhike to the venue. Joining them at the "Captain Consciousness Presents: The Trip: An Electronic Performance" was the Grateful Dead, who'd brought along its soundman and premier LSD chemist, Owsley Stanley; Janis had once sampled his potent crystal meth. When not running the band's sound, Owsley wandered the concert, giving away blue tabs of acid. Getz "took a hit and got very, very high," he recalled. Janis, according to Sam Andrew, "distrusted psychedelic drugs because [she told him] they make you think too much."

Janis had devoured J. R. R. Tolkien's *The Hobbit* and *The Lord of the Rings* trilogy, so performing at "Bilbo's Birthday" celebration at San Francisco's California Hall in late July was a gas. Big Brother's sets—recorded, bootlegged, and released on CDs decades later—document her evolving sound, less than two months after she joined the band. Janis had taught them Powell St. John's "Bye, Bye Baby," its loping tempo and spare arrangement showcasing her vocals. Judging from the applause, it was a crowd favorite. The group also performed a kind of psychedelia-dosed vaudeville set piece that began with an off-key a capella "Amazing Grace" (with Albin, Andrew, and Janis on vocals). Then Albin's zany rap spoofed an LSD trip in which a Haight Street prophet offered "a holy sacrament, 350 mg Owsleys," promising, "You'll see God, maybe hell, and a lot of other things."

While Janis added exclamatory *yeahs*, Albin's tale unfolds with the LSD tablet stuck in a recipient's throat, while modulating and accelerating guitars build into a sonic frenzy. In character, Albin describes vividly a hallucination in which "I saw a whole Bill Ham light show." The band then segues into "Land of 1000 Dances" before veering back to "Amazing Grace." Janis ends the traditional spiritual with a vocal solo and her newly developed *yowl*. "It was nearly impossible not to stare constantly at her," Great Society's Darby Slick recalled. "She pranced, she strutted, she shrieked, she whispered. The word of mouth was: a star is born."

With each successive gig, Janis's self-assurance grew. After playing a high-profile bill, she wrote home about Big Brother's reception among established musicians: "Two of the bands have hit records out—the Grass Roots (who incidentally are big fans of ours and even wear our buttons when they play) and the Jefferson Airplane—and were very well received, but I/we got an ovation, bigger than any other groups, for a slow blues in a minor key. Wow, I can't help it—I love it! People really treat me with deference. I'm somebody important. SIGH!!" Janis had never had this kind of acclaim in her life, and it felt better than any drug. She had been including "SIGH" in letters for years, but now the contentment and happiness the word radiated nearly jumped off the page. She realized she'd made the right decision to join the band.

The "slow blues in a minor key" came from one of Janis's favorite artists, Willie Mae "Big Mama" Thornton. She, too, had relocated to the Bay Area, where she played the Monterey Jazz Festival and local venues. Janis, Peter, Sam, and James saw her at the Both/And, a small jazz club on Divisadero Street. She sang her famous "Hound Dog," but the song that really grabbed their attention was her original composition "Ball and Chain." Riveted, Janis jotted down the lyrics, and after the show, they went backstage to meet the thirty-nine-year-old singer and ask if they could cover her song.

"She was a tough woman with a truck-driver style," Andrew recalled. Thornton gave her okay but warned, "Don't fuck it up." At its next rehearsal, Big Brother recast the song in a minor key, slowing it to a glacial pace. Janis squeezed every bit of hurt she'd suffered into "I wanted to love you and I wanted to hold you, yeah, till the day I die." "Ball and Chain" became a Big Brother showstopper; one year later, the song would introduce Janis to the world.

>─┼─◇─○─◇─┼─◁

Big Brother, like other groups on the scene, had evolved into a kind of family. Following the lead of the Grateful Dead, the members decided to move to Marin County and live communally. Not far from the Dead's compound at a former children's camp, they found a rustic cottage amid a redwood forest up a long drive outside of tiny Lagunitas. The home was built in 1904 by botanist and ornithologist C. Hart Merriam as a base to study plants and wildlife. The erudite naturalist became friendly with local Miwok Indians, who helped him choose the bucolic spot atop a hill surrounded by in-ground springs. Early visitors to the exceptional property included naturalist John Muir, botanist Alice Eastwood, and President Theodore Roosevelt. By the 1960s, a forest ranger owned the place, and when his marriage broke up, his former wife rented it to Big Brother for six months. "Out in Marin, they still frowned on long hair and the whole hippie scene," said Albin, who signed the lease. Near the bottom of the driveway sat a large propane tank, on which someone had scrawled "Carlos Is Alive and Well in Argentina," so the house became known as "Argentina."

The August day she moved in, Janis wrote her parents, who had not yet replied to her previous letters. She remained determined to be seen as their dutiful daughter:

At last a tranquil day & time to write all the good news. I am now safely moved into my new room in our beautiful house in the country. I'm the only member of the band out here so far . . . sitting in a comfortable chair by the fireplace, doors wide open and a 180 view of trees, redwood & fir. Bliss! I've never felt so relaxed in my life. This is the most fantastic house & setting. . . . Of course part of my comfort is due to the fact that this is the first day in 10 or 11 that I've had to relax at all. We've been working every night for 11 days. . . . I've got the best

*bedroom in the house (I got here first) w/ sunshine all day. The weather
up here is much warmer than in the city. In S.F., you have to wear a
heavy coat even in the afternoon, but it's just perfect here. I plan on
getting a wonderful tan. And it's not too hot like Texas. Just lovely—
75–80°, don't you envy me? If you have a map, look on the coast for
Stinson Beach—we're about 10 mi. inland from there.*

Though small, the house comfortably fit Big Brother and the musicians'
partners. Dave Getz carved out a space behind the kitchen; Janis's sunny
alcove, with a wall of windows, was on the second floor next to the
room with Peter and Cindy Albin and their young daughter. The three
Gurleys bunked in a third room upstairs. Living in a shack behind the
house were Sam Andrew and his girlfriend Rita Bergman—a friend of
Nancy's from Detroit whom everyone called Speedfreak Rita. As much
as Janis had tried to avoid methamphetamine, the drug was all around.

Her new living situation influenced Janis's wardrobe, and she emulated Nancy Gurley's style and that of other women on the scene. Her
mother's daughter, she wrote Dorothy about San Francisco fashions,
illustrated with her sketches:

*A fashion note—thought y'all would like to know what everyone looks
like out here. The girls are, of course, young and beautiful looking w/
long straight hair. The beatnik look, I call it, is definitely in. Pants,
sandals, capes of all kinds, far-out handmade jewelry, or loose fitting
dresses & sandals. The younger girls wear very tight bell-bottoms cut
very low around the hips & short tops—bare midriffs. But the boys
are the real peacocks. All have hair at least Beatle length [sketch], most
rock & roll people have theirs about this long [sketch] & some, our
manager Chet's for example as long as this [sketch], much longer than
mine. And very ultra Mod dress—boots, always boots, tight low pants
in hound's tooth check, stripes, even polka-dots! Very fancy shirts—
prints, very loud, high collars, Tom Jones full sleeves. Fancy print ties,
Bob Dylan caps. . . .*

Conforming to the style to the extent of my budget, I have a new

pair of very wide-wale corduroy hip-hugger pants which I wear w/
borrowed boots. Look very in. On stage, I still wear my black & gold
spangly blouse w/ either a black skirt & high boots or w/ black Levis &
sandals.

Janis planned already to make her onstage image more distinctive by
dressing up and creating a performance persona—like Bessie Smith
with her beaded gowns and feather hats, and Rose Maddox with her
colorful embroidery and fringe. "I want to get something out of gold
lame," she wrote. "Very simple but real show biz looking. I want the
audiences to look at me as a real performer, whereas now the look
is 'just-one-of-us-who-stepped-on-stage.'" Soon she'd have a sleeveless
shift made of gold metallic fabric.

><⊙><

Living in Lagunitas, Big Brother often partied with the Grateful Dead
and Quicksilver Messenger Service, which had moved to a run-down
ranch in nearby Olema. At one of the gatherings at the Dead's compound, Janis took up with Pigpen, who shared his bottle of Southern
Comfort. So far, she'd stayed away from drugs, except for weed, but
she had started drinking again and enjoyed the sugary whiskey Pigpen
favored. Though he looked tough like a Hells Angel, Pigpen was a shy
man, and, like Janis, found booze the best way to loosen up. Eventually the two consummated their friendship, and usually spent the night
together at the Dead's place. "On many a night, they would kill off a
couple of bottles of Southern Comfort, play and sing themselves into
a romantic mood, and retire to Pig's room," the Dead's Phil Lesh recounted, "which was situated just above mine. I could hear them grunt-
ing and screeching ecstatically very clearly, and I often wonder if the line
'Did you ever waken to the sound of street cats making love?' from Bob
[Weir]'s song 'Looks Like Rain' was inspired by the music Pig and Janis
made in the dead of night."

Though their fling was short lived, Janis and Pigpen remained fond
of each other, sharing a bottle, playing pool, and singing the blues to-

gether. Janis sent her parents a magazine photo spread that included the Dead, and circled his picture: "Isn't Pigpen cute? They make Pigpen T-shirts now with his picture on it—for fans. I have one—red." On double bills with the Dead, Janis sometimes joined Pigpen on a duet of Bobby Bland's "Turn On Your Love Light." The extended jam was usually the show's finale.

At the "Argentina" house, Big Brother rehearsed every day, working up new original songs. The group diligently prepped for a high-profile opening slot for its hero Bo Diddley at the Avalon Ballroom on August 12–13. "Everybody just committed themselves completely to the band," according to Getz. "It was just 'This is gonna be it!'" That weekend, the Avalon's "Earthquake" dance was packed, with two thousand tickets sold. Big Brother played one of its best shows, and Janis strutted and sang like she was born for the stage. "Everybody got a sort of high," said Getz. "The whole place just took off like a rocket ship."

Afterward, in the cramped dressing room, Elektra Records A&R man Paul Rothchild visited the band. In just over two months with Big Brother, Janis's talent and stage presence were attracting interest from the music business. Rothchild had made a name for himself producing the 1965 debut LP for Chicago's Paul Butterfield Blues Band, a big attraction in San Francisco. Rothchild and Elektra owner Jac Holzman requested that Janis attend a meeting with them to discuss her joining a "supergroup" of blues musicians, based in Los Angeles. A few days later, they invited her to a Berkeley studio to jam with the possible lineup: on acoustic guitars, Janis's old friend Steve Mann and the Even Dozen Jug Band's Stefan Grossman, a New Yorker. Joining Janis on vocals was blues vocalist/guitarist Taj Mahal, most recently a member of the LA-based Rising Sons (with Ry Cooder).

"We were all excited about playing together," Stefan Grossman recalled. "We played and talked for about three or four hours, and the vibe was friendly. We did the Lee Dorsey tune 'Get Out of My Life, Woman,' and the combo of Taj's and Janis's voices was pretty amazing."

Janis was excited about this turn of events. But if she joined the Elektra group, she'd have to leave her Big Brother family, whom she loved but thought lacked commercial prospects. She wrote to the Joplins about her dilemma, astutely assessing such a career move and asking their advice.

> *Rothchild feels that popular music can't continue getting farther*
> *& farther out & louder & more chaotic, which it is now. He feels*
> *there is going to be a reaction & old fashioned music blues, shuffles,*
> *melodic stuff is going to come back in. Well, Elektra wants to form*
> *the group to BE this—and they want me. They want to rent us a*
> *house—in L.A.—& support us until we get enough stuff worked out,*
> *then, first, they want us to do a single & an album. Now they're a*
> *good company—& since we'd be their group, they'd push the hell out*
> *of us. . . . And, he says, we couldn't help but make it. Now I don't*
> *know what to do! I have to figure out whether R&R is going to go*
> *out, how deep my loyalties to Big Brother go (the band is very uptight*
> *at me for even going to the meeting & I can understand it) & for*
> *another, I'd be under contract to a record co. from the beginning—I'd*
> *be starting on the top almost and I'm not sure yet whether the rest of*
> *the band (Big Brother) will, indeed, want to work hard enough to be*
> *good enough to make it. We're not now, I don't think. Oh god, I'm*
> *just fraught w/ indecision! And let's face it, I'm flattered. Rothchild*
> *said I was one of the 2, maybe 3 best female singers in the country &*
> *they want me.*

When she reported Elektra's offer to Big Brother, Peter Albin flew into a rage. As the group gathered outside on the large sunny deck of its home, he argued for why she should not quit Big Brother. "It was a terrible, traumatic experience," Albin recounted. "We were all living together, and we were like family. She said that what she always wanted was to make records and be famous and a star." The group's philosophy was "a band is like a sacred trust," according to Getz. "We assumed she was making a life commitment."

Big Brother had been offered a monthlong residency at a Chicago club near the end of August. The other four urged her to join them for the gig. "I put it to her in such a way that she should make the right decision—going east to Chicago was a big deal for us," Albin explained. Janis broke down in tears and agreed. But she was still torn about her prospects: "I'm hoping . . . the Chicago job will show me exactly how good Big Brother is . . . & then I can make up my mind," she wrote home.

Complicating matters further, the band decided to fire Chet Helms, its manager of sixteen months. Helms, who named the band, was linked so closely to the group that in 1965 he was considered "Big Brother" and the musicians "the Holding Company." But now that the Family Dog dances at the Avalon were so time consuming, Helms had less time to focus on Big Brother's career. The band members wanted a more professional manager who could elevate them to the next level of success. They hoped this would also entice Janis to stay.

"We had to sit down and decide who was going to go over and tell him," Albin recalled. "He was very involved with the Avalon and the Family Dog. It was obvious we were playing second fiddle. We needed somebody to just concentrate on our career." Helms took the news calmly, expressing no ill will toward the group to which he'd introduced Janis. "I wasn't into this to make money," Helms once said idealistically. "I was into it for the revolution."

With no manager and a conflicted lead singer, but with plane tickets in hand, Big Brother set off for what it hoped would be a new chapter in Chicago. Janis would get her first taste of band life on the road—as well as its inherent diversions.

CHAPTER 12

"THE IDOL OF MY GENERATION"

*Either we are all going to go broke and split
up, or else we'll get rich and famous.*

—JANIS JOPLIN

D espite the confusion and confrontation in the days before leaving California, Janis was optimistic about the band's trip to Chicago, her ambition blazing. "Chicago is Blues Heaven & I can hear & be heard by some important people," she wrote her parents. "I really dig flying & being a R&R band & flying to a gig is even more exciting. SIGH!!" Janis hoped to use the Chicago residency, away from San Francisco trendsetters, to test and increase her musical skills and contributions to the band. Big Brother wanted to expand its audience outside the cocoon of the West Coast fan base. Instead, the Chicago residency became a crucible for the band, a case study in dues paying. Janis dealt with this latest disappointment and rejection by drinking heavily, a habit that would accompany her back to San Francisco in September. Throughout, though, she developed an onstage persona and became the essential voice of the group.

The trip went badly from the moment Big Brother landed at O'Hare International Airport in the heat of August 1966. The band members had no place to stay, no manager to call for help, and very little money. They made it into Old Town, near the North Side entertainment district, lugging their bags and their equipment, searching for a hotel that would take them. "We got lots of the 'Is it a boy or a girl?' sort of crap," said Peter Albin—an early sign of the baffled reception they'd receive in the Windy City.

Albin contacted his aunt Leslie and uncle Roger Rush in suburban Glenview, and they invited the marooned group to stay at their Pleasant Lane home. (Sam, with Speedfreak Rita in tow, opted to couch surf in Chicago.) The Rushes were appalled by the band's disheveled appearance, though their teenage children, Nicky, Cathy, and Chris, were thrilled to meet real-life hippies. The senior Rushes decided to take a vacation to Florida, leaving the house to their kids and the Californians—a fact Janis omitted when writing the Joplins: "They're really nice people w/3 super-creative & bright kids. Have a big air-cond. house in the suburbs, loaned us a car. We're all kind-of sad about having to leave our house in the country, though."

Mother Blues, a well-known folk music venue at 1305 North Wells Street, was expanding into rock shows. Just before Big Brother's residency, Jefferson Airplane played a fairly successful weeklong stint—though their female vocalist Signe Anderson, who traveled with her infant, left the band soon after. But with no advance advertising or press, Big Brother's opening night, on Tuesday, August 23, was a complete bust. The sparse audience gaped from the back of the room. Chicago, like much of America at the time, did not have a counterculture to support Big Brother's "freak rock." They were booked to play five hourlong sets a night, beginning at eight, with the first two hours open for those under twenty-one. But "the teenagers wouldn't dance or hoot or holler or cheer or anything," according to Peter Albin; then at ten o'clock, when the bar served drinks, "the older crowd [came] in and they were white-collar drunks—a bad scene."

"They don't get stoned," Janis complained later to a journalist. "Nobody was having any fun, man, they were all just drunk." Instead of finding blues heaven, she'd landed in what she called a "strange town . . . really the Midwest!" In a letter home, she admitted that "5 sets a night, 6 nights a week GASP! [is] really hard work. . . . Our music isn't really going over either. There are so many good blues bands in Chicago that we pale beside them and that makes playing all the harder." Janis's bandmates cast blame elsewhere. "They didn't understand the music, couldn't dig it at all—hated it, in fact," Albin said later. Meanwhile, after a night of heavy drinking, Janis and James Gurley rekindled their affair, sharing a bedroom at the Rush home.

While in Chicago, Janis finally heard from her father for the first time since she'd left Texas more than two months earlier. His steely note inquired about her future: "As you have so studiously avoided the topic, we are assuming that you feel your present venture promises success and that you will not be back here for college next month. If this assumption is incorrect, let us know immediately, as we need to know. On the other hand, if the assumption is correct, all we can do, I guess, is to wish you the very best of luck and all the success you hope for."

In her reply, Janis attempted a lengthy explanation of her decision to focus on music and the positive effect performing had on her mental state, enabling her to stop taking the Librium prescribed to her for anxiety. She began:

> Daddy brought up the college issue which is good because I probably would have continued avoiding it, in my own inimitable adult fashion, until it went away. I don't think I can go back now. I don't know all the reasons, but I just feel that this all has a truer feeling. True to me. A lot of the conflicts I was . . . going to [therapist] Mr. Giarratano about I've resolved. Don't take my tranquilizers anymore. I don't feel like I'm lying now. . . . I'd like to go back to school. I really would, but I somehow feel that I have to see this through first, and when I can, put myself through. If I don't, I'd always think about singing & being good & known & feel like I'd cheated myself—you know? So, although I envy many aspects of being a student and living at home, I guess I have to keep trying to be a singer. Weak as it is, I apologize for being so just plain bad to the family. I realize that my shifting values don't make me very reliable and that I'm a disappointment and, well, I'm just sorry.

Her comfort with Big Brother and her limited success thus far seemed to provide the affirmation she needed. In reporting on her relationship with the band, she emphasized her professional goals. Just as she struggled between her own ambition and her parents' wishes, she made it clear that if the band—her new family—couldn't cut it, she would eventually leave them behind as well. "The record thing I wrote you about caused quite a bit of emotional trauma within the group," she wrote. "All sorts of questions of loyalty came up. I decided to stay w/ the group but still like to think about the other thing. Trying to figure out which is musically more marketable because my being good isn't enough, I've got to be in a good vehicle."

Unresponsive Chicago audiences pushed Janis to go further to get the attention she craved. And she and Big Brother were quite literally hungry, so she was desperate to deliver. Mother Blues's long, narrow stage became Janis's workshop. Without much room to move, she still managed to magnify her stage presence by experimenting with her persona. During instrumental breaks and while singing, she put her considerable energy into the tambourine or maracas, improving her rhythmic chops, tapping ever deeper into her innate musicality. She took up the Cuban guiro, a gourd-shaped, open-ended wooden instrument with notches, played by rubbing a stick alongside the rough edges to create a scratching sound. "She had a great sense of rhythm," according to Dave Getz, who gave her the percussion instruments. "Even when we played really fast, when it's hard to stay on tempo, she did a pretty good job of it. Her ear for rhythm was very good, and she always knew where the beat was."

With five sets a night to fill, the band expanded its repertoire to nearly forty songs. Big Brother would go from Chuck Berry and Little Richard covers to Nina Simone's "Rags and Old Iron," "which Janis sang just beautifully," said Getz. Janis wrote an anguished blues tune "The Last Time," with changing time signatures and a stop-and-start rhythm. They also incorporated older songs from Janis's Austin set, including "Turtle Blues," using it as a launchpad for James Gurley's long, fuzzy, psychedelic guitar riffs. Her acoustic "Women Is Losers," which she told them she'd initially called "Whores Is Funky," became a stomping psychedelic blues with a military cadence. Gurley, in his quiet baritone, handled lead vocals on a couple of numbers, including a cover of "All Is Loneliness," an obscurity by Moondog, an eccentric New York street musician and avant-gardist who wore Viking-horn headgear while busking. Janis and Peter harmonized on the Moondog song's haunting choruses. Gurley's other lead was an electrified version of the old Appalachian ballad "Coo Coo" (also known as "The Cuckoo"), to which Janis added her gliding soprano, as she had in her Austin days covering the song. Sam Andrew's spotlight was his amped-up version of the Norwegian composer Edvard Grieg's "In the Hall of the Mountain King," catapulted by the dual guitars into a lengthy noise fest, culminating in a storm of feedback generated by Gurley picking up his amplifier and then purposely dropping it.

Janis soon became friendly with a Mother Blues waitress, a beautiful African American woman who played R&B records between sets and "was very hip and knew what was happening," Getz recalled. A favorite among the 45s was the hit ballad "I've Been Loving You Too Long (To Stop Now)" by Otis Redding, whose music would have a major impact on Janis's evolving vocal style.

Another hip local, Nick Gravenites, spotted Big Brother walking down Wells Street one day. While previously living in San Francisco, he'd seen both Janis and Gurley perform individually at the Coffee Gallery. Now back in Chicago, he managed a local blues club. "I had a short haircut, and they thought I was some big, greasy gangster coming over to fuck with them, beat them up or something," Gravenites recounted. "They were getting a lot of weird reactions in town." An aspiring singer and songwriter, Gravenites caught their show that night and saw that "people didn't know what the fuck to make of them. They were so freaky at the time. The audience was dumbfounded [and] didn't know whether they should get up and dance. They didn't know whether they should like them or not. I was no different. They scared the hell out of me. Especially Janis—reeking of patchouli and a long granny gown on and covered with pimples. She had this weird, shrieking voice—I think she had a sore throat at the time, and it sounded even weirder. Maybe one daring person would get up and dance. It was just one of those scenes like they were from Mars." Despite these initial misgivings, Gravenites would become one of their future collaborators when he returned to San Francisco.

Occasionally, local teenage musicians the Shadows of Knight, who'd recently had a hit with "Gloria," stopped in to see Big Brother, along with their producer, George Badonsky, who co-owned local Dunwich Records. Afterward, Badonsky "[shook] his head, saying, 'Gee, they're nice—too bad no one will pick them up,'" Gravenites recounted. "It was obvious to him they were too outrageous for any sane-thinking person to even consider recording."

In San Francisco, a couple of record labels had, in fact, approached Chet Helms, while he was still their manager, about signing his charges. In mid-August, before her Elektra offer, Janis had written home that "we're talking to ESP Records—they want us to do an album." The tiny New York–based label (ESP-Disk) recorded primarily free jazz, including Albert Ayler and Sun Ra, as well as the Fugs, whose cofounder Ed Sanders complained about the label's "shackling" contract and nonexistent royalty payments. Janis acknowledged that ESP was "sort of an underground record company. Not big and flashy, only does albums [rather than 45s, the record industry's main currency in 1966] & only does slightly out-of-the-way groups, which I admit we are. We wouldn't get a big nat'l following like the Lovin' Spoonful, but we'd have a steady following among the hippies."

A wary Helms had rejected the ESP deal, and, presciently, he had also turned down a recording contract from Bobby Shad, forty-six, founder of Mainstream, an independent jazz label. (Born Abraham Shadrinsky, his grandson is film director Judd Apatow.) Shad began his career as a producer in the 1940s at the jazz and R&B label Savoy and then became an A&R man at Mercury Records, working with such notable artists as Sarah Vaughan, Carmen McRae, and Gerry Mulligan, among others. The New Yorker established Mainstream in 1964 to reissue Commodore Records jazz 78s. Sniffing out the San Francisco rock underground back in July, Shad set up auditions at the historic former Spreckels Mansion near Buena Vista Park. While Big Brother auditioned in the building's four-track studio, Helms sat next to Shad, who was interested in recording them and other groups live at the Avalon.

"They played about three tunes," Helms recalled, "and he says, 'Hey, this is pretty hot.'" Shad offered a six-month, three-single deal. "He starts outlining how he's going to screw the band out of their publishing," Helms recounted. "'We're gonna screw them out of this, screw them out of that. They'll never know the difference.'" Appalled, Helms signaled to the band that the audition was over; Big Brother, not sure if he'd made the right decision, followed him out the door.

In September Shad learned that Big Brother was in Chicago and approached the group again—this time, crucially, without Helms as a liaison. The result was the worst disaster to hit the band during its Chicago sojourn. Shad's timing couldn't have been more fortuitous. After two frustrating weeks, Mother Blues had stopped paying the band its contracted fee, and Big Brother earned only the meager proceeds from the door, usually less than $100 a night. Meanwhile, the band members had no return plane tickets or money to buy them. They were stuck. The musicians' union couldn't help them, informing the group that its only recourse was to file a complaint, which would close down the club. It was at this point that Bob Shad offered a contract and a recording session in Chicago. Thinking that an advance could finance the trip home, the band was receptive; in Janis's case, she wanted to prove to her parents, via a record contract, that she'd made the right decision to stay with Big Brother and that "she could keep a commitment," according to Dave Getz. "And we saw it as a way of locking the band together with Janis. I remember thinking, *If this Chicago thing turns into a total disaster, she's going to call Paul Rothchild, and we're finished as a band.*" Janis had indeed phoned Rothchild from Chicago but told him she'd fallen for one of her bandmates—Gurley—and couldn't accept his offer.

"This real far-out cat from New York was pushing us," Sam Andrew recalled later about the contract that would take an ungodly sum of money to undo. Big Brother's attorney, who had been referred by Shad, assured them the five-year contract, which turned out to offer no advance and assign half the song publishing rights to Mainstream, with the band earning a mere 5 percent royalty on sales, was the non-negotiable industry standard. "We were naïve kids," Andrew recounted. "We asked him for a thousand dollars [advance], and he said no. We said, 'Five hundred?' He said no. 'Well, can we have plane fare home?' He said, 'Not one penny.'"

Mainstream did book a session in a Chicago recording studio, for which the band was paid union scale, around $90 each. Janis enjoyed "quite an experience" there, she wrote her parents, with the group recording four songs, each featuring a different member singing lead: Gurley on "All Is Loneliness," Albin on his self-penned "Blindman," Janis on "Down on Me," and Sam Andrew and Janis duetting on "Call on Me," a soulful ballad he'd written in Lagunitas. "It took us 9 hrs. to get less than 12 minutes," she wrote home about the recording. "And we didn't mess up a lot either."

No one in Big Brother had ever worked in a professional recording studio before, and the engineer had never recorded a loud rock band. Their volume quickly posed a problem. "The engineer [kept] the VU meters from going into the red," according to Andrew, which prohibited the band's trademark sonic distortion. "The guitar sound was pure 1950s, and James and I were unhappy with it but didn't know how to correct it. We didn't know how to ask for what we wanted, and they were not about to volunteer anything." Shad instructed the engineer to keep the songs brief, around two minutes—the length needed for 45 rpm singles—which meant no long guitar breaks.

An eager student, Janis embraced the recording process. "She did very well on the sessions," said Andrew, which included singing her parts exactly the same way twice, to "double track" her vocals. Janis detailed the proceedings in a letter home: "First of all, you record the instrumental part alone. Then when you have it to your (and your engineer's) satisfaction, you lay the vocal on another track over the instrumental. Then for a dynamic effect you dub another vocal track, same voices, same words, over the first to give the voice a deeper sound." Janis bragged about the impression she made on Shad, who told her she "came out very well on the first ones & thinks I am the most marketable aspect of the group & wants to get some of my songs." Shad planned to release a single in the fall, with Big Brother then returning to do another session in a Los Angeles studio. "It was exciting," Getz recounted. "We all believed we were going to get the band to another level, to make us famous."

>-+-●-○-<●-+-<

At Mother Blues, Big Brother finally began to build a modest following, including a few locals and a crew of roving hippies traveling the country in a van—an "entourage of very strange and odd characters," according to Getz. Their "head honcho was a very pretty, sweet guy" who had a fling with Janis. "She just adored him." The hippie vagabonds smoked DMT, which Janis, who still enjoyed weed, also tried. (DMT is an ingredient found in ayahuasca, a natural hallucinogen.) "One hit, and you were high like on acid for fifteen minutes," recalled Getz. "You'd hallucinate, have some kind of brain flash, an amazing epiphany, and then all of a sudden—*boom*—you're back in reality." Still afraid of hard drugs, Janis generally stuck to alcohol and later told friends she detested DMT, warning them not to try it.

Big Brother enlisted one of its new fans, a tall blond woman from New York, as its onstage go-go dancer. "Miss Proton, the Psychedelic Girl" wore a Saran Wrap turban and a skimpy leotard, her skin covered with Day-Glo paint and glitter. "I'm standing there singing," Janis recounted, "and there's this half-naked chick dancing right in front of me. I was really cracking up. It was very hard to sing."

During the last week of the club engagement, Big Brother received its first major newspaper coverage: a mixed review in the *Chicago Sun-Times*, on September 16, 1966, some of which stung Janis deeply:

Lacking the finesse and the drive of the Jefferson Airplane, this group still is exciting . . . and ugly! I mean it's not the same as the Grateful Dead, another Bay Area rock group led by a 300-pound former Hells Angel [Pigpen], but no one in Big Brother and the Holding Company would win beauty prizes either. The group's real beauty is audible as in Howlin' Wolf's "Moanin' at Midnight" or [Gurley's] "Easy Rider" or any other strong blues. We would have stuck around to hear more than one set but the drummer played with such unbelievably corny licks that we were driven up Wells St.

Janis took the review personally, asking, "But what about Sam? He's not ugly!" Back in San Francisco, she'd refer to it again, repeating to a writer: "They said we weren't as ugly as the Grateful Dead, but that we were still pretty ugly."

After nearly a month in Chicago, the assorted difficulties led to fights and bad feelings among band members. Just a few days before leaving, Janis had a particularly nasty spat with Peter Albin—after she stole a cashmere sweater from an apartment above Mother Blues where the band hung out. "She said it was because the club 'isn't treating us right,'" according to Albin. "I saw her [steal] it, and I said, 'You've got to return that.' She said, 'This guy owes us money and this is what he gets.' I said, 'It's [the club owner's] friend, not him.' That's when we had one of our first shouting matches, and she used the F-word several times at me—that didn't sit well with me."

When the gig was finally, mercifully, over, the band signed up for a free drive-away car, delivering someone else's vehicle to the West Coast. Excluding Albin, whose aunt bought him a plane ticket, on September 19 Big Brother plus Speedfreak Rita squeezed into a 1965 Pontiac Grand Prix. "It was a big sedan, and in the trunk we had our two Danelectro amps, my trap case, guitars, and some luggage," Getz recalled. "My bass drum was in the back seat. Sam and Janis did all the driving." The journey home went no more smoothly than their weeks in Chicago. Passing through Nebraska, Janis noticed the turnoff for Clay Center, her mother's ancestral home. "I almost drove in to meet my relatives," she wrote Dorothy from the car, "but I couldn't remember their names, so we're still on the road."

Farther west in Nebraska, the car squealed to a stop. Someone had spotted a huge field of what appeared to be marijuana. Everyone jumped out, grabbed handfuls of the cherished plants and stashed the weed inside Getz's bass drum. The excitement, however, was short lived. Just a few miles down the road, with Andrew behind the wheel, a police car pulled them over. The guitarist's driver's license had expired, but he was down-on-his-knees thankful that the car wasn't searched before being ordered into the town of Ogallala to see the judge. In the makeshift courtroom, the guys were polite and deferential, but Janis, infuriated, as if back in Port Arthur, argued compulsively with the cops. "They warned us, 'Get the hell out of here—don't stop,' after the band paid a fifty-dollar fine," said Getz. "'If you stay anywhere within Keith County, we're going to arrest you and throw you in jail! We don't want to see your kind around here again!' Janis was just chomping at the bit the whole time."

By the end of September, they were at last back at the Avalon Ballroom, playing a weekend of packed shows. "*Wheeee!* Now *these* are our people!" Janis proclaimed onstage. Big Brother immediately jumped into frequent gigging, while settling into a rhythm in Lagunitas, which included daily rehearsals and songwriting sessions. Albin's catchy new acid rock number, "Light Is Faster Than Sound," became a crowd-pleaser that Janis kicked off with her distinctive "*whoaaaaah*"s.

"She worked with him on her part," Getz recounted. "Just like she'd worked with Sam for her vocals on 'Call on Me' and James on his 'Easy Rider.' At one point, she said, 'Dave, why don't *you* write a song?' I wrote 'Harry'—an abstract kind of thing. I said to everyone, 'Okay, it's going to be a rhythmic phrase; play whatever notes you like.' The next day I gave them two more bars, and we evolved this concept." The chaotic instrumental—an edgy slap of noise—ended with Janis's spoken "*Harry, please come home,*" like a mom beseeching her runaway teen. "She had a great time with 'Harry,'" according to Getz, "doing funny stuff with her voice. People loved it."

Janis's domestic side—cooking and sewing—blossomed at Lagunitas. She wrote her mother, asking her to mail items she'd left behind, including her knitting bag and yarn, her partially made Lone Star quilt, and her cookbook and recipe cards. She helped prepare communal dinners, and she bought a secondhand Singer sewing machine to make

costumes to go with the $35 boots she bought in Chicago. ("So groovy!
They're old-fashioned . . . tight w/buttons up the front. Black. I'm
going to make myself some sort of beautiful/outlandish dress to go
w/them.") Writing home about fashion continued as her main connection to Dorothy.

With Nancy Gurley's and Speedfreak Rita's encouragement, though,
Janis also slipped back into her dark side. Nightly, the three engaged in
marathon bead-stringing sessions—necklaces, bracelets, ornamental
window shades, room dividers—the feverish pace fueled by shooting
speed. Before long, Janis returned to the drug she'd feared most. "Nancy
Gurley kind of promoted . . . other people . . . doing a lot of speed,"
according to Janis's old friend from the Haight, Pat "Sunshine" Nichols,
with whom she'd reconnected. "The women around Nancy were really
influenced by her." Whether Janis's relapse just happened one night,
or whether her resolve had weakened gradually as her heavy drinking
resumed, is unknown. Perhaps she thought that after being clean for
more than a year, she could dabble without getting strung out again.
Regardless, like her friends, she seemed enthralled by the ritual of tying
off, preparing the syringe, and shooting up. At one point, Dave Getz,
having never injected a drug, asked the women if he could join them.
"They all got into a big argument about who was going to shoot me
up," he recounted. "I think Nancy Gurley won. She gave me a shot of
methedrine, and I stayed up for about three days."

><+>+<>+<>+<

To drive between Lagunitas and San Francisco, Janis bought a used Sun-
beam compact convertible. She got her occasional lover, poster artist
Stanley Mouse, to paint "Big Brother & the Holding Company" and the
God's-eye symbol on the driver-side door. But with little money coming
in from gigs, she could barely cover the British import's constant repair
costs. "It was a nice clean healthy little car," she wrote her mother, "and
now it's an out-&-out beatnik car & it knows it. . . . The starter motor
burned out, so I have to push it to start it. Poor thing. It's out front,
parked on a hill."

In Haight-Ashbury, she sometimes spent the night at Sunshine's apartment at 640 Ashbury Street. "Pretty soon we started going out to places together," Sunshine recalled. "She always put me on the guest list." Sunshine, though only an acquaintance, had held on to Janis's belongings left behind when she'd returned to Texas the previous year. Seeing the remnants of her former life must have stirred bitter memories. "She was really surprised she got them back," said Sunshine. "Quite a bit of jewelry, clothes she had made out of shawls, and a decent-sized FM radio." Sunshine would remain one of Janis's most loyal friends—and eventually a drug buddy.

Janis was becoming well known around the Haight, particularly after Big Brother's first interview was published on October 5 in the eighth issue of the typed, mimeographed fanzine *Mojo-Navigator*. Edited by David Harris and Greg Shaw, *MN* was the mouthpiece for Bay Area music, founded in August 1966, five months after the nation's first serious rock music zine, *Crawdaddy*, was launched on the East Coast by a Swarthmore College student named Paul Williams. *MN* and *Crawdaddy* did for rock & roll what *Downbeat* had done for jazz and *Sing Out!* did for folk. *MN* ran extensive interviews with bands; the previous issue included a Grateful Dead Q&A that found Jerry Garcia calling Janis "an incredibly powerful singer . . . her knowledge of style and her control is really phenomenal, as well as her range." He went on to suggest that "they need more material that's adapted to her style . . . [and to] find a way to showcase Janice [*sic*] and get good material for her as well as her and Peter working together. . . . Mostly what they need is experience, and I think they'll come back from Chicago a lot tighter."

Garcia's prediction was spot-on. As Big Brother settled back into West Coast life, gigging constantly, the fruits of their Chicago labors became apparent. When the five of them sat down with Shaw and Harris, they described their unpleasant Windy City residency, as well as answered *MN*'s questions about the San Francisco scene. Though Garcia had diplomatically told *Mojo* that he equally admired the Fillmore—operated by impresario Bill Graham—and the Family Dog's Avalon,

Albin and Janis both emphatically said they preferred the Avalon, a declaration in print that would come back to haunt them.

An aggressive New Yorker and sharp businessman, Graham, originally business manager for the San Francisco Mime Troupe, had begun promoting shows at the Fillmore with Chet Helms in early '66. Soon after, he took control, ousting Helms, who moved on to the Avalon. The two had been rivals ever since, each booking weekend shows. Loyal to Helms, Janis told *MN* that the Avalon was the real deal, while the Fillmore, where Big Brother rarely played, appealed more to "tourists and drunken sailors looking to pick up chicks."

Mojo-Navigator carried news stories about the Haight scene, including coverage of the impending law criminalizing LSD possession in California, effective October 6, 1966. In protest, a Love Pageant Rally was organized for Golden Gate Park's Panhandle, where costumed revelers led by Acid Test originators, the Merry Pranksters and Ken Kesey—the latter disguised as a cowboy, since he was wanted by the police on drug charges —tripped on acid. Janis and Sunshine made the scene, sharing cheap wine. "Everybody took acid," Sunshine recalled, but "she and I didn't. She said [LSD] put her in a place she didn't like to be: not in control of herself." Shooting speed, conversely, returned Janis to that initial euphoria and intense degree of concentration she'd sought before.

At the Love Pageant, Big Brother and the Grateful Dead each performed on a flatbed truck surrounded by "thousands of high-loving heads out there messing up the minds of the cops and everybody else in a fiesta of love and euphoria"—as described by Tom Wolfe in *The Electric Kool-Aid Acid Test*. Numerous free concerts in the park would soon follow, culminating in the Gathering of the Tribes, or Human Be-In, the following January.

"Something's gonna happen," Janis predicted to *MN* when Mainstream released the band's debut 45, "Blindman," with the flipside featuring "All Is Loneliness." Though Janis did not sing lead on either track, she was thrilled by the *idea* of having a record out. "It isn't just going to carry on like this," she said. "Either we are all going to go broke and split up, or else we'll get rich and famous." After the label sent a single copy to the band in Lagunitas, Janis wrote the Joplins that "we're supposed to get 50 free records & I'll send you one. We haven't received any yet—they were due 2 wks. ago. . . . We have one copy which we've played so much I can't stand it any more. I can't even tell if it's any good." Clocking in at two minutes, "Blindman" begins with Albin's baritone, Janis's chiming in on each chorus, backed by straightforward guitar, drums, and bass. "All Is Loneliness" showcases Gurley's raga-style drone guitar behind the Gregorian-chant-like vocals, with Janis taking over, her vibrato echoed by whirring sonics. At 2:16, the song fades out with the return of the chorus harmonies.

In its positive review, *Mojo-Navigator* questioned "why the 45 is not already being played around here." Contrary to Janis's opinion, David Harris found the record "excellent both in terms of commercial potential and actual re-creation of their in-person sound. The vocal harmony is if anything better than what they achieve live, and the ensemble sound of the band cuts through the recording technique well. 'Blind Man' is almost reminiscent of the Mamas and the Papas. . . . 'All Is Loneliness' is done in a very interesting four-part harmony utilizing overdubbing. The only complaint . . . is that the guitar solos are a good deal simpler than those . . . they use in person, and this is understandable for commercial reasons."

Though the single got no AM radio play, the band was featured in a glossy new photo magazine, *I.D. 1966 Band Book: First San Francisco Edition*, which Janis mailed to her family, along with a picture "of me looking beautiful off a proof sheet a photographer did of us." Still seeking her parents' approval, she introduced the freaky-looking people in the photo spreads as her new friends, so "you can see how groovy the people in California look," she wrote the Joplins. "The bands that are friends of ours are the Grateful Dead, the Quicksilver Messenger Service, the Charlatans, the Outfit, & the P.H. Phactor Jug Band. Take a look at them . . . and the Family Dog picture. The Family dog is Sancho on top of the truck—the symbol for all those people that form a rock & roll corporation & put on dances every weekend. Those people are all friends of mine! Aren't they amazing?! The people w/ stars after their names are members of [Big Brother]. I'm in the back on the right. . . . They aren't dressed up—they look that way all the time. Now, taken in perspective, I'm not so far out at all, eh?"

Janis's growing popularity did not protect her from the wrath of Bill Graham. After fleeing the Nazis in his native Germany, Graham (born Wulf Grajonca) grew up tough on the streets of the Bronx before heading west, where he made a failed attempt at becoming an actor. Instead, he found his calling as a shrewd concert promoter aggressively capitalizing on the burgeoning counterculture. Janis soon discovered that crossing Graham was much worse than picking a fight with a typical club owner: when she arrived at the Fillmore in mid-October to see the Butterfield Blues Band, Jefferson Airplane, and Big Mama Thornton, Graham was stationed at the top of the stairs. *"You're not coming in here!"* he screamed at Janis. *"After what you said about the Fillmore in that rag! Get out of here!"*

Yelling back, *"You motherfucker!"* and sobbing, Janis was ushered— some witnesses said pushed—down the stairs and onto the street. Nick Gravenites, in town from Chicago with the Butterfield Band, was appalled. Graham "had this habit of throwing people out of his club," Gravenites told writer John Glatt. "He'd scream and holler and humiliate you and run you out of the place like you was dirt. It would be ugly. . . . Janis ran off down the street crying." Her vulnerability made such rejections almost unbearable, but Graham did not hold grudges for long—especially when there was money to be made. After Janis and Big Brother's ascent, all would be forgotten.

In October Janis learned her mother had been diagnosed with breast cancer and had already undergone surgery. Janis was unable, or perhaps reluctant, to travel to Texas to check on her. She wrote her, "Gawd, I feel so delinquent not having written in so long"—though she'd actually sent several letters home in previous weeks. "And you just getting over a serious operation. I'm sorry, sorry. I'm so thankful that you're doing okay— your letters sound chipper—& that they feel they caught it in time. I really am relieved & also very proud of you for the stoic way you handled everything. I know it's rather late to be saying all this, but since I have my car I'm highly mobile, so if you ever need me or want me, call, please."

Life in Lagunitas had become frantic. The Albins, early risers who liked a tidy house, did not get along with the Gurleys, who slept late and never cleaned up, with their toddler Hongo and un-housetrained German shepherd adding to the chaos. Janis explained to her mother that "we all just stumble from one day to another, not getting much of anything done. I've discovered I can't do anything unless there's a modicum of quiet & w/eight people in one house—talking & carrying on w/their babies, I can't do any little things, like writing letters, mending, sewing, anything. For example, everyone is gone now (Allah be praised!) so I can do this."

Janis also felt isolated in Lagunitas, with the Dead having decamped for a Victorian house at 710 Ashbury Street, in the center of the action. By the fall of '66, Haight-Ashbury had become a countercultural beacon, with "freaks" gathering on "Hippie Hill" in Golden Gate Park. (Most locals hated the word *hippie*, coined by *San Francisco Chronicle* columnist Herb Caen to describe "baby hipsters.") An underground newspaper the *Oracle* had just published its first issue, and soon its offices moved into a funky poster shop, the Print Mint, managed by Janis's former beau Travis Rivers, who would become the *Oracle*'s publisher. Down the street, brothers Jay and Ron Thelin opened the Psychedelic Shop, America's first head shop. Janis became friendly with a group of street activists called the Diggers, particularly cofounders Emmett Grogan and Peter Coyote, a pair of charismatic East Coast transplants. The self-described "radical anarchist group" believed everything should be free. They gave away food in the Panhandle and opened a free store where you paid nothing for goods. Railing against capitalism and materialism, the Diggers' projects and happenings resulted in the "Haight becoming a city within a city," according to Stanley Mouse, "a real community."

Around this time, Janis also met Peggy Caserta, a Louisiana-born beauty who opened Mnasidika, the first boutique on Haight Street. She often gave clothing to bands to wear onstage and in photo shoots. During Big Brother's weeklong residency at the Matrix club, the two became acquainted. "I was knocked out of my chair," Caserta remembered. "The hair stood up on my arms because I had never seen or heard anything like Janis—that kind of raw, soulful, gut-tearing. Afterward, I walked over to her and said, 'You're going to be a superstar!' She laughed and said, 'You really think so?'" Caserta returned the next two nights, and the following week, Janis dropped by Mnasidika and asked her if she could buy a pair of $7 jeans on layaway, putting down 50 cents. Shocked that a woman with such talent couldn't afford the pants, Caserta gave them to her. Thus began a relationship that would eventually turn passionate.

Caserta's reaction to Janis's onstage performance was increasingly common. "People had told me that the chick could really sing, but I didn't believe them," Ed Denson wrote in the underground weekly the *Berkeley Barb*. "The chick really *can* sing. She is a blues wailer . . . with the ability to scream and throw her body into the music." Grace Slick, who'd just replaced Signe Anderson in Jefferson Airplane, recalled being awed by Janis: "A white girl from Texas singing the blues? What gumption! What spirit! I don't think I had that fearlessness."

After Big Brother played the Avalon with the East Coast–based Jim Kweskin Jug Band, Janis chatted with the group's vocalist-violinist, Maria Muldaur. "She blew me away, completely," Muldaur recalled after seeing Big Brother do "Ball and Chain." "Then we bonded over a joint and her saying, 'Hey, you like Etta James?' We became friends in that moment."

Janis relished the upswing in her visibility. "This business just isn't any fun unless you can perform," Janis wrote her mother. "The monetary aspects of not working are important, too, of course, but the real value is just in being appreciated. It's worth all the hassles and bad rehearsals just to have 1,500 kids really digging you. And for me to have a musician from another band [it could have been one of many] tell me that I'm the best chick blues singer, bar none—not even Bessie Smith. Happened this weekend. SIGH!!" Between the respect she earned from other musicians and the increasing chorus of praise from audiences, Janis's thwarted dreams for the Chicago trip had become reality in San Francisco.

CHAPTER 13

"HAIGHT-ASHBURY'S FIRST PINUP"

*The best of all was Monterey. Ain't nothing
like that ever gonna happen again.*

—JANIS JOPLIN

The months between the fall of 1966 and Janis's transformative performance at the Monterey Pop Festival in June 1967, after which she became a national star, were the happiest of her life. "I'm becoming quite a celebrity amongst the hippies & everyone who goes to the dances," Janis wrote the Joplins in late '66, one of a burst of letters she sent chronicling her achievements and pleasures. As she evolved from being "one of the boys" in Big Brother to becoming the group's central focus, the correspondence made clear her personal ambition. Of course, her carefully composed missives accentuated the positives, leaving out her renewed drug usage and increased drinking. While reporting on the band's growing popularity, though, Janis dropped hints about her own changing identity—one that would ultimately separate her from the band and her family.

By the end of 1966, Haight-Ashbury was attracting nationwide media attention, with a focus on the rising rock bands, as well as the expanding counterculture reflected by the increasing numbers of young people making the scene. Venues proliferated, and the Avalon and Fillmore began booking more diverse acts, including the R&B star Otis

Redding. The epicenter of a new kind of spiritual consciousness, San Francisco was attracting devotees of Eastern religions and philosophies, and, in the spirit of the Diggers, Big Brother played benefit after benefit, gratis, for all of them: from the Buddhists and the Hare Krishnas to the Haight-Ashbury Free Clinic and the Hells Angels.

The band became particularly chummy with the San Francisco chapter of the Angels, a major component of "Hashbury." Enamored of the motorcycle gang's outlaw image, Janis actually felt more kinship with bikers than with practitioners of Eastern mysticism, declaring to her parents that Big Brother's gig at an Angels party was "our crowning achievement here-to-fore." This seesawing between peace-and-love endeavors and the decidedly macho outsider Angels was oddly common. Few sensed that the two subcamps of the Haight scene would eventually clash, with deadly results. The same weekend that Big Brother played a "Zenefit," benefitting the San Francisco Zen Center, it headlined a November 12 Angels event at Sokol Hall. Organized by Angel "Chocolate George" Hendricks—a lover of vodka-spiked chocolate milk—it was "a complete madhouse," Janis wrote the Joplins.

"You thought you were going to a hippie party," recalled Buddhist poet Larry Litt, then nineteen. "But you had to go through this gauntlet of Angels at the door. I was with a girl wearing a fishnet T-shirt with nothing underneath, and the Angels liked that, so we got in." The Angels milled about the lobby, "flowing in and out all night, never dancing, but drug dealing and beer drinking," said Litt. Dave Getz discovered that his drum heads, left unattended, had been stamped with the slogan "When we do something right, no one remembers. When we do something wrong, no one lets us forget."

During the middle of Big Brother's set, a large man shuffled onstage, grabbed the mike from Peter Albin, and screamed maniacally before wandering off. Janis's shrieks seemed subdued in comparison. When the bassist asked a nearby Angel, "Who was *that*?" he said, "Oh, that's our friend Gary the Deaf Mute."

"There was a lot of drinking and rowdy partying," Getz recounted. "I remember being a little scared, but I felt protected by the Angels. Free-

wheelin Frank and Chocolate George were poetic characters, into the romance of the road." At night's end, the bikers roared off simultaneously,
making "this huge noise, like a jet plane." Befriended by Beat writer
Michael McClure, Freewheelin Frank Reynolds made art, wrote verse,
and penned a memoir, cowritten with McClure and published by Grove
Press. Before long, Janis was perched behind Freewheelin Frank on his
bike. She'd take him and other Angels to bed, but overall, they treated
her as their "little sister"—lead singer of their very own house band (acknowledged by the Angels' insignia being emblazoned on Big Brother's
Cheap Thrills album cover). Janis would remain close to the Angels for
nearly four years, even after their violent rampage at the 1969 Altamont
festival resulted in their being cut off by other previously friendly bands.

>─+◦>─◦─<◦+─<

Though Big Brother's Mainstream single had flopped, Bob Shad booked
the band for a December 1966 recording session in Los Angeles, "to
feature me," Janis wrote the Joplins, "so we're working on my stuff."
Even the revered jazz critic Ralph Gleason noticed Janis, mentioning her
for the first time in his *San Francisco Chronicle* column, On the Town:
"heard a bit of [Big Brother] at the Avalon a while back, and they are
really getting into shape. Janis Joplin is a remarkable singer with a wild,
strong voice."

Though Janis had become the focal point onstage, Peter Albin still
assumed leadership duties for the band, negotiating contracts and handling press interviews. He was prominently quoted in a December 19
Newsweek story on the San Francisco scene, "The Nitty Gritty Sound,"
in which he said, "People are getting into the nitty gritty of emotional
and personal life. They're expressing themselves through physical
movement, and this creates a real bond between the musicians and the
audience." Janis was paying attention. Within a year, she would assume
Albin's role, becoming a master of the sound bite and a sought-after
interviewee.

After Chet Helms's dismissal, Big Brother looked for a new manager and briefly hired a local named Jim Killarney, who left after being

injured in a car accident. The band was "all disorganized," Janis wrote the Joplins. They performed constantly, but most gigs were either benefits or low paying, so money was tight. They had to rent cars and drive themselves to shows in Sacramento and Santa Cruz, and sleep on floors because they couldn't afford motels. Much of Janis's meager earnings went into car repairs, visits to the dermatologist, who'd prescribed tetracycline for her acne, and food for her new love: a puppy named George. "So cute! Only 8 weeks old and fluffy as a dandelion!" she reported home. "Part German shepherd and part English shepherd. He's going to be pretty big. . . . Also, while in Santa Cruz this weekend, I caught a mouse. . . . Really cute. I haven't named him yet." George became Janis's constant companion, with the two often photographed together.

Seth Joplin routinely sent his daughter money, since she often complained, sometimes humorously, about financial problems: "My car suffered a tragic breakdown on the streets of Berkeley and is now parked in the alley behind the repair shop waiting for me to raise $75 (!!). Should have it as soon as we get paid for the Stanford job. But as my finances are tenuous, I think I'll keep Daddy's [$20] check to be sure I can get to L.A. After that, I'll destroy it! After memorizing the contents, of course." Confessing that she would have to miss the upcoming holidays in Port Arthur, Janis tried to soften the blow by focusing on what to buy her family for Christmas, and requesting for herself a "good, all-round Betty Crocker or Better Homes" cookbook and some colorful tights—like she'd worn in high school.

The Mainstream recording session, over two days in mid-December, found Big Brother in a Los Angeles studio much like the one in Chicago, saddled again with a staff completely inexperienced at working with loud freak-rock. Veteran engineer Jackie Mills, who had recorded Fred Astaire and numerous film scores, was impressed by Janis, however. She "had such a great quality," he recalled. "When she sang, you could hear the freedom." On a tight budget, there was no time for preproduction or redoing songs or fixing botched notes. The group had to cut its material quickly, in one or two takes, with minimal soloing and no songs running longer than two and a half minutes.

Over some twelve hours in the studio, Big Brother recorded Jim Gurley's loping, countryish "Easy Rider" and surreal take on "Coo Coo"; Peter Albin's soaring "Light Is Faster Than Sound" and child-like "Caterpillar"; and Janis's ominous "Intruder," bluesy "Women Is Losers," and herky-jerky "The Last Time." Before releasing an album, though, Shad insisted on issuing a single in early 1967, pairing two of the Chicago recordings prominently featuring Janis's vocals, "Call on Me" (with Sam Andrew) and "Down on Me."

While in LA, Big Brother played the Shrine Auditorium, after which Janis spent the night with her aunt Barbara Irwin, their first rendezvous since 1961. In a letter sent before her arrival, Janis tipped off her aunt that "I'm a new-breed-swinger now, the idol of my generation, a rock-n-roll singer," and invited her and the family to the Shrine "dance." Barbara insisted Janis wear a bra during their visit, but the reunion was otherwise joyful; they even played a round of golf. As proof, Janis mailed her mother "a scorecard from Barbara & my golf match," commenting that her cousin Donna "reminds me very much of Mimi—just like her . . . same mannerisms, everything." Though swiftly becoming the queen of the counterculture, Janis still craved her parents' love, even as her fan base grew, perhaps even more so. Her letters at the time read not only as a chronicle of her rising fame but also as a testament of her need to be tethered to her family. It was a need that neither Janis nor the Joplins consciously realized.

Big Brother rushed back to San Francisco to attend a run of eagerly anticipated concerts at the Fillmore, where Janis had been forgiven by Bill Graham. The promotor had booked Otis Redding—after flying to Georgia to convince him to play for his hippie clientele—for three nights in late December. Before Graham took it over, the Fillmore Auditorium primarily presented black artists, and Redding had performed there in 1965 on a bill with B. B. King. For his December shows, Graham commissioned two posters, one catering to the African American community, and another for his usual crowd, with a typically psychedelic design, prominently listing opening acts the Grateful Dead and Country Joe and the Fish.

Already a Redding fan, Janis became an Otis devotee after seeing the twenty-five-year-old Stax/Volt recording artist and his eight-piece band all three nights. In addition to possessing a legendarily soulful voice, Redding masterfully worked the crowd with a sensual yet downhome style. *"Wanna jump some more?"* he'd holler after an up-tempo number. *"Wanna get sweaty some more?"* His balladry affected Janis the most: "Pain in My Heart" where he massaged the words, using a subtle force to differentiate each verse, with occasional "uncontrollable" shouts of emotion. According to Country Joe McDonald, who would soon become her lover, Janis "told me she invented her *'buh-buh-bah-baby'* [stuttering vocals] after seeing him."

Redding's latest single "Try a Little Tenderness," a gut-wrenching version of the pop standard covered by Bing Crosby and Frank Sinatra, was, according to Redding biographer Jonathan Gould, "the most harmonically complex song that Otis would ever record, chock full of minor second and sixth chords. . . . The track is a musical microcosm of the Stax sound, a seamless synthesis of the pleading ballads and pounding grooves." Janis watched, listened, and learned. "She wanted to *be* Otis," McDonald remarked later.

To get a front and center seat, Janis arrived long before each nine o'clock show. One of the nights, she was tripping on acid after being dosed at a party, according to Dave Getz. But that didn't distract her total focus on Redding. Bill Graham later described one moment during the set—possibly while Redding sang "I've Been Loving You Too Long"—when the singer spotted "a gorgeous young black lady in a low-cut dress" who "started sighing like she just could not hold on. . . . He walked across the stage, leaned down and looked at her, and he was a big, good-looking guy, and she was going, 'Oh! Oh!' and he said, 'I'm gonna s-s-sock it to you, baby.' One, two, and the whole place went *'Hah!'* All together." Janis took note.

In his *Chronicle* column, Ralph Gleason described the Redding vocal style as "heavily emotional, overtly sexual singing that makes his slow ballads almost orgiastic in performance . . . oozing sex and swinging like mad." Surely Janis read the review. Dusty Street was a regular at the Fillmore, then a college student and soon to become a pioneering FM radio DJ. "It was more fascinating for me, almost, to watch Janis watching Otis," she recalled. "Because you could tell that she wasn't just listening to him, she was studying something. There was some kind of educational thing going on there. I was jumping around like the little hippie girl I was, thinking *This is so great!* and it just stopped me in my tracks—because all of a sudden Janis drew you very deeply into what the performance was all about. Watching her watch Otis Redding was an education in itself."

From that week until the end of her life, Janis invoked Redding as her favorite singer. "You can't get away from him; he pounds on you; you can't help but feel him," she would tell Nat Hentoff. She'd feign a swoon when citing Redding before TV cameras. Her own erotically charged delivery would leave her audiences aroused—cries of *"I want to fuck you, Janis!"* rang out occasionally from the audience. Some of Janis's male counterparts, such as Led Zeppelin's Robert Plant—then a teenager toiling in blues bands in rural England—would later emulate Janis the way she did Otis.

>-+-0-+-<

Before their Lagunitas lease expired and band members moved into separate San Francisco apartments, Big Brother threw a massive Christmas bacchanal. They bought cases of wine, cooked pots of food, and rolled a hundred joints of the marijuana they'd picked in Nebraska. The weed turned out to be only hemp, so not a single person got high from it, but plenty of acid circulated. Janis drew Christmas cards for her housemates—that's how Getz discovered her artistic talent, he said later—and the band decorated a Christmas tree, around which members of Moby Grape, the Airplane, the Dead, and Quicksilver played music and partied. Other guests included assorted Hells Angels, Chet Helms, Travis Rivers, and former Waller Creek Boy Powell St. John, who'd recently moved to San Francisco from Mexico. Someone brought a pet goat, which ate half of Getz's bedspread, and the Christmas tree toppled over more than once. December ended with a blur of near-nightly gigs and benefits for various causes, during which there remained "a communal feeling of taking responsibility for ourselves and solving problems on our own," Sam Andrew explained.

The year 1967—one of the most eventful in rock—began with another Hells Angels party, this time a thronged free gathering in Golden Gate Park's Panhandle. A harbinger of what was to come, the "New Year's Wail" ("Whale" on some handbills) was paid for and promoted by the Angels as a token of gratitude to the Diggers, who'd bailed out bikers Chocolate George and "Hairy Henry" Kot after an October arrest. "The Angels pay their debts," Digger Peter Coyote recounted. "They asked us to arrange the details, but they footed the tab, including free beer, and offered the Grateful Dead, Janis Joplin, and Big Brother and the Holding Company as a huge thank-you to the community. It was the first large-scale free rock concert in any city park, and it was a grand day." Writer Charles Perry remembered "a mind-boggling sight—the feared outlaws drinking and dancing with hundreds of mystical acidheads in a foggy San Francisco park." The Angels now resided in a house across the street from the Grateful Dead's home on Ashbury Street.

"Played a hippie party in Golden Gate Park yesterday," Janis wrote the Joplins on January 2, 1967. "Co-sponsored by the Hells Angels who, at least in S.F., are really very nice. They have a different social code, but it seems to be inner-directed and they don't try & impose it on anyone." She also thanked her family for their Christmas gifts—including the requested cookbook, a candlestick ("my favorite . . . just lovely"), and another $20 from her father. She apologized for not calling home on Christmas: "People started coming for the party at 2 in the afternoon & I just couldn't."

Looking forward to what she projected would be a successful new year, she told her parents about a recent photo session with photographer Lisa Law, who "did a whole bunch of things of me & I think they're going to use one on a poster for the Family Dog! Gawd, I'm so excited! Also, [Stanley] Mouse, who has a button machine, has made Janis Joplin buttons. Oh thrill of thrills—very rare, only the IN people have them, my dear. No name, just a picture, so you have to be in to know who the hell I am. But I dig it. FAME, FAME, heh, heh." It was a goal she could declare to her family but kept under wraps among her hippie friends.

Big Brother was one of the bands invited by editors of the underground paper the *Oracle* to perform on Saturday, January 14, in Golden Gate Park at "A Gathering of the Tribes for a Human Be-In." Word spread through posters and *Oracle* ads that "all SF Rock Groups" would be appearing, alongside Beat poets, LSD acolytes, and campus radicals. But Big Brother was already booked elsewhere and missed the event of the year: the Dead, the Airplane, and Quicksilver played for an unpredictably huge crowd of forty thousand, who frolicked peacefully on the Polo Fields that afternoon. Covered widely by the media, the Be-In sounded a clarion call for would-be hippies, freaks, and heads to flock to the Haight—kicking off the soon-to-be-named Summer of Love. Big Brother was down in Los Angeles performing at the Shrine with, ironically, the group whose Acid Tests gave birth to the Be-In: Ken Kesey's Merry Pranksters.

The new year brought Big Brother what it needed most: a manager. Julius Karpen, a friend of Quicksilver manager Ron Polte—both hailing from Chicago—had returned to San Francisco after traveling in Mexico with Kesey. The former business agent for the San Francisco chapter of the powerful American Federation of Labor and Congress of Industrial Organizations, better known as the AFL/CIO, had checked out Big Brother during the mid-January run at the Matrix. Karpen recognized Janis, celebrating her twenty-fourth birthday onstage, as a girl he'd seen at a North Beach party in 1964, singing "stunning country-western . . . that blew everyone's minds." He also fell in love with Big Brother's sound. "They were so powerful, and the Matrix was so small," he recounted, realizing in a flash the band would be "the biggest thing happening in rock & roll." After meeting with Karpen, Big Brother, impressed by his credentials as a former Merry Prankster, hired him.

"Got ourselves a manager who is so fine," Janis optimistically wrote the Joplins, "does everything & really knows his business—really helped a lot, bought a '52 Cadillac hearse for transporting band & equipment, and looking for new places to live in the city—we move out of here on the 15th. . . . Our new record is coming out soon & best of all, we're really getting better. New material & new proficiency—it has us all turned on. We have a lot of confidence in our ability now & we're irrepressible! (sp?) Well, we're awfully excited anyway."

One of the first problems Karpen had to solve was a stack of unpaid parking and traffic tickets that Janis had accrued. She refused to pay the hundreds of dollars she owed and, instead, elected to spend the night in jail. "The more we argued over it, the more stubborn she got," recalled Karpen, who opposed her choice. "We can pay the fines," he told her, but she said, *"No! I'm not giving them any money!"* When Karpen said, *"You're tough!"* he recalled that she answered, *"I don't just sing this way, you know!"* Janis's up-against-the-man stance echoed that of her outlaw friends in the Diggers and Hells Angels.

Janis's next letter home didn't mention her brief incarceration but touched on other developments: "So far, moving into the city has really hung us up—we have no rehearsal hall. Very hard to find a place where you can make a lot of noise, don't have to pay much rent, and the equipment will be safe overnight. So, we're all sitting in our respective places trying to find something to do and waiting. And it's come at a very inopportune time—we were really getting into a good thing together—we're getting lots better and it's so frustrating!"

No doubt, some of Janis's frustration was due to enforced distance from her drug buddies. Separation—serendipitous, it turned out—from Nancy Gurley and Speedfreak Rita resulted in Janis weaning herself off speed. While looking for an apartment, she crashed with a friend who lived on Haight Street across from the Mnasidika boutique, where she frequently stopped to chat with Peggy Caserta.

"I sit around . . . and play folk songs on my guitar and watch television and make beads and take George for walks," she wrote her parents. "George! Now, he is my salvation. He gets me out of the house when I'd have just sat & moped. And he's so nice to come home to after a job when I'm feeling especially lonely. I come home & he's so happy to see me! Just can't contain himself—he's so sweet. He's getting bigger & bigger, but is really a good dog. When I take him in the car, he won't get out unless I tell him to, never runs away & is housebroke. And so sweet—all he wants is to be petted & loved. (That's about all anyone wants though, isn't it? . . .)." An animal lover since childhood, Janis would adopt a succession of dogs and cats. But unlike George, her need to be "petted & loved" would seemingly never be satisfied.

Janis had enjoyed countless flings over the past six months with infatuated fans, Hells Angels, and fellow musicians, but she longed for, in hippie parlance, "an old man." Then, in Berkeley one February weekend, Big Brother played the Golden Sheaf Bakery with Country Joe and the Fish. "I was on acid that night, and I just fell in love with Janis," Country Joe McDonald recounted. "She was so cool. We were clowning around and dancing, and at one point, all [the] bands jammed together."

A year her senior, McDonald had become a folksinger at twenty after three years in the navy. He moved from Los Angeles to Berkeley, participated as an activist in the Free Speech Movement, and joined the SDS (Students for a Democratic Society). Forming Country Joe and the Fish with Barry "the Fish" Melton in 1965, they played politicized folk music, electrified with psychedelic sonics and a frenetic rhythm section. Janis dug the handsome McDonald's magnetic stage presence, intelligence, and bravado. He'd just divorced his wife of five years when he and Janis became a couple soon after their bands played a benefit together on March 5.

"Things happened fast," McDonald told filmmaker Bob Sarles. "We just fell in love . . . and started hanging out, and I wound up living with her in the Haight." A Berkeley resident with no car, McDonald often hitchhiked across the bridge to San Francisco. Almost giddy, Janis wrote the Joplins: "I have a boyfriend. Really nice. He's head of Country Joe and the Fish, a band from Berkeley. Named Joe McDonald, he's a Capricorn like me, and is 25 & so far we're getting along fine. Everyone in the rock scene just thinks it's the cutest thing they've ever seen. It is rather cute actually." Janis pasted a photo of her and McDonald—looking very much alike—in her newly put-together scrapbook, labeling it "Country Brother and the Company Fish."

Mainstream at last released Big Brother's second single, the soulful "Call on Me"—Janis's duet with Sam Andrew—with the B-side the fiery "Down on Me," featuring her soaring vocals double tracked on both songs. Janis's voice and the tunes' straightforward melodies made the single more accessible than the previous record—though still not representative of the band's noisy live sound with extended guitar breaks. Big Brother was again disappointed by the recording's clean pop sound, and they now seriously regretted having signed a five-year contract with a low-budget label that had no traction in the marketplace and no particular interest in their musical vision.

"Our new record is out," Janis wrote her parents. "We seem to be pretty dissatisfied w/ it. I think we're going to try & get out of the record contract if we can. We don't feel that they know how to promote or engineer a record & every time we recorded for them, they get all our songs, which means we can't do them for another record company. But then if our new record does something, we'd change our mind. But somehow, I don't think it's going to. But we'll see. . . . More importantly, I feel we're playing better than ever. Seem to have more of an idea of working together, not fighting each other w/ our instruments."

When Big Brother met with an attorney to see if they could break their Mainstream contract, he was "fairly negative" about it," Janis reported. Feeling "used & abused" by the label, which was incommunicado, according to Janis, the band tried to contact Shad but to no avail, the lack of support leaving the band feeling "hung up."

Mainstream did send the 45 to AM radio stations, the primary means of breaking hit singles. But in San Francisco a tiny FM station was beginning to get attention by drawing Haight-Ashbury listeners away from the AM dial. KMPX 106.9 was a foreign-language station when DJ and music entrepreneur Tom Donahue began broadcasting there four hours a day, spinning San Francisco bands and other artists who didn't get AM airplay. And rather than stick to the AM format of rapidly paced brief singles, interspersed with commercials, he kept the needle on vinyl for album tracks stretching upward of fifteen minutes. In his deep baritone, Donahue also informed audiences about Haight happenings, antiwar protests, and concerts. He was soon joined by Detroit native Larry Miller, who spun discs from midnight to six and also rapped to his listeners, more like a fellow head than a commercial DJ. As their audiences increased, Haight businesses began advertising during Dona- hue's and Miller's programming.

"Janis had a room in a flat right above the Haight," McDonald re- counted, "and that's where we spent a lot of time, and I remember us listening to KMPX radio—a tiny little station then. Tom Donahue and Larry Miller would be the DJs, and we were lying in bed listening to the radio to hear our songs, because Big Brother had a [single], and we had an EP, and they would play a Big Brother track, and we would go, 'Wow! Wow! This is so cool!' And then they played Country Joe and the Fish, and it was like, 'Wow, this is too much!'"

The B-side, "Down on Me," got the most local airplay, eventually reaching number thirty-nine in San Francisco. Back in Texas, the *Hous- ton Post* reviewed the single, noting, "The girl's voice knocked me out. Little did I know that it is Janis Joplin, a girl who used to sing here at the Jester and Sand Mountain."

San Francisco's mainstream press was now noticing Big Brother, including music critic Phil Elwood of the *San Francisco Examiner*, who wrote that "the most dynamic of the musical performers is granny- gowned Janis Joplin. . . . She sings everything as a blues and bases her style on the Ma Rainey–Ida Cox tradition of the 1920s, with a bit of Bes- sie Smith thrown in. Miss Joplin warms the heart of a lifelong old blues fan like this reviewer. And the Big Brother band is in good shape these days, too. Their guitar-bass blend has become an harmonic fascination and the once ponderous rhythm is now moving in a rolling, good danc- ing pattern."

Big Brother was in demand among San Francisco's up-and-coming rock photographers, including Herb Greene, known for his distinctive portraits of the Grateful Dead and Jefferson Airplane. Noted photog- rapher Jim Marshall developed a rapport with Janis as he shot the band onstage in the Panhandle. Former New Yorker Bob Seidemann was particularly friendly with Big Brother and caught the group in their brand-new rehearsal studio, "the Warehouse," a cavernous space on the second floor of a three-story building on Golden Gate Avenue. As the band's confidant, Seidemann later captured intimate portraits of Big Brother's two main draws, James Gurley and Janis. First he shot Gurley, wearing an Old West–style shirt, his long hair accented with a large feather. Janis loved the photo and sent a Big Brother handbill with the Gurley image to her parents, with a note explaining that "James is quite a romantic figure in the hip scene in S.F. (which numbers from 5-10,000 people, according to the S.F. Chronicle), & reports are that soon 3 x 5 posters of his face will be on sale around. Fantastic, eh?"

During Janis's session with Seidemann, she had her own ideas about creating an iconic image. After he took a few photos, she began removing her clothes until she was wearing nothing more than a dozen bead necklaces and a sparkly black cape draped around her shoulders. Artfully shot in shadow, the provocative black-and-white portrait shows Janis, with a hint of one nipple exposed through the beads, staring boldly into the lens with a hungry look on her face. The photograph would become Janis's defining image, immortalizing her as the Queen of Haight-Ashbury. Another shot, never published during her lifetime, was Janis, sans cape, her nakedness obscured only by beads, her hands crossed and covering her mons veneris. The portraits came to represent a woman to whom the whole country would soon be introduced: a woman unafraid to express naked emotion onstage and in her recordings.

>-<>-0-<>-+-<

Janis found her first home in the Haight when Julius Karpen rented her a "really fine!" apartment on Lyon Street, composed of two large rooms, a kitchen, a bath, and a curved bay window and balcony overlooking the lush, green Panhandle, a hippie hangout and the site of frequent free concerts. "I'm right across the street from the park," she wrote her parents. "Here, you can go 10–20 blocks without ever seeing a living plant, and I just look out my window or step out on my balcony & I've got fresh air and trees and grass!! So wonderful. SIGH." A respiratory infection had motivated Janis to give up cigarettes, a habit she'd acquired at fourteen, and she reported the news to the Joplins, demonstrating that she was taking care of herself as her career was taking off:

Guess what (special for Dad) I've done—I've quit smoking!!! Still want one now & then but it's been about a month now. I felt it was just too hard on my voice. I'd been smoking for 10 yrs! I got a real bad cold & bronchitis & I just couldn't smoke for about a week & when I got well, I refused to start again. I may break down but I hope not. This is really better for me.

As articles about Haight-Ashbury and Big Brother proliferated, Janis sent her family a stream of clippings, as well as band merchandise. She mailed her brother Mike a T-shirt emblazoned with the Family Dog logo featuring its canine mascot, Sancho, on the front, and "Big Brother and the Holding Company" across the back. Janis's Bay Area fans had become more expressive in their affection, and she drank in the attention she'd always wanted. After the band played on April 15 at the massive Spring Mobilization for Peace gathering at Golden Gate Park's Kezar Stadium, she didn't write the Joplins about the speeches by Coretta Scott King (the wife of Martin Luther King Jr.) and Julian Bond (a founding member of SNCC then serving in Georgia's House of Representatives). Instead, she focused on her feeling of impending stardom: "A simply amazing thing happened," she explained. "As the boys were tuning, I walked up to the front of the stage to set up the microphones and as I raised the middle mike up to my mouth, the whole audience applauded! Too much! And then as we're getting ready to play, a girl yelled out, 'Janis Joplin lives!' Now you can't argue with that, and they clapped again. Also a rock publication named *World Countdown* had a collage on its cover using photographs of important personages in & about the scene and I'm in there."

The following week, Janis and Big Brother made their second television appearance. Previously, in November '66, they had lip-synced their Mainstream debut single on *Pow!*, a local program, but this time they played live in the studio, broadcast on the April 25 episode of *Come Up the Years*, on future PBS affiliate KQED. The producers built a set resembling the Avalon Ballroom, with light-show-style graphics behind the band. Looking comfortable and relaxed on camera, Big Brother played a typically egalitarian set, with Albin, Gurley, Andrew, and Janis each getting a featured spot, performing "Down on Me," "Light Is Faster Than Sound," "Coo Coo," "Blow My Mind," "In the Hall of the Mountain King," and "Ball and Chain." Janis, dressed in a capelet, leather miniskirt, print blouse, beads, and boots, sat with the guys for an on-camera Q&A with the show's host. Between joking around, Janis earnestly described her boring life in Port Arthur, brief career as a folksinger, and admiration for San Francisco, where "playing [music] is the mostest fun there is." The show signed off with Janis looking into the camera and quipping, *"Hello, Mom!"*

Though Dorothy couldn't view her daughter's bid for parental approval, since it aired only in San Francisco, Janis soon wrote to let her know that "Things are going so good for us & me personally I can't quite believe it! I never ever thought things could be so wonderful!" She reported that the band's playing was "better than ever," its constant gigging was reaping good reviews, and its finances had improved, with the band earning more than $1,000 for a weekend's work and $500 to $900 for one-off shows. "Not bad for a bunch of beatniks, eh?" Janis remarked. "And our reputation is still going uphill. It's funny to watch—you can tell where you are by the people that are on your side. Y'know, the scene-followers, the people 'with [a] finger on the pulse of the public.' . . . Guess who was in town last week—Paul McCartney!!! . . . And he came to see us!!! SIGH! Honest to God! He came to the Matrix and saw us and told some people that he dug us. Isn't that exciting!!!! Gawd, I was so thrilled—I still am! Imagine Paul!!!! If it could only have been George. . . . Oh, well. I didn't get to see him anyway—we heard about it afterwards. Why, if I'd known that he was out there, I would have jumped right off the stage & made a fool of myself."

McCartney, it turned out later, was not in the audience that night, but in attendance at Big Brother shows was another British Invasion star, Eric Burdon of the Animals, as well as Peter Tork and Mickey Dolenz of pop-rock sensation the Monkees—all drawn by Janis's voice. New manager Julius Karpen, stoked about the group's potential, thought "they were on a mission from God, helping lead the San Francisco revolution," as they generated near hysteria at gigs such as the Avalon's Tribal Stomp. "My motto was to guide them, to let the band stay true to itself." With so many bookings, Big Brother hired its first employee, Dave Richards, an artist, carpenter, and cab driver who became their equipment manager and a close friend of Janis's. Karpen increased Big Brother's performance fees, budgeted its earnings, bought new equipment, and put the members on a weekly salary of $100 each (roughly $329 today), about which Janis gleefully wrote her parents ("good heavens!").

Most exciting of all was her newfound status as "Haight-Ashbury's first pinup," which she began calling herself: "They're bringing out a poster of me!" Janis crowed. "Maybe you've read in TIME magazine about the personality posters. They're big, very big photographs, Jean Harlow, Einstein, Belmondo, Dylan, & Joplin. Yes folks, it's me wearing a sequined cape, thousands of strings of beads & topless. But it barely shows because of the beads. Very dramatic photograph & I look really beautiful!! If it wouldn't embarrass you, I'll send you one. I'm thrilled!!"

><-•->-○-<•-><

With each performance, it became clearer that most in the audience were there to see Janis. Rehearsing almost daily, Big Brother added to its set and reworked older arrangements to avoid the guitars getting in the way of her vocals. They had built a repertoire of nearly fifty songs, and the new ones prominently featured Janis. She and Peter Albin collaborated on "Road Block," a frenzied rocker with male-female vocal interplay. Sam Andrew wrote "Combination of the Two," an ode to the San Francisco scene, his vocals punctuated by Janis's psychedelic scatting—*"whooh-whooh-whoo yeah"*s and *"whoah whoa whoah"*s—and her Otis-inspired *"We're gonna knock ya, rock ya, sock it to ya!"*

Before Janis joined Big Brother, the group had attempted George Gershwin's "Summertime," from his 1935 opera *Porgy and Bess*, as both an instrumental and with Peter Albin on vocals. Janis had loved the song since girlhood, singing along to the *Porgy and Bess* soundtrack LP. More recently, she'd discovered Nina Simone's 1959 version. Sam Andrew, who crafted an introductory vamp to the song, averred that "'Summertime' was a particularly effective tune for Big Brother because it was a change from our usual harum-scarum romp. It gave Janis a chance to show what she could do with a classic tune: a minor key with its major sixth." To introduce Janis's softly sung vocal, he devised a guitar part based on Bach's Prelude in C Minor, from Seth Joplin's favorite, *The Well-Tempered Clavier*. "I played the theme of this prelude at half tempo," said Andrew, a student of music theory, "and it was the perfect starting point and central motif for 'Summertime.'" Andrew later wrote of Janis's vocal "achievement" in her interpretation: "It was as if molten metal had been poured into the rather conventional form of the song. Her voice was so high in emotional content that it split into two lines . . . one modal line accompanying another at an exotic distance we felt rather than heard."

Sam Andrew also praised "what Janis could do with a consonant." In her phrasing, she "hangs on that initial *n* in 'nothing's going to harm you.' . . . It is one thing to stretch out a vowel, but elongating an *n* is something else. The mouth is closed, and there seems to be nowhere to go with the sound," but Janis "sang a sort of consonantal melisma: *n, n, n, n. nnnn.*" After months and months of practice, Janis was stretching her vocal vocabulary, adding nuance and texture to her timbre. In rehearsals, she finessed techniques such as breaking her vocal over a syllable. On "Combination of the Two," Janis experimented with adding vibrato and a gravelly rasp to her vocalizing. She also continued working on her interpretation of "Ball and Chain," adding more dynamics to the song's slow, burning emotional build.

At Karpen's insistence, Janis studied briefly with San Francisco vocal teacher Judy Davis, who'd coached Judy Garland, Barbra Streisand, and Grace Slick. Janis apparently didn't click with the legendary teacher, an expert in the physiology of vocal sound projection. But Janis saw her often enough to learn exercises that strengthened vocal cords and aided projection. Davis taught Janis how to breathe properly, to engage her diaphragm to support her singing. Though the lessons were short lived, Janis gained stamina and learned how to control her instrument. Eventually, in the words of Bowdoin College musicologist Tracy McMullen, Janis "could take a scream through several dynamic levels (from *ppp* to *fff* and everything in between) at will, and turn from a clear, powerful tone to a rich, gravelly one on a dime."

><+>-0-<+><

Big Brother finally got a booking at the Fillmore, though Karpen and Bill Graham locked horns in a contentious relationship, quibbling over fees and other details. Nonetheless, Graham hired the group for a coveted spot opening three of six nights for Howlin' Wolf, the blues icon Big Brother had seen once during its Chicago residency.

The last weekend in April, they performed with another blues idol, Willie Mae "Big Mama" Thornton, at California Hall. Though always jittery before a gig, Janis was particularly anxious about singing "Ball and Chain" with its composer present. From the stage, she enthusiastically acknowledged its author—since her folkie days, Janis always identified to audiences the originator of the songs she sang. Thornton apparently appreciated Janis's version and told a journalist, "That girl feels like I do." Big Mama respected the way Janis made a song her own, as Thornton herself was inclined to do: "When I do a song by Jimmy Reed or somebody," Thornton once said, "I have my own way of singing it. . . . I want to be me. I like to put myself into whatever I'm doing, so I can feel it." Janis saw herself as being part of a sisterhood of song: from her early influences Ma Rainey and Bessie Smith (both of whom influenced Thornton), to Odetta, Nina Simone, Etta James, Billie Holiday, and eventually Aretha Franklin and Tina Turner—all of whom she would praise onstage and in interviews.

While Janis's local fame was on the rise, her relationship with Joe McDonald had fractured. From the beginning, McDonald was attracted to her looks, sense of humor, and intellect, he said, but though they "seemed to get along very well on almost everything," they ran into problems over politics and LSD. Janis mostly abstained from taking acid, preferring drinking, while McDonald enjoyed tripping. His anti-war stance was all-consuming, and for the most part, Janis "wasn't into political trips at all," he explained. "She was suspicious of them. That was the one big thing we used to argue about." Like the Grateful Dead, Janis and Big Brother concentrated on their music rather than protesting the Vietnam War.

But perhaps the biggest problem with their relationship was their competitive egos, both "control freaks," as McDonald put it. When Janis and McDonald strolled the Haight, adoring fans often approached her, to Janis's obvious delight. During Big Brother gigs, she was treated like a goddess, mobbed after shows. McDonald may have chafed at the attention she got. Though Country Joe and the Fish had a strong following, theirs was nothing compared with Janis's. She was driven and ambitious, focusing hard on her music and career rather than catering to her "old man."

Janis and McDonald's arguments escalated until finally he packed his bags and moved back to Berkeley. Though McDonald recalled that "our careers began to take over, and we just didn't have time to be a couple anymore," Janis's friends remember her being deeply hurt by the split, her skyrocketing popularity offering no balm. "Joe dumped Janis," said her old Austin friend Jack "Jaxon" Jackson, who now worked for the Family Dog. "She was vulnerable, and it really fucked her head up." Janis was learning that the fame she coveted could not fulfill all her needs.

About a month after their breakup, Janis approached McDonald with a request. "She said, 'Before we get too far apart, would you do me a favor and write a song for me?'" he recalled. So he composed the ballad "Janis," with the lyrics "Even though I know that you and I could never find the kind of love we wanted together/alone I find myself missing you and I."

The tune lent itself to Janis's "pretty ballad voice," McDonald said, but Big Brother never played it because the song was too sweet and folky for their style. Though Janis didn't want to sing it, she placed the vinyl 45 recorded by Country Joe and the Fish into her scrapbook. The track also appeared on the band's second album, issued in late 1967, around the time McDonald remarried.

Janis poured her anguish over the broken relationship into her music, cowriting with the band the gut-wrenching "I Need a Man to Love." She varied her vocals on the song, beginning with a straightforward blues approach and gradually building into an emotional torrent, screaming, "this loneliness, baby, surrounding me!" Big Brother also collaborated on an exorcism of loneliness, "Catch Me Daddy," which kicked off with Janis's banshee vocals, a full-throttled scream that became a hard rock standard in the 1970s, via Joplin acolytes Robert Plant, Deep Purple's Ian Gillan, Aerosmith's Steven Tyler, and David Johansen (who glammed it up in the New York Dolls).

When not rehearsing or performing, Janis looked for distractions elsewhere, sometimes with Hells Angels and young male fans at the Avalon. One afternoon strolling the Haight with her dog, George, she met twenty-year-old San Francisco State College student Mark Braunstein, the son of influential Bay Area art dealer Ruth Braunstein. He organized free concerts in the Panhandle and worked at the Psychedelic Shop.

"We struck up a friendship, just chatting and talking," Braunstein recalled. Janis often visited him at work, where she bought candles, posters, and other exotica to decorate her apartment. Occasionally, the pair went to the movies, with Janis usually choosing foreign films, and loaned each other books; a Janis favorite was Thomas Hardy's tragic *Jude the Obscure*, its doomed protagonist surely resonating with her Saturday Night Swindle philosophy. Though Braunstein had a girlfriend, he and Janis eventually became casual lovers. "She just couldn't face being alone," he explained. Braunstein was later hired on to work with Big Brother's road crew.

>-I-<>-O-<>-I-<

Janis found more affirmation from film director Richard Lester, who asked Big Brother to appear in his new movie to be filmed in San Francisco. The Englishman—who directed the Beatles' *A Hard Day's Night* and *Help!*, as well as the black comedy *How I Won the War*, featuring John Lennon—cast Big Brother to appear in *Petulia*, starring Julie Christie, Richard Chamberlain, and George C. Scott. The drama examined issues such as spousal abuse and mental illness, against a flower power backdrop. Manager Julius Karpen, who obtained a $1,500 fee for the band, hired LA-based lawyer Bob Gordon to negotiate with Warner Bros.– Seven Arts to retain ownership of the Big Brother song used in the film. Gordon would become Janis's confidant and longtime attorney.

Janis relished the moviemaking experience, during which she learned how to make an impression on camera. Big Brother's scene in *Petulia* was filmed at the venerable Fairmont Hotel, where they performed during the movie's opening scene. "Richard Lester was trying to get a signature San Francisco vibe into his movie," Dave Getz explained. "He got the Grateful Dead playing at the Fillmore, and he got us playing at the Fairmont for all these rich people who supposedly hired a psychedelic hippie band for their big fund-raiser." In her scene onstage, clad in a short black dress and purple tights, Janis sings, shakes, and plays percussion on "Road Block," with the song sounding like "hill country church music," according to Sam Andrew. "Janis's voice is high, lonely, and haunting, with an inflection that sends chills up the spine." After her a cappella opener, Big Brother jumps in with a "rhythm and blues lick [reminiscent of] Louis Jordan's 'Rag Mop.' The song's style contrasted strangely with the dinner jackets and evening gowns who were dancing to it." Though *Petulia* was no blockbuster, it holds up well today and is a rare visual document of a prefame Big Brother performance on the cusp of the Summer of Love.

In May '67 Chet Helms and other hippie provocateurs and entrepreneurs held a press conference officially announcing and naming the impending "Summer of Love," predicting that some hundred thousand people would flock to San Francisco in June. Haight-Ashbury had exploded from a small community of like-minded freaks and heads coexisting with racially diverse residents, to a sea of runaways, homeless people, the mentally ill, and drug dealers. Like North Beach and the Beats, now the neighborhood had become a tourist attraction, with

Gray Line "Hippie Hop" buses crammed with gawking tourists navigating the congested streets. Such "Hippieland" jaunts were advertised as "the only foreign tour within the continental limits of the United States."

Almost as foreign to Haight residents, emissaries from Los Angeles came calling to beseech San Francisco bands to play their music festival planned for mid-June. Producer and record label executive Lou Adler and his partner John Phillips, founder of the Mamas and the Papas, hoped to enlist San Francisco bands for their Monterey International Pop Festival. The promoters offered to pay artists' expenses but no performance fees, with profits donated to various charities. Most San Franciscans saw this as an attempt to cash in on their scene. "It looked as if Hollywood wanted to tie up the San Francisco counterculture with a pretty pink ribbon and sell it to America," according to Sam Andrew.

After meeting with the promoters and their team, Grateful Dead co-manager Rock Scully reported, "We all [got] the same vibe.... [They're] here to exploit the San Francisco hippie/love phenomenon by building a festival around us and Janis and Country Joe and Quicksilver and the Airplane." Bay Area artists disdained the crassly commercial John Phillips–penned Scott McKenzie hit "San Francisco (Be Sure to Wear Flowers in Your Hair)." To vouch for their credibility, the promoters enlisted festival committee member Paul Simon, festival publicist and Beatles PR man Derek Taylor, and consultants Bill Graham and Ralph Gleason to convince the San Francisco bands to perform. Big Brother would be among thirty-three acts playing a total of five concerts over three days: seven San Francisco bands; LA pop stars like Phillips's group, board member Johnny Rivers, and the Association; folk rock stalwarts the Byrds and Buffalo Springfield; and numerous artists flying in from New York and London, including the then-obscure Jimi Hendrix Experience and a little-known UK band, the Who.

On June 16 Big Brother and its entourage—including Janis's dog, George, recently hit by a car—caravanned down the coast. The Monterey fairgrounds, where Janis had performed twice over the past four years, looked nothing like before. The "midway" ($1 admission for those without concert seats) resembled an exotic bazaar, filled with purveyors of posters, candles, crafts, clothing, and incense. Tickets for the recently refurbished seven-thousand-seat arena ranged in price from $3 for the bleachers to $6.50 for a folding chair in the orchestra section. Large areas were sectioned off for record executives, VIPs, and the media, to whom Taylor issued a thousand press passes. The festival brochure promised that "the matchless hi-fi sound system" ensured that "the sound carries well beyond the arena into the strolling area," with acclaimed engineer Wally Heider recording the performances.

Opening night featured primarily LA pop, plus Eric Burdon and the Animals and Simon and Garfunkel. On the twenty-four-acre fairgrounds, bands mingled with fans—some wearing hippie finery, others sporting short hair and crew necks—with late-night jams on makeshift stages at a nearby college camping area. Crowd estimates range from twenty-five to eighty thousand, as fans arrived over the course of the weekend to wander the fairgrounds. Owsley dispensed thousands of tabs of "Monterey Purple" LSD. "Those were real flower children," Janis later recounted wistfully. "They really were beautiful and gentle and completely open."

Big Brother played second on Saturday afternoon, deemed "Underground Day," and few in the audience knew the band. "Janis was so nervous, it was crazy," John Phillips remembered. "Backstage, Lou Rawls was telling her, 'It'll be fine. Don't worry about a thing.' She was rattling, just shaking. But then just as soon as she hit that stage, she just stomped her foot down and got real *Texas*."

After Chet Helms enthusiastically introduced the band, singling out Janis, she let loose a strong and confident "Down on Me," her vibrato immediately engaging the crowd. All those afternoon shows in Golden Gate Park had prepared her and the band for this moment. "Combination of the Two" opened with Janis's rhythmically scratching the guiro alongside Sam Andrew's guitar solo, followed by her joyful whoops as he sang his ode to San Francisco. Her soaring scatting sailed along between the verses; the audience remained riveted as James Gurley played an edgy solo to close the number before Janis's *"We're gonna sock it to ya!"* Big Brother immediately segued into the chaotic "Harry" and finished it before the audience could figure out what hit them. Peter Albin, doing the song introductions, signaled the start of "Road Block." Backed only by Dave Getz's drums, Janis's and Albin's voices blended well on the folky intro, "Trying to find my road." Then as the tempo picked up, Albin took over lead vocals, with Janis's call-and-response adding energy.

For their last number, Gurley let loose his long, twisted guitar lines to open the slow blues "Ball and Chain." Transported, as if singing to herself instead of thousands, Janis, eyes closed, softly intoned the opening lines, building gradually from her vulnerable alto, to soulful stuttering, to the cathartic climax's multitextured screams and howls. The audience was stunned. The crowd's intensity pushed Janis further, with the song's dynamics enhanced by her pauses followed by her wounded yowls. Fans leapt from their seats, ecstatically applauding her vocal acrobatics. Janis wrung every ounce of emotion out of the song, sliding effortlessly from bell-like vibrato to fervently testifying *"Tell me why!"* She stomped her foot in time with the words, ending the bloodbath with "I'm gonna love you till the day I die." While Janis softly sang the titular line, explosive applause drowned out the sound.

"It was as if the earth had opened up," Joel Selvin wrote twenty-five years later in his chronicle of the festival, *Monterey Pop*. "The audience was spellbound, startled at the crude power unleashed. . . . She was the first real hit of the festival, a taste of what everybody had come to see." Documentarian D. A. Pennebaker captured the reaction on film, by zooming in on Mama Cass Elliott's face, her awestruck expression and lips mouthing the word *Wow!* Janis "had everybody riveted," said Cass. "I'd heard from David Crosby about this girl from Texas who could sing her ass off. And I'd never seen anybody work without a bra before. She was sexy. It was an electrifying performance."

"When she came offstage, she was crying," John Phillips recalled. "She couldn't believe she'd gone over so well. It was such an emotional experience for her. Janis stole the show—she just *took* it!" Later, standing in the wings, she asked Butterfield Band keyboardist Mark Naftalin, "Do you think I'll make it?"

What Pennebaker and his camera crew did *not* capture was Janis and the band's actual performance. Adler and Phillips had hired the director of the cinema verité *Dont Look Back,* documenting Bob Dylan's 1965 UK tour, to make an ABC-TV *Movie of the Week* (for a $400,000 deal between the network and producers). The San Franciscans, still suspicious of being burned by LA "sharpies," had refused to sign the release form handed to them before they went onstage. Since the bands were performing gratis, their managers—Karpen, Scully and Danny Rifkin (the Dead), and Ron Polte (Quicksilver)—wouldn't allow them to be filmed without being paid or given creative control over the footage. But Pennebaker, a thirty-five-year-old New Yorker by way of Chicago, was determined to get Janis in his movie.

"She came out and sang, and my hair stood on end," he recounted. "We were told we weren't allowed to shoot it, but I knew if we didn't have Janis in the film, the film would be a wash. Afterward, I said to [Dylan's manager] Albert Grossman, 'Talk to her manager or break his leg or whatever you have to do, because we've got to have her in this film. I can't imagine this film without this woman who I just saw perform.'"

Backstage, Dave Getz overheard members of Grossman's clients the Paupers, who'd played the night before, saying, "Wow! Did you see Big Brother and the Holding Company?" John Phillips immediately approached Janis, telling her that she and the band could perform a second set on Sunday night if they agreed to sign the film contract. Janis spotted Grossman, whose clients Paul Butterfield and Mike Bloomfield's Electric Flag were also on the bill Saturday afternoon. She ran over to him and asked, "Should we allow ourselves to be filmed for the ABC movie?" The forty-one-year-old manager known for his shrewd deal making said simply, "Yes, I think you should."

Janis, who'd evolved from band newcomer to main attraction in one year, urged Big Brother to participate. But Julius Karpen absolutely refused to allow the group to sign without being paid or given creative control. Over several hours, Janis became more frantic and determined, pleading her case that such national exposure was much more important than a payment. Karpen refused to budge. Getz recalled: "All these meetings. Janis would talk to us, then she'd talk to Albert. Then we'd meet with Julius. It came down to a face-off between Janis and Julius. She said, 'We have to be in this movie, and if it means getting rid of Julius, so be it.'" The band finally agreed, and Karpen was forced to acquiesce.

Big Brother was scheduled to return to the stage on Sunday, the last evening of the festival. During that day's matinee, the buzz among the packed throngs remained focused on Janis's performance the day before. "I was in the front row, the press section," recounted the *Village Voice*'s Richard Goldstein, one of rock's pioneering critics. "[Journalist Robert] Christgau was sitting right next to me. When we saw her, we were knocked over. From the first notes, her voice stunned me with its primal drive. . . . I knew instantly that Janis would be a big star."

"The first big hit was Janis Joplin," Christgau reported in his Monterey coverage for *Esquire* magazine, "a good old girl from Port Arthur, Texas, who may be the best rock singer since Ray Charles, with a voice that is two-thirds Willie Mae Thornton and one-third Kitty Wells, and a fantastic stage presence. Her left nipple erect under her knit pantsuit looking hard enough to put out your eye as she rocked and stomped and threatened any moment to break the microphone, or swallow it. She got the only really big nonhype reaction of the weekend, based solely on her sweet, tough self."

Michael Lydon, a *Newsweek* reporter who'd been transferred from London to San Francisco, wrote: "In the bright sun of Saturday afternoon . . . came one of the most fantastic events of the whole shebang: the voice of Janis Joplin. . . . Janis leapt, bent double, and screwed up her plain face as she sang like a demonic angel. It was the blues big mama style, tough, raw, and gutsy. . . . The group behind her drove her and fed from her, building the total volume, a sound that has become a San Francisco trademark. The final number, 'Ball and Chain,' which had Janis singing (sing? talking, crying, moaning, howling) long solo sections, had the audience on their feet for the first time."

Record label execs also took notice, including Columbia's new president, Clive Davis. "Janis had no billing," he recalled. "It was just 'Big Brother and the Holding Company.' She was absolutely riveting and hypnotic and compelling and soul stirring in such a way that she clearly was representative of an epiphany that changed the rest of my life."

Janis's own favorite set of the weekend was Saturday night's climax: Otis Redding, reaching an audience that had not yet experienced his bracing, soulful sound. Since Janis had seen him at the Fillmore, he had successfully toured Europe, backed by the superb Stax/Volt Records house band Booker T. and the MG's, and the Mar-Keys horn section, both of whom accompanied him at Monterey. *"Shake!"* Otis, resplendent in a sharp green suit, demanded, and the audience leapt to its feet for the first time since "Ball and Chain." Following "Shake," Redding sang only four more songs, due to the late hour and a sound curfew, but each was potent: his composition "Respect" had just spent two weeks at number one for Aretha Franklin, the second from her Atlantic Records debut. Introducing "I've Been Loving You Too Long," Redding, who'd smoked a joint before going onstage, asked, "Y'all are the love crowd, right?" With horns blaring, Redding turned the Rolling Stones' "Satisfaction" into an R&B song. Janis swayed, standing on her folding chair next to Mark Braunstein, as Redding finished around one in the morning with a throbbing "Try a Little Tenderness." In his memoir *Living with the Dead*, Rock Scully gossiped that Janis made her way to Otis's motel room that night, but Peter Albin discounts the tale, certain that Janis would have boasted about such a conquest to her bandmates. Regardless, she once again absorbed the great singer's emotional punch and sexually charged showmanship, translating it into her own style of soul power.

Finally, Sunday evening, after a workmanlike set by New York's Blues Project, Big Brother returned to the stage, this time introduced by hip comedian Tommy Smothers, cohost of the CBS variety show *The Smothers Brothers*. Clad in flared leggings that matched the clingy white minidress with gold threads she'd worn on Saturday, Janis glowed in the lights. She lined her blue eyes with kohl and fluffed her hair out around her shoulders. She adorned herself with just a few strands of beads and a couple of buttons. The band was given half as much time as before, with Pennebaker requesting "Combination of the Two" and "Ball and Chain." Those who saw both shows declared the second inferior to the first, but, nevertheless, the film crew's cameras documented a powerful, life-changing performance.

"When you see what she does at Monterey when she sings 'Ball and Chain,'" Pennebaker related, "it was so amazing, yet so simple. I was onstage behind her watching her wiggle her butt, and she just took that song to the cleaners." Bob Neuwirth, working with Pennebaker that weekend, recalled, "Watching her perform was like watching a great violinist—it was the reaching for the notes that held the drama."

Still on camera, Janis skipped offstage, ebullient, hopping up and down when she reached the wings. Between sets, at one point, she sat on the stage edge with Pennebaker, chatting about the band's future. Soon after, she joined an under-the-stage jam session led by Jimi Hendrix that included Mama Cass, Brian Jones of the Rolling Stones, the Who's Roger Daltrey, and Eric Burdon. Singing "Sgt. Pepper's Lonely Hearts Club Band," the musicians were boisterous and loud. "We were making a lot of noise," Eric Burdon said, "and Bill Graham came down from the stage and said, 'Shut the fuck up! You're killing the other acts!'" Hendrix and the Who would play explosive sets that night, but most journalists and fans left with the name Janis Joplin on their lips.

Another breakthrough that weekend, Indian sitar maestro Ravi Shankar, was impressed too. "I felt her energy and her feeling of being tortured," he said, "and at the same time, her tremendous musicianship. Very, very strong." According to Lou Adler, "Otis Redding got their souls, and Ravi Shankar drove them out of their seats. Janis tore their hearts out."

CHAPTER 14

WOMAN ON THE VERGE

I just may be a "star" someday. You know, it's funny:
as it gets closer and more probable, being a star is
really losing its meaning. But whatever, I'm ready!

—JANIS JOPLIN

Janis was no longer just a local sensation poster girl for the exciting new music represented at Monterey. National and UK newspapers and magazines ran her photo alongside articles praising her voice. The Monday-morning headline in the *San Francisco Examiner* that accompanied Phil Elwood's coverage, "Dreams Come True in Monterey," seemed particularly appropriate. He called Janis "the real queen of the festival," who "repeated her triumph Saturday afternoon . . . in an encore performance last night." Most journalists lauded Janis while ignoring her bandmates, or at best, describing them as her backup musicians. The *Village Voice*'s Richard Goldstein referred to them as "sidemen" who "focused on Janis, cradling her with their riffs and coaxing her vocal flights." One of the most meaningful validations for Janis arrived on June 22, via a telegram from her parents: "Congratulations on being first page *Los Angeles Times* Monterey Festival report. Barbara's sending us a copy." The telegram was signed: "Your Port Arthur fan club." Also came word that the Joplins were planning a family trip to the city where their daughter had become a star.

As much as her bandmates relished their commercial breakthrough, they weren't eager to cede control of Big Brother to Janis and clung to the idea of the group as a democracy. But her position had changed almost overnight, with the group's attorney Bob Gordon noticing that "she was serious about her career. There was a lot of input from everybody in the band, but Janis was clearly the leader." Firmly established as Big Brother's focal point, she became the band's spokesperson—journalists primarily wanted to talk to her. When Peter Albin and James Gurley lost their status, low-level resentments began to escalate. As for Janis, her "entire personality attained an almost frightening intensity," is how Sam Andrew saw it. The fame she'd always wanted was at hand, and she knew it.

In the weeks following Monterey, Gordon and Julius Karpen began fielding calls from Clive Davis at Columbia Records, as well as scouts from Mercury and Atlantic Records. They were invited to attend Columbia's annual convention in Florida, where Davis made an initial low offer to sign the group. But Mainstream's Bob Shad remained unwilling to discuss selling the band's contract. Instead, to capitalize on the rapturous Monterey press, he quickly assembled and rushed out *Big Brother & the Holding Company*—again, with no input from the band. Today the album has a certain charm, with a folk rock sound and quirky songs showcasing Janis's fresh, self-assured vocals, the album's most obvious attribute. But the ten tracks recorded in August and December 1966 did not accurately convey the group's current music; the entire LP was shorter in length than just one of Big Brother's live jams.

The band members denounced the album immediately and refused to participate in any publicity efforts. They told a *Berkeley Barb* reporter they hoped it would flop so they'd be released from their Mainstream contract. Regardless, the LP debuted on the *Billboard* album chart on September 2, eventually reaching number 60, though band members received no royalty checks. Most reviews were lukewarm, noting that the recording did not sound like the live band. *Playboy* complimented Janis's "superb" vocals on "Bye, Bye Baby," "Women Is Losers," and "her own intense 'Intruder,'" but nonetheless called it "disappointing" and complained that she didn't sing lead on every track.

In July Janis's cousin Jean and her husband, visiting from LA, attended one of Big Brother's nonstop string of concerts, a double bill with sixteen-year-old singer-songwriter Janis Ian, whose controversial "Society's Child," about a biracial romance, was then a hit, although many radio stations banned it. Janis and the Bronx-born Ian, on her first West Coast tour, bonded and stayed in touch. "She was seven or eight years older than me," Ian recalled, "but it didn't matter. We both had bad skin, we both felt overweight. We were both outsiders." Afterward, Big Brother went to a "Come as a Hippie" party thrown by Gurley's sister-in-law. Big Brother dressed as straights, with Janis's relatives costumed as freaks—"a gas," Janis recalled.

By then, she hadn't written home in months. But her cousin's visit motivated her to send off a lengthy letter with enclosed clippings "that mark a real shift," she noted. "I do hope you remember me after all this while—what can I say? . . . Since Monterey, all this has come about. Gleason has been plugging us and has used me as a description for style (the inimitable Joplin style). . . . Now we're getting interviewed and my picture will be in *Esquire* and *Playboy* (not the center fold-out but something about the festival) and Julius (our manager) said some lady from *McCall's* called and might use me in an article about 'Young Women Breaking Down Barriers' or something like that. Oh, you saw the thing in *TIME*, but you didn't see *Newsweek*—it had a picture of me! I hope all this and my excitement doesn't seem shallow to you. It really thrills me. Wow, I met two of the Rolling Stones, most of the Animals . . . (and these are big groups—well respected and rich, baby), and they say I'm the best they've ever heard! E Gawd!! . . . Well, anyway I'm ecstatic!! . . . This band is my whole life now. It is to all of us. I really am totally committed and I dig it. I'm quite proud of myself because I'm really trying."

Janis openly embraced her ambition but also revealed her profound insecurity at her good fortune suddenly being taken away: "Before when I came out here, I just wanted to hang out & be wild & have a good time, but now that's all secondary (I still want to have a good time, you understand) but singing gives me so much satisfaction. Well, the recognition gives me a lot of satisfaction, too, I must admit. Well, to summarize, Big

Brother is doing great and I just may be a 'star' someday. You know, it's funny—as it gets closer and more probable, being a star is really losing its meaning. But whatever, I'm ready!"

Janis may have questioned the meaning of her celebrity because she already feared Seth Joplin's "Saturday Night Swindle"—leading to a letdown or unhappiness, or worse, a life-threatening development. Clearly, though, as illustrated by her name-dropping, Janis enjoyed the approbation of rock luminaries, including Jimi Hendrix. Just after Monterey, he had played six nights at the Fillmore, drawing ecstatic crowds. Big Brother performed on the bill the last night, on June 26. "The audience went nuts over him," Peter Albin recalled about Hendrix's erotically charged performance. Afterward, Janis reported to her bandmates that women waited in line to duck into the backstage bathroom for a quickie with Hendrix—but she declined to wait her turn. Still, rumors have persisted that Hendrix and Janis "got it on" backstage at the Fillmore, according to Hendrix biographer Charles Cross, whose research found that "neither principal ever directly confirmed this tryst."

Jimi and Janis did make a connection, whether sexually consummated or not. When Hendrix asked her advice about playing a free show on a flatbed truck in the Panhandle being organized by Mark Braunstein, Janis said, "Do it!," and Hendrix put on a concert that has since been counted among his best. Whenever their paths crossed, Janis and Jimi showed affection and respect for each other—their careers and lives seemed headed down parallel tracks.

She did not get along so well with another hot new artist: Jim Morrison. In July Janis met the Doors' lead singer when they played a weekend of shows at the Fillmore. The LA-based band's second single, "Light My Fire," had just become a pop smash, with Morrison being cast as a cross between a teen idol and Dionysius. Janis joined the band for dinner one night, and afterward, Morrison, his girlfriend Pamela Courson, Sam Andrew, and Dave Richards congregated at Janis's apartment. After hours of drinking, Morrison and Janis escaped to her boudoir; Courson fled in tears, and Andrew escorted her back to her hotel room. Later, Janis complained about Morrison's unresponsiveness in

bed and habit of slugging down booze the moment he woke up. A pair
of battling egos, Janis and Morrison's relationship was toxic from the
start and would only worsen.

>-←·→-○-←·→-←

In mid-August the Joplins—Seth and Dorothy; Laura, eighteen; and
fourteen-year-old Michael—arrived in San Francisco. Months earlier,
Janis had encouraged the trip, brimming with enthusiasm: "You'll just
love San Francisco, I know you will. Actually I've always hoped Laura
would try and go to college out here, so maybe she could see some of
the campuses while here. And of course I'll take you to one of the big
dances. . . . And you can see us perform! Oh, I'd really like for you to . . .
I have so many places to take you to and show you!" Yet Janis worried
to friends about making a good impression, particularly on her mother.

"We were the only teenagers who went to the Summer of Love
with their parents," Laura quipped later. On the day the Joplins arrived,
Big Brother had recently returned from an inaugural concert at Chet
Helms's new venue in Colorado, the Denver Dog. After playing the
previous night in Santa Clara, Janis arose very early on Sunday, August
13, to meet them. "She was giddy with excitement," Laura recalled in
Love, Janis, "proudly showing off the Haight-Ashbury scene and her
exalted status within it. We strolled the streets, with Janis pointing to
favorite head shops, dress shops . . . and the attire of interesting people
on the street. She couldn't stop sharing her excitement over [her favorite
Beatle George Harrison's] recent visit to the neighborhood, that he had
strolled the sidewalks right where we walked."

The previous week, on August 7, Harrison; his wife, Pattie; and
their entourage had spent the afternoon in the Haight with Pattie's sister Jenny Boyd, then living in San Francisco. Tripping on acid as they
strolled, they caught the attention of fans who wanted Harrison to sing.
"One minute there were five, then ten, twenty, thirty, and forty people
behind us," Pattie recounted. "It was horrible . . . ghastly drop-outs,
bums, and spotty youths, all out of their brains. Everybody looked
stoned—even mothers and babies—and they were so close behind us

they were treading on the backs of our heels. It got to the point where we couldn't stop for fear of being trampled. Then somebody said, 'Let's go to Hippie Hill! And we crossed the grass [of Golden Gate Park], our retinue facing us, as if we were onstage. They looked at us expectantly, as if George was some kind of Messiah.'"

The Joplin family's experience was not as harrowing as the Harrisons' but troubling in a different way. Janis invited them up to her apartment to meet the "family" she'd written them about: "George [and] . . . a new kitten, no name yet, gray with a little brown and white and very aggressive—when she's hungry she follows me around and shrieks at me. George takes really good care of her—licks her, carries her around in his mouth and she in turn eats only dog food and chews on his bones. It's a strange family, but it's mine."

To the Joplins, her apartment—adorned with swaths of silk, brocade, lace, Indian-print spreads, and Family Dog and Fillmore handbills—looked as exotic as *The Arabian Nights*. Janis's friends admired the way she had artfully decorated her home, but her parents were aghast. They stood silently before one wall she'd papered with multiples of her seminude poster, while Janis preempted any comment about her exposed nipple: "It hardly shows, Mother. . . . I'll give Mike one if you'll let him keep it." Unlike the female nude Janis had painted on her closet door as a teen, Dorothy could do nothing about this breach in propriety. She refused to let Mike—the same age Janis was when she first rebelled—take home any posters his big sister offered.

That night, Big Brother wasn't booked at the Avalon, but Janis arranged for them to play a few songs during Moby Grape's slot so that her family could see her onstage. In an earlier letter, she had tried sweetly, in vain, to convince her parents to "slightly alter your travel plans so you can . . . see us play somewhere. You see we work every weekend . . . and you can all come to a dance and wear beads and see us and see a light show and be proud of me." Trudging up the Avalon stairs, the Joplins were welcomed inside by Chet Helms, who "waived the admission charge," Laura recalled, while "Janis danced with glee, telling him we were her family. Entering the dance hall, the overpowering sounds and cruising bodies stunned me. . . . I felt like a stranger . . . set apart by my clothes and by not being stoned. . . . Big Brother performed a few tunes, working in synchronized fashion with the swirling lights. . . . I was awed by the whole experience, though the music was only a bit of it."

The other family member who commented publicly on Big Brother's Avalon performance that night was the understated Bach and Beethoven fan Seth Joplin, in a 1970 interview with *Rolling Stone* reporter Chet Flippo. "I couldn't imagine the volume of sound—truly incredible," he said. "But she was good. The band put on a special performance free for our benefit."

After Big Brother played, Mike, who recalled being "very excited," tried unsuccessfully to coax some pot smokers to share a joint with him backstage. With Janis sending a signal not to indulge him, "no one would relent to his pleading," said Laura, and the visiting family made a move toward the door. As Laura related later to filmmaker Amy Berg, "I remember overhearing one of my parents tell the other one, 'You know dear, I don't think we're going to have much influence anymore.'"

Outside on desolate Sutter Street, Janis saw her parents' negative reaction to the Avalon and took it as a personal rejection, as if their dislike of the experience meant they also disapproved of her and her status as the scene's reigning queen. She was a Joplin, capable of being as judgmental about her parents as they were of her. From this moment forth, just as she was separating from being "one of the boys" in Big Brother, she began to withdraw from her family. Janis would look to her increasing fan base, an expanding circle of friends, and various numbing agents—alcohol and eventually heroin—to anesthetize herself from the pain of having lost that connection. Though she called home occasionally, she would not write the Joplins for some five months—and her family never visited her in San Francisco again.

>─┤◄►─○─◄►┤─◄

Soon after, Janis added to her Lyon Street family: Linda Gravenites, the estranged wife of Big Brother's Chicago friend Nick Gravenites, had moved to San Francisco in 1959. Like Dorothy Joplin, Linda was an excellent seamstress, and she designed and made costumes for the improv group the Committee. Janis commissioned an ensemble for the band's upcoming performance at the Monterey Jazz Festival. A statuesque brunette who'd briefly been a North Beach topless dancer, Gravenites had seen numerous Big Brother gigs but didn't click initially with Janis, finding her "unapproachable," she recalled. "I felt like she would bite my head off—she scared me."

Now the pair clicked, particularly when Janis discovered that Linda's first husband was North Beach denizen Patrick Cassidy, a fond fling of Janis's back in 1964. "She said, 'Oh, how wonderful! One of my mythic men!'" Gravenites recounted. "That connection was really why she got interested in knowing who I was, and we became friends." Linda, four years older than Janis, had been housesitting at 710 Ashbury for the touring Dead, and after their return, Janis invited her to crash on her couch while she finished the outfit for Monterey. Gravenites's position as Janis's roommate and helpmate became "official" when one day Janis "was looking around at the dirty dishes and said, 'I need a mother,' and I said, 'I can do that,'" Linda recalled. "I could take care of the things she didn't want to—or didn't think about." The timing couldn't have been better. Janis needed a replacement for the always energetic and organized Dorothy Joplin, as well as a support system and a voice of reason. Over the next few years, Gravenites was much more than Janis's costume designer, surrogate mom, and roommate; she was her closest companion, who would always voice her opinion whether Janis wanted to hear it or not.

Gravenites, to her surprise, discovered that Janis kept an organized house, carefully maintaining a budget—definitely a trait learned from her mother. Paying $75-a-month rent, "she knew exactly to the penny" her expenses, Linda noted, and where her $100 weekly salary was spent. At home, Janis read constantly, and that fall, she couldn't put down *Ecstasy and Me: My Life as a Woman*, a ghostwritten memoir from the misunderstood actress Hedy Lamarr. The Austrian sex symbol never got the credit she deserved for her intellect (in the 1940s, as part of the U.S. war effort, she helped invent a radio guidance system that led the way to Wi-Fi and Bluetooth), a problem that hit home for Janis, whose wild-woman persona overshadowed the fact that she had a keen mind. A voracious reader, Janis always traveled with books; Gravenites eventually designed and made a gorgeous beaded bag for Janis to carry everything from bestsellers such as Ira Levin's *Rosemary's Baby*, to favorite novels by Thomas Wolfe and F. Scott Fitzgerald, to nonfiction, including a collection of Fitzgerald's letters and Nancy Mitford's biography of his wife, Zelda.

Linda Gravenites had many male friends, one of whom, charismatic Milan Melvin, became Janis's latest lover. Tall and lanky, with long black hair, he sold ads for radio station KMPX and hung out with members of the Committee. No one knew it then, but as a Berkeley student from 1960 to 1964, Melvin had been a paid FBI informant, infiltrating Communist and student activist groups. Eventually he quit informing and attempted to disappear in the Nevada desert, where he discovered the Red Dog Saloon and adopted the cosmic cowboy look of Stetson, boots, Western shirt, and turquoise jewelry. A bit of a hustler, but no Peter de Blanc, he had moved into Committee member (and future screenwriter of *Jaws*) Carl Gottlieb's apartment, where he and Janis connected.

"The first thing that attracted me to Janis was her laugh," Melvin recounted. "Only bad girls threw their heads back and belted out a laugh like that. I remember Janis and me coming together like crazed wildcats in heat, just kicking and clawing and biting and scratching and making love . . . until we were near dead and then getting up and taking some more drugs and then doing it again." Melvin was among the few with whom Janis dropped acid.

When not performing, Janis prowled the Haight with Linda, often accompanied by Sunshine and Suzy Perry, guzzling beer and flirting with passersby. "Four Capricorn ladies getting louder by the minute," Gravenites recalled. "People would just sort of part as we came down the street with our paper bags of Rainier Ale." Sometimes they ventured to North Beach, teasing the longshoremen and playing eight-ball at the Gino & Carlo pool hall. Janis usually won.

Her new circle of friends also included Philadelphia-born artist Robert Crumb, whom she met through her Austin pal Gilbert Shelton, both now leading lights of the underground comics scene then under way in San Francisco. Janis "liked me and S. Clay Wilson and these other cartoonists," recalled Crumb, a shy and awkward man who was the creator of *Mr. Natural* and, along with Wilson and Shelton, contributed regularly to *Zap Comix*. Janis, seeing in Crumb her erstwhile, geeky visual-arts self, was drawn to the talented artist and blues fan. She could be herself around them: kick back, drink, laugh, and flirt. "I even made out with her once," recalled Crumb, who was admittedly stunned by Janis and "this group of . . . loudmouthed, hard-drinking hippie-Okie girls, kind of tough and rough, kind of intimidating." If she were in town and got a call from Crumb, she'd head right over "with these girlfriends of hers," said Crumb. "They were tanked up, they were wild, they were game for anything." Becoming famous for the lewd, big-bottomed, braless women he drew, Crumb seemed inspired by Janis and her pals, who would "jack . . . me around for a couple of hours," he said. "They were the ultimate, hippest, coolest girls around."

According to Linda's estranged husband, Nick Gravenites, "I called them the 'Capricorn women'—wild and crazy, loud, hard-drinking, liberated women! They'd go out and raise hell, cussed like lumberjacks. Nobody could keep up with them."

Meanwhile, the remaining camaraderie between Big Brother and manager Julius Karpen frayed further after Monterey. Janis had not forgiven him for his dogged opposition to their being filmed by Pennebaker, and she began to think that Karpen, a heavy pot smoker, was too much of a hippie to handle their affairs properly. She wanted national stardom, and he seemed out of his league in pursuing that goal. He often nagged Janis about her drinking, which further annoyed her. The band all agreed there was a problem when he wouldn't allow them to see his accounting ledger or report how much money they had earned. Instead of increasing their salaries, Gurley recalled, "He said we needed to accumulate a good stash to cover band expenses. We'd say, 'How much money is in there, Julius?' And he'd say, 'I don't know,' and we just never got anywhere with him." Peter Albin reported to

Big Brother that his uncle Henry, a shrewd businessman, told him they "deserved to be robbed blind" if they didn't insist on inspecting their manager's ledger.

The breaking point came in mid-September 1967, when Bill Graham booked Big Brother to open at the prestigious Hollywood Bowl for the marquee event "Bill Graham Presents the San Francisco Scene," starring Jefferson Airplane and the Grateful Dead. Since it was scheduled the night before their set at the Monterey Jazz Festival, Graham offered to charter a plane for the band members. Posters and advertisements listed Big Brother, but, at the last minute, Karpen wouldn't sign the contract because Graham gave them only twenty minutes onstage. When the promoter offered to increase their fee to compensate for the short set, Karpen refused. Graham then contacted Albin and got him to sign the contract, but Karpen, incensed, demanded they not play. Big Brother "backed out without notice," *Los Angeles Times* music columnist Pete Johnson noted in his coverage of the Hollywood Bowl concert.

Janis was livid over the missed opportunity, but she became even angrier over a later incident involving Karpen at the Monterey Jazz Festival on September 16. Big Brother was included in the Saturday afternoon "Big Blues Bag" segment, along with B. B. King, influential Texas guitarist T-Bone Walker, and gospel greats the Clara Ward Singers. Legendary Columbia Records A&R man John Hammond—who signed Billie Holiday and Bob Dylan—invited Janis to join him in his box seats when not onstage.

The audience, a mix of black and white jazz and blues fans, was more sedate than the Pop Fest crowd three months earlier. Janis had taken up cigarettes again and smoked nervously until it was time for Big Brother to hit the stage. "She was scared silly," according to Ralph Gleason, who booked them at the jazz fest. "I think she was scared silly every time she went onstage."

As he wrote later, "There she was, this freaky-looking white kid from Texas onstage with all the hierarchy of the traditional blues world, facing an audience that was steeped in blues tradition, which was older than her ordinary audience and which had a built-in tendency to regard electric music as the enemy. The first thing she did was to say, *'shit,'* and that endeared her right away. Then she stomped her foot and shook her hair and started to scream. They held still for a couple of seconds, but here and there in the great sunlit arena, longhairs started getting up and out into the aisles and stomping along with the band. By the end of the first number, the . . . arena was packed with people writhing and twisting and snaking along. . . . It was an incredible sight. Nothing like it had ever happened before in the festival's ten years. . . . It was Janis's day, no doubt about it. . . . . Old and young, long hair or short, black or white, they reacted like somebody had stuck a hot wire in their ass."

After the set, Janis asked Gleason about the cameramen capturing the proceedings for a San Francisco TV special. " 'Did you film it?' she asked, quivering, when she got offstage," Gleason recalled. "I had to tell her no. She was disappointed. She knew what it had been. And God knows, the world has less than it might have because we couldn't film that incredible performance. . . . [But] Janis's manager at the time, in a burst of paranoia still to be equaled, had refused to okay our filming of Janis's performance."

Enraged, Janis demanded the band fire Karpen. Back in San Francisco, when Big Brother again asked to see the books, he still refused. As it turned out, he'd kept piles of receipts rather than maintain any kind of professional ledger. The band and Karpen agreed to part ways six weeks later.

Adding to the tension, Janis's bandmates got a nasty review in the influential underground paper *Los Angeles Free Press* following their six-night run at the Golden Bear club in Huntington Beach. In "Janis Joplin Too Full of Soul for Holding Company Partners," Larry Kopp singled out Janis for her talent, writing that she had "the guts of Ma Rainey and Bessie Smith, with the control and precision of Nancy Wilson or Billie Holiday and with a style that makes James Brown look like the Ziegfeld Follies." In contrast, Kopp complained that Big Brother "doesn't come up to her level" and then dissected each instrumentalist's foibles. He observed that Janis "starts out as if she is playing a game, making drug references, pointing the index finger of each hand upward like Betty

Boop, making cute expressions that don't seem to have any relation to the music. Her style looks put on until something clicks and . . . her hands find the beat and . . . she becomes her music." The review confirmed Janis's worst fears about her bandmates: they weren't up to her talent.

The Huntington Beach run was fraught for other reasons, too. Because Big Mama Thornton opened for Big Brother, Janis felt guilty being the headliner and also worried that she would "look terrible next to her," according to Karpen. She drank more than usual, to the point that Thornton, herself an alcoholic, told Janis backstage, "Honey, you better stop drinking. It'll kill your voice."

Then one night after a show, Janis's life took an ugly turn that would lead to the worst possible Saturday Night Swindle: James Gurley turned her on to heroin. Certainly the same burdens that escalated her drinking contributed to her shooting up with Gurley: the high-wire pressures of her now-explosive career, the painful distance from her parents, and Big Brother's growing jealousy of her star power. "When I discovered [the heroin use], it really brought me down," Karpen later told writer Joel Selvin. "Janis was already into alcohol problems, but this seemed major."

When Janis confessed to Linda Gravenites that she had shot up smack, her roommate urged her to stay away from it. But Janis had stumbled onto a blanket of numbness that she would soon crave again. Better than anything else, heroin briefly cured her loneliness, anxiety, insecurity, and sense of dislocation—all in one shot. Gurley, who idolized junkies such as legendary jazz saxophonists John Coltrane and Charlie Parker, neither of whom lived past forty, later shrugged off his own heroin use as a "new world to explore . . . more of an adventure thing." He claimed its usefulness as a tool "that would cool you out . . . trying to burn off the energy. To knock you down so you could go to sleep. We'd be so tanked up after the show with adrenaline. I would never be able to go to sleep till past dawn." Just as Janis had jumped back into shooting speed with Nancy Gurley the previous year, she now followed James, who had been dabbling with heroin for a while.

Soon after, Janis shot heroin again, according to Linda Gravenites, with Paul Whaley, the twenty-one-year-old blond-haired drummer for Blue Cheer—named for a brand of LSD and managed by Gut, a former Hells Angel. Janis sometimes stayed at the hard rock trio's communal house in Marin. Blue Cheer guitarist Leigh Stephens remembered her and Whaley once finding a scorpion and, as a prank, placing it next to Stephens's toothbrush. Heroin and playing around with "cute young boys," said Gravenites, helped Janis deal with her life's mounting pressures.

The Haight had veered out of control with noise, crime, and drugs, and the police started cracking down. In October Big Brother was nearly busted for disturbing the peace while performing at the Matrix. The club was shuttered briefly because of neighborhood noise complaints. The narcotics squad raided the Grateful Dead's house at 710 Ashbury. Though police uncovered only a bit of cannabis, they arrested employees, friends, and two band members, Pigpen and Bob Weir, neither of whom smoked pot. On October 6 the Diggers staged a "Death of Hippie" parade that ended at the Psychedelic Shop, where afterward owners Jay and Ron Thelin gave away all the merchandise and closed the store. For Janis, it hurt to watch the destruction and loss of her formerly beautiful community—another reason to get numb.

In November the most famous rock manager in America, Albert Grossman, arrived in San Francisco from New York to meet with Big Brother. Before contacting him, the band had heatedly discussed management possibilities among themselves and with friends. They had even approached Bill Graham about handling them, but the promoter nixed the idea. "[Janis] needed somebody to really lock into her career and her life," he reflected later. "I wasn't qualified to manage Janis. . . . I remember saying if they wanted somebody of strength, they should go with Albert." Karpen claimed later that *he'd* recommended they hire Grossman and called his office to set up a meeting.

Linda Gravenites also knew Grossman through Nick and other Chicago musicians. When Janis asked her opinion whether they should go outside the San Francisco bubble and sign with him, Gravenites told her bluntly, "If you want to just keep playing around here, no. If you want to become an international star, *absolutely*." With intermediary Bob Gordon, who'd previously done legal work for Grossman, they made the call to New York.

The arbiter of hip, Albert Grossman was known for his excellent taste, shrewd negotiating skills, and inscrutability. Born in 1926 in Chicago, he got his start in show business by cofounding the Gate of Horn club, and then moved into management, handling folk artists Bob Gibson and Janis's early inspiration, Odetta. In 1959 he collaborated with jazz impresario George Wein on the first Newport Folk Festival, after which he moved to New York in 1961. He put together the trio Peter, Paul and Mary, with whom he enjoyed his first big commercial success. He signed Bob Dylan just after his 1962 Columbia Records debut, with the two becoming nearly inseparable—Grossman, looking like a cross between Benjamin Franklin and a wise old owl, a father figure to Dylan, his scruffy and brilliant young upstart. At the negotiating table, Grossman's impenetrability worked in his favor, his opponents often scrambling to offer better terms in response to his frequent silences. Among many other achievements, Grossman was the first music manager to insist his client be referred to in contracts as "Artist"—rather than "Act" or "Entertainer"—which today is an industry standard.

By late 1967, Grossman had accumulated a stable of artists hailing from Chicago, New York, and Canada. He had not yet seen a San Francisco act that interested him—until he saw Janis at Monterey. When they convened at her Lyon Street apartment in November, the reserved Grossman's cool demeanor unsettled the band. He didn't say much but asked them questions and listened intently. The only topic that seemed to arouse emotion in him was heroin. His client Michael Bloomfield, among others, had started using smack, and Grossman's first wife had been a junkie. A requirement of working with him, he told Big Brother, was "no *schmeeze*." Recognizing the old-school term for the drug, they all nodded their heads in agreement.

"He was a very intimidating, strange guy," recalled Dave Getz, down to the way he held his cigarette between his little finger and his ring finger. "He didn't say a lot, but he was big, and he had a lot of presence and charisma. We were, of course, intimidated by the fact that he was Bob Dylan's manager. Bob Dylan was like a god to most of us—beyond human." Tacked to Janis's wall, in fact, was a large black-and-white poster of a saluting Bob Dylan.

Also at the meeting was attorney Bob Gordon, still serving as Big Brother's lawyer. Their prospective new manager demanded 20 percent of his clients' earnings, rather than the typical 15 percent. When asked about the higher percentage, Grossman responded with a challenge: If he couldn't make them $100,000 the first year, they could tear up the contract and not owe him a penny. It was a huge sum for a band that, according to Dave Getz, made barely $25,000 that year.

After they signed the paperwork on November 11, Grossman began putting their finances in order. As with his other clients, he set up a Big Brother publishing company, with Bob Gordon as secretary and each band member designated an officer and receiving shares of stock. This was so they could earn more from their songwriting. He also retrieved the receipts from Karpen so that his accountant could organize their business records. And he began negotiating with Clive Davis to pony up enough money to release Big Brother from its Mainstream contract and sign the group to Columbia. Meanwhile, band members' salaries were doubled to $200 a week.

Back in New York, Grossman hired the band's first road manager, John Byrne Cooke, a twenty-five-year-old folk musician, Harvard graduate, and the son of British-born journalist and broadcaster Alistair Cooke. Cooke was referred by his former roommate and Dylan confidant Bob Neuwirth, who had turned down the gig. An aspiring filmmaker, Cooke had worked for Pennebaker at Monterey and witnessed Big Brother's breakthrough. Though a novice at road managing, the New Yorker had tired of Cambridge and was game for something new. Cooke's $150 weekly salary would come from Big Brother's performance fees, with the Grossman office setting up West Coast bookings and an upcoming East Coast–Midwest tour beginning in February 1968. Before venturing west, Cooke asked Neuwirth for insight into his newfound profession. "Don't carry their guitars or do beer or cigarette runs," Neuwirth advised. "Keep it businesslike: you're the road *manager*, not the roadie. And don't make friends with them, or you won't be able to tell them what to do." The well-bred Cooke's authoritative manner made him the perfect candidate for the job.

During their first meeting at the band's rehearsal space on December 1, Cooke appeared the complete opposite of the hippie road crews to which they were accustomed. At six foot one, with short dark hair and a neat mustache, he dressed like the Ivy Leaguer he was. He was a "connoisseur, a raconteur, and quite a good photographer," according to his former flame and longtime friend singer Judy Collins. After Janis asked Cooke his astrological sign (Libra), she replied dismissively, "I don't care much about Libras one way or the other." Still, his chiseled good looks appealed to her, and she confided later to Getz she thought he was cute.

In December Big Brother traveled back and forth to Los Angeles, beginning with a performance at the Cheetah Club, followed by several bookings at the famed Whisky a Go Go on the Sunset Strip in West Hollywood. The packed opening night at the Whisky didn't go as well as the band had hoped: Sam Andrew broke a string and played out of tune, and Janis drank too much Southern Comfort. But they still managed to "permanently alter . . . the emotional atmosphere of the city," according to Ron Koslow in the tip sheet *KYA Beat*. "We won't be the same until Janis and her voice come back to us. She's a cross between Bessie Smith, Joan of Arc, and a Bengal tiger, a very, very beautiful animal who all at once makes you want to laugh and cry and shriek with terror."

›‹•›‹•›‹•›‹

For the first time in sixteen months. Janis flew home to Port Arthur around the holidays. Her family welcomed her back, and longtime friends Adrian and Gloria Haston threw a party in her honor. Janis was thrilled to see the old gang, who were so proud of her success. Things hadn't changed much in Port Arthur, though: dressed in her freaky finery, she stopped into a convenience store to buy cigarettes and was jeered at by the clerk.

Janis "flew into the guy," according to Gloria, "but she didn't come back and cry about it. There was a great deal of brashness and bravado."

She handed out copies of Big Brother 45s, and showered her family with Christmas gifts. Sitting on the Joplin coffee table were numerous magazines featuring Janis, including a copy of *Look,* with a full-page portrait of Big Brother and the Dead shot by famed photographer Irving Penn. A color insert from the *San Francisco Examiner* featured Janis modeling a yellow poncho—her dog, George, at her feet—alongside other Bay Area women clad in ensembles by an up-and-coming San Francisco designer. Dorothy had notified the *Port Arthur News* about the triumphant return of her daughter, and reporter Leonard Duckett spent an afternoon with the family interviewing Janis about her career. A photograph of a rather shell-shocked-looking Dorothy and Seth, with a beaming Janis, Mike, and Laura, accompanied the article, "Janis Joplin Drawing Acclaim, Blues Singer with Soul," in which he described her as wearing "her hair long and wild, hippie fashion, and her clothes too fall in the style of what she wears when performing . . . long strings of beads, and rings, rings, rings."

"I don't want to do anything outside the band," Janis assured Duckett. "I've had a few offers to leave, but this is what I want to do. The band is making money. That's what it's all about, isn't it?" Duckett ended his story noting that "by now, Janis Joplin is back in San Francisco, doing the music she loves." What Duckett couldn't have known was that she had left behind Port Arthur and the Joplins for good. She would visit again, but she had moved far beyond their influence; her comment about finances may have been a way to send that message. While her parents were proud of her success, they disapproved of her life—and Janis knew it. The more provocative remarks and insults about Texas she uttered to the press, the angrier they'd become. But she had discovered a new family of admirers who would shower her with the approval and advice she needed. Between Albert Grossman and Linda Gravenites, she may well have felt she'd found stand-ins for Seth and Dorothy Joplin.

>→·→·○·←·←<

Back in Los Angeles for another Whisky residency, Janis got more of the star treatment. Her now dear friend Peter Tork hosted a party for Big Brother at his Laurel Canyon estate, where "everyone was wearing bright Indian clothing and crashing on a floor filled with pillows and hashish pipes," according to Janis Ian, also a guest. "There were dozens of naked people lolling around; I shrugged it off, trying to look cool."

Big Brother had purchased an equipment truck for Dave Richards and roadie Mark Braunstein. Both would join them on the upcoming East Coast tour. Band and crew stayed at the low-budget, seedy Hollywood Sunset Motel, but John Cooke made it clear that in the future they would choose better lodgings.

Big Brother saw vividly what pop stardom could bring when invited to the Bel Air mansion of John and Michelle Phillips. With Mamas and Papas hits and songwriting royalties, the couple could afford an estate previously owned by the 1930s silver screen star Jeanette MacDonald, complete with roaming peacocks. "John was totally hosting us like stars," Dave Getz recounted, "getting us high, showing us around. It was that kind of moment where we felt like we'd arrived in LA at the top echelon. We were being stroked by everyone."

In the screening room, the group gathered to watch Pennebaker's rough cut of the Monterey Pop Festival. When shown footage of Jimi Hendrix humping his amp and lighting his guitar on fire, ABC had nixed the *Movie of the Week* plan and given Lou Adler and Phillips the rights to the film. The producers then made a distribution deal for a theatrical release of the movie for 1968, which would feature Janis's face in ads and Big Brother's "Combination of the Two" as the title track.

John Cooke had "seen much of the footage, but not the edited film," he recalled, though Big Brother had not yet viewed anything. He noticed Janis's eyes grow wide as the film revealed Big Brother's performance of "Ball and Chain." Though the segment opens with frames of Getz playing drums, followed by Albin on bass, the cameras then fix on Janis—and that's where most of the footage remains. Gurley's long guitar break was edited out. The film captures powerfully Janis's magnificent performance and vocal talent, while her band fades into the background. When Janis saw the close-up of the rapt Mama Cass watching her onstage with amazement, she exclaimed, "Far out! How did he get that shot?"

The band, understandably, was not pleased by the camera's focus on Janis. "It wasn't the *group* everyone wanted," Getz said. "It was Janis. We assumed we'd appear in the movie as a band, but seeing it was a shock. It was all Janis. They saw her as a superstar in the making. I realized that though we were finally going to be making money and go to another level, it also meant our little family was being separated—there was Janis, and there was the band."

Big Brother's epiphany in that screening room marked the beginning of the band's real success—and also the band's end.

CHAPTER 15

"ROCK STAR BORN ON SECOND AVENUE"

*What we've had to do is learn how to control
success, put it in perspective, and not lose the
essence of what we're doing: the music.*

—JANIS JOPLIN

Working with the most famous music manager in America and about to sign with the world's top record label brought Janis as much anxiety as it did joy. Could she live up to the promise she engendered and the accolades she received? Could she do so while tethered to less-talented musicians whom she still loved like brothers? As her position of power within the band had increased, the family of equals started to come apart. With a new record to cut and an East Coast tour looming, Janis intended to work harder than ever. One of her most beloved bandmates and, perhaps not coincidentally, the man who introduced her to heroin—James Gurley—did not share this determination.

Before leaving for New York City in February, the group added new material to its repertoire. Jefferson Airplane's bassist, Jack Casady, an avid R&B fan, brought Big Brother a song that would be its commercial breakthrough. "Piece of My Heart," written by Jerry Ragovoy and Bert Berns, had been recorded by Erma Franklin, sister of Aretha. Under the radar on pop radio, it had just debuted on the R&B chart in November, rising to number ten. When Casady heard Franklin's record, slow and jazzy vocals backed primarily by keyboards and sax, he imagined Janis's voice on the wrenching ballad.

"Erma's an alto, not a soprano like Aretha, so she had a much huskier vocal presentation," Casady observed. "Peter Albin came over to visit, and we'd listen to records, and I'd show him stuff on the bass. I said, 'This would be a perfect song for Janis.' I played it for him and gave him the 45, and he took it to Janis. It was perfect for her kind of excitement and adrenaline."

"We 'Big Brotherized' it," Dave Getz said about the band's reconstruction of the song. Andrew crafted a jagged opening guitar line, with Janis's beseeching *"Come on! Come on!"* segueing into her plea "Didn't I make you feel . . ." The band doubled the song's two-and-a-half-minute length via Andrew's guitar-skronk solos. "Piece of My Heart" showcased Janis's spectacular vocal range and diverse textures, including "her stuttering repetition of words and phrases, the shotgun rat-a-tat-tat delivery of a line," and her ability to suddenly soar to a "screaming tessitura," wrote Bowdoin College professor Tracy McMullen in an academic study of the song.

A line Janis "Otisized"—*"Never, never, never, never, never, never* hear me when I cry at night, babe / and I cry all the time!"—took on special meaning for Janis, grieving the tragic death of Otis Redding and several bandmates on December 10, when their twin-engine Beechcraft crashed into a Wisconsin lake on the way to Madison for a show. She and Sam Andrew held their own private memorial, playing Redding's records all night at Janis's apartment.

Adding to her emotional distress, Janis discovered she was pregnant. According to Linda Gravenites, Janis considered having the baby, whose father was probably "that drummer from Blue Cheer," Paul Whaley, who had already moved on. But with her career ascending and her personal life in flux, Janis made the decision to terminate the pregnancy, though she felt "lousy about it," Gravenites recalled. In 1967, six years before the *Roe v. Wade* Supreme Court decision, abortion was widely illegal in the United States. It had been legalized in California, but solely for extreme cases: women who'd been victims of rape or incest, or whose lives were endangered by pregnancy. Mexico became Janis's alternative—a dangerous one, it turned out—and she planned a trip for the procedure following a run of shows in LA.

Big Brother had gotten off to a rocky start with its patrician road manager, John Cooke, whose aloof attitude and bossiness irritated the band. After complaining to Albert Grossman, the band met with Cooke to discuss their "difference in lifestyles," Cooke recounted. "I said, 'Look, man, if you want somebody whose hair is as long as yours and who just hangs around and smokes dope all the time and carries the guitar cases, we can hire somebody to do that for thirty or forty dollars a week. But I have to have a certain degree of autonomy. I can't just be hanging out. Let's try this a little longer.'" Cooke would eventually bond with the group—though he'd be nicknamed the "road Nazi"—and work with Janis for much of the next three years.

Grossman was deep in negotiations with Mainstream's Bob Shad and Columbia's Clive Davis over Big Brother's contract. Davis eventually agreed to Shad's demand for $200,000 to release the band (half of which Columbia would recoup from Big Brother's royalties); Shad would receive a 2 percent royalty from the group's first two Columbia albums. Davis offered a $50,000 advance to cover the costs of its first LP for the label. At the time, most San Francisco bands were signing for a total of $20,000 to $50,000. In order to land Janis and Big Brother, "Columbia was putting up a quarter of a million dollars—a fortune back then—with 40 percent of that money a straight [nonrecoupable] expense," Davis would write (with Anthony DeCurtis) in his autobiography. "I clearly knew this was an aggressive move, and possibly unprecedented in the talent marketplace, but on the rare occasion when you're dealing with an extraordinary—if not, historic—artist, then you have to be bold." He expected a bestselling debut album and agreed to Grossman's choice of producer, John Simon.

Born in 1941, the son of a doctor who founded Connecticut's Norwalk Symphony Orchestra, Simon was an accomplished keyboardist with perfect pitch. After attending Princeton, he trained at Columbia Records as a staff producer, scoring a pop hit in 1966 with the Paul Simon–penned "Red Rubber Ball" by the Cyrkle. John Simon's diverse early production work included the debut albums by Leonard Cohen (the stark, seismic *Songs of Leonard Cohen*) and Blood, Sweat and Tears (the horn-drenched jazz-blues-rockish *Child Is Father to the Man*). Grossman hired Simon to produce demos for the Band, which led to their being signed to Capitol Records. He was working on the Band's debut, *Music from Big Pink,* when he first met Big Brother at Golden State Recorders in San Francisco. Not a fan of psychedelic music, Simon immediately nixed Sam Andrew's suggestion they work up a "freak-rock" version of "The Star Spangled Banner" (which, of course, Jimi Hendrix famously would do in 1969). Simon was "mincing," according to Andrew. "He was disapproving of everything . . . like we were supposed to feel privileged that he had come from the East to clean up this rough Western product. You couldn't have chosen someone more unlike Big Brother."

As the stakes for the band rose, James Gurley continued his decline, drinking heavily and using heroin and downers. He had lost his primacy, and after having witnessed Jimi Hendrix's prowess, he felt insecure. Andrew took over much of the lead guitar work and contributed new material such as "Flower in the Sun" and "Farewell Song," while Gurley's creativity shriveled. Meanwhile, the media focus on Janis intensified. "James suffered the most as she ascended," Dave Getz observed. "He pulled back and started self-destructing, getting really fucked up, almost dysfunctional."

In mid-January 1968 an incapacitated Gurley nearly fell off stage at the Golden Bear while Grossman, visiting from New York, watched. Afterward, their new manager called an impromptu Big Brother meeting—without Gurley—and suggested they replace the guitarist and give him $10,000 and a six-month leave to clean up. The band immediately vetoed the idea, with cries of "We're a band! He's an important member! We can't do this without him!" The others never confronted Gurley, according to Getz. "Everybody tried to avoid it, deny it, look the other way."

Janis and Sam Andrew were dabbling in heroin, too, like "dilettantes," said Andrew, but keeping it hidden and after hours. "We took heroin because we thought you were supposed to—that's what Charlie

Parker did, all these greats," he recounted. "It had this mystique like the Holy Communion about it. . . . It's like a warm bath on the inside." Janis had devoured *Lady Sings the Blues*, Billie Holiday's 1956 autobiography, which detailed the addiction that would contribute to the singer's death three years later at the age of forty-four. According to Linda Gravenites, Janis romanticized shooting smack, seeing it as a mark of authenticity— as if it took a hole in her arm to express a hole in her soul.

Janis spent her twenty-fifth birthday onstage at the Kaleidoscope club in Los Angeles and was feted by her entourage. Cooke arranged for champagne and birthday cake, and the club owners covered the stage in three dozen red roses. Four dozen more arrived from the band and friends, including Peter Tork. She was thrilled.

Soon after, Janis sneaked away to Mexico for her abortion. She returned in time for another Los Angeles performance, but she was hemorrhaging and racked with pain. Booking agent Todd Schiffman told the band members they could cancel, citing problems with the club's sound system as an excuse. But Janis rallied. "I couldn't believe it!" Schiffman told writer Alice Echols. "She put on an hour show, and you wouldn't have known she was sick. I couldn't believe my eyes. That tells us what kind of dedication and craziness she had."

Back in San Francisco, Janis took time to recuperate from the ordeal. On January 31 she wrote the Joplins for the first time in months and reflected on turning twenty-five: "A quarter of a century! Oh, it's all too incredible. I never thought I'd even survive this long." She informed them she had been ill for a week and a half, costing the band $8,000 in canceled bookings at the Fillmore:

I finally had a wonderful rest. . . . I feel so nice & calm now. The first time off I've had in months! Very fun, this was the first time I've ever been stay-at-home preferably in bed sick since I was away from home. I didn't really realize it until one afternoon lying in bed drinking a beer, I suddenly flashed on the fact that lying in bed drinking a beer is the way to be sick! . . . People sent me flowers (3 vases full) and very many charming young men came to call. Linda and I had a fine time.

Her mother had sent a clipping about Aretha Franklin, a year Janis's senior, who had broken through in 1967, redefining soul music with her magnificent "I Never Loved a Man (The Way I Love You)" and "Respect." Janis worshipped Franklin's voice—"she is by far & away the best thing in music right now"—and aspired to sing with that kind of power. Beginning to see herself as approaching the great Franklin's league, Janis wrote the Joplins that "Rolling Stone, a national rock & roll newspaper," which launched in San Francisco in November 1967, "called me 'possibly the best female voice of her generation.' But I suppose [Franklin] & I are different generations." About to record for Columbia, Franklin's label before she signed to Atlantic, said Janis, "should certainly test our mettle."

In the same letter, Janis, no doubt empathizing with her brother, Mike, a fledgling artist, gave him exactly the kind of openhearted praise and encouragement she herself perpetually craved:

> *Your poster was GROOVEY & really good luck w/ your light show. Sounds like a great idea. If you need any advice, write, because I know lots of people that do them. Some of them the originators of the whole thing. Do you plan to start with liquid projections? They're the best because they can reflect the mood of the music & keep the tempo. If you can get this & incorporate slides with it, you'll really have something. You & your friend should get the equipment & rehearse w/ records. Again, good luck, it's a good idea.*

Janis would continue to send loving messages to her brother, whose endeavors starting an underground paper clearly had been motivated by the San Francisco trip, saying in one note, "honey, just congratulations & pride & all the love I have for your work, in *Agape*, particularly the poem—oh so fine!!! I have it on my wall."

⤙⤛⊙⤜⤚

The second week in February 1968, Janis, in a white puffball hat, and Big Brother, bundled in coats, at last flew into New York City, with

John Cooke, Dave Richards, and Mark Braunstein. They set up camp at the venerably funky Chelsea Hotel on West Twenty-Third Street. Janis wrote the Joplins of her "famous literary type intellectual hotel" where Dylan Thomas and Brendan Behan had lived. The Spanish restaurant-bar El Quijote, adjoining the hotel lobby, and the nearby club Max's Kansas City would become Janis's headquarters while in New York.

Max's, originally a hangout for abstract-expressionist painters, had a back room where Andy Warhol, rock stars, and their coterie held court. As Big Brother walked in the first time with Albert Grossman, Country Joe's "Janis" blared on the jukebox: "Into my life on waves of electric sound and flashing light, she came." Necks craned to see the crème de la crème of the Haight's hippie scene, or as Janis labeled her contingent: "a sloppy group of street freaks." A Max's waitress commented, "They all seem so happy compared to everyone in New York." Janis and Big Brother would find Manhattan "uptight" in contrast to laid-back San Francisco. "[The] city . . . made us all crazy," Janis said a few weeks later. "It was dividing the unity of the band."

At Grossman's offices in a town house on East Fifty-Fifth Street, Janis and Big Brother met Myra Friedman, who was newly hired to handle their publicity. A thirty-five-year-old classical music major from St. Louis, Friedman had previously worked in public relations at Columbia Records. She was dazzled by Janis, describing her as "grand, raw, powerful, simply bed-rocked in defiance and sexuality." Friedman would evolve into another Dorothy Joplin, scolding Janis for her misbehavior while caring for her deeply, and Janis would embrace another surrogate mother.

Janis felt at home in Grossman's inner sanctum—"a somber room, sort of a mausoleum wherein lay queer and ominous secrets . . . its dark quietness a reflection of his personality," in Friedman's words. After an extended hug, Janis held on to Grossman's every word—though there weren't many. Like her father, Grossman radiated a sharp intelligence and a shrewd cynicism, usually saying less than anyone else in the room.

Grossman had set up a rehearsal space for Big Brother at a downtown loft to prepare for its East Coast debut at the University of

Pennsylvania's Palestra gym on Friday, February 16; to be followed the next night by its New York premiere at the Anderson Theater, an old Yiddish theater at 66 Second Avenue that had recently turned into a low-rent rock venue. Big Brother headlined two shows, at eight and eleven, with B. B. King opening. Janis was anxious during sound check, and operations director John Morris tried to calm her nerves. It had been eight months since her triumph at Monterey, and though she'd gotten plenty of press since then, Janis still had to prove herself in New York City.

With the Joshua Light Show pulsating behind them, Big Brother kicked off the set with Janis's vocal fireworks on "Catch Me Daddy," the band jumping in with a loud roar. The audience went nuts as Big Brother ripped through "Magic of Love," "Brownsville," and "Light Is Faster Than Sound." "She tore the place apart!" Morris recalled decades later. "I've done about four hundred concerts in my life and probably seen eight hundred, and that would have to rank with the top two or three of all of them."

Snapping photos, twenty-six-year-old Elliott Landy was a fledgling photographer who'd shot primarily for an underground Boston paper. He was floored: "What a gorgeous lady to photograph! I'd never seen anyone like Janis! She was so fearless, brave. She put it all out there." Also in the audience were recording engineer Elliot Mazer (another Grossman client) and Columbia staff engineer Fred Catero, both of whom had been prepped in advance by an absent John Simon "about the lack of musicality and untogetherness of the band," according to Mazer. But Catero and Mazer found Big Brother's performance exciting, particularly Janis's powerful voice.

Afterward, the backstage filled with musicians and journalists, including Richard Goldstein and Linda Eastman, a photographer friend of Sam Andrew's who'd shot the Rolling Stones and would eventually marry Paul McCartney. Goldstein wrote an exuberant review for the following week's *Village Voice*, and a few months later, in *Vogue*, he'd describe Janis as "staggering"—she "assaults a song with her eyes, her hips, and her hair. She defies key, shrieking over one line, sputtering over the next, and clutching the knees of a final stanza, begging it not to leave." Goldstein was personally taken with Janis, and one night, after blintzes at Ratner's deli, he walked her to the Chelsea and enjoyed a good-night kiss.

Robert Shelton, the *New York Times* critic whose 1961 review of a Bob Dylan gig led to Dylan's recording contract with Columbia, wrote a piece that ran with the headline "Rock Star Born on Second Avenue," illustrated with Janis's photo, the rest of the band cropped from the picture. "As fine as the whole evening was, it belonged mostly to sparky, spunky Miss Joplin," Shelton said. "[T]here are few voices of such power, flexibility and virtuosity in pop music anywhere. Occasionally Miss Joplin appeared to be hitting two harmonizing notes at once. Her voice shouted with ecstasy or anger one minute, trailed off into coquettish curlicues the next. It glided from soprano highs to chesty alto lows.

"In an unaccompanied section of 'Love Is Like a Ball and Chain,' Miss Joplin went on a flight that alternately suggested a violin cadenza and the climax of a flamenco session. In 'Light Is Faster Than Sound' and 'Down on Me,' she unleashed more energy than most singers bring to a whole program."

On Monday, after scooping up a stack of the *New York Times*, Janis and the guys headed to Black Rock, the formidable skyscraper on Sixth Avenue and Fifty-Third Street that housed CBS and Columbia Records. Grossman, whom Janis had jokingly propositioned postgig on Saturday night—"Albert, I'm so happy I wanna fuck you"—called Clive Davis to let him know that Janis wanted to "ball him," too, to seal the deal. Davis politely declined.

After touring the offices and meeting Bob Cato, the art director who would design their album cover, Big Brother proceeded to the twenty-sixth floor to sign the contract with Davis. It's hazy in everyone's memory, but at some point, James Gurley either stripped naked to change clothes for the press party that night or was nude while seated at the conference table. In Davis's telling, he'd just been explaining how informal the label could be, when he realized the shirtless Gurley, seated at the table, was also pantless. "Janis saw how taken aback I was and laughed," Davis recalled in *The Soundtrack of My Life.* " 'Well,' she said with a twinkle, 'this is how informal *we* are!' "

At the packed party that night at Piraeus, My Love, a Greek restaurant on Fifty-Seventh Street, the band got drunk while surrounded by journalists and cognoscenti attracted by that day's *Times* review. Janis was the toast of the town. The next day, she wrote a rapturous letter to Linda Gravenites: "Look! Our first New York review after our first New York performance! Too much! Really wonderful! . . . We signed [with Columbia] and made the big announcement, so you can tell anyone— it's official! We start recording *live* as soon as possible so it all seems to be falling into place really rapidly. So far we've really dug N.Y. People have been very friendly & we've had a lot to drink. That's the key to adjusting in N.Y. Drink a lot & get used to spending time in bars &, wow, we're the right group!"

Janis also sent the review to the Joplins, with a buoyant note:

Too much, eh? So now we're in the process of taking the East Coast by storm. Also, as of yesterday afternoon we're with Columbia, official. Signed the contract on the 26th floor of the CBS building, met the president, had a press party, & got drunk. Am now in Albert's office, just completed an interview. From all indications, I'm going to become rich & famous. Incredible! All sorts of magazines are asking to do articles & pictures featuring me. I'm going to do every one. Wow, I'm so lucky—I just fumbled around being a mixed-up kid (& young adult) & then I fell into this. And finally, it looks like something is going to work for me.

Janis's self-mythologizing—emphasizing her troubled youth and downplaying her ambition and years of work to become a great singer—had begun. She quickly perfected the art of the interview, giving journalists outré quotes and feeding them exaggerated stories of tortured adolescence and accidental success. She learned quickly that she could wow them in print just as she did onstage. No woman had ever performed like her—or talked like her to the press. "When I'm singing . . . it's like an orgasm," she would tell writer Michael Thomas after a concert in Providence, Rhode Island. "You can't remember it, but you remember it."

At the band's first outing to Boston—a weekend gig at the Psychedelic Supermarket—thieves stole $5,000 worth of Big Brother's equipment from the club after the Friday night show. Cooke had to scrounge up gear for their next two concerts. Four days later, they flew to Detroit. For the planned live album, Columbia sent engineer Fred Catero to record Big Brother's shows at the Grande Ballroom, a funky old venue similar in vibe to the Avalon. Inside the ballroom, he set up a mobile recording unit to capture their two-night stand in early March. The opening act, the fiercely political protopunk-hard-rock band MC5 (Motor City 5), unleashed a roaring set that undermined Big Brother's own attack. Intimidated and likely tired, Big Brother had an off night, hitting more bad notes than usual, missing cues, and failing to connect—quite the opposite from the New York triumph. The Grande audience's lackluster response defeated the whole purpose of recording live, where crowd feedback can inspire a band to new heights, even mask mistakes. After the set, Janis stopped by the control booth to hear a playback. Catero recalled playing her the tape, to which Janis responded with, *"Oh, fuck!,"* spilled her drink, and then abruptly stomped off.

The next night's gig wasn't much better, though Catero recalled her "singing like you never heard" and the band playing "okay." Later, sitting disconsolately with Catero at a bar, Janis gulped five drinks in a row. When Gurley stood up from his barstool, a packet of heroin fell from his pocket. So far on this first trip east, Janis, obeying another Grossman ultimatum, refrained from using; she wrote Linda Gravenites about "a big lecture coupled w/ an implied threat from Albert about smack (no more or he drops us)." Another letter confirmed, "so far, at least, I've put down smack." Though she had continued to chip in San Francisco, she had not yet developed a habit. And knowing how much was at stake during the upcoming weeks of recording and performing, she avoided heroin for now.

Back in New York, Big Brother gathered in Grossman's office to listen to the Grande recordings. Aware of how badly they'd played, the band members heard only their mistakes, out-of-tune guitars, and irregular tempos. Their annoyed manager suggested that Andrew switch to bass, with Albin, who played guitar on a few songs, taking over his leads. The band nixed that idea, but all agreed the recordings were a useless, expensive mistake—the album would have to be cut in Columbia's studios in Midtown Manhattan and Los Angeles.

After the meeting, Grossman took Janis aside and told her she could do better with seasoned musicians. Years later, however, when Columbia released live tracks from the botched Grande sets, influential critic Lester Bangs raved about the "ragged but right" version of "Piece of My Heart" and the "rush of metal thunder" on "Down on Me," asserting that "James Gurley's guitar solo [on "Ball and Chain"] is one of his best on record, as searing a storm of noise as [on] *Cheap Thrills,* but speeded up, directed with a kind of joyous fury."

At the time, though, the disappointing recording resulted in backbiting and finger pointing. The mood of Janis's next note to her mother, on March 5, contrasted greatly with her earlier one: "So very busy & N.Y. is very strange—competitive & ugly & is turning us all around. On my evening off, I went & saw *Hello Dolly* w/ Pearl Bailey. She's wonderful."

"Lots of trouble in the band," Janis wrote the next day to Linda Gravenites, "revolving around the fact that I think I'm hot shit (as I'm told behind the band's back by everyone from Albert on down) and the band's sloppy. I guess we'll survive, but the live recording is off now after one attempt because we were so terrible (but I was okay). God I'm so fucking confused!"

All hoped for redemption on March 8, when Big Brother headlined the debut concert at the Fillmore East. Bill Graham's brand-new venue, his first outside San Francisco, was located in a converted Yiddish theater at 105 Second Avenue. The much-ballyhooed event featured opening sets by singer-songwriter Tim Buckley and electric bluesman Albert King. Graham, in town for the opening, wanted to single out Janis's name on the theater marquee, but she insisted the Fillmore East list only the group name.

For many of those who'd never seen Big Brother, the concert was revelatory. "When Janis started singing, I was stunned," photographer Bob Gruen recalled. "She wasn't so much performing—as just *being*, like she was possessed. Just *feeling* and sharing that feeling. It didn't seem like an act—it was *real*. The only other time I've had that experience was seeing Tina Turner." A young usher, budding artist/photographer Robert Mapplethorpe, raced home to Brooklyn and told his roommate Patti Smith about the amazing singer he'd seen. But compared with their exhilarating New York debut at the Anderson, the band's playing was off. The sound system malfunctioned, and the guitars occasionally drowned out Janis's vocals, forcing her to overcompensate by screaming shrilly "like a fishwife," said one male writer. Yet Nat Hentoff was intrigued enough to set up an interview with her for a major story in the Sunday *New York Times*.

The following weekend, *Voice* critic Richard Goldstein accompanied Big Brother to a two-night stand in Philadelphia at the Electric Factory, "a huge garage turned psychedelic playground filled with straight kids come to gape at the hippies," he wrote. He observed Janis's preshow jitters: how she "stalks around the tiny room, her fingers drumming against a tabletop. . . . [She] peers through a crack in the dressing room door and scowls, 'Oh shit. We'll never be able to get into those kids. Want to see death? Take a look out there.' " Yet after sipping Southern Comfort mixed in a cup of tea, and snuggling backstage with a man dressed in a gorilla costume, her mood brightened. She again wowed the audience: "Kids surround the stage, spilling over with the joy of being reached," Goldstein reported. "Because to hear Janis sing 'Ball and Chain' just once is to have been laid, lovingly and well."

><+>-O-<+><

Big Brother entered Columbia's Studio B on March 19 at seven in the evening to begin recording the album the band wanted to call *Sex, Dope and Cheap Thrills*—inspired by a line on a poster for the campy 1936 antidrug film *Reefer Madness*. The group slogged away until four in the morning, trying numerous takes of "Combination of the Two" and then failing to capture "Catch Me Daddy."

"Every time she did a take, it was killer, perfect," Fred Catero observed. "But the band just weren't there yet. They needed another five years, at least, to be considered on [her] level." The musicians couldn't remember their parts, he recalled, or made frequent mistakes each time they tried a new take. John Simon showed his displeasure, warning them, "You got to get together here."

To counter what the instrumentalists considered the studio's sterile environment, technicians built a mock stage to simulate a club setting. Big Brother returned the next night to cut "Piece of My Heart" and "Summertime." Also adding to the live ambience, the members used a PA to hear what they were playing rather than wear headphones. They performed together on the "stage," unlike typical sessions where individual parts were recorded in isolation booths to prevent the sound of one instrument from bleeding into another, thereby limiting a producer's ability to blend the individual "tracks."

"James was having the hardest time," Dave Getz recalled. "It was really excruciating sometimes to get a good solo out of him without screwing up or striking a bad note." At first, Janis didn't criticize Gurley or the others. "She was resigned that she couldn't direct everybody," the drummer recounted. "She couldn't give personal direction and say, 'Dave, you play this, Peter play this.' It was out of keeping with Big Brother. No one directed anybody else. It was not the way we operated." At times, though, she lost patience, according to Catero: "She was singing her heart out, then she stopped and walked into the control room and said, 'I'm not gonna sing with those motherfuckers out there!'" and grabbed her bottle of Southern Comfort.

Simon's exasperation added to the pressure, as did D. A. Pennebaker's presence in the studio. He filmed Big Brother recording "Summertime" for a possible documentary on Janis, although he would later drop the project. In the footage, Janis argued that a missed note on guitar wouldn't affect the overall sound, since her vocals were the main thing people wanted to hear anyway. Caught by Pennebaker's cinema verité,

Sam Andrew defended his Bach-inspired guitar parts to Simon in a bid to prove his classical training and his ability to read music. Sometimes, during playbacks, Janis chatted with Gurley, distracting him from listening to them. When Pennebaker focused his lens on her, she mugged for the camera. Yet "Janis was a very strong force in the studio," John Simon related later. "She definitely didn't keep quiet when she had opinions," which pertained to everything from guitar parts and tempos to sound mixes and song choices.

"Things still very weird here," Janis wrote Gravenites about the sessions. "Recording's hard—put down 2 tracks—'Combination of the 2' and 'Piece of My Heart.' It's gonna be a long haul drag but will make it." During her interview with Nat Hentoff, Janis described their problems in the studio. "Making this record hasn't been easy," she told him. "We're not the best technicians around. We're not the kind of dispassionate professionals who can go into a studio and produce something quick and polished. We're passionate—that's all we are. And what we're trying to get on record is what we're good at—insisting, getting people out of their chairs. What also makes it hard for John Simon . . . is that we're kind of sloppy at the same time as we're happy. Last night, he was trying to get something done and said, 'Come on! Who's the head of this band?' There was a pause because . . . no one is. We vote on things. We're democratic." As criticism of her band of brothers intensified, Janis initially doubled down on her insistence they were a unit, fearing yet another fracture of family, all the while knowing in her heart it was inevitable. "She was trying to be the same," Dave Getz noted, "but she couldn't be the same."

The band took a break from recording for a gig in Chicago, its first time back since the 1966 Mother Blues residency. At the Agora/Cheetah, the audience numbered three thousand, with a young Bob Seger's band as the opener. Much to Big Brother's displeasure, they discovered the concert's ads and posters said, "Janis Joplin/Big Brother." They began the gig in a huff. But "the minute we walked offstage after the first set, it all fell back into place," Janis said. "We looked at each other, like, 'Remember me?' We remembered what it was all about." That night,

Janis wore one of Gravenites's sexy new creations: a gold minidress with matching garter. (When interviewed by fashion magazines *Vogue* and *Glamour*, she raved about Linda's designs.) In a piece for *Downbeat*, Mark Wolf focused on her physical exertion and messy appearance: "her hair is unkempt, she is sweating profusely, and she breathes heavily as if she has just run the four-minute mile."

In her interview with Wolf, Janis downplayed the hard work and planning that went into her performance. "Music is just about feelin' things," is how she put it. "What we're trying to do in our music is just get back to old-time havin' a good time, jumpin,' gettin' stoned, carryin' on—'Hey, baby! Come on up here, and let's do it! Out onstage!'" Afterward, true to her word, she took a "really groovy guy," as she described him, to her hotel room.

Back in New York, recording sessions resumed. One late night Janis stepped into the Chelsea elevator with a professorial-looking man with a hangdog look—thirty-three-year-old Leonard Cohen. He would later memorialize the tryst that followed in two variations of his "Chelsea Hotel"—#1 and #2—with #2 featuring these lines about their sexual encounter: "You were talking so brave and so sweet / giving me head on the unmade bed / while limousines wait in the street."

Janis's view of their encounter was less tender. The following year, during a session with acclaimed photographer Richard Avedon, while being interviewed by his assistant/writer Doon Arbus, Janis spoke about the ups and downs of her sex life. "Sometimes . . . you're with someone and you're convinced that they have something . . . to tell you," she confided. "Or . . . you want to be with them. So maybe nothing's happening, but you keep telling yourself something's happening. You know, innate communication. He's just not saying anything. He's moody or something. So you keep being there, pulling, giving, rapping. . . . And then, all of a sudden, about four o'clock in the morning, you realize that, flat ass, this motherfucker's just lying there. He's not balling me. I mean, that really happened to me. Really heavy, like slam-in-the-face it happened. Twice. Jim Morrison and Leonard Cohen. And it's strange 'cause they were the only two that I can think of, like prominent people, that I tried to . . . without really liking them up front, just because I knew who they were and wanted to know them. . . . And then they both gave me nothing . . . but I don't know what that means. Maybe it just means they were on a bummer."

Leonard Cohen, it turned out, observed more than "nothing" about her. In his song's lyrics and wistful melody, composed in the months after her death, Cohen captured her wit and lifelong, tortured relationship with beauty, writing: "And clenching your fist for the ones like us who are oppressed by the figures of beauty / You fixed yourself, you said, 'Well, never mind we are ugly but we have the music.' "

Cohen later publicly named his paramour in "Chelsea Hotel," though anyone who knew Janis—whose other hotel trysts included a "charming" Irish guitarist, a nineteen-year-old "from the N.Y. street gang school" (in Janis's words), and a member of the band the Chambers Brothers—recognized her from such lines as: "You were famous, your heart was a legend / You told me again you preferred handsome men but for me you would make an exception."

Janis had another run-in with "handsome man" Jim Morrison while hanging out at Steve Paul's The Scene, an insiders' rock & roll club on West Forty-Sixth Street where musicians jammed after hours. Hendrix was a regular, frequently playing until dawn. Around three o'clock one night, while Janis watched Hendrix onstage with the Chambers Brothers, Morrison drunkenly stumbled in. According to Danny Fields, then the Doors' publicist, "Jim bellied his way up to the low stage, threw his arms around Jimi's thighs, and said, 'I want to suck your cock.' " In defense of Hendrix, Fields continued, "Janis ran over to the stage, yelling, 'You asshole!' She banged a bottle down on Jim's head. The three of them were on the floor in a ball, like little fish. Their handlers came running up and pried them apart and took them home." No stranger to violent brawls in Louisiana roadhouses, Janis shrugged off the drunken episode as just another night out.

After Big Brother finally finished tracking "Summertime" on March 28, Janis was in good spirits, writing Dorothy Joplin that "the 3 tracks that we have down really sound good." The toast of New York still craved af-

Janis's main New York hangouts were the Chelsea Hotel and Max's Kansas City. She is joined in Max's backroom by director Paul Morrissey, Andy Warhol, and Tim Buckley (with whom Big Brother shared a bill at the Fillmore East), 1968.

Janis always traveled with books, reading in airports and between gigs; her oversized fur bag was roomy enough for a book and a bottle of booze. Elliott Landy accompanied the band to their Grande Ballroom gigs in Detroit and snapped this shot of Janis backstage in March 1968.

Janis often repaired to the twenty-four-hour Jewish dairy restaurant Ratner's, at 111 Second Avenue, after Fillmore East performances for late-night noshing. Bill Graham stocked his venue's food concession with Ratner's baked goods.

Janis maintained a long friendship with Pigpen (behind her in hat), with whom she often duetted on "Turn On Your Love Light" when Big Brother and the Grateful Dead shared a bill like this one at the Northern California Folk-Rock Festival in Santa Clara County on May 18, 1968.

Janis was photographed so often with a bottle of Southern Comfort that the liquor company rewarded her with a fur coat. Jim Marshall shot this iconic photo in the dressing room at Winterland in 1968.

After their East Coast sojourn, Big Brother gladly returned in May 1968 to their Cali stomping grounds, where they performed on a bill with the Dead, Jefferson Airplane, and the Doors at the Northern California Folk-Rock Festival. At one point, Janis cornered Marty Balin and Jerry Garcia for career advice.

"Janis was the goddess in San Francisco," said Mick Fleetwood, whose band opened for Big Brother in 1968.

© DAVID GAHR

Janis met a conquest soon after arriving at the Newport Folk Festival, with Sam Andrew and road manager John Cooke looking on, July 1968.

© DAVID GAHR

Big Brother sound-checking at Newport, a festival Janis had longed to attend since 1961. The band headlined to a sold-out audience on Saturday, July 17, 1968.

© DAVID GAHR

Among the joys of Newport, Janis reconnected with her Austin, Texas, mentor Kenneth Threadgill, also performing at the festival.

The Queen of Rock & Roll in the lobby of photographer Baron Wolman's studio. During one session with Wolman, then chief photographer for *Rolling Stone,* she brought a microphone and a tape player that she could sing along to. "She started off by lip-synching for about five minutes," Wolman recalls, "then the next five minutes she was singing out loud so she could hear herself, and after that she just went into a full concert for me, for an hour—just for me."

Janis in furs with a symbol of her success, her very own Porsche— a 1965 Super-90 cabriolet convertible—custom-painted by her close friend and former roadie Dave Richards.

For her first gig after leaving Big Brother, Janis performed in Memphis at the Stax-Volt Yuletide Thing concert, and attended a party at Stax President Jim Stewart's home in December 1968, where she was photographed with Stax artists Judy Clay, William Bell, Carla Thomas, Rufus Thomas (*front row, left to right*), Steve Cropper, Donald "Duck" Dunn, Ben Cauley, and James Alexander (*back row, left to right*).

Janis lounging in her favorite room at the Chelsea Hotel, on West Twenty-Third Street in New York City. Photographer David Gahr had a special rapport with Janis beginning with their first session, when she learned he shot for *Time* magazine, a staple in her childhood home.

Members of the as-yet-unnamed Kozmic Blues Band (keyboardist Richard Kermode, guitarist Sam Andrew, and saxophonist Snooky Flowers, from left) join Janis at rehearsal before appearing on *The Ed Sullivan Show,* March 16, 1969.

Janis was thrilled to chat onstage with legendary impresario Ed Sullivan, whose TV show she'd watched religiously with her family in the 1950s.

Onstage with the Kozmic Blues Band at the Fillmore East, 1969. Amalie R. Rothschild, a member of the Joshua Light Show and the unofficial house photographer at the Fillmore East, photographed Janis numerous times.

In Chelsea, Janis posed in front of a distressed billboard advertising an off-Broadway play about conservative Georgia politician Lester Maddox.

One of the highlights of Janis's 1969 European tour was a concert in Frankfurt, Germany, in April 1969; bassist Brad Campbell was knocked out by her performance—as was the audience, some of whom flocked onstage by set's end.

Janis socialized in the artists pavilion at Woodstock, sharing bottles of champagne, August 1969.

Janis was joined at the Woodstock festival by her friend and lover Peggy Caserta, August 1969.

During Janis and the Kozmic Blues Band's Woodstock set, which started at 3 a.m., Snooky Flowers sang "Don't Turn Me Loose" while Janis danced barefoot.

Janis relaxed with members of the Kozmic Blues Band and their entourage (Richard Kermode, road manager Joe Crowley, Snooky Flowers, Linda Gravenites, and saxophonist Terry Clements, from left) on days off in Florida.

Janis joined Tina Turner onstage at Madison Square Garden on November 27, 1969, when the Ike and Tina Turner Revue opened for the Rolling Stones.

During the Kozmic Blues Band's final performance, at Madison Square Garden on December 19, 1969, Janis shared the stage with Beaumont, Texas, native Johnny Winter. The two had enjoyed a fling earlier that year, and he was her date to the premiere of *Myra Breckenridge,* starring Raquel Welch and Mae West.

Kozmic Blues's swansong: Janis flanked by Terry Clements (*at left*); guitarist John Till (*right*) and bassist Brad Campbell would join her next group, Full Tilt Boogie, in 1970. They went out rocking, with one reporter writing that the Garden nearly caved in "under the weight of all that frenzy and jumping around."

A clear-eyed Janis photographed in her One Fifth Avenue hotel room on December 19, 1969; later that night, after her Madison Square Garden concert, she relapsed on heroin.

In her new home in Larkspur, Janis enjoyed playing pool in her garage. She'd soon run band rehearsals in the garage with her new group.

Janis fell madly in love with Ohio native David Niehaus (*at right*), whom she met with Ben Beall (*left*) at Carnival in Rio de Janeiro, Brazil.

The belle of Carnival, February 1970. Janis and Niehaus tried unsuccessfully to put on Brazil's first rock festival to keep the party going.

Janis became friendly with New York–born singer-songwriter Eric Andersen on the Festival Express tour, seen here at a stop in Winnipeg. Shortly after the tour, he wrote the song "Pearl's Good Time Blues" about her.

In Truchas, New Mexico, Janis visited the ranch of her friends Lisa and Tom Law after filming a cigar commercial in nearby Taos. She was "looking for a mountain man," she told Lisa Law, and bonded with their neighbor Tommy Masters, who later became Bob Dylan's bus driver. The 1970 photo was the last one of Janis that Law ever took.

Janis won the respect and love of *Pearl* producer Paul Rothschild. He told her, "Let's fuck on tape."

Janis adored Kris Kristofferson and spent time with the footloose author of "Me and Bobby McGee" in California.

Before playing Full Tilt's concert at the Garden State Arts Center in Holmdel, New Jersey, Pearl (as her new band called her) relaxed with keyboardist Ken Pearson and bassist Brad Campbell, captured by drummer Clark Pierson's camera, on August 11, 1970.

Being Janis Joplin on the roof garden of the Chelsea Hotel, 1970. She once said, "Don't compromise yourself. That's all you've got."

firmation from her mother: "I just can't tell you how much your letters have meant to me here—so nice. Your firstborn is really doing great in the music business. Did I tell you about all my reviews? Can I tell you again? This is all so *exciting* to me." After a detailed, lengthy annotated list of her voluminous press coverage, she added: "ISN'T THAT TOO MUCH?!" and paraphrased a line from the 1960 televised musical *Peter Pan*, "I just have to crow."

As in the past, Janis still attempted to connect with her mother on fashion and—now that she could afford it—home décor: "Just bought $115 worth of fur—a deer skin for the wall, 5 used coats to cut up & sew back together for a huge rug & a fantastic white alpaca rug about 3" thick & huge! Fantastic, I love fur & soft things. I didn't get any clothes while I was here—just some shoes. In fact I didn't do anything except the music bizness. Recording, gigs, interviews & picture sessions took all of our time. . . . Bye for now—[I'll] try to write again when I'm not so enamored w/myself."

The week before Big Brother's return to California, the group was booked on a bill with B. B. King for a residency at Generation, a hip new club in the Village. The East Eighth Street venue didn't have a liquor license yet. Two years later, Hendrix would turn Generation into his Electric Lady Studios. Pennebaker captured Big Brother's opening night, filming a well-played version of "Summertime." On April 4, following the shocking assassination of Martin Luther King Jr. in Memphis, the club became a gathering place for musicians to mourn. "B. B. King [sat] on his guitar amp onstage and [played] gospel songs," according to John Cooke, "moving . . . the audience to tears." The club stayed open all night, with Hendrix and bluesman Buddy Guy stopping by to play. For a more organized tribute to Dr. King, John Cooke invited musicians to join Big Brother on its last night there, including Jimi Hendrix, Buddy Guy, Al Kooper, Paul Butterfield, Elvin Bishop, Richie Havens, and Joni Mitchell.

>-+∘-○-∘+-<

By spring 1968, Big Brother had arrived. In fewer than two months of concerts, the band earned more than $40,000, nearly $250,000 today, and everyone got a raise. Back in California, the pace didn't let up. The day after an April 10 date at the Anaheim Convention Center, they returned to San Francisco. *"We're so glad to be here with you!"* Janis proclaimed during the band's three-night stint for Bill Graham, first at the Fillmore and then, to accommodate the crowds, the larger Winterland. "She walked across the stage cackling maniacally and stomping her foot, which she did when she was really happy," Sam Andrew recalled.

"Coming home triumphant was a great time for all of us," Dave Getz reflected. "For a moment, it really felt like we had gone and conquered the world." Recorded for possible use on the album, the sets documented the reenergized band in top form. "The live versions have more of the pure, insane, raw energy that was [our] stock and trade," said Getz, "which had to be toned down in the studio." Peter Albin, still sharing onstage patter with Janis, thanked the enthusiastic crowd for being "patient"—unlike New York audiences.

Cradled in the arms of San Francisco, Janis restarted her fling with cosmic cowboy Milan Melvin, who'd moved to the hip new FM rock station KSAN. Then, at Peggy Caserta's Stinson Beach cabin, her friendship with the boutique owner evolved from platonic to sexual. They had earlier spent the night together at the Chelsea in New York, when Caserta was in town on a buying trip. As Janis and Caserta became more intimately involved, Janis introduced her to heroin, which she'd taken up again. As Janis injected her the first time, she murmured, "Say goodbye to your pain," recalled Caserta, who at the time was in a long-term relationship with a physically abusive woman. "I couldn't understand Janis's affinity for heroin until this night," Caserta wrote in her memoir *I Ran into Some Trouble*. At the time, Caserta was "desperate to ease the raw wounded feeling," and Janis "was offering me, with tenderness and kindness, the solution . . . one she herself had been employing to ease her own pain and maybe some fears, too." Caserta detailed Janis's well-kept set of works: her syringe, spoon, and purple silk scarf for tying off her arm. As Caserta herself became a junkie, the drug "would bond us in yet another way," she wrote. Occasionally, the two women indulged—in smack and sex—in a ménage à trois with Milan Melvin, who would soon marry Joan Baez's sister, Mimi Fariña. Janis jokingly referred to herself, Caserta recalled, as the Queen of Unrequited Love. Amid all her lovers, Janis continued to yearn for the one who would give her that complete unconditional love, pouring her anguish into her performances. "Look at all the love songs," she told Caserta. "How many are happy?"

While on tour, Janis had lost her lease to the Lyon Street apartment (due to her dog, George), and she and Linda Gravenites moved to a larger two-bedroom place on Noe Street, between the Castro and Mission districts. Perched on a hilltop, the third-floor flat featured sweeping views of Noe Valley. On their new kitchen wall, they hung a picture of "Uncle Albert": an image of William Penn cut out from a Quaker Oatmeal container, which they thought resembled Grossman.

Throughout the rest of April and into May, the band performed in California, while making trips to Columbia's LA studio to finish the album. Tension returned as all five struggled to please the merciless Simon. He told Janis she sang off key, and he particularly disapproved of the way she used identical phrasing on each vocal take—a practice she'd perfected double tracking her vocals during the Mainstream sessions. For the Columbia recordings, she had rehearsed her vocals to the point that, during the sessions, she could repeat herself flawlessly take after take. Simon argued that Janis was being inauthentic, since blues and jazz singers tend to improvise each time they sing.

Janis's soon-to-be iconic and influential style, however, was the result of much thought and practice. As she explained in an interview with Nat Hentoff: "I don't feel quite free enough with my phrasing to say I'm a jazz singer. I sing with a more demanding beat, a steady rather than a lilting beat. I don't riff over the band. I try to punctuate the rhythm with my voice."

Simon, a perfectionist in the studio, appreciated aspects of Janis's talent and hard work. But he seemed not to fully realize what he was dealing with. The two simply had no chemistry. Her abrasiveness and profanity bothered him: "She said, 'Hey motherfucker'—that's what she always called me, never 'John,'" he later groused. When she heard

Simon on keyboards during an Electric Flag session he was producing, she insisted he play barrelhouse piano on "Turtle Blues." They attempted a live-sounding track, with Gurley and Andrew bringing a tape recorder to their favorite watering hole, Barney's Beanery, to capture the saloon's sonics. Then in the studio, John Cooke, Bob Neuwirth, and Howard Hesseman—who'd moved to LA with fellow Committee cast member Carl Gottlieb—smashed glass and whooped it up for the recording. Though most listeners were fooled, and the Beanery was credited on the LP for the song's "vibes," Simon scoffed at the track, calling his piano playing "one of my two embarrassing performances on record." Big Brother finally completed the album, polishing off a torrid "I Need a Man to Love" and "Oh, Sweet Mary," a reconstructed "Cuckoo" with new lyrics surely inspired by Janis's life in Texas: "Why is it so hard?/Breathing in the air."

During recording sessions, the band had taken up residency at Hollywood's Landmark Motor Hotel, on Franklin Avenue, a hip rock & roll hostelry recommended by Neuwirth, then working for the Doors. Its ersatz tiki décor and shag carpeting added a kitschy touch, and management didn't frown on late-night parties. Hendrix and the Chambers Brothers often lounged around its secluded swimming pool. For each of her stays there, Janis selected room 105, near the lobby, with quick access to the pool. It would become her home away from home in LA. While there, Janis grew closer to Neuwirth, who introduced her to a new circle of friends, including Michael J. Pollard. The actor had become hot property after his Oscar-nominated role as C. W. Moss in 1967's *Bonnie and Clyde*, and soon he was pushing for Janis to play a part in an offbeat Western that never came to pass.

One crazy afternoon, Janis and her entourage wound up at a party thrown by female friends of Hesseman and Gottlieb, caretakers for the Calabasas home of crooner John Davidson. After hours of drinking, Janis engaged in yet another showdown with a wasted Jim Morrison. As she played pool and tried to ignore him, the Doors' singer suddenly grabbed her by the hair and then pushed her facedown onto a coffee table. Janis ran crying to the bathroom. A while later, she returned, picked up a whiskey bottle, and when Morrison staggered toward the door, she broke it over his head. "The next day," according to Doors producer Paul Rothchild, "Jim said, 'What a *great* woman! She's *terrific.*' He was in love. He loved violence."

The feud between Morrison and Janis would persist. Sometime later, as a guest on Dick Cavett's TV show, Janis exploded with laughter when Cavett lit her cigarette, saying, "Let me light your fire." "That's my *favorite* singer," she said, dripping with sarcasm but giving no further explanation.

Onstage, Janis began creating a persona; an exaggerated version of herself. Privately, she'd ask Linda Gravenites, "What if they find out I'm only Janis?," but in public and onstage, her bravado increased. Between songs, she sometimes cracked wise, putting on a kind of Mae West meets W. C. Fields accent, irritating her bandmates. "I started noticing Janis believing all her publicity," Peter Albin recounted about the press's focus on her talent. She was becoming a diva, partially due to the "encouragement from her entourage, this clique of LA people—Paul Rothchild, Bobby Neuwirth, Michael Pollard. Janis started to become a phony; a caricature of herself."

Clive Davis planned to list Janis's name above the band's on their album jacket—but Grossman, speaking for Janis, nixed the idea. The debut Columbia release had been renamed *Cheap Thrills*, with the label eliminating the words *Sex* and *Dope*. In New York, Big Brother had participated in a photo session for a proposed cover in which the band frolicked naked in bed together—excluding Albin, who wore long underwear. "We were much amused to find a Madison Avenue version of a psychedelic bedroom," Sam Andrew recalled about the set, "like something Peter Max would do, all in pink . . . the complete antithesis of the real thing, which would be . . . in dark shades, if not totally black." When Janis arrived on set, according to Andrew, "she took one look and let out a whoop and a Texas cackle . . . 'Let's trash it, boys!'" That added more authenticity, but Janis's bare breasts were exposed in the photos, so Columbia ruled against the concept.

Big Brother turned to Janis's pal R. Crumb for a solution, and his bold illustrations of the album's song titles and portraits of each band member became the eye-catching cover. A collector of 1920s and 1930s blues 78s, Crumb combined his own style with the exploitative imagery of early blues, or "race records," advertisements, including a "mammy" for "Summertime" and voluptuous images of Janis, with accentuated cleavage, nipples, and hips. For the back cover, the label chose a black-and-white portrait of Janis—smiling broadly, her hair flying, and her legs planted in a wide stance—taken by San Francisco photographer Thomas Weir. The interior of the gatefold album sleeve featured the entire band shot by Elliott Landy while bathed in a light show onstage at the Fillmore East.

Clive Davis rejected John Simon's initial rough mixes of *Cheap Thrills,* so Big Brother reconvened in June with Elliot Mazer in the studio to complete the sound mixing. Simon had chosen the anarchic rush of "Harry" to kick off side two, which Davis vetoed, though Crumb's illustration of the song—a bug-eyed swami, for *"Hare* Krishna"—stayed on the cover. At that point, Simon quit the project and went on tour with Taj Mahal. He told Columbia he wanted no producer credit on the LP sleeve, although he received royalties on album sales. Over the years, Simon gave various reasons for his decision: early on, he told a reporter he was "just helping the band out" and that it wasn't his "kind of music."

Janis was among the names listed in the engineering credits on the LP sleeve. As with Big Brother's Mainstream sessions, she became absorbed with the mechanics of the studio, writing her parents that the sound mixing process "means setting the balances of all instruments & voices to each other. It could be a very simple or a very complicated procedure." Mazer described Janis's involvement as "incredibly on top of it. For two weeks, only Janis, myself, and the engineer would stay, from two in the afternoon until seven in the morning. . . . I never knew an artist that worked harder." Sam Andrew recalled Janis spending thirty-six hours straight with Mazer on the LP's final mixing session.

In the end, *Cheap Thrills* re-creates the roar and rough-edged spontaneity of Big Brother in performance, with Janis's vocals soaring above the fray. The album's sonic wizardry included snippets of live material edited into the mix, creating the impression of a live recording. The LP opens with Bill Graham's booming announcement, *"Four gentlemen and one great, great broad,"* before a studio recording of "Combination of the Two." Many reviewers mistakenly thought the entire album was live. With the deletion of "Harry," side two consisted of only three tracks, with the live-at-the-Fillmore "Ball and Chain" bringing the LP to a close. "A lot of editing had to happen, but what's on *Cheap Thrills* is incredible," said Dave Getz. "You don't hear all the torturous [bits]. There were some takes that were just so awful they were painful to listen to. But somehow John Simon and all of us together—with millions of takes being edited together—got something unique."

The album's rawness, captured via fastidious production techniques, set it apart from most Columbia recordings at the time. To help promote its August 1968 release, Clive Davis invited the band to play the annual CBS convention in Puerto Rico in late July. Janis spent most of her time there strolling the convention with Grossman, who clearly doted on her. The guys in Big Brother were treated like backup musicians while Janis schmoozed with the corporate execs. Equipment chief Dave Richards was so troubled by the animosity among the band members that he quit after Puerto Rico. "There was no friendship anymore," he recalled. "It used to be everybody kidded around, but it turned into this icy thing, before every gig." The performance at the convention went well, eliciting enthusiasm from Columbia staffers, but "resentment ran through the band," said Dave Getz. With such high stakes, "mistakes weren't taken lightly anymore—there was a lot of blaming toward each other too. It wasn't just Janis versus everybody else."

However, any sense of conflict was absent from Janis's cheery postcard to her parents: "Had to write you a card from Puerto Rico. So far all I've seen, unfortunately, is the inside of 3 hotels & a short stretch of beach—but lots of free rum punch on Columbia. We play tonite 7, leave tomorrow morning for Newport, but at least I'll get to see the island from the air."

›‹•›‹—0—›‹•›‹

Performing at the Newport Folk Festival had been a long-held dream for Janis. While in the Waller Creek Boys, she'd tried to find someone to hitchhike with her from Austin to Rhode Island. Known for its acoustic blues, old-timey country, bluegrass, gospel, and folk, the festival rarely booked electric bands—Dylan was famously booed when he went electric there in '65. Janis's affinity for Bessie Smith, touted in the festival program, and Grossman's longtime association with the festival helped get Big Brother on the bill—as did its increasing popularity among college students.

Janis traversed the grounds, checking out the afternoon workshops. She delighted in reconnecting with Kenneth Threadgill, who was yodeling Jimmie Rodgers songs and other C&W numbers. Janis hugged and kissed the man she considered her first booster. She hung out with the Kweskin Jug Band's Maria Muldaur and also attended a set by Appalachian balladeer Jean Ritchie, whom she'd admired as a teen. And she managed to snag hip publicist Danny Fields's "gorgeous" male assistant to accompany her back to her hotel room.

"I've been watching everybody; it's been groovy—but I've been horny to play," Janis told the audience during Big Brother's sold-out headlining slot on Saturday, July 27. Dressed in Linda Gravenites's latest design—a tight black minidress with an embroidered, very-low-cut bodice and mesh tights, Janis radiated excitement. The set, which was recorded, veered from wobbly to killer. The opener, their new single, "Piece of My Heart," sounded shaky, but they got into the groove on "Summertime." The traditional "Cuckoo"—rather than the revised version, "Oh, Sweet Mary"—worked well, but "Combination of the Two" lost momentum during a long, dissonant guitar jam. Big Brother finished with a dynamic "Ball and Chain"—the crowd of twenty thousand applauding wildly. Back for an encore, Janis confessed, "I've been wanting to come to this festival since I was seventeen years old, and I never had the bread. That's the truth." Then, still being cheered after an emotion-drenched "Down on Me," they reprised the chorus of "Piece of My Heart," executed better than before. "Thank ya, that's all we got time for! You're so groovy, man!" Janis yelled into the mike as the sound curfew brought the show to a close. Boisterous applause continued to ring out long after they ran offstage, triumphant.

But for Peter Albin and Dave Getz, the lyrics to "Down on Me"— "Everywhere I go, they're down on me"—really hit home when they saw their manager backstage. *"Wasn't it great?"* they asked him. Grossman frowned, saying, "The rhythm section is still not up to par." Making their humiliation worse, he delivered his verdict while standing with members of the Band, who looked embarrassed.

"It was a shock," Albin recounted, "such a comedown." John Cooke, who'd loved the performance, gave Grossman his positive appraisal, but the manager just shook his head. In Cooke's telling, Grossman never asked for his musical opinion again.

A few days later, back in New York at the Chelsea Hotel, Janis called a band meeting.

CHAPTER 16

KOZMIC BLUES

*Playing another kind of music is what you have
to do to grow as a musician. That's what we're
supposed to be all about—get better at what we do.*

—JANIS JOPLIN

Janis knew she had to leave Big Brother. The question was when. Albert Grossman had first planted the idea of her forming a new band some four months earlier in March, when the Grande Ballroom recordings failed. He saw her as Big Brother's only real talent and her bandmates as replaceable. Grossman either didn't recognize their important role as her surrogate family or thought Janis had outgrown that need. He simply saw them as a liability to Janis's—and his—success. Since 1966, when Janis almost joined Paul Rothchild's proposed blues group, she'd known such opportunities existed. But having the history and familiarity with Big Brother, the sense of having come up together as a unit, compensated for the group's failure to live up to her musical standards. In her next venture, leading her own band, she would discover that playing with excellent musicians could cause its own set of problems.

By the summer of 1968, however, the intraband animosity had all but shattered Big Brother's familial bond. "We were in our own worlds," Dave Getz recounted. "When we weren't playing, everybody became really isolated, and there was no unity." For months, Janis discussed with friends the possibility of leaving Big Brother. She'd cornered Jefferson

Airplane's Marty Balin and the Dead's Jerry Garcia on May 18 at a northern California festival. The three climbed into the cab of a pickup truck, with Garcia behind the wheel, and Janis told them Grossman urged her to play with a better band.

"She wanted our advice on whether she should leave her old buddies or not," Balin remembered. "Janis was upset because they were her friends. There was something so raw and funky about Big Brother. They just fit her so perfectly, with Jim Gurley on that crazy heroin guitar of his. But Grossman was telling her he was going to make her a big, big star. We told her to follow her heart and to follow the path that would be best for her music."

Other musicians didn't see Big Brother's attributes. "Janis was the goddess in San Francisco," recalled drummer Mick Fleetwood. On its first US tour, Fleetwood Mac opened shows in June for Big Brother at the Carousel (soon to become Bill Graham's Fillmore West). Fleetwood and the group's leading light, blues guitarist Peter Green, criticized Big Brother's chops: "As musicians, we really didn't understand where they were at," Fleetwood observed. "Things were out of tune and sloppy. We said, 'Wish she had a better band.'"

Most of all, Grossman had had enough. In New York, after Newport, he called Janis for a meeting. Peggy Caserta, visiting Janis at the Chelsea Hotel, accompanied her to his office. "It was after a night of debauchery," Caserta recounted. "He said, 'I think there should be some changes—now.' She's looking at him, and he says, 'The band's got to go.' She gasped, but she knew this was coming. She said, 'But Albert, those are my boys. I can't do this.' She got upset, and he said, 'Listen, you've hired me to do a job, and I intend to do that job. They're not up to par. I can get you musicians who are up for this job. We'll handpick them.'" Janis felt terrible. "When we left, she was trembling. She grabbed my hand in the elevator and started to cry, and mascara was running down her face, and she said, 'Peggy, I can't do this.'"

Janis then contacted Clive Davis. "I was careful to stay out of the deliberations about Janis leaving the band," the label head said later, "beyond discussing it with Grossman when he brought it up. Then Janis called me personally. . . . I got the impression that she had made a decision already and was simply looking for my support. Her desire to work with more accomplished and versatile musicians seemed right to me. . . . She was clearly the star of the band, and critics and even other musicians were openly critical of Big Brother's musical limitations."

Before confronting the band, Janis waited until after their sold-out return engagement at the Fillmore East the weekend of August 2. Janis was both nervous and excited about performing with the Staple Singers, whose dynamic lead singer, Mavis Staples, was another favorite vocalist. "I'll never be able to sing like that," she whispered to Myra Friedman while watching the gospel-soul group. The Staples returned onstage after their set to join Big Brother on Sister Rosetta Tharpe's "Down by the Riverside."

"The Staple Singers had to catch a plane that same night," Sam Andrew recalled. "We wanted to jam with them, so we brought them on in the middle of our set. It was an incandescent moment. Mavis Staples shared the mike with Janis. They were very different singers. Mavis sings in a very calm, deliberate manner, and her voice is deep and richly resonant, which made an interesting contrast to Janis's supersonic style."

The following week, the band gathered in Janis's room at the Chelsea. She broke the news that she'd be leaving Big Brother after their *Cheap Thrills* tour, planned to run until December. Similar to the Lagunitas showdown exactly two years earlier, Peter Albin exploded with anger. "He said it was a dirty, lowdown thing to do," recalled Dave Getz. But the drummer wasn't surprised by Janis's announcement and took the news calmly, as did Gurley and Andrew. After all the conflict, "We were relieved," Gurley admitted. In November, following one of their final concerts, Janis would tell a journalist, "They're my family. I really love 'em. But we've just been together too long. We spent two and a half years really getting close. I've never been this close to anyone."

⊱⊶⊙⊷⊰

To help neutralize her anxiety about the future, Janis quickly found diversions in old friends—and heroin. The charismatic ringleaders of subversive street activists the Diggers—Emmett Grogan and Peter Coyote—arrived in Manhattan to "check out the scene, see what we might accomplish there, and . . . have some adventures," Coyote recalled in his memoir *Sleeping Where I Fall: A Chronicle*. "Janis Joplin, a good friend, sometime lover, sometime dope partner, always steady pal, was in New York when Emmett and I arrived. We ran around . . . together, taking her out to hear great jazz and blues singers." Grogan and Coyote regularly used heroin, which had become as widely available in the Haight as LSD.

"Started seeing Emmett & Peter," Janis wrote Linda Gravenites that week. "1st night had an incredible shooting party—dope—in my hotel room. Mostly my dope, too, come to think of it. Oh but I was so in love! w/ all of them! They've got such interesting heads—I just love to sit & listen! God. So that night I ended up w/ Emmett (just 2 years late, was all he said & it was groovey), so spending a lot of time w/ them & so happy. One afternoon last week I called Emmett & told him I was bored so, lo, he sent Peter over & honey!! Now I know our tastes are alike. God I'm really in love w/ him."

In mid-August, when Big Brother left for its Midwest tour, the Diggers stuck around. "Emmett and I stayed on in their rooms at the Chelsea Hotel, pretending to be 'managers,'" Coyote, who would become a successful actor, recounted. "That ruse wore thin, and we were forced to move from room to room, jimmying the flimsy locks to find an empty room and greasing the palms of the maids with bottles of Southern Comfort that well-wishers sent Janis by the case." Coyote and Grogan were chummy with Grossman, who supported progressive causes and gave them gratis office space. From there, the Diggers eventually "brokered a peace meeting" between New York gang leaders and city detectives—with a treaty of sorts agreed to late one night at the CBS penthouse boardroom, also arranged by Grossman.

>─I─◄♦─O─◄♦─I─◄

Deciding she wanted a close friend in her band-to-be, Janis surprised Sam Andrew by inviting him to join her. She was nervous about being on her own and finding skillful—and simpatico—musicians to back her up. "I want a bigger band with higher highs, a bigger ladder, and I want more bottom," she told journalist Al Aronowitz for a *Life* magazine profile. "I can really sing, but I also know I've got a lot to learn. I guess it happened too soon for me. That means that I gotta do all my learning in front of people. That's scary."

Janis dealt with that fear the way she always had: by drinking heavily and doing drugs. After a gig in Cincinnati, the band—excluding Albin—went to a party at a hippie house and shared syringes of smack with their hosts. "There's a certain kind of freedom that one gets from heroin in the beginning," Dave Getz offered. "All of a sudden all the pain and worry and stress are removed. You're totally relaxed, you're not tense, you can just hang out and chat with people. For a performer, someone as high-strung as Janis, she found it had a positive payoff."

When the others learned that Sam would be joining Janis, they were outraged. "That was the biggest blow," Getz revealed, "when Sam said, 'Oh, I'm going with Janis too,' after we'd discussed continuing the band with a new singer. That really floored me." At Minneapolis's Guthrie Theater, the tensions spilled over onstage. After furiously dancing and singing, Janis breathed heavily into the microphone. Albin, "feeling a little malicious," he recalled, "started making fun of her," saying into his mike, "Here she is doing her Lassie imitation," followed by his own loud panting. Mortified, Janis screamed, *"Fuck you!"*

"It was said in jest, and she took it the wrong way," Albin explained. "Then I got pissed off after she yelled at me onstage." A *Rolling Stone* writer witnessed the exchange and noted the angry vibe backstage, all of which he reported in his concert coverage. In New York, Big Brother played a high-profile concert with Jimi Hendrix, the Chambers Brothers, and Soft Machine at the Singer Bowl, attended by eighteen thousand. "That great singer, Miss Joplin, was not in top form," Robert Shelton wrote in his *New York Times* review. "She was not mixing too well with her quartet. . . . [She] will be leaving that group at the end of November to form a new band."

The demoralizing gig coincided with the highly anticipated August 31 release of *Cheap Thrills* and its first single, "Piece of My Heart," with the flip side "Turtle Blues." To get AM airplay for "Piece of My Heart," Clive Davis had his engineer make some edits, including cutting Andrew's guitar break. The truncated version was now a radio-friendly two minutes and change instead of four minutes plus. Though Big Brother condemned Mainstream's similar actions, this time Janis gave her permission for the edit—anything for a hit. "Piece of My Heart" immediately entered the Hot 100, where it remained for three months, reaching number twelve. Even without the psychedelic guitar break, it was a gripping slice of blues rock—unlike anything else on the radio.

Cheap Thrills had so many advance orders that it shipped gold, topping the *Billboard* album chart two months later. It stayed there for eight weeks, remaining on the album chart for more than a year and quickly selling a million copies. The label promoted the record with radio ads such as: "Nobody can tell you about it. You've got to feel it for yourself. Get your *Cheap Thrills* on Columbia Records."

The album crackles with excitement and passion, Janis's voice cutting through the occasional guitar sludge. The seven diverse tracks sound live even though, excluding "Ball and Chain," they were painstakingly pieced together in the studio. The loud-fast sonics predate punk and grunge, and Janis's vocal style would influence Robert Plant, Steven Tyler, David Johansen, Ann Wilson, Axl Rose, Kurt Cobain, and other rock singers.

Yet upon its release, many critics panned *Cheap Thrills*. *Rolling Stone*'s Boston-based Jon Landau (Bruce Springsteen's future producer and manager) did not like most San Francisco bands, and he'd written a negative review in the magazine of Big Brother's Newport performance. His review of the "disappointing" *Cheap Thrills*—"a fair approximation of the San Francisco scene in all its loud, exciting, sloppy glory"—noted the omission of producer John Simon's name from the credits. Simon, Landau wrote, "feels that this album is as good as the band and that's about it. In fact, he likes the Mainstream LP better." Landau agreed with Simon's assessment. Three decades later, however, *Cheap Thrills* would be listed among *Rolling Stone*'s Top 500 Albums of All Time, and "Piece of My Heart," one of its Top 500 Singles.

One of the most scathing critiques ran in the *New York Times*, with jazz critic William Kloman calling Big Brother "middle-class white kids with long blond hair pretending to be black. The whole thing comes off as bad parody, a kind of plastic soul that lacks the humor and relative integrity of, say, the old 'Amos n Andy' shows." This theme of appropriating black music was echoed in a *Downbeat* review, "Burnt Cork Again," which called Big Brother "embarrassing blackface" and "impostering."

Al Aronowitz, in his *Life* profile of Janis, "Singer with a Bordello Voice," also panned the LP yet took her to task for leaving Big Brother: "Janis Joplin had decided to send Big Brother . . . back to San Francisco while she shopped around for another band. 'They don't help the words, they either fight 'em or just lay there like dead fish,' she said." Janis was taking her frustration with Big Brother public.

What few at the time realized was Janis had a clear idea of what she wanted in a new group: an R&B–inspired band with horns—a cross between the funky-soul sound of Stax/Volt Records and the "brass rock" of fellow Columbia artists Blood, Sweat and Tears and, particularly, the seven-piece group Chicago, whom she'd befriended when they shared a bill. In September she wrote her parents about "my hardest task. I told you, you remember, that I was leaving Big Brother & going to do a thing of my own. Well, I have to find the best musicians in the world . . . & get together & work. There'll be a whole lot of pressure because of the 'vibes' created by my leaving Big Brother & also by just how big I am now. So we've got to be just super when we start playing—but we will be."

Janis first eyed a rhythm section composed of Electric Flag bassist Harvey Brooks and Canadian drummer Skip Prokop, who'd played with Grossman clients the Paupers. "Albert called me into his office and told me, 'I want you to put Janis's new band together,'" Prokop recounted. "He said, 'I want this band to be so tight and so hot—like they're from Muscle Shoals and could play with Aretha Franklin.'"

Janis immediately bonded with Prokop, who suggested that instead of Brooks they hire Paupers bassist Brad Campbell, a twenty-three-year-old Canadian. Grossman arranged a demo session at a studio in

Midtown Manhattan with producer Elliot Mazer and session players. "We did stuff that people have never heard Janis do," said Prokop, " 'Hey Joe' and a couple of Aretha tunes. She was amazing. The engineer said, 'She's incredible!' "

On September 7, the day after Big Brother headlined the Hollywood Bowl, Janis signed a simple letter stating, "I hereby tender my resignation as a Director and a Vice President of Big Brother and the Holding Company effective this date." Bob Gordon set up her own Fantality organization (the word, her mash-up of *fantasy* and *reality*) and Strong Arm Music. "A lot of pressure," Janis wrote the Joplins, "because of the way it's going to be set up this time—I'm now a corporation called Fantality, which also has much more chance of making money for me as my price goes up, I pocket the extra, or rather Fantality does. Albert told me—are you ready?—that I should make 1/2 million!! next year counting record royalties."

Gordon took Janis to Zipper Motors in Beverly Hills where, for $3,500, she bought a used 1965 Porsche Super-90 cabriolet. "They had just put on seventeen coats of oyster lacquer, each rubbed down separately," Gordon recalled. "It was gorgeous, looked like a pearl." She reported to the Joplins about her purchases: "I'm already doing pretty well for money. I have a tendency to spend whatever I have as soon as I get it, but I've been getting so much recently that I just can't—I have everything I need plus several thousand in the bank. Last week I bought a 1965 Porsche convertible—very fancy & high class & a great car too. And a new stereo & a color TV & more clothes & Linda and I are now on a vacation—Lake Tahoe & Reno. Incredible. Who'd have thought?!!"

Janis commissioned her former equipment manager Dave Richards to custom paint the Porsche. He turned it into a kaleidoscopic collage, with a portrait of Big Brother, a Marin County landscape, and the cosmos, among other surrealistic imagery, calling it "The History of the Universe." Every inch was covered, including under the gas flap and on the dashboard. Her Porsche became the most recognizable car in San Francisco—possibly in the state of California.

Janis's elevation to rock star status had hit home for her when a few months before parting ways with Big Brother, the band performed at the American Music Show festival at the Rose Bowl in Pasadena, California, on September 15. They headlined a bill with a dozen acts, such as the Byrds, Country Joe, and Buddy Guy, as well as artists who had influenced Janis, including Buffy St. Marie, Joan Baez, and Wilson Pickett. "The most fantastic thing of all happened," she wrote the Joplins:

> We closed the show on a big Pop Festival—lots of the bigger acts. The stage was set in the middle of the football field & the cops wouldn't let the kids out on the grass near us—rules. But on our encore I kept asking them to let the kids dance, they wouldn't so here I am, looking at the audience singing "Down on Me" & all of a sudden they broke, just like a wave & swarmed onto the field. They ran to the edge of the stage & started trying to touch me. I reached down & shook a few hands, then turned to go down the backstairs but when I got there nothing but kids, thousands of them reaching, reaching. They were pulling on my clothes, my beads, calling, 'Janis, Janis, we love you.' I was completely surrounded & being buffeted around when the cops rescued me & put me in a car—had to drive to the dressing room. Car was surrounded at all times by kids on the windows, roof, fenders, hood. Made a Beatle type entry into the dressing room as they were trying to break down the back door. Incredible! Can't say I didn't like it though. Man, I loved it!!

Dorothy typed a congratulatory card: "GOOD NEWS to your report of singing being happiness and your own dream come true! While we do not know what part of each of the many news stories are quotes, etc., we do KNOW that you have achieved a tremendous success in a field of your own choice and every one of the steps you have taken have made it possible."

Dorothy's card continued with unmistakable notes of concern for her daughter: "So, your family salutes your happiness and your success and your developing business acumen and even your awareness of the continued need to grow in the field of your choice as you mentioned when you phoned about adding new instruments to your band and getting it professional as well as native talent. So, we would like to hear from you regularly about each of the steps, plans, itinerary, formats, styles and continued happiness. Glad to talk to you.—Mother."

Janis treasured and saved Dorothy's card, but her days of arranging clippings and photos in a scrapbook had ended. There were too many articles, and she no longer had the time, or the energy, to compile them. She wrote fewer letters, communicating more often by phone—since she could now afford long-distance calls. Her mother's pointed allusion to the validity of news stories' quotes was in response to the Joplins' increasing discomfort with reports in the press of Janis's tales of adolescent woe in Port Arthur. It's unlikely Janis even noticed Dorothy's concern.

As Big Brother played its last two months of gigs, Janis began working with her new musicians. Skip Prokop relocated to San Francisco, where he met with Janis to develop material. One night after Prokop jammed at the Fillmore, a Hells Angel approached him. "He comes right up in my face and says, 'Somebody wants to talk to you!'" Prokop recounted. "I'm escorted into this sea of black leather jackets, that's parted and closed like the Red Sea, and this guy says, 'So you're Skip Prokop? You're putting Janis's new band together, right?' I said, 'Yeah, that's what I'm here for,' and he said, 'And you're gonna take care of our little sister, right?' I said, *'Yeah, sure!'*" It dawned on Prokop that Janis, in a sense, had her own set of bodyguards.

Prokop also discovered that she used heroin fairly regularly. "We were at her place, and her girlfriend comes over," he said. "The next thing you know they're pulling their dresses off and saying, 'We're gonna shoot up.' Janis got more and more stoned till she was about to fall off the chair. So I picked her up and put her to bed, making sure she was okay before I left. I remember her grabbing my arm and saying, 'Skip,' in that Janis whisper, *'please don't tell Albert.'*"

>⊷⊶⊷

On September 29 Big Brother performed its one and only national TV appearance. ABC's glitzy *Hollywood Palace* variety show clung to another era, as if the counterculture didn't exist. That week's guest host, sitcom star Don Adams of the popular spy spoof *Get Smart*, gave the group a corny intro: "Okay, kids, here they are, the hottest group in the country, Big Brother and the Holding Company, with Janis Joplin!" The band then launched into an abbreviated "Summertime" and "I Need a Man to Love" on a set with a bogus "light show" projecting swirling colors. The instrumentalists mimed playing—to a backing track—while Janis sang live.

Looking lovely and poised in a purple satin blouse and elephant-leg pants, she was briefly interviewed onstage by their clearly dismissive host. Adams's voice dripped with condescension as he read to his seated, straight-laced studio audience a quote from Janis in a *Life* magazine feature. Feigning confusion about her stated preference for audiences that dance rather than sit, Adams asked Janis to explain what she meant. "When an audience is dancing," she told him earnestly, "they're communicating with you." Adams rolled his eyes, shook his head, and the audience guffawed.

"I was crushed," she told a journalist later. "You can't get any love out of that place. I knew it was going to be hard, so I said, 'Just close your eyes . . . and sing. . . . Don't play any games with them, just try and sing, and then it will work, right?' I got about halfway through the chorus of one song, and I was concentrating with my eyes closed and I felt I was really getting it together, so I opened my eyes and looked at the audience, and they were laughing. All those little old ladies from Kansas were laughing at me. It just destroyed me." They may not have actually laughed during her performance, but the provincial crowd's obvious derision brought back painful memories.

>–◆–○–◆–◃

The band's schedule was packed with dates to capitalize on the successful album and to enable Big Brother to earn as much as possible before the tour ended. "I'm making a hundred dollars a minute," Getz realized at a show at Philadelphia's Spectrum indoor arena. Janis didn't hold back, "swearing, moaning, screeching, stomping, jumping, crashing, twisting, swinging and tearing herself and 17,000 others to pieces as she belted out the blues like no one else can," reported the University of Pennsylvania's daily newspaper. Before the show, she told a reporter her new music would be "something more subtle. Horns and organ. . . . The kind of things that milk you rather than hammer you."

But Ellen Willis reported in the *New Yorker* what could only be considered as hammering during the band's Fillmore East gig in August: "Janis Joplin put on the most exalting, exhausting concert I have ever been privileged to see, hear, and feel. Euphoric from Bill Graham's champagne, she sang four encores, and the audience, standing on the seats, wouldn't go home. Finally, she came back onstage. 'I love you, honey,' she said, gasping, 'but I just got nothing left.' Someday, we were sure, it would really be true—someday soon, if she kept giving like that. I didn't know if I wanted the responsibility of taking; I felt a little like a vampire. From now on, I decided, after two encores I stop clapping."

Big Brother's final New York City show, on November 15, at Hunter College, found the band "severely disjointed," according to the *New York Times* review. Spirits were low: Republican Richard Nixon had just won the presidential election. Janis had been up all night on speed. Getz took LSD before going on. Another conflict erupted onstage. During Getz's extended drum solo on "Mr. Natural," his bandmates exited while he got the spotlight. Then Janis danced back onstage carrying a small conga drum, which she set down near Getz. "I couldn't reach it, so I kicked it, and it flew about ten feet," the drummer recalled. When it sailed by, Janis mistakenly thought it was aimed at her, so she screamed, *"Fuck you, man!"* Afterward, she and Getz began loudly arguing backstage, with Janis saying, "I was just trying to be nice to you, man, bringing this drum to you, and you embarrassed me in front of three thousand people!"

After a Long Island performance the next night, Janis could barely get out of bed and called her publicist, Myra Friedman, for help. She was diagnosed with acute bronchitis; Big Brother canceled its next few shows, including one in Austin, Texas, which Janis had been looking forward to. A week later, she had recovered enough to perform a makeup date in Houston. The Joplins drove the ninety miles from Port Arthur, as did old friend Kristin Bowen; Houstonites Dave and Patti McQueen also attended. After the concert, her family and friends witnessed Janis fly into a rage backstage, yelling at a stagehand. He had closed the curtains before she finished singing, trapping her alone and embarrassed out front, with the band hidden behind the drapes. Also, the theater enforced a strict noise curfew, like most US venues, and it did not permit seated audiences to leave their chairs and dance, another of Janis's pet peeves. Soon after, the city banned all rock concerts. Even when the ban was lifted, the city of Houston—her old stomping grounds—still barred Janis from performing there "for her attitude in general."

The Joplins' visit was additionally strained because Dorothy and Seth resented Janis's negative comments to the press about her hometown and troubled adolescence, as well as her quips comparing singing to taking "heavy dope" and having an orgasm. "One went so far as to say that her family kicked her out of the house at age fourteen," Laura Joplin wrote in *Love, Janis*. "Our parents were crushed. Not only was Janis flouting most of the morals that their generation prized, but she was lying about her relationship to her family in a very public way. They felt powerless and wronged." When autograph seekers chased Janis and her family to their car, the Joplins were further rattled, and their late-night dinner together at Janis's motel was uncomfortable for all.

>·+◆>·0·◆+·<

On December 1 Big Brother's final tour ended where it had all begun two and a half years earlier: a Family Dog benefit for the Avalon—which had closed in November due to financial and legal problems. The crowd didn't hide its anger at Janis's decision to quit Big Brother, with close-knit residents of the Haight's good old days feeling particularly betrayed. Graffiti popped up on neighborhood walls urging Janis not to leave the group. Some fans and friends personally confronted her about dumping the band and leaving behind the hippie community that had supported Big Brother. Having won their love, Janis now risked losing it—an excruciating proposition for her. Even her champions, such as

Ellen Willis, questioned her future: "We worried: Will Success Spoil Janis?" she wrote in the *New Yorker*. "Will she become overconfident, lazy, mechanical? Did Big Brother perhaps give her more than we realized? Will she lose it—*it*—without them?"

Janis's hometown paper *Rolling Stone* predicted that her new band would be a slick Vegas-style revue; a November feature described Janis onstage as "posing like an imperious whore." "I thought they were my friends," she would tell a reporter, "but [*Rolling Stone*] abandoned me." Though Linda Gravenites urged her to lay off the heroin, Janis continued to use it as a buffer against the tumult: "I just want some fucking peace!"

Janis had no downtime. She immediately had to transition from playing Big Brother concerts to rehearsing with the new group, and that band was not gelling. Skip Prokop had withdrawn from the project after Janis insisted on including Sam Andrew in the new band. "I said to her, 'I don't think Sammy's good enough to play in this kind of band,'" Prokop explained. When she told him, "Sammy is nonnegotiable," Prokop quit, returning to Canada and starting the band Lighthouse.

On keyboards, Grossman had enlisted Indiana native Bill King, who played the Hammond B-3 organ in Village clubs with drummer Roy Markowitz, who replaced Prokop. The two flew to San Francisco to meet bassist Brad Campbell, staying at Mark Braunstein's mother's apartment. "The three of us were on the same wavelength and totally into it," King recalled. "Roy and Brad were really straight and not screwed up on drugs." When Janis invited them to her apartment for dinner, the first thing they noticed was a sculpture of a large phallus in the living room. Then several rowdy Hells Angels arrived, the drugs and booze consumption increased, and "things started to get really out there," King said, "so we left."

For Janis's horn section, Grossman hired the erstwhile Electric Flag's tenor saxophonist, Terry Clements, and trumpeter Marcus Doubleday, the latter of whom was addicted to heroin. On the first day of rehearsal, Doubleday arrived late, with a syringe jammed into his horn. Adding to the pressure, Grossman had already booked a gig for the band. They were to play in the soul capital of Memphis at a "Yuletide Thing" concert organized by Stax Records, Otis Redding's label. Grossman enlisted Mike Bloomfield to oversee a mere three days of rehearsals before they flew to Memphis. Although Bloomfield and the Band's drummer, Levon Helm, who checked out a rehearsal, reported to Grossman that the group was coming together, Terry Clements recalled otherwise. The twenty-nine-year-old Englishman found the rehearsals "chaotic and unproductive, with no one taking a strong leadership role." Sam Andrew's strongest memory was of buying balloons of heroin prior to each rehearsal. Janis continued to slide toward addiction, alongside Andrew and her paramour Peggy Caserta.

On December 20, 1968, Janis and her new band arrived in Memphis to rehearse at Stax. Being in the studio where Otis Redding recorded was thrilling but unnerving for Janis, who tried to take charge at rehearsal. "There she was—hair flying—jumping around, yelling and screaming, 'Too slow!' 'Still too slow!' 'No, too fast!'" reported Ralph Garcia, a fledgling writer and photographer covering the band's debut for *Circus* magazine. "They rehearsed for almost four hours with Bloomfield riding herd, jumping, shouting, and slowly bringing them together."

It had only been eight months since Martin Luther King's assassination at the Lorraine Motel, a gathering place for Stax artists. The concert poster listed Janis as the headliner above "all these great Stax artists underneath," said Bill King, "and that put a bad feeling in the air. I think some people thought, 'Here's this Janis Joplin coming to town and demanding top billing. She felt just horrible and wanted to apologize to everybody." Janis and the band joined Stax artists at a party at the home of label president Jim Stewart; there, she sipped cocktails and posed for pictures with stars Rufus Thomas and daughter Carla, Judy Clay, William Bell, and members of the MG's and the reconstituted Bar-Kays (Redding's surviving band members). She also met journalist Stanley Booth, who was covering the concert for what she called "those shits at *Rolling Stone*."

Things did not go well on Saturday night. During sound check, Janis and the band were thrown off by the Mid-South Coliseum's sonorous acoustics, and they encountered persistent technical difficulties with their amps and the PA. Clad in a feather-trimmed cerise jumpsuit, Janis "looked sort of like a big, sexy bird," according to Garcia. After a high-energy opening slot by the Bar-Kays, in matching zebra-striped outfits and doing a dance called the sideways pony, their Stax labelmates followed in rapid succession, each polishing off highly entertaining sets, appreciated loudly by the crowd.

Following Eddie Floyd, Janis's band took its time, fumbling with equipment while the restless audience waited impatiently. Janis finally opened with new covers they had worked up: Floyd's "Raise Your Hand" and the Bee Gees' "To Love Somebody," which Janis delivered Otis style. Applause was tepid: the primarily black audience wasn't familiar with Janis's sound, and the small number of teenage rock fans knew only Big Brother's "Piece of My Heart" and "Ball and Chain"—the songs Janis planned to sing as an encore. After a sluggish "Summertime," Janis and company shuffled offstage, with no calls for their return. Instead, Stax's Johnnie Taylor rushed out to close the show with a dynamic version of his current smash, "Who's Making Love." Though well-wishers offered reassurance backstage, Janis was devastated. "At least they didn't throw things," she muttered to Stanley Booth.

Afterward, Janis, Doubleday, and Andrew all shot heroin and nodded out. "It was insanity for us to play at the Temple of Soul," Andrew reflected later. "We'd just started this band, and we played very badly." Though Garcia's *Circus* feature raved that Janis's performance was "fantastic," Booth chided her in *Rolling Stone*, recommending she "might start over with some musicians who know already how to do the sideways pony."

The Memphis fiasco was an omen of the year to come: a band with a revolving-door membership and no real leadership. Between her drug and alcohol consumption and her inexperience directing a band, Janis found herself the captain of a rudderless ship. She wanted the camaraderie of early Big Brother but with her, the star, calling the shots. It turned out she couldn't have it both ways—at least not for now.

A week later, Bill King vanished. Unbeknownst to the band, the FBI had detained him for draft evasion, and to avoid jail, he enlisted in the army (then went AWOL to Canada, where he remained). The drug-addicted Doubleday also left the band. In San Francisco, Janis discovered keyboardist Richard Kermode, twenty-two, playing at a North Beach topless joint, and someone recommended trumpeter Terry Hensley, a part-time cab driver. The new band spent the next month rehearsing Big Brother songs and new material. In addition to the Memphis numbers, they added a song by "Piece of My Heart" coauthor Jerry Ragovoy, "Try (Just a Little Bit Harder)." Nick Gravenites, another band "advisor," taught them his bluesy scorcher "Work Me, Lord."

Despite the worthy material, Janis was not yet able to articulate to her band the music she heard in her head: the swamp of Jerry LaCroix's roadhouse R&B mixed with her interpretation of the Stax sound. Vocally, she aspired to Etta James, Aretha Franklin, and Tina Turner, women whose music she now name checked as inspirations—just as she had Bessie Smith and Big Mama Thornton. "She gave me respect," James later said about Janis. "When I heard her sing, I recognized my influence, but I also heard the electricity and rage in her own voice." Janis was beginning to acknowledge being in striking distance of her role models' artistry, but this prospect also intimidated her.

Janis's drinking and drugging didn't help matters. While alcohol and dope offered relief from anxiety, guilt, and insecurity, they blunted her ability to communicate and deeply connect with her musicians, sapping her of the strength needed to commandeer a band. She also now had the means to indulge in expensive intoxicants as much as she wanted. In the contest between her ambition and her self-destructiveness, self-destruction was winning. When writer Michael Lydon interviewed her for a *New York Times Magazine* feature, she told him, "I'm scared," about her new musical direction, "but I never hold back. I'm always on the outer limits of probability." During their lengthy chat, which started at a boozy rehearsal and then continued at a pool hall and her apartment, she acknowledged her drinking was a crutch: "When I get scared and worried, I tell myself, Janis, have a good time. So I juice up real good." She added a prophetic statement: "Man, I'd rather have ten years of superhyper-most living than live to be 70 by sitting in some goddamn chair watching TV." She pointed to her new lynx coat: "That fur coat, too. Know how I got that? Southern Comfort. Far out! I had the chick in my manager's office photostat every goddamn clipping that ever had me mentioning Southern Comfort, and I sent them to the company, and they sent me a whole lotta money. How could anybody in their right mind want me for their image? Oh, man, that was the best hustle I ever pulled—can you imagine getting paid for passing out for two years?" Lydon's article asked, "Will she make it? . . . Janis Joplin has changed signals. Instead of rock, it's rhythm & blues."

In February 1969, two weeks after Janis's twenty-sixth birthday, she and her new six-piece band flew to the East Coast to try again. John Cooke continued as road manager, and Bobby Neuwirth signed on informally as Janis's aide-de-camp, the role he'd held with Dylan. Joining Braunstein were roadies George Ostrow and Vince Mitchell, the latter of whom would be Janis's occasional lover. With a blizzard raging, they returned to the Fillmore East midweek for four sold-out shows beginning February 11. Backstage Janis gave an interview to Mike Wallace of the CBS-TV newsmagazine program *60 Minutes*, then in its first season, for a segment on the Fillmore called "Carnegie Hall for Kids." Like a student trying to convince an elder, she earnestly touted the honesty of the blues, explaining to Wallace why young people were "getting into black music, any kind of music that tells the truth."

Adding to the stress of opening night in New York, bassist Brad Campbell's visa had expired, and they worried he'd be recognized onstage and deported back to Canada. To hide him in plain sight, Friedman told the press that "Keith Cherry" had replaced Campbell. Neuwirth used an eyebrow pencil to darken Campbell/Cherry's blond mustache and sideburns, with sunglasses and Janis's fur hat completing the ridiculous disguise.

Onstage, the loud horn section sometimes drowned out or competed with Janis's vocals. Extremely nervous, she overcompensated, straining her voice, and "strangled the songs to death," according to *Rolling Stone* critic Paul Nelson. He compared her to both actor Richard

Burton and a Radio City Music Hall Rockette and complained that Janis and band "failed to mesh." Andrew's guitar did not always work with the horns, and some of the new arrangements of Big Brother songs were awkward. Emulating the performance style of Stax artists and the Ike and Tina Turner Revue, Janis, tambourine in hand, boogalooed while the instrumentalists soloed. Afterward, against Myra Friedman's wishes, she gave Nelson an interview. In his cover story, "Janis: The Judy Garland of Rock?" (Garland would die of a drug overdose in June), Nelson painted the picture of a neurotic mess painfully defensive about her new approach, which he said resembled "a brass burlesque show."

Six weeks later, when they performed back in San Francisco at Bill Graham's Winterland, the subdued audience did not call for an encore—a first on her home turf. Joining her afterward in the dressing room, journalist John Bowers noted, "She is pale, as if in shock, saying, 'San Francisco's changed, man. Where are my people? They used to be so wild. I know I sang well! I know I did!'"

She should "scrap this band and go right back to being a member of Big Brother," hissed Ralph Gleason at the end of his spiteful *Chronicle* review, "if they'll have her." The next night, she added a couple of Big Brother songs to the set list, and the response improved. But Janis took such slights hard, escaping into a heroin haze with Caserta and her old friend Sunshine, now a junkie and living with Janis and Gravenites. Shortly after the Winterland shows, Janis's roommates found her unconscious with blue-tinged skin; they managed to resuscitate her from an overdose of heroin, her first. In December Janis would tell a doctor that she had OD'd several times that year, revived by Gravenites and others. But the grip of heroin was such that even these near-death experiences didn't deter her from using.

Janis's band still had no permanent name (she'd use "Main Squeeze" for it and her next band, on occasion), perhaps because it didn't really have a group vibe but was rather an aggregation of players chosen to back her. A notable new addition was alto sax player Cornelius "Snooky" Flowers, a former member of Oakland soul group Johnny Tolbert & De Thangs and who had worked with Mike Bloomfield. An African American navy veteran, Flowers grew up in Leesville, Louisiana, near Port Arthur. In September Janis would invite him to stay with her family—the first time a black man slept in the Joplin home—and he squired Janis to R&B clubs in Port Arthur's segregated black district.

"I had never heard a white girl sing that good," Flowers recalled about first seeing Janis in '67 with Big Brother. "But that band was the sorriest I ever heard. I said, 'Man, she singin' funk, and that band is playing some other kind of shit.'" Janis and Flowers became close soon after he joined the tour in New York in mid-February. "She opened her hotel room door wearing nothing but her bra and panties and said, 'Hey, baby!'" he recounted. One night they went to the Village to see jazz multi-instrumentalist Roland Kirk, who announced from the stage, "We got a star among us tonight." "It freaked her out," Flowers related, "but he said, 'Come on up here and play with us.' She was scared to death, but they played 'Piece of My Heart' better than we played it."

Flowers's take-charge personality made him a natural leader, and his contributions to the group increased until he was singing a couple of songs during each set. On *The Ed Sullivan Show* on March 16, Janis and the band played live, and Flowers was featured prominently—in an era when there were few biracial bands on TV. They had performed in Ann Arbor, Michigan, the day before, and afterward, Janis stayed up all night partying at a blues club. "I wanted to look as funky as I could for Ed Sullivan tonight," she told John Bowers, "but damned if I don't think I may be too funky now."

Yet on the *Sullivan Show*, she appeared energized, though raspy voiced, on the two songs the group performed: "Maybe," the 1958 Chantels ballad she'd loved as a teen, and "Raise Your Hand," during which she shimmied while the horn section vamped. When Sullivan, whom she'd watched so often with her family, grabbed her hand afterward, she was elated—his handshake a sure sign of approval, she told the band. John Bowers, who'd been traveling with the group, noted that Janis had slept only one and a half hours over the past forty-eight.

Soon after, days before the band departed for a European tour, veteran trumpeter Luis Gasca—who'd worked for Count Basie, Mongo Santamaria, and others—replaced Hensley. During the first three weeks in April, the band jelled in Europe, performing in Stockholm, Amsterdam, Frankfurt, Copenhagen, Paris, and London. The latter city, where the band spent its first eight days rehearsing, greeted Janis as if she were visiting royalty—from a different planet. Accompanied by Ian Kimmet, a Grossman protégé who worked for his UK publishing company, she tantalized tabloid journalists and broadcasters with her heavy drinking and flirtatious bravado, while perfecting her bawdy blues mama persona. "She boasts a façade of utter shock," sniffed one scribe, "a constant barrage of 4-letter non-descriptive adjectives. This week she was to have been the cover story on *Newsweek*, but [former president Dwight] Eisenhower's death meant that the feature on her had to be postponed. She had some very un-American things to say about Eisenhower: 'Goddamn it, fourteen heart attacks, and he had to die in my week!'" Janis would appear on a May issue of *Newsweek*, with the cover line "Rebirth of the Blues."

Linda Gravenites was on hand to take care of her wardrobe, and the two were invited to join George and Pattie Harrison for dinner—Janis finally got to meet her favorite Beatle. During rehearsals, Janis took on the demeanor of drill sergeant, Kimmet recalled, screaming orders and whipping the band into shape. With the group's newfound tightness, European audiences did not look back and yell for Big Brother, and the positive feedback contributed to the growing cohesion of the ensemble. The horns joined Sam Andrew's guitar on the intro to "Summertime" and "Combination of the Two," where they added punch even if Janis occasionally could not hit the high *"whoah whoah"*s. While she gave her voice a rest, Flowers sang two numbers: a song he wrote called "Me"—on which Janis thwacked a cowbell—and a cover of Otis Redding's "I Can't Turn You Loose," with Janis doing the Louisiana dirty bop. In Copenhagen, she joined the opening act, Fleetwood Mac, onstage for a song.

Several of the European concerts were recorded, and in Frankfurt, the band played a second show for television broadcast. "I make it a policy not to tell anyone to sit down, so they'll all stand up!" she told the audience, composed of US enlisted men, their wives, and a few longhaired Germans. *"I wanna see you people move!"* she demanded. By show's end, during "Piece of My Heart," Janis was surrounded onstage by deliriously dancing GIs and miniskirted women.

At the sold-out finale at Royal Albert Hall, Janis successfully drove the usually staid British audience to get out of its seats and dance. Eric Clapton and Fleetwood Mac were among the musicians in attendance, though Mick Jagger reportedly sniped he wouldn't be going because, "If I want to hear black singing, then I'll listen to black singers." The high-energy performance was an unmitigated triumph, and afterward, Neuwirth and Cooke recorded Janis's happy chatter, "God, I'm so happy! I got 'em all off their asses!! I think I'll call my mother!"

Instead she excused herself from the soiree in her suite to join Sam Andrew in the bathroom to shoot up. She'd been covertly doing heroin on the tour, taking the risk of sneaking it across borders. San Franciscans Bob Seidemann and Stanley Mouse, in London and attending the packed party, realized something was amiss: they discovered Andrew had overdosed, with Janis and Gravenites plunging him naked in a bath of ice-cold water, where a groupie named Suzie Creamcheese straddled him. He revived. Seidemann warned Eric Clapton, who'd started using heroin, to leave the party in case the police arrived.

For Linda Gravenites—always opposed to Janis's heroin use—the harrowing scene was the last straw. She decided to stay on in London rather than return with Janis. Pattie and George Harrison had hired her to make a beaded purse and jacket, and she moved into the Harrison manor. "I'll come home when you stop doing smack," she told Janis.

Back in the States, touring continued, but Janis, angry over Gravenites's defection, took it out on the band members, haranguing them about their playing, while the demoralized musicians criticized her performances. Markowitz quit, replaced by LA rock drummer Maury Baker. Janis's longtime pal Mark Braunstein, disturbed by the dissension, also resigned. Janis had taken up with keyboardist Richard

Kermode, but that relationship soon fizzled. Throughout, she remained closest with Sam Andrew, whose musical contributions suffered from his own heroin use.

In June Janis—now on a salary of $300 a week, with much of her earnings invested—returned to Columbia's LA studio to record a new album. This time Grossman selected Gabriel Mekler, who'd produced the Paupers' second album, as well as hits by Three Dog Night and Steppenwolf. In an attempt to clean up and prepare, Janis moved in with Mekler and his family. Her voice was shot from touring, screaming on-stage, smoking, and drinking. A classically trained pianist and "a likable guy," according to Three Dog's Night's Chuck Negron, Mekler wanted to collaborate with her on the preproduction and recording process. Negron, whose first meeting with Janis at the Whisky had ended in a drunken argument, stopped by Mekler's Hollywood home while she was in residence. "She was standing in the kitchen helping his wife with the cooking," he recounted in his memoir *Three Dog Nightmare*. Wearing an apron and with her hair up, Janis seemed "this whole other person without the . . . drugs and booze . . . with a certain awkwardness, shy-ness, and vulnerability. She was actually very nice, very sweet."

Recording sessions took place over ten days in mid-June. Mekler saw the album as Janis's debut solo effort, and her musicians as mediocre sidemen, nothing more. They clashed in the studio when he tried to direct them. Mekler had never worked in Columbia's Studio D, where only union engineers were allowed to touch the equipment. At one point, an engineer accidentally erased an entire take, angering the band. And the group's unheeded request for a raise from Grossman stirred more resentment. "Everybody was putting down everybody else," said bassist Brad Campbell. "It was a total mess." Still, they managed to cut fine versions of songs they'd been playing live: "Try," "Maybe," "To Love Somebody," and "Work Me, Lord."

While at Mekler's, Janis had been writing new songs, including "One Good Man," her update of a Bessie Smith blues. It came to life in the studio with magnificent guitarwork—bottleneck slide and a blistering solo—by Mike Bloomfield, uncredited on the LP. Nick Gravenites's "As

Good as You've Been to This World" began with a long opening vamp by the horn section, featuring Gasca's trumpet and the saxophones of Clements and Flowers. Janis's raspy testifying vocals came in halfway through, with lyrics voicing her philosophy: "Live your loving life / Live it all the best you can."

During the final sessions, they perfected the album's standouts. The Richard Rodgers–Lorenz Hart song "Little Girl Blue," which Janis named as a favorite among her repertoire, was a challenge for all. Bloomfield and Mekler arranged parts for a string section, and Janis's voice never sounded more vulnerable. Inspired by the 1959 Nina Simone recording, she truly made it her own. (Simone, notoriously critical, praised Janis's version while playing the song at the 1974 Montreux Jazz Festival and name checked her again at the same fest in '76.) Andrew's guitar licks, similar to his "Summertime" intro, were kept spare. The strings flow in, while the drums remain soft. Janis gives one of her strongest vocal performances on record, with just the right amount of melisma near the song's end. She *almost* used the "pretty" voice her mother loved so much. "God! Did she ever just want to sing rather than just scream it out," Mekler recalled. "She wanted to develop her voice and go to a high level of art."

For a while, Janis had been talking about the kozmic blues: the existential darkness spun from the Saturday Night Swindle letdowns that tormented her. She finally put those black-dog thoughts into the lyrics of a devastating song that would inspire the name of her new album, *I Got Dem Ol' Kozmic Blues Again Mama!*

> *Time keeps moving on*
> *Friends they turn away,*
> *Well, I keep moving on*
> *But I never found out why*
> *I keep pushing so hard a dream,*
> *I keep trying to make it right*
> *Well, I'm twenty-five years older now*
> *So I know it can't be right*

> *And I'm no better baby, and I can't help you no more*
> *Than I did when I was just a girl.*
> *I'm gonna hold it yeah,*
> *I'm gonna use it till the day I die.*

Mekler cowrote the music for "Kozmic Blues" and brought in two members of Steppenwolf, drummer Jerry Edmonton and keyboardist Goldy McJohn, to play on it. Following Mekler's gorgeous piano melody, Janis's vocals come in with restrained emotion: "I keep pushing too hard." She stretches out and finds that her initial restraint adds to the building emotion of the song. The horns join piano and guitar for the poignant chorus. Janis's distraught vocals end the ballad with a wrenching pathos.

>––•–••–○–••–•–<

Janis would dedicate the album "to Nancy G." On July 4, 1969, Nancy Gurley died of a heroin overdose after James had injected himself and his wife during a wilderness camping trip. When he was arrested for second-degree murder, Janis contributed $20,000 for his legal defense; he was later acquitted. When Janis and Sam Andrew learned of Nancy's death, they immediately shot up—an addict's typical response to such trauma. Soon after, perhaps heeding Grossman's advice, Janis fired Sam. After doing dope together again, she told him bluntly, "Your services are no longer required." The guitarist did not react. When she asked him, "Don't you want to know why?," Andrew said, "What difference does it make?" As part of the farewell, they made love for the first—and only—time. Andrew agreed to teach his parts to her new guitarist, Canadian John Till, poached by Grossman from Ronnie Hawkins's backing group, the Hawks, whose alumni included all five members of the Band.

John Till, twenty-three, joined in time for the Atlanta Pop Festival, which included Led Zeppelin at one of its first US festivals. Janis and the newly named Kozmic Blues Band then played the Forest Hills Tennis Stadium, where Dylan had been booed when backed by the Band in 1965. It would be Andrew's last gig and John Till's second. "Janis came on to thunderous ovation," reported journalist Ellen Sander. "She performed, all blues and dues and spitfire bitch, crooned and wailed and gave herself inside out. She danced into every number, the band cooked hard behind her." Nationally, security had been cracking down on concertgoers, trying to prevent fans from storming the stage. Janis couldn't abide such rules. At Forest Hills, when the audience demanded more after her last song, "the rentacops marched out in dignified single file from both sides of the stage and stood in front of it in a solid line," according to Sander. "Janis's eyes popped at the sight of them. She held the microphone away from her face and let out a stream of curses that stopped them dead. 'GO!' she demanded. 'Get the hell out of here!' she screamed, this time right in the microphone. Her command echoed around the stadium and the audience cheered. The cops went back the way they came and a great cheer went up. Janis said, 'They got to understand, these pigs, that what's going on here is for us—it's not for them!'"

Such proclamations would not turn out so well in Tampa four months later, on November 16. When a cop stepped onstage with a bullhorn during "Summertime" to demand the concert end before the curfew, Janis went ballistic. *"Get off my stage, motherfucker! How dare you stop me in the middle of a song!"* she blared into her mike. Afterward, she was arrested and booked on obscenity and other charges. Her mug shot was taken at a quarter after one—her first since getting busted in Berkeley for shoplifting six years earlier. The charges were eventually settled out of court (with the obscenity claim being dropped due to the First Amendment), with Janis paying a $200 fine and hefty legal fees. By then, she was on the FBI's surveillance list, under suspicion of inciting riots.

Throughout the late spring and early summer of 1969, the buzz was that "three days of peace and music" at a bucolic gathering in upstate New York would be monumental. On August 15 Janis and the band arrived at the Liberty Holiday Inn the day before their appointed slot to play the Woodstock Music and Arts Fair. Janis and pals from the Grateful Dead and Jefferson Airplane hung out in the motel lounge, drinking, playing poker, and repeatedly selecting the Beatles' "Hey Jude" on the jukebox. Joe McDonald had a brief reunion with Janis in her motel room that ended with "a blow job," he recalled. Then, following Janis's liaison with her roadie Vince Mitchell, Peggy Caserta arrived and took over as Janis's playmate. At one point, while talking to the press, Janis flirtatiously grabbed Caserta's breast. By some accounts, the lovers shot heroin during the long wait for Janis and the band's performance. Yet, in the artists' area at the festival site on Saturday, Janis remained vivacious and engaged, continuing the party, flitting around and pouring champagne for all.

After late-night sets by the Grateful Dead and Creedence Clearwater Revival, the Kozmic Blues Band finally went onstage in the wee hours of Sunday, August 17. Peering into the darkness, populated by a half million people, tiny lights twinkling as far as the eye could see, Janis reached out to the crowd like an earth mother: "Do you have enough water and a place to sleep?" It would be John Till's first gig as the lone guitarist, and he rose to the occasion, interplaying his leads with the horn section and keyboards. At three in the morning and after days of little sleep, Janis didn't have her usual high energy when opening with "Raise Your Hand," though her shrieks and screams surely awakened those nodding out. She spent much of the instrumental vamp "As Good as You've Been to Me" dancing barefoot, clad in a Technicolor tie-dyed ensemble with a long gold-trimmed vest (soon removed). Janis delivered a soulful "To Love Somebody" and a sultry "Summertime." She blasted through "Try (Just a Little Bit Harder)" and then slowed down for "Kozmic Blues," which she introduced by warning, "Talking about the kozmic blues. If you don't know what I mean, you will soon enough."

Onstage for nearly sixty minutes, she was spent by the time she began "Ball and Chain"—her voice scorched and then depleted as she drew out the ending while her bandmates veered into dissonance. Still, she came back for an encore of a sped-up but strong "Piece of My Heart." Ellen Sander reported that "Janis Joplin danced with [the audience] as if they were one. They shouted back at her, they wouldn't let her off until they'd drained off every drop of her energy." Because Grossman refused to allow Janis's performance to be included in the original Woodstock documentary, released in March 1970, it was rumored that she'd bombed—but the recordings and existing footage prove otherwise for much of the hour spent onstage.

Festivals proliferated during the summer of 1969, and Janis and the Kozmic Blues Band played gatherings in Texas, Ohio, and Louisiana. Nineteen-year-old Bruce Springsteen and his band Child opened for Janis at Convention Hall in Asbury Park, New Jersey. He was just her type, and she made that clear, but Springsteen would have none of it. "Help, she's after me!" he pleaded with his guitarist "Little Steven" Van Zandt, who recalled with a chuckle how his bandmate hid out to avoid Janis's advances.

The constant touring hadn't helped band morale. When saxophonist Terry Clements had a rare moment alone with Janis, he confessed he wanted to quit. Luis Gasca left, and trumpet player Dave Woodward replaced him. Then her trusted friend and road manager John Cooke tendered his resignation, effective October 5, following the band's return to Winterland. A young Seattle-based promoter, Joe Crowley, was enlisted to take over for Cooke.

Fortunately, Janis still had Neuwirth in her camp, and that fall he gave her the most wondrous gift. At Grossman's office one day, Neuwirth had been chatting with Canadian singer-songwriter Gordon Lightfoot, who turned him on to a fantastic song he'd just learned in Nashville. "He took out his guitar and played 'Me and Bobby McGee,'" Neuwirth recounted. "I said, 'Damn! That's a good song. Teach it to me.' So I wrote down the words, and I said who wrote it? He said, 'Some guy down in Nashville named Kris Kristofferson. He's got a whole bunch of good songs.' This was before Kris was getting cut— maybe Roger Miller had cut it, but I hadn't heard it. That very night, I was having dinner with Janis. I went down and picked her up, and while she and her girlfriend were getting ready, I played the song on her guitar. She goes, 'What is that song, man? Teach it to me!' So I did."

Janis began practicing "Bobby McGee" on her acoustic guitar, and by the time she and the band played Nashville's Fairgrounds Coliseum on December 16, she felt the time was right. Without warning, she started strumming the captivating song, and the band fell in behind her. When she told the audience that "Me and Bobby McGee" was by a Nashville songwriter, the applause was thunderous.

Janis had been listening to country rock, performed by the Flying Burrito Brothers and others at the Palomino club in North Hollywood. Like Gram Parsons of the Burritos, she'd ordered some custom designs from Nudie the Rodeo Tailor, inventor of the rhinestone cowboy. "Did you read about him in *Rolling Stone?*" she wrote Linda Gravenites in London. "He makes the incredible flashy western clothes—real gaudy stuff. Just what I wanted! I'm getting a pants & vest outfit. Purple w/ flowers & scroll-work, encrusted w/ all sorts of colored rhinestones. I'm so excited—Real flashy colored rhinestones!" Janis had pleaded with Gravenites to return to California. "I'd rather have something by you." But Linda stayed away for the time being.

I Got Dem Ol' Kozmic Blues Again Mama! debuted on *Billboard* on October 11, remaining there for twenty-eight weeks and gradually moving up to number five. It produced only one minor hit, the song "Kozmic Blues," which stalled just outside the Top 40. Reviews were lukewarm, with Janis, again, being taken to task for her new musical direction. Some male critics accused her of being "bent on becoming Aretha Franklin" and derided her for dumping Big Brother. "Writers rape her with words as if there weren't any other way to deal with her," Australian critic Lillian Roxon lamented. An exception was an insightful piece in the *Village Voice* by Johanna Schier, who wrote that Janis "was singing stronger and better. . . . The top of her range is more solid and her vocal control is maturing. . . . She breaks through into greatness by anyone's standards." Indeed, the album still sounds fresh today and includes some of her best vocal performances, particularly on "Little Girl Blue," "Maybe," and "Kozmic Blues."

But the record's relative lack of success confirmed Janis's and Grossman's instincts to disband the group. The Kozmic Blues Band had played the most high-profile dates of her career and also appeared on several national television programs, including a jaw-dropping live set on Tom Jones's variety show. Janis did a breathtaking "Little Girl Blue," and the chemistry between her and the soulful Welshman on their duet of "Raise Your Hand," during which they boogied together during the horn vamp, was unlike any other prime-time fare, before or since.

The Kozmic Blues Band's final stop would be at Madison Square Garden, where Janis had recently danced to the Rolling Stones after singing an impromptu duet with Tina Turner during Ike and Tina's opening slot on the Stones' first US tour in three years. During Janis's sold-out concert on December 19, she was joined by old friends for a freewheeling "Bo Diddley": Beaumont's guitar prodigy Johnny Winter, who'd just signed with Columbia, and blues harmonica player and singer Paul Butterfield. It was a crazy night, with John Bowers recalling the Garden nearly "caving in under the weight of all that frenzy and jumping around" by the ecstatic audience. Janis dedicated the show to the New York Jets: she'd recently had a one-night stand with the team's shaggy-haired quarterback "Broadway Joe" Namath.

There was a fabulous after-party hosted by Clive Davis and his wife at their deluxe Central Park apartment, where Janis, clad in black chiffon and high on heroin, encountered Bob Dylan for the first time since introducing herself to him at Monterey in 1963. "I'm gonna be famous one day," she'd told him then. Whether or not they commiserated at the party on the downside of fame is unknown, but according to Davis, Dylan never removed his gloves or coat.

CHAPTER 17

PEARL

*Onstage I make love to twenty-five thousand
people, then I go home alone.*
—JANIS JOPLIN

Janis spent what would be the last year of her life looking for new songs and collaborators—but most of all trying to find a way to reconcile her ambition as a singer with her desperate need to escape the Saturday Night Swindle with some kind of loving attachment. She told a journalist in spring 1969 that she sought "to be true to myself." But "true" to which Janis? The one who finally embraced her ambition to excel as an artist and wanted to give herself completely to her music and career? Or the Janis who was conditioned to believe, partially by her own father, that nothing would ever bring lasting happiness, although she wanted badly to try? These questions were on her mind when she wrote her parents a few days after her twenty-seventh birthday:

"I've been looking around and I've noticed something. After you reach a certain level of talent . . . the deciding factor is ambition, or as I see it, how much you really need. Need to be loved & need to be proud of yourself . . . & I guess that's what ambition is—it's not all a depraved quest for position . . . or money, maybe it's for love. Lots of love!" Janis's realization: the success and fame she'd always wanted could not fill that well of loneliness.

For the past two years, Janis's life had been spent primarily on the road. In 1969 she wanted to put down roots, and by the fall, she'd pur-

chased her first home: a modest one-story house at 380 West Baltimore
Avenue in the Marin County hamlet of Larkspur. Situated among redwoods on a cul-de-sac, the bucolic setting was similar to the property
she'd shared with Big Brother in Lagunitas. Also, like "Argentina," the
wood-shingled house featured a stone fireplace and exposed beams—
"real strong and rustic," in Janis's words. There were two spacious bedrooms, each with its own bath, in separate wings of the house. Janis
particularly loved her new home's large deck with "benches all around,
a built-in barbeque, overlooks a stream, and . . . redwood trees growing right up through the floor," she'd written to Linda Gravenites in
London.

To Janis, the Marin property represented both success and a need to
escape that success. Again imploring Gravenites to return to the States,
Janis wrote her that the "beautifully quiet" house would provide sanctu-
ary, helping her stay off drugs:

> Y' know how we discussed the two ways of facing the Kozmic Blues . . . ?
> One to get stoned & try and have as good a time as possible & two,
> to try & adjust to it? Well I'm going to try #2. No dope, walks in the
> woods, learn yoga, maybe (don't laugh) horseback riding, try to learn to
> play piano—I think all this & the excitement of having a house & the
> incredible peace you feel there ought to be wonderful. We could really be
> happy there. I know it, & I really need you. Please come.

Janis's belief that a secluded, beautiful home could aid in her recovery
wasn't entirely a self-delusion. Just before the Woodstock festival, she
had spent a week with friends relaxing—and partying—on the Carib-
bean island of Saint Thomas. Then during the fall, she'd gone camping
with roadie Vince Mitchell in the Texas hill country, where she wore
silver cowboy boots with her Levi's. Sleeping under the stars and cooking over a campfire had rejuvenated her. Soon after, however, when she
at last performed at the University of Texas in Austin, she drank heavily. Backstage, she told former lover Julie Paul, "It's not easy living up
to 'Janis Joplin,' you know." She needed a break from constantly being

the rowdy blues mama she'd created, but her onstage persona was now rooted in her everyday life, gaining more control over her judgment and sense of her true self. "If you wear the mask long enough, sooner or later you become the mask," is how Bob Neuwirth put it when discussing Janis with Laura Joplin.

In November Linda Gravenites flew back to the States to once again serve as Janis's roommate, confidante, and designer. As she'd feared, she soon discovered that Janis was still doing heroin. Gravenites and Janis's publicist, Myra Friedman, angrily confronted her about it. Over the course of a long, traumatic night, Janis screamed in denial but finally relented and promised once again she would quit. Albert Grossman recommended a New York endocrinologist, Dr. Ed Rothschild, who specialized in treating drug addiction.

On December 9, 1969, Rothschild examined Janis and prescribed a ten-day supply of Dolophine, a tablet form of methadone, to take while she underwent withdrawal. But Rothschild suspected that though she was willing to kick, Janis had not fully committed to staying clean. "She indicated that other people wanted her to come and that she was here reluctantly," he recounted. When Janis's blood test indicated normal liver function, she exclaimed to Rothschild, "That just shows that I'm a really strong, healthy person. Because the way I've been drinking, you'd think my liver would be shot!" The doctor noted that Janis's "diet was terrible, that she ate a lot of sweets and had wide weight swings . . . from 115 to 155 pounds." Her excessive intake of alcohol, drugs, and sugar composed part of "a behavior pattern that was going to hurt her," Rothschild recalled telling her. He could help her get off heroin, he said, but "beyond that, it was up to her." Janis would eventually visit Rothschild's office for further help, but after her Madison Square Garden concert on December 19, someone offered her heroin backstage, and she relapsed.

<hr/>

With the disbanding of Kozmic Blues after the New York show, Janis took a three-month leave from performing. Living in her new home with Gravenites, she started 1970 still occasionally shooting smack, usually with friends Sunshine and Peggy Caserta. "As long as I think you'll quit sometime, I can stand it. . . . I'll stick around," Gravenites told her. "But if I think it's gonna be all the time forever, I can't do it. . . . I'm gone." Janis focused on "doing . . . fantastic & expensive work on the house," she wrote the Joplins. "It's turning into a palace—all fur & wood & stained glass & velvet couches & chaise lounges & even a chandelier hanging in the middle of an eye-full of redwoods." She also took piano lessons for the first time since her mother had taught her as a child. She had kept on retainer two Canadian members of the Kozmic Blues Band—bassist Brad Campbell and guitarist John Till—and Grossman began recruiting candidates to join them in a new band when she went back to work.

Janis spent her birthday—January 19, 1970—amid her first extended break from the stage since joining Big Brother in June 1966. She wrote her family that "I managed to pass my—gasp—27th birthday, without really feeling it. Not doing much now—just enjoying the house. I'm one month into a supposedly 3 month long vacation."

Janis also pondered the vicissitudes of rock stardom: "Ah, such a funny game . . . when you're nobody & poor, you don't care—you can just drift but when you get a little position & a little money, you start really hustling to get more & then when you're numero uno, you've gotta really break ass so nobody catches you! Catches you?! Two years ago I didn't even want to be it! No, that's not true . . ."

Janis seemed at last to understand her complicated mix of needs and how easy it was to conflate career ambition and her yearning for love. But understanding intellectually didn't fill the hole, relieve her fundamental loneliness, or significantly alter the destructive behavior that caused many of her problems. Later that spring, she would presciently tell a journalist, "I had the kozmic blues real bad. . . . You've got to realize that you'll never have as much as you want, and that when you die, you'll be alone. . . . Once you've really accepted this, then it doesn't hurt so much." She quoted a lyric from a new song she'd begun singing: "*Get it while you can*—'cause it may not be there tomorrow." These sentiments were, in effect, a reframing of Seth Joplin's Saturday Night

Swindle lesson. Janis compulsively told herself that accepting this dark worldview relieved some of the pain.

Her kozmic blues were compounded by the loss of another "family member" the previous year: her beloved two-year-old dog, George, had vanished from her Porsche while it was parked outside her rehearsal space. She placed ads, offered a reward, and announced he was missing on KSAN radio, all to no avail. Grossman gave her a fluffy white pooch, which she called "the daughter of George." She wrote her parents that she wanted "lots of dogs." That spring, Janis adopted two cats and three dogs, including a Great Pyrenees, "a cross between a St. Bernard & a Mastiff," she wrote home. She told them she'd named her huge new dog Thurber after humorist James Thurber, whose work her father had long admired. In May she remarked to a reporter, "Dogs are better than people. They're my best friends." The unconditional love the animals offered, combined with their own uncomplicated needs, gave Janis a taste of family.

Ever since seeing the French film *Black Orpheus*, shot in the late fifties in Brazil during Carnival, Janis had wanted to experience the Rio de Janeiro festival. She decided it would provide the perfect opportunity to get off heroin as well. This time she vowed to stay clean and gave away her stash to Caserta, who had no intention of quitting. With another ten-day supply of Dolophine, Janis and Linda Gravenites flew to Rio in the beginning of February. The first female rock star to visit Brazil, Janis was feted by local officials and invited to exclusive parties. She wired Myra Friedman that she "felt like Brigitte Bardot. I've never had such an incredible press reception . . . so much paparazzi that I held a press conference. Every paper, every magazine, all glowing." At the press conference, Janis described San Francisco's "beautiful" free concerts where "everybody would come and dance." Saying she loved Brazil "because people seem nicer to each other here than in New York," she also claimed she'd "be a beatnik" if not a singer, and that if her voice gave out, she'd become "a beach bum."

One afternoon lounging on the beach of Ipanema, Janis and Linda Gravenites met Americans David Niehaus and Ben Beall. Sandy haired and bearded, Niehaus had been traveling the Amazon solo for a year before meeting up with Beall, a college friend from the University of Notre Dame. A Cincinnati native, Niehaus, who was Janis's age, had volunteered for the Peace Corps in Turkey after college, and then attended law school. Spotting Janis sunning herself in a bikini, he was charmed by her friendly "Hi, you cute thing!" and soon discovered "she was smart and had a good sense of humor," he recalled. Niehaus didn't realize who Janis was until the second day they were together. Though her celebrity was gratifying to her, it meant more to Janis that David was attracted to her for herself rather than her rock star status.

Carnival's revelry—the samba parades, amazing costumes, and joyous dancing—captivated Janis. She perfected Rio's sensual dance moves as she and Niehaus boogied in the streets. "We laughed a lot," he recalled. When Carnival ended on February 10, she wanted to keep the party going by organizing a free concert in Rio. Naming it Unending Carnival, Get It On, she wrote Friedman, "There's never been a free thing here before—the theme of our festival. Strangely, Carnival lasts . . . four days only—after that, it's illegal. Hence our plan." But the authorities would have none of it, and their plans "to put on the first rock concert in South America," according to Niehaus, fell apart. "It was a military dictatorship, and they just made it impossible. They didn't want a bunch of longhairs rocking and rolling." Though the festival came to naught, the couple wanted to continue exploring Brazil. Gravenites returned to California to supervise house renovations, while Janis and Niehaus planned a trip to the northeastern state of Bahia.

When Janis's methadone ran out and the pain of withdrawal debilitated her, Niehaus embraced the opportunity to help. He shepherded her through a harrowing detox that "almost killed her," he said. This experience bonded them tighter. Once clean, Janis seemed determined to stay that way. The first flush of falling for Niehaus and the distance from her drug buddies and supply helped her stay off dope. She wired Friedman: "I finally remembered that I was a beatnik, and we're going to hitch-hike around, sleep on the beach, just live for a while. And I don't even think about drugs." Friedman alerted *Rolling Stone*'s Random

Notes editor that Janis was "going into the jungle with a big bear of a beatnik named David Niehaus," and quoted her as saying, "I finally remembered I don't have to be onstage twelve months a year. I've decided to go and dig some other jungles for a couple of weeks."

Simultaneously, Janis sent a telegram to Albert Grossman, alluding to being clean and finding her true self, yet still begging for her manager's paternalistic support: "I'm real Janis . . . so Janis again, and so happy for awhile, or forever. . . . Please don't desert me, but can you be happy for me?" Leaving their belongings behind at their hotel, the lovers rented a motorcycle for a five-day trip. "We slept on a beach called Cabo Frio, south of Rio, and we rode down there on the motorcycle after dark," Niehaus recounted. En route to Bahia, they hit a concrete median in the road and swerved out of control, with the pair flying off the bike. Knocked unconscious, Janis suffered a concussion. Niehaus flagged down a car and took her to the hospital, where she was treated and released. She and Niehaus continued on their journey, hitchhiking to Salvador, stopping in tiny villages along the way—"just like a regular ole beatnik on the road," she would later tell talk-show host Dick Cavett. In one town, they heard "Piece of My Heart" wafting out of speakers attached to a ramshackle bus station. Janis loved the African culture in Bahia, and in Salvador she bought locally made jewelry, including a bracelet and red-beaded choker with a small heart pendant. She would wear the pieces unceasingly, as mementos of her happiness in Brazil.

After their adventures, they planned to fly to California together, but, at the airport, it was discovered Niehaus had overstayed his visa. Janis screamed in vain at officials, but Niehaus had to stay behind to straighten out the paperwork. Suddenly alone again and back in the land of easy access to heroin, Janis stopped in Los Angeles, called her dealer, George, and scored a bag. A few days later, when Niehaus arrived in Larkspur, she was high. They argued, she promised to stop, he believed her, and the love affair resumed.

Considering her his "first love, his first real lady," Niehaus recorded in his journal that Janis told him she'd experienced "real [love] before, but it turned to blue and [she] chose to love no more." Whether she was

referring to Peter de Blanc's betrayal or some other lover is unclear. But
as much as she cared for Niehaus, her past disappointments, insecurity,
and, most of all, her inherited fatalism prevented her from committing
to him fully. His devotion and desire for her to get clean, which she welcomed in one part of her heart, threatened her always-lurking "blues
mama" persona that had brought her the career she'd longed for—and
which she believed, at age twenty-seven, she had to maintain to succeed.

Still, just as she'd reinvented herself in 1965 as a budding housewife
for de Blanc, she tried to be an "old lady" to Niehaus: "She treated me
really good," he reflected, "better than any woman ever had. She went
out of her way to make me happy—cooking dinner at night and scrub-
bing my back when I took a bath." The other side of Janis's personality emerged when the couple was awakened by noises in the kitchen
one night. When Niehaus investigated, he discovered several large Hells
Angels rummaging through the refrigerator. "They had guns in their
belts, and they wanted to know who the fuck I was," he recalled. He
ran back to the bedroom to inform Janis, who stomped into the kitchen
and cursed out the bikers. "Janis took control," Niehaus explained. "She
could be this indomitable force. They not only left, but they came back
later with bags and bags of groceries. Those guys were not nice guys—
but she made them nice guys."

From domestic earth mother to tough biker chick, both sides of
Janis attracted Niehaus. But he wasn't prepared to handle her celebrity.
"We'd go out to a bar," he remembered, "and I'd park the Porsche, and
by the time we came back, there'd be a hundred fifty people around the
car. It got old pretty quick." To clear his head, he left for a weekend of
skiing, and when he returned, he discovered Janis and Peggy Caserta in
bed together and high on smack. Fed up, he told Janis he'd had enough
and was leaving to continue his travels in North Africa and Asia. "She
said, 'I'll stop doing heroin, I'll never do it again if you stay,'" he recalled. He turned down her offer to road manage her upcoming summer tour, and asked her instead to travel the world with him.

"David really loved her," according to Linda Gravenites. "Janis loved
him too. . . . She was saying, 'Stay with me,' and he was saying, 'Come

with me.' She couldn't, and he couldn't." Niehaus told her, "'You meet me in the Himalayas, and we'll take it from there.'" Finally, in an *Affair to Remember* moment, they agreed to go their separate ways but promised each other they would reconnect in a year and a half.

Janis and David Niehaus spent their final days together in Los Angeles. On March 28, with her lover in tow, Janis returned to Columbia's Studio D in Hollywood to cut a song backed by Paul Butterfield and his seven-piece band. The producer on the session was another Grossman client, twenty-one-year-old Todd Rundgren, who'd had a minor hit, "Hello It's Me," in 1968 with his band Nazz. Grossman considered the iconoclastic multi-instrumentalist, producer, and singer-songwriter "a boy wonder." But Rundgren chafed at the restrictions working in Columbia's studio, where only union engineers could operate the board. He didn't particularly like Butterfield's band and found them "difficult to direct." Nor did he and Janis click: he judged her "temperamental." Regardless, as she usually did in the studio, she focused on singing and blocked out everything else, drinking hot chocolate and tequila cocktails between takes.

Backed once again by a horn section, as well as Butterfield's blues harmonica, Janis's voice sounded rested and strong on the soulful "One Night Stand." Listening to the song's lyrics, Niehaus recognized the loneliness she'd experienced as a touring musician: "Playin' in a town without a name and I'm feelin' low an' everybody looks the same / Well, you catch my eye, and then you come on strong an' try to make your play / Just because we loved tonight, please don't you think it's gonna stay that way / Don't you know that you're nothin' more than a one night stand / Tomorrow I'll be on my way, an' you can catch me if you can." Barry Flast, signed to Grossman's publishing company, came up with the concept for the song, with Janis tweaking the lyrics to suit her, which included singing frankly as a woman about her sexual encounters on the road.

At one point, alone with Niehaus in the studio, Janis asked the engineer to roll backing tracks of songs she'd previously cut. "We got in this sound booth with perfect sound," Niehaus remembered. "She put the earphones on and sang me love songs. She made me feel like I was 'the only man,' as the words go in one song."

When she drove him to the airport, they embraced and kissed good-bye with a "promise of love and family, which I wanted as much as she did," Niehaus reflected later in his journal. "We were in love," he said about the two months they spent together. "We thought it was going to be forever, but first she wanted to do more of her career, and I wanted to travel the world."

Still craving her parents' validation, she wrote them about Niehaus: "I met a really fine man in Rio, but I had to get back to work, so he's off finding the rest of the world—Africa or Morocco now I think, but he really did love me & was so good to me & he wants to come back & marry me! I thought I'd die without someone besides fans asking me. But he meant it & who knows—I may get tired of the music biz, but I'm really getting it on now."

The passionate relationship with Niehaus continued to haunt her. She told the *San Francisco Chronicle*, "There's a man I'm in love with. . . . He wanted to see the world and I wanted to be a singer. We're trying to see what we really want." Niehaus began "appearing" in new songs she added to her repertoire. In Jerry Ragovoy's "Cry Baby," she called out a man who left her "to go find myself," ad-libbing, "but like the Capricorn I am, I'll be standing there waiting" when he "returns from Casablanca." He also inspired a new original, Janis's first in a while, "Move Over," with lines such as: "Make up your mind / You know you're playing with me." After performing the song on *The Dick Cavett Show*, she would explain it as the story of a woman frustrated by a man "offering more than he is willing to give." In Janis's mind, though Niehaus said he wanted to spend his life with her, he chose to travel the world rather than stick around.

In San Francisco, on April 4, Janis joined Big Brother at the Fillmore West for a reunion show orchestrated and recorded by Bill Graham. Before a euphoric crowd, they played eight songs from their two albums together, starting with a chaotic "Combination of the Two." Though she had a cold, Janis sounded terrific, and she alternated songs with Nick

Gravenites, who was now singing with the group. Her old band joined her on stripped-down versions of Janis's *Kozmic Blues* tracks "Try," with Brad Campbell on bass, and "Maybe." During a jazzy twenty-minute version of Big Brother's "All Is Loneliness," Janis improvised lines about "the loneliness waiting for me at home." A highlight was a jam with Gravenites on another long blues improvisation she called "Ego Rock," where she ripped her home state: "I had to get out of Texas baby, Lord it was bringing me down / I been all around the world but Port Arthur is the worst place that I'd ever found." Janis ended the first verse with the declaration "I'm going to live to be an old lady and never go back to Texas."

Playing with Big Brother for the first time in fifteen months "was so much fun," she said, "drinkin' tequila, kissin'." But she had come to accept, with no small measure of sadness, that she'd likely never have that again: "You can't go home again," she said, quoting Thomas Wolfe. Big Brother and their hometown fans knew the nostalgic enjoyment of that night would not—could not—be replicated. That it came off at all was testament to their deep bond.

Nevertheless, the approximation of such a bond became Janis's goal as she hired new musicians to play alongside Campbell and Till. Grossman enlisted Canadian keyboardist Ken Pearson, who'd been on an album with his client Jesse Winchester, and twenty-four-year-old Richard Bell had played the organ in the Hawks with Till. Bell and Pearson auditioned for Janis at her house, and their organ and piano styles fit perfectly in her sonic plan. Janis's former sax player Snooky Flowers recommended drummer Clark Pierson, a Minnesota native who played with him at a North Beach topless joint called the Galaxy.

Janis began holding rehearsals in her garage, where they tried out new material. The four Canadians and one American felt naturally at ease among themselves; they were an organic unit rather than a forced aggregation of session players. Janis felt comfortable around them, and she and they treated each other with mutual respect. Though she was unquestionably the bandleader, she could also be "one of the boys" again.

In a bid to create an alternate persona to the rock star "Janis," whose name she'd heard screamed and seen printed, sometimes in disdainful, sexist articles, Janis cast about for a nickname—a sobriquet to be used only by those who knew her best. Perhaps this persona would help her harness the more grounded version of herself. She seized on "Pearl." Originally suggested by Dave Richards, this became her nickname, intended for use only by her new bandmates and close friends—those who knew the *person*, not the celebrity. "Don't use the word *star*," she'd told Dick Cavett after he referred to her as one. "It drives me up a wall."

Sometimes attending band rehearsals were Johanna and John Hall, the latter a musician and singer-songwriter. Janis had become friendly in New York with twenty-two-year-old journalist Johanna Schier Hall after her positive review of *Kozmic Blues* ran in the *Village Voice*. A few weeks later, she and Janis spent twelve hours together for a proposed *Voice* profile (that never ran). "She was incredibly bright and funny, a lot of fun," Hall recalled. Janis often dropped by the Halls' East Village apartment. "I look at Janis with a feminist filter," Hall offered. "She invented herself as this bawdy blues mama—there wasn't anyone like her. She created herself and walked her own path, and that was difficult. There was a lot of sexism."

After the recently married Halls relocated to Mill Valley, they reconnected with Janis, who was "pining about this guy, the love of her life, who'd gone to Kathmandu," Johanna Hall recalled. "She said, 'Write me a song! You're a woman. You're a writer. . . . *You can do this!*'" For the first time, Hall began writing lyrics to a melody her husband had composed. "I thought, 'Maybe she'd like to sing to this guy,' so I cast the song that way. I wanted it to be like singing an incantation." Hall finished the lyrics to "Half Moon," originally titled "Seven Song," with yearning lines such as "I hope to bring your sweet love home to me." It was one of the first songs Janis's new band learned. As John Hall taught it to the group, Johanna observed a "bratty" Todd Rundgren "making faces behind Janis's back. I had a great respect and reverence for her, and I felt protective about the way Todd was behaving. I don't think he liked Janis, and that bothered me." Soon after, Janis "took charge very quickly" and fired Rundgren, said Hall. She wanted a seasoned producer with whom she could collaborate—one who could help her get on tape the distinctive mix of soul, blues, country, and rock in her head—and decided to choose one herself.

Janis had gotten lucky with her new down-to-earth bandmates. They were as enthusiastic as Janis about working together, and they quickly formed a close friendship. The easygoing personalities meshed well, and musically they were pros, delivering a kind of soulful rock in which Janis could express herself more fully. Campbell and Till, as former members of the Kozmic Blues Band, offered guidance to the others, showing them the ropes. In an April letter to her parents, Janis sounded thrilled: "Really rushing through rehearsals, have a new (2 of the same guys. 3 new) smaller band & it's really going fantastic! Great new songs—really needed new songs—so we'll do an album while on the next tour. Albert is lightening up on my schedule a little because of my old age & because I put my foot down! 2 mos on the road then 2 off, etc. So I can have a little personal life, I hope!"

Yet backsliding seemed inevitable. During their time together, she'd told Niehaus that heroin was the only way she could find peace when her feelings tormented her. To critic Nat Hentoff, she had described the effect of such emotion: "I never seemed to be able to control my feelings, to keep them down. . . . When you feel that much, you have superhorrible downs. . . . I'd do wrong things, run away, freak out, go crazy. Now, though, I've made feeling work for me, through music, instead of destroying me. It's superfortunate. Man, if it hadn't been for the music, I probably would have done myself in." But after three years of playing, recording, and touring, music was no longer enough for Janis. She couldn't resist crawling back under that blanket of numbness offered by heroin.

Another binge included a night in Larkspur with Peggy Caserta and Mike Bloomfield, ending with the guitarist overdosing and being revived by the women (he would finally succumb to a heroin overdose eleven years later, in 1981). At that point, Linda Gravenites snapped. She assumed Janis was never going to quit for good, and true to her word, she moved out. "Linda just got really sick of watching the abuse," Johanna Hall recalled. "Janis told me, 'Linda left behind all these outfits I bought her—*like indictments.*" She also took $300 she felt she was owed. Janis was devastated; Gravenites was much more than just her right hand. She'd filled in for Dorothy Joplin, counseling Janis and telling her the truth. Though Janis complained of Gravenites's nagging her about smack, she also needed that putative savior just as she'd needed her mother to nurse her back to health in 1965. But Janis had driven away Linda's maternal force.

When she left, Gravenites warned Janis she'd be a junkie for life. The devastation of losing such a crucial tether and the intensity of her prediction pushed Janis once again to summon her willpower and try to quit heroin. Grossman attempted to help by sending her to a health spa—the closest thing to a rehab facility at the time. Soon Janis was back on methadone, and she informed Sunshine and Peggy Caserta that she couldn't see them again until they got clean too.

Janis did not want to live alone and contacted Lyndall Erb, a young clothing designer from San Francisco who'd just moved back to Marin from New York. Erb had looked after Janis's Noe Street apartment the previous year, made Janis a few costumes, and was friendly with Country Joe and the Fish. She accepted Janis's invitation to move into Gravenites's room.

Not long after, a pair of drunken houseguests arrived at their door: Bob Neuwirth had finally met the composer of "Bobby McGee"—Nashville-based singer-songwriter Kris Kristofferson. The two clicked, and after several nights of barhopping in New York, they drunkenly boarded a plane to San Francisco to visit Janis. During the bender that Neuwirth called "the Great Tequila Boogie," Janis took one look at the ruggedly handsome, blue-eyed Texan in his leather pants and shirt and was smitten. After more partying, they tumbled into bed, where Kristofferson stayed on and off for the next couple of weeks. Janis would later laugh about his cowboy boots shredding her satin sheets.

While tapering off methadone, Janis drank heavily. "I'd get up, intending to get out," Kristofferson recounted, "and in she comes with the early-morning drinks, and pretty soon you're wasted enough and don't care about leaving." Music kept him there too. She learned his devastating "Sunday Mornin' Comin' Down," a portrait of the dissolution he and Janis knew all too well. Kristofferson greatly admired her version of "Me and Bobby McGee," which she'd strum on her Gibson Hummingbird acoustic guitar and sing. "I would always rather hear Janis sing 'Me and Bobby McGee,'" Kristofferson said years later. The line "Freedom's just another word for nothing left to lose," he explained, "expressed the double-edged sword that freedom is: you may be free, but it can be painful to be that free."

Thanks to Bobby Neuwirth, Janis also scored a name for her band: *"Is everybody ready for a full tilt boogie?"* he yelled out one night. *"That's it!"* Janis said. The Full Tilt Boogie band members, along with Neuwirth and Kristofferson, were among the revelers at Janis's Dionysian tattoo party in mid-May. Ever since getting a blue cornflower inked on her right foot by an English beau, Janis had wanted another tattoo. In San Francisco, she discovered Lyle Tuttle, a veteran tattoo artist who had inked a small red heart on her left breast. On her left wrist, Tuttle tattooed a bracelet resembling one she'd bought in Bahia while traveling with Niehaus. Janis was one of Tuttle's first female clients, and after she spread the word, women began flocking to him for tattoos. "That put tattooing back on the map," Tuttle observed. "With women getting a newfound freedom, they could get tattooed if they so desired. For three years, I tattooed almost nothing but women." On Dick Cavett's talk show, Janis raved about Tuttle, tattooed from the neck down, and gleefully described hiring him to tattoo her party guests, eighteen of whom left with new embellishments.

By mid-May, Janis had remained clean, and the band was ready for their debut gig—the first of two dozen they would play over the next three months. Bennett Glotzer, Albert Grossman's new management partner, traveled to San Francisco to oversee Janis's progress. He was not keen on her choice of venue to premiere Full Tilt Boogie: a Hells Angels party at a dance hall in San Rafael. The previous December, upon recommendation by the Grateful Dead, the Rolling Stones had hired the Angels as "security" for their free Altamont festival, which organizers hoped to be a kind of Woodstock West. Bikers viciously beat up audience members and even knocked out Jefferson Airplane vocalist Marty Balin, who'd tried to stop the violence. During the Stones' set, an Angel stabbed to death an eighteen-year-old black man, Meredith Hunter. The murder and much of the brutality had been caught on film for the documentary *Gimme Shelter*. Since then, the members of the Dead, who refused to perform at Altamont because of the assaults, had put distance between themselves and the bikers.

Nevertheless, loyal to the end, Janis agreed to play for the Angels on a double bill with Big Brother. That night, as she approached the stage with a fifth of tequila in hand, a biker from another motorcycle club demanded her bottle of booze. She shot back, *"No way, man! I'm saving this for onstage."* Before he could jump in to help, Brad Campbell witnessed Janis being attacked: "the guy grabbed the bottle and just smacked her to the ground," he recalled. "Then all hell broke loose. All these Hells Angels jumped on the guy and said, '*Hey man, that's Janis Joplin!*' They beat the shit out of the guy. I thought, *Oh my God, these people are animals!*"

Though bruised and dazed, Janis somehow managed to sing, but she downed so much tequila that she couldn't remember her performance the next day. Her bandmates told her that during the show, a Hells Angel forced drummer Clark Pierson to remove his shirt while playing. Standing behind him, the menacing biker "started poking him on the shoulder—'*You look hot! Take your shirt off,*' " said Campbell. Pierson tried to ignore him and kept playing, but the Angel demanded, *"I said you look real hot—take that shirt off!"* This time Pierson did as told.

On May 23, after she'd called John Cooke and told him she'd quit heroin, he returned to California to work for her again. On her behalf, he contacted Doors producer Paul Rothchild, whom she'd gotten to know in LA. Janis wanted him to produce her new album, and Grossman agreed with the idea. Yet Rothchild was reluctant to produce Janis because, he told Cooke, "Last time I saw her, she was a junkie and couldn't focus on her art and was abusive to people around her. At that point, I was listening to the last shards of her voice." He agreed to check out a live performance in July before making his decision.

Janis was reinvigorated by band rehearsals, during which she began trying a more subtle vocal approach. She told the *San Francisco Chronicle*'s Julie Smith, who visited her in Larkspur, "Man, I never had more fun in my life! I'm just like a kid jumping up and down. I'm learning how to sing. I've got the power—now I'm learning how *not* to use it." Janis also tracked down Ben Fong-Torres, a *Rolling Stone* editor and writer moonlighting at a Chinese American newspaper, phoning him around midnight. "Janis and *Rolling Stone* had had a pretty tough relationship," Fong-Torres observed, so he was shocked to hear from her, especially after having tried unsuccessfully to interview her in the past. She chatted amiably about her Brazilian adventures, her tattoos, and her new musical direction and band; Fong-Torres titled his article, "Hey, Janis Is Feeling Great." Soon after, the magazine assigned writer David Dalton to accompany Janis on her upcoming tour, beginning May 29, with *Rolling Stone* giving her its first extensive coverage since Paul Nelson's derisive cover story in March 1969.

Janis assumed a real leadership position among her bandmates while touring, offering musical direction in a diplomatic way, which they accepted. "She always presented this very up, very happy, very ready-to-rock, ready-to-play, ready-to-do the job, make-the-music [persona]," recalled Full Tilt guitarist John Till. "It wasn't Janis and the Full Tilt Boogie band. She was a member of the band . . . and she liked it that way." Janis would tell a reporter that she hadn't enjoyed herself so much since the year she joined Big Brother. She was finally able to convey to experienced yet fresh players the subtleties and nuances of the music within her, and they could take that direction and run confidently with it.

With bookings through August 12, Janis typically worked weekends, taking plenty of days off in between. "The minute we went out on the road with Full Tilt Boogie," John Cooke observed, "Janis was a changed woman. . . . She had figured out how to be the bandleader." After five initial concerts in Florida and the Midwest, Dalton joined the tour on the way to a stop in Louisville, Kentucky. "The tangible affection that flowed between Full Tilt and Janis showed itself in the playfulness they generated on stage," wrote Dalton, who'd catch a half dozen shows and grow close to Janis.

"These guys are on the same wavelength as me," Janis explained. "It's more of a family thing again." She told a Louisville reporter of the band's "really big talent" and that "I'm so fuckin' proud of them. I'm just so jacked to work with them, every day I just kiss 'em and tell 'em I love 'em." Full Tilt Boogie "was a great band for her," according to Johanna Hall, who saw Janis perform with all three of her groups. "They really loved her."

In June Janis and Full Tilt Boogie introduced a new song, "Get It While You Can," nationally on *The Dick Cavett Show*. The hot-pink and teal feathers in Janis's hair contrasted greatly with the plaintiveness of the song, as she implored the audience to "take a gamble" on love, "because we may not be here tomorrow." Written by Janis's favorite songwriter, Jerry Ragovoy, the ballad was originally recorded by soul singer Howard Tate. Janis turned it into a dramatic showstopper a la "Kozmic Blues," propelled by organ and piano. Janis and Cavett, a Nebraska native, had great rapport, and she gossiped to friends that she'd slept with television's hippest talk-show host. Cavett, who has neither denied nor confirmed the rumor, was clearly taken with Janis, and she would appear only on his talk show, refusing offers from *The Tonight Show*'s Johnny Carson and others: in 1969 with Kozmic Blues and twice in '70 with Full Tilt. She gamely held her own in conversations with other guests: statuesque actress Raquel Welch (Janis: "Everyone wants to be liked; no one gets tired of fans"); Gloria Swanson, the star of *Sunset Boulevard* and other classics (discussing skirt lengths); and actor Douglas Fairbanks (whom she quizzed about F. Scott Fitzgerald in Hollywood). When the Committee made an appearance, she joined their improv performance, with each member acting out an emotion. Janis expertly played "frustration."

In conversation with the well-informed and witty Cavett, who treated Janis seriously while joking with her, she earnestly answered his questions:

"Why aren't there more ladies that do what you do?"

"It seems so natural to me. It's not feminine, maybe . . . to get into the bottom side of the music, the feeling of the music."

"Is it a contradiction to make money and still be miserable?"

"Music doesn't have anything to do with money—playing is about feeling, letting yourself feel inside what you're trying to push aside."

"Do you hate the road?"

"You're alone a lot—but you get to play a lot. Ultimately that's one of the dues you pay to play music."

"Ever tired of it?"

"It's the best thing that ever happened to me."

The highlight of Janis's summer was from June 28 to July 4, on a train tour across Canada, named the Transcontinental Pop Festival, which kicked off in Toronto, stopped in Winnipeg, and ended in Calgary. For what John Cooke called "Woodstock on wheels," promoters leased a train—later known as the Festival Express—to transport more than a dozen acts. Janis and Full Tilt were paid $75,000 to headline an eclectic bill that included the Grateful Dead, the Band, New Riders of the Purple Sage (NRPS), Chicago bluesman Buddy Guy, Canadian folksingers Ian & Sylvia (Tyson) in their new country-rock band Great Speckled Bird, singer-songwriter Eric Andersen, and country-soul band Delaney and Bonnie (Bramlett), among others. In Toronto, Janis told *Circus* magazine that she'd "never been so happy" than with Full Tilt. "They rock and roll and ass-shake when I do, and when I sing a ballad, they're quiet and sensitive. And they just love to play, any hour of the day, as long as I want. . . . For those few hours [onstage], I feel like I can do anything. I feel like the Empire State Building."

Not long before, in Maryland, Janis's onstage acrobatics had landed her in the emergency room. She was rushed to the hospital by ambulance after she left the stage in extreme pain. During the last number, she had executed such an extended leg kick that she pulled a muscle deep in her groin. But by the time of the Festival Express, she had recovered fully, and during her Toronto performance, *Circus*'s Roger Keene noted that "she is pure energy, emoting, belting . . . . You realize that Janis is possibly the most exciting pop performer in North America today."

John Cooke, David Dalton, and a film crew hired by the producers documented Janis's Festival Express experience onstage and on the train: two bar cars filled with drunken musicians jamming; even the Dead, who rarely drank, guzzled down booze. Four hundred bottles were consumed, according to NRPS guitarist David Nelson. But "you could get shots of vitamins and speed so you make it through your show," recalled Eric Andersen. "They had, like, five doctors on board. They thought of everything."

One bar-car jam session captured on film shows a sloshed Janis strumming her acoustic while wedged between a wasted Rick Danko and a smiling John "Marmaduke" Dawson (NRPS), with whom she was having a fling. Across from Janis sat Jerry Garcia and Bob Weir, guitars in hand. With the vibe of a family reunion, the fivesome literally howled along to the old prison work song "Ain't No More Cane." When someone mentioned the train was nearing Alberta, Janis leaned into Garcia and requested the chestnut "Alberta, Let Your Hair Hang Low," at which Garcia smiled and murmured, "Janis, I loved ya since the day I saw ya."

Janis bonded with Bonnie Bramlett on board, and during one conversation, which Janis insisted Dalton record, they compared notes about their experiences as women on the road, their bands, and the sacrifices they'd made as musicians. Bramlett, a midwesterner who began her career as an Ikette with the Ike and Tina Turner revue, told Janis she'd struggled to be a singer her whole life. In response, Janis repeated her mythologized story of accidental success—that she'd never had that ambition but had only dreamed of being a "beatnik" until "all of a sudden someone threw me in this rock & roll band. They threw these musicians at me, man, and the sound was coming from behind. The bass was charging me. And I decided then and there that that was it. I never wanted to do anything else. It was better than it had been with any man . . . maybe that's the trouble."

Onstage during the last stop, in Calgary, Janis joyfully presented the tour promoter with a miniature train, thanking him effusively for the amazing experience. But the venture had been a financial disaster, with hippies protesting the $10 ticket prices and threatening to crash the gate, resulting in smaller crowds than expected. For the performers, though, it was a chance to hang out, jam, and have a blast. Buddy Guy, who preferred whiskey to weed, recalled, "There were so many drugs on that train that it's a wonder the thing didn't go off the track and float up into the sky." He was charmed by Janis, "who couldn't have been sweeter," Guy recalled. "She sang black. She proved that the color of our skin don't have shit to do with the depths of your soul." He echoed earlier words from B. B. King, with whom she'd also shared stages: "Janis Joplin sings the blues as hard as any black person."

Another high point of Janis's summer was a quick trip to Austin to join the sixty-first birthday celebration for Kenneth Threadgill. She'd cut short a Hawaiian sojourn, leaving soon after her performance in Honolulu and flying all night with John Cooke to arrive on July 10 for the outdoor hoedown at the Party Barn west of town. Word had circulated that she might show up, and the pasture filled with thousands of Austinites hoping to see the hometown-girl-made-good. Appearing on the primitive stage midway through Threadgill's set, she gave her overjoyed mentor a souvenir from Honolulu, saying with a cackle, "Here ya go, Mr. Threadgill, I wanted to give you a good Hawaiian lei." His band—including Julie Paul and her husband guitarist Chuck Joyce—backed Janis, who sat on a hay bale and played acoustic guitar on her country-tinged numbers. She introduced "Me and Bobby McGee" as being written "by a good friend of mine . . . he's gonna be real famous, I'll give him about a year." She followed with Kristofferson's melancholic "Sunday Mornin' Comin' Down"; in her intro, she acknowledged the kozmic blues that dogged her no matter what: "it's just as bad . . . *every day*."

A young Houston native, Bill Bentley—a music fan and writer who would go on to a career in the recording industry—caught Janis's eye. "She kind of picked me up," Bentley recounted. "I was shy and didn't have many girlfriends, but I thought, *Let's go!* She had that aura—she was just electric onstage. No other white girl has ever had that electricity. She was magic. This was her homecoming in Austin, and she really was the queen—on top of the world. She was drinking beer, but she wasn't fucked up." The pair hit a couple of after-parties, where they talked about the Beats and the blues, and ended the evening at the Holiday Inn. "Janis just loved music," said Bentley, who later worked with Neil Young and ZZ Top, among others. "It was her reason for living."

The next night, Janis's prospective producer Paul Rothchild attended her concert in San Diego. Seeing her live with Full Tilt for the first time, the thirty-five-year-old Rothchild, son of an opera singer, was impressed. "Her eyes were bright and clear, and her spirits were up," he recalled. Backstage before she went on, she handed him a stopwatch and said, "Look, I've only got thirty-five good minutes in me. When I sing my first note, start it. Once in a while, I'll turn around and look at you, and you flash me how much I got left." Janis reminded the experienced producer of a marathon runner "pacing" herself: "Within the first ten seconds, I heard 'the voice' again . . . the depth of understanding of the songs and how much the song relied on her—rather than she relied on the song. I was enraptured because I was listening to one of the most brilliant vocalists I'd ever heard in classical, pop, or jazz music." Her ability to communicate to the audience—which evolved from what Rothchild recalled as "3,000 couch potatoes" to "standing up screaming like crazy for the next forty minutes"—also convinced the producer that she was "a singer totally immersed in the magic of that moment of creativity."

Rothchild agreed to join Janis in Larkspur to discuss working together. While sipping piña coladas she'd learned to make in Hawaii, he was impressed by her intellect and willingness to stretch vocally. He directed her to sing "in the church-choir voice from when she was ten," according to John Cooke, who sat in on the meetings. Rothchild told Janis, "What we want to do is work that part of your voice into songs and develop it into the full passionate one, so the effect is more dramatic."

"Great, let's do it!" Janis said. When he asked what she wanted to be in thirty years, Janis told him, "Like the world's greatest blues singer, Bessie Smith." Rothchild promised her that she would be that and more—and he officially signed on as her producer.

Though she'd moved on from her folkie days interpreting the work of the singular blues singer, Janis still treasured Smith's music. Just recently, she had helped pay for a headstone for Bessie Smith's grave, previously unmarked since her burial on October 4, 1937. The stone read: "The Greatest Blues Singer in the World Will Never Stop Singing— Bessie Smith—1895–1937."

>-+-+-0-<-+-<

Janis had not forgotten her wandering lover, David Niehaus, and wrote him while en route to New Mexico. She led with the news she thought might impress him most: "I kicked!!! 4 Mos. Ago! . . . So I get Janis back! She's absolutely (and if I do say so myself) delightfully crazy but I love it! . . . Hope you dig the fact that I'm no longer a junkie and am again full of feelings. It's fantastic and it hurts, but I wouldn't go back to sleepin' for nothin'." She hoped to join him on his far-flung adventure in October, she wrote, when recording was finished.

Janis was excited about the upcoming sessions. Rothchild had convinced Clive Davis to let Janis record at Hollywood's Sunset Sound, where he'd cut the first two Doors albums, rather than at the CBS studio in Los Angeles. "We want to do this right," he told Davis, "in an environment that will be rock & roll." Like Todd Rundgren, he didn't want to work with Columbia's staff engineers, and Janis liked the casual atmosphere at Sunset, a garage-like space in a seedy neighborhood. In July Rothchild and the band did a trial session at each studio, with Sunset Sound's results—a version of "Me and Bobby McGee"—preferred by all involved. "All the players were good," bassist Brad Campbell observed. "You just need the right players around you for the magic. And Paul knew how to work with musicians. He could get the best out of us." Plans were made to begin recording at Sunset in September.

In West Hollywood, while staying at the Tropicana Motel, Janis rendezvoused with Kristofferson one last time. She hadn't heard from

Niehaus, and she longed for more than just a lost weekend with Kristofferson—but the footloose singer-songwriter, whose career was about to
take off, let her down easy. He "loved" her—but wasn't in love with her.

Later that summer, back in Larkspur, Janis hooked up with a well-
heeled coke dealer she'd met in May. A senior at UC-Berkeley, Seth
Morgan, twenty-two, was an Easterner and the son of poet and literary critic Frederick Morgan. Subsisting on a small trust fund and his
drug-dealing income, Seth Morgan led people to believe he was related
to J. P. Morgan. Though Janis eschewed cocaine, she dug the roguishly
handsome hustler, who drove a "baroquely chromed" Harley-Davidson
"painted gold with orange flames," according to Morgan. Janis was "attracted to my brusqueness," he related later, "and I learned early on to
play to that weakness." He made it clear that he did not care for her
music, but Janis didn't seem to mind. Perhaps she also liked the fact that
he shared a first name with her beloved father.

By summer's end, Morgan was spending every night at her Larkspur
home—"not in love, but with a compelling physical and emotional kinship," he recalled. He enjoyed "stepping out" at Marin hotspots, drawing attention as Janis's new boyfriend. She preferred "an out-of-the-way
suburban drinkery with laminated tables and Frank Sinatra on the juke
and a neon martini glass outside," he complained. "But all this soon
wore thin, and we stayed home more and more, watching TV, shooting
pool on her antique Brunswick, and drinking. Always drinking."

In early August Janis departed on what became her last tour, which
kicked off with a triumphant return to New York, performing to fifteen
thousand at the Forest Hills Tennis Stadium. "If the concert on Sunday
evening . . . was any indication, Janis Joplin finally has a backup band worthy of her," wrote Mike Jahn in the *New York Times*. "Full Tilt Boogie, as
the name implies, has the emotion and drive needed to back Miss Joplin,
and also is composed of fine musicians. It's hard to pick out individual
performances in the midst of such a great evening, but John Till on guitar and Richard Bell on piano seemed particularly outstanding. . . . Full
Tilt Boogie took a basically blues format and drove it with tremendous
power, matching its leader's shouts, moans, and gasps with true soul."

Their final New York area gig was at Port Chester's Capitol Theater on August 8. Beforehand, she joined Bobby Neuwirth and friends actors Rip Torn and Geraldine Page at the nearby Vahsen's saloon, where Janis started riffing on a Michael McClure ditty she'd learned from Digger Emmett Grogan. She began sing-talking the twangy number, "like a sea shanty," Neuwirth recounted—"Oh, Lord, won't you buy me a Mercedes Benz"—while he jotted down lyrics on bar napkins, and Torn and Page banged their beer mugs to keep time. Janis "came up with the second verse, too, about a color TV," said Neuwirth. "I suggested words here and there, and came up with the third verse—about asking the Lord to buy us a night on the town and another round. Janis and I were giggling and showing off a bit."

Onstage that night, Janis surprised everyone—especially her band—with the introduction: "I'd like to do a song of some significance. . . . I just wrote it at the bar on the corner, so I don't know all the words yet. I'm going to do it *Acapulco*"—the joking way that Neuwirth referred to "a cappella." "Janis stomped off the beat and began belting out the lyrics," Neuwirth recalled, "the way she had done at the bar. The band soon tried to fit in as best they could."

"Mercedes Benz" made it onto the set list two days later at the sold-out Garden State Arts Center, where they surpassed the attendance record of 8,500 previously held by crooner Andy Williams. During the ninety-minute show, Janis took audience requests, with her second encore "Get It While You Can" keeping the crowd in a "near frenzy." Then, the next afternoon, on August 11, they played their final public performance at Harvard Stadium, in Cambridge, to a crowd of forty thousand. An outdoor show and a hot August day were not the best conditions for a performance. Also, police patrolled the area—Janis still on the FBI's surveillance list. But the concert went off without a hitch, and Janis and Full Tilt left their audience screaming for more. "My music ain't supposed to make you want to riot!" she told the *Boston Phoenix*. "My music's supposed to make you want to fuck!"

Then Janis flew to Texas. In May she'd decided to attend her tenth high school reunion. All summer, she'd tried in vain to talk friends into joining her, including Beaumont's Johnny Winter—with whom she'd had a fling in 1969—and Tary Owens, who'd become addicted to heroin while living in San Francisco. In June she'd spoken both ominously and with dark humor about the reunion to Dick Cavett, whom she also invited. She had said on his national TV show that "they laughed me out of class, out of town, and out of the state, so I'm going home," which elicited loud applause from the studio audience. When she ran into artist Robert Rauschenberg at Max's Kansas City that summer, he tried to talk her out of returning to their bigoted hometown. "I couldn't convince her not to go," he reported later. "I knew that it was going to be a disaster."

For company, Janis enlisted her pals Neuwirth, Cooke, and John Fisher, the owner of the New York car service Love Limousines who had become a dear friend after two years of driving her. She always preferred sitting up front with Fisher, peering out the lavender-tinted side windows. Texas newspapers had been reporting on Janis's impending visit for weeks, with one article stating that "locals are surprised that Janis, so well noted for her antiestablishment views, [would] come to something as establishment as a high school class reunion." Janis's friends were baffled by her determination to attend. Some thought she wanted to show off her stardom to former classmates eking out a living "pumping gas," as she told one reporter. Possibly still craving approval from those who'd scorned her a decade before, she wanted to prove she could win them over just as she had audiences across the country. In 1969 she had said of those in Port Arthur who hurt her, "I just wanted them to love me."

As Rauschenberg predicted, the weekend turned into a series of gut-wrenching disappointments soon after the Joplins picked her up at the airport on Thursday evening. Perhaps to punish her for the Cavett show comments or to humble her in some way, she was given a cot in the den, rather than offered Michael's or Laura's bedroom to sleep in. "My parents treated her pretty cold," her brother reflected. "They were pretty upset with the way she'd been talking about them and the town, so that was a real tense situation around the house." The next night, after her entourage arrived, the Joplins hosted a dinner at their country club, with John Cooke's date, from a well-to-do Austin family, making most of the small talk.

Afterward, Janis and her posse went across the Sabine River to go juking in Louisiana. She wanted to show them the places where she'd partied as a teen, but some, including the Big Oak, had closed down. They settled for a packed roadhouse with a country band onstage. But Janis's mood darkened when she was mobbed by autograph seekers. It was not the kind of attention she wanted that night.

The next morning, Seth and Dorothy pointedly left town for a wedding. Janis cooked brunch for her guests, who were staying at a nearby motel. For the zine her brother founded, *Agape*, she wrote the message: "Never compromise yourself. It's all you've got!"

At the reunion itself, it became clear that Janis craved ultimate redemption from her hometown, but she didn't know how to ask for it. Instead, she put on an act as the rejected outsider who had triumphed and returned to flaunt her success. When approached by a local TV reporter as she sashayed down the street, Janis used her Mae West–W. C. Fields voice to flippantly answer his questions. Prior to the evening's reunion festivities, in the Petroleum Room at the then swanky Goodhue Hotel, Janis, with her sister, Laura, seated next to her on the dais, participated in a press conference. Though she began by cracking jokes and making snide remarks like a cocky star, she became flustered when asked about her alienation in high school. As if she were back in the principal's office a decade before, she snapped, "I don't know—why don't you ask *them*?" when asked if her classmates "made you different." "I f-felt apart from them," she stumbled, as if about to cry. When Laura piped up and said her parents considered her "exceptional," Janis looked surprised.

During the reunion dinner, no one really knew how to treat Janis. She received only polite applause when she was singled out merely for being the alumnus to travel the greatest distance and awarded a gag tire. Generally, she was either snubbed or approached by sycophants whom she barely remembered. None of her good friends attended, including Karleen and the rebel guys; they saw no reason to show up for something as corny as a high school reunion—not even to spend time with, and to support, Janis.

Soon after the reunion dinner, Janis and her cohorts headed to the Pelican Club, a beer joint with headliner Jerry Lee Lewis—whom Janis, at fifteen, had written a letter to *Time* defending. Earlier that summer, she had seen "the Killer" perform in Louisville, where she'd tried to pick up his teenage bassist—who happened to be Lewis's son. She and Jerry Lee had exchanged words then, but he'd hardly been cordial, even when she mentioned their mutual friend Kris Kristofferson. Lewis, at a fairly low ebb in his career, playing low-paying gigs like the Pelican, was surly when Janis gaily trounced backstage to "welcome" him to her hometown and introduce him to her sister. Lewis generally did not like hippie women like Janis who looked disheveled and wore no makeup. When he made a nasty comment about their looks, Janis yelled, *"You mother-fucker!"* and slapped him across the face. Lewis slugged her back, hard: "If you're gonna act like a man, I'll treat ya like one," he snarled. Cooke and Neuwirth quickly ushered her out, while she cried hysterically. Back at the Joplins' house, they finished off another bottle of tequila, with Neuwirth passing out in the car—with the motor running—and Fisher crashing on the couch next to Janis's cot. When the Joplins woke up the next morning and discovered the inebriants, they were furious.

After her friends left for the airport, Janis and Dorothy clashed, with her mother screaming at her, "I wish you'd never been born!" Though Janis had so wanted to redeem herself in her family's eyes by being celebrated by her hometown, the opposite had occurred—with more pain and hurt being thrust upon one another. "The reunion was really when we had our worst break with Janis," Seth Joplin recalled later. "She gave two or three interviews. . . . Dorothy didn't like what she said and told her so. She got mad and left—got an earlier plane . . . and I can't blame her either." Even her adored father did not try to persuade her to stay.

"I was a real pessimist, a real cynical bitch," Janis told a journalist soon after the Port Arthur disaster. "Then I read somewhere this definition that said, 'A pessimist is never disappointed, and an optimist is constantly let down.' So by that definition, I'd be an optimist."

Back in California, Janis threw herself into her relationship with Seth Morgan until early September, when recording started in Los Angeles. Morgan stayed in Larkspur, where he entertained women in Janis's bedroom. Occasionally, he flew to LA, but he didn't like the Landmark Motor Hotel, with its "gruesomely schlocky sprawl with orange carpets and ersatz Polynesian artifacts hanging everywhere," he wrote in the *Berkeley Barb*. He considered Janis's hotel room, 105, "a single with a kitchenette . . . markedly inferior to the quarters assigned to the musicians, roadies, and . . . John Cooke." He also disliked the "endless and stupifying rotations between the room at the Landmark, Barney's Beanery, and the recording studio." The friction between Janis and Morgan increased with each visit, but she always begged him to come back. She couldn't stand being alone.

At Sunset Sound, however, Janis usually appeared happy and focused. As she and Rothchild worked on song arrangements, tempos, and instrumental parts, he listened thoughtfully to her ideas. The veteran producer was so impressed with Janis's direction and musical vision that he told her she would make a great producer—a statement she took to heart. The opportunity to independently direct a recording session became another goal.

"Paul was very much in love with Janis," according to engineer Bruce Botnick, who'd worked with Rothchild on the Doors LPs. "He told me that during the recording, right as it started, they realized there was a serious attraction. But he realized that if he [started an affair], he wouldn't get an album. So he said to Janis, 'Look, I really love you very much, and I'd like to be with you, but let's fuck on tape.' " Occasionally, after hours, they raced each other in their Porsches along the Pacific Coast Highway.

Janis remained elated with her band, telling Ken Pearson, "If you guys leave me, I'll kill ya!" But still she couldn't cut back on her drinking, even though she realized it adversely affected her voice. In 1969 she had to redo vocal takes during the *Kozmic Blues* sessions when her voice was wrecked from drinking the night before. She knew she had to prove herself with Rothchild, and if she couldn't cut it vocally, he would quit the project. So she tried to pace herself, limiting herself to a few drinks at the studio. Afterward, at Barney's Beanery, restraint was more difficult. Then one evening in the Landmark lobby, she spotted her dealer, George, on a call to Peggy Caserta, who, unbeknownst to Janis, was staying there too. Janis ended up at Caserta's door, they got back together, and Janis shot up heroin for the first time in some five months. Afterward, she rationalized her relapse to Seth Morgan by claiming the drug would help her refrain from drinking. After no longer "being so goddamned drunk all the time," she insisted, "we're laying down some good tracks."

At Sunset Sound, she remained engaged with the music. "Fun was the underlying thing," Rothchild remembered. "It was all about smiles and laughter." One night Janis and the band recorded an exuberant version of "Happy Birthday" for John Lennon's upcoming thirtieth (on October 9), segueing into a twisted "Happy Trails," with Janis singing like Dale Evans—the song's composer—in a boisterous soprano.

They had begun the sessions cutting material the band had road-tested all summer: "Move Over," "Get It While You Can," "Half Moon," "Cry Baby." On songs such as "Me and Bobby McGee," they focused on what Janis called "more of a country blues feel."

"Am I getting my Texas accent back?" she asked Rothchild.

"I hope so," he replied.

In addition to Gram Parsons and the Burritos at the Palomino, she'd discovered Linda Ronstadt belting her country rock repertoire at the Troubadour. Meanwhile, Rothchild had connected with Alabama-born songwriter and keyboardist Spooner Oldham at an Everly Brothers session and requested a song for Janis. On piano, Oldham played "A Woman Left Lonely," which he'd started with songwriting partner Dan Penn. "Paul said, 'You finish that, and I'm sure I'll record it with Janis,'" the affable Oldham recalled. The California transplant flew to Penn's home in Tennessee to cut a demo.

"I took the tape to Sunset Sound and met Janis, who was sitting in the sound booth with Paul," said Oldham. "She was real congenial to me," he recalled, "and I hugged her and said, 'You're doing great, Janis, you've got a great career goin'. I'm so proud of you.' And she looked at me as if I'd stabbed her and said, 'You know, Spooner, I think it's going to end any day.'" Perhaps failing to stay clean gave Janis a sense of dread. She was beginning to realize that she was not immortal; as strong as she considered herself, she had also seen friends and peers meet an early demise, some of whom were her age, twenty-seven.

One of them, Jimi Hendrix had just died in London, on September 18, choking to death on his own vomit after a barbiturate overdose. When Myra Friedman called Janis for a comment for the press, she blurted out, "There but for the grace of God . . ." Then she pondered, "I wonder what they'll say about *me* after I die?" Two weeks before Hendrix's death, blues guitarist–vocalist Al Wilson of Canned Heat, who had also performed at Monterey and Woodstock, died of a drug overdose. The year before that, another twenty-seven-year-old blues lover, Brian Jones, recently jettisoned from the Rolling Stones, had drowned in his swimming pool.

Still, Janis remained optimistic about her music and relished the results of the sessions. "There's always a lot of growth during recording," she told Richard Bell. She phoned Clive Davis at Columbia and played him some rough mixes. "She seemed so thrilled about the record," he recalled. "She was so upbeat, so positive about her beautiful version of 'Me and Bobby McGee.'"

When Janis ran into Jefferson Airplane vocalist Marty Balin in LA, she insisted he come to Sunset Sound to hear some tracks. "Janis was the best singer I'd ever heard," reflected Balin, a recording artist since his teens. "No one could match her." After the pair "killed two bottles of booze" while listening, Balin recalled, she turned to him and, pleading for affirmation, asked, "Aren't I the greatest singer?"

"Yes, you are," he said, and he meant it.

Though she'd already added a third Ragovoy song, "My Baby," to the album, Janis called the songwriter to see if he had anything new. Perhaps inspired by Hendrix's death, he'd written "I'm Gonna Rock My Way to Heaven," which he sang over the phone, promising to send a demo. She also enlisted Nick Gravenites, who brought a composition he'd started, cryptically titled "Buried Alive in the Blues," to Sunset Sound. He taught it to the band, and he and Janis worked on lyrics. Eerily, death was in the air.

Another songwriter Janis approached was twenty-six-year-old soul singer and guitarist Bobby Womack, whose "It's All Over Now" was an early Rolling Stones hit in 1964. Womack arrived at Sunset Sound with his acoustic guitar to play Janis some uncut songs. "I started off with 'Trust Me,'" Womack recalled. "When I got to the end, she was out of her chair. 'I love it! . . . That's the song!'" Womack sang a scratch vocal so that the band could work it up in the studio on the spot. Janis quickly learned the words, and they recorded it with Womack playing along on acoustic guitar.

During the session, he saw Janis's kozmic blues emerge. "Jimi Hendrix had recently died, and she was in a fix about that," Womack recalled. "Crying and talking about death. . . . Janis was down. She was on the phone to her boyfriend. From what I heard she wanted him to come out and see her, but he refused unless she wired him some money. I heard her scream into the phone, *'You always want money from me! That's all you want!'* "

Janis got drunk, and Womack offered her a ride to the Landmark, he recalled in his 2006 memoir. While cruising in his Mercedes, she was singing, "Oh Lord, won't you buy me a Mercedes Benz?," when inspiration struck, and she had Womack turn around to go back to the studio. No one was there but Rothchild, who agreed to record Janis doing an off-the-cuff spoken intro followed by a twangy a cappella "Mercedes Benz." At one point, Janis called Michael McClure and sang it to him, and then asked if he minded her cutting the song he'd originated. He said he liked his version better, but "go ahead."

Afterward, back at the Landmark, Womack and Janis commiserated; he confessed he had a thing for cocaine. She preferred heroin, he remembered her saying, because it could "bury her thoughts and deaden her from the world."

For all her progress as a musician and her joy over the band, Janis could not let go of the need to feel connected to a person and have a normal "civilian" life. She told guitarist John Till she "wanted to be more than a rock singer. She wanted to have a family. She wanted to get married." Though Janis had either forgotten or buried her promise to Niehaus, along with her pride over quitting heroin, she had not given up on her difficult relationship with Morgan; Janis brought up marriage nearly every time they spoke. He agreed half heartedly, under the condition that it be an open marriage. During one of the couple's numerous arguments, he recalled taunting her with "You'll have to find someone else to be Mr. Joplin." Still, Janis, desperate for stability, persisted, calling LA's city hall to get marriage license requirements, and asking her attorney Bob Gordon to draw up a prenuptial agreement.

As if she knew what was coming, she and Gordon had discussed revising her will, which she'd signed in 1968, leaving most of her estate to her brother and bequeathing some money to Linda Gravenites, now absent from her life. Her new will would leave half her estate to her parents, and a quarter each to Laura and Michael. Linda was omitted. Janis also added a provision that, upon her demise, $2,500 be provided for a party for her friends. By late September, Gordon had incorporated the revisions she requested.

Janis spent the next week—the last of her life—recording at Sunset Sound and making plans. The month before, she'd introduced Morgan to Caserta and to heroin, and they'd set up a date for a ménage à trois at the Landmark for that Saturday. She went to a hairdresser to get blond streaks added to her light brown tresses, and on Friday, October 2, she drove her Porsche to Beverly Hills to sign her revised last will and testament in Gordon's office. He gave her the prenup for Morgan to sign that weekend.

On Saturday afternoon, October 3, Janis scored heroin and stashed it in the bureau drawer in her hotel room alongside her works. She then met the band at Sunset Sound to listen to their recording of "Buried Alive in the Blues." While there, she argued on the phone with Morgan, who'd called to postpone his trip by a day. That night, Caserta would also stand her up. Planning to cut her vocal track on Sunday, Janis and keyboardist Ken Pearson ended the night with screwdrivers at Barney's Beanery. Then they returned to the Landmark, where she went to her room alone. Around one o'clock in the morning, on Sunday, October 4, she skin-popped her usual dose—injecting it under the skin of her left arm, rather than mainlining into her vein as she typically did. It is unclear why she chose to skin-pop, which delays the effects of the heroin by some ten minutes—rather than the instantaneous high of mainlining, her preference. Afterward, she strolled to the lobby with a $5 bill to get change for the cigarette machine.

She chatted briefly with the desk clerk, who didn't realize a long-awaited letter was in her mailbox—from David Niehaus, dated August 17 and mailed from Asia: "Come on, Mama! Sure would dig that you were here. . . . Come over and see some of the East. Nepal in October is said to really be something . . . write me . . . if you can come for a few weeks or a few years. . . . Really miss ya. Things aren't the same alone. . . . Love ya, Mama, more than you know."

Back in her room, the heroin suddenly hit as she sat on the edge of her bed, the pack of Marlboros just placed on the nightstand. Janis collapsed, her $4.50 still clutched in her hand. She hit her face on the nightstand, drawing blood, and fell to the floor, her body wedged between the bed and table. The heroin shut down her heart and lungs, and she died—thirty-three years to the day of Bessie Smith's burial.

Janis had no idea the heroin she'd injected was China white, brought into the country by a young French count whose customers included Keith Richards of the Rolling Stones. The batch Janis had scored without realizing its strength was 40 to 50 percent pure, rather than the usual 10 percent or so. Her tolerance was probably lower as well, since she had been clean for months. Unlike the times she had overdosed in the past, there was no one there to revive her.

Eighteen hours later, around seven thirty Sunday evening, John Cooke found her body after having been alerted by Rothchild that she never arrived at the studio. In shock, Cooke asked Vince Mitchell to accompany him back to Janis's room before he called Bob Gordon, who notified the police. After the authorities arrived, it didn't take long for the media to swarm in. At first, the press didn't know what to make of Janis's death because of her hard-drinking image, with not many journalists aware of her heroin use. Some believed Janis committed suicide; others theorized murder, with conspiracy theories spread due to her death coming so soon after Hendrix's. Though Cooke had spotted Janis's set of works in her dresser drawer, the evidence vanished at one point. Later, an empty balloon of heroin appeared in the trash can—a friend had apparently removed it, then thought better of the idea. The subsequent police investigation, an autopsy, and a second coroner's report supervised by Thomas Noguchi, the medical examiner who handled the deaths of Judy Garland and Marilyn Monroe, declared the cause of death an accidental overdose of heroin.

On October 7 Dorothy and Seth Joplin held a private funeral in Los Angeles, without Janis's siblings, bandmates, or friends. As specified in her will, her cremains were scattered by air off the coast of Marin County, and on October 26 the party she funded was held at the Lion's Share in San Anselmo, where grieving members of Big Brother and other musician friends performed, attended by some two hundred people, including her sister, Laura.

Eight days earlier, on October 18, Janis's final album, *Pearl*, was completed. After her death, Rothchild and Full Tilt had returned to the studio to recut instrumental backing for several of Janis's vocal tracks. From unfinished recordings, Rothchild spliced together various vocal performances to construct final versions of songs. The instrumental track of "Buried Alive in the Blues" was also included. When Rothchild remembered Janis's spur-of-the-moment "Mercedes Benz," it became the tenth track, ending with her spoken *"That's it!"* followed by her joyous cackle. Janis's band and friends such as Kris Kristofferson gathered to hear the finished album. "We all believed she was somehow there," Brad Campbell asserted. "We felt her there."

Pearl was released three months after Janis's passing, in January 1971, and became the most successful album of her career, going on to sell more than eight million copies. Of the three 45s released, "Bobby McGee" lodged at number one for two weeks, the second time in pop history a posthumous single topped the charts. "Cry Baby" and "Get It While You Can" also entered the Hot 100. "A Woman Left Lonely" had been planned for release on 45, but after Janis's death, it was determined by Columbia to be just too sad.

Every time Paul Rothchild heard Janis's songs on the radio, it was excruciating. "Janis's death was the most devastating thing in my life," he reflected later. "We decided we'd be together forever. It was the most fun we'd ever had in the studio. She was always one hundred ten percent there." Still in a deep funk months after Janis's death, he broke his contract with the Doors and declined to produce their sixth album, *L.A. Woman*; Jim Morrison died of a heroin overdose—allegedly supplied by the same drug dealer whose wares killed Janis—in Paris in July 1971. He, too, was twenty-seven.

Albert Grossman, who'd already cut back on his management duties after his relationship with Dylan ended in 1969, focused his attention on his Hudson Valley recording studio and new label, Bearsville Records. Those close to him believed that Grossman, who died from a heart attack in 1986, never got over Janis's death.

Seth Morgan became addicted to heroin and eventually served time in prison for armed robbery. Upon his release, he published an acclaimed novel, *Homeboy*, in 1990. He died days later in a motorcycle accident, when he drunkenly sped into a bridge post in New Orleans, also killing his girlfriend.

David Niehaus learned about Janis's death in a back issue of *Time* magazine while in Kabul, Afghanistan. "My entire being has been aching the past few days since hearing about Janis," he wrote in his journal. "Both of us were fools to allow that last moment in each other's arms to be the last moment." Today, he believes that Janis "was so sensitive to the world. That's what killed her. 'Cause she had to turn it off." Niehaus continued to travel the globe, visiting more than a hundred countries, and later wed a doctor, to whom he's been married for more than forty years.

In 1969 *Newsweek* called Janis "the first female superstar of rock music." In the nearly five decades since her death, few artists have matched the power of her onstage performances. Her music lives on, embraced by yet another generation of fans. Her influence continues in those artists who saw her perform in the 1960s and those who've discovered her in the intervening years. One of those, Alicia Keys, told the *Chicago Tribune*, "I use Janis Joplin as a point of reference—I look at the total abandonment in her singing style. You feel like she's holding nothing back."

Ray Charles once said that singers don't reach their full potential until the age of fifty because a whole life shows up in the voice at that age. Perhaps, as she once aspired, Janis would have become "like the world's greatest blues singer, Bessie Smith" or even taken a turn into a whole other genre.

Three months before she died, Janis described music as the one aspect of her life that had never let her down; it had never succumbed to the Saturday Night Swindle. She also expressed the belief that her singing was the true expression of her self. People "ask me, 'How did you learn to sing the blues like that?'" is how the discussion began. "I just opened my mouth, and that's what I sounded like," Janis said. "You can't make up something that you don't feel." In a conversation aboard the Festival Express with singer Bonnie Bramlett, in 1970, Janis acknowledged, with a new, deeper degree of self-realization, the choice she had made to become who she was, as well as the limits imposed by that choice:

"You give up every constant in the world except music," she explained. "That's the only thing in the world you got."

ACKNOWLEDGMENTS

While putting together these acknowledgments, it suddenly dawned on me: the roughly four years I've worked on this biography is about equal to Janis's much too brief career: from June 1966, when she joined Big Brother, to her death in October 1970.

The genesis of my book goes back even further than four years, though: it would not exist if not for my literary agent, Sarah Lazin, who first brought up the idea of a Janis Joplin biography as far back as 2009 or so. Sarah actually saw Janis perform numerous times in San Francisco in the sixties, and I'm honored that she thought I was the right person to tell the story of Janis's life and music. Sarah, thank you so much for your belief in me—and your patience!

My research into Janis's work began even earlier: former vice president of education and public programs at the Rock & Roll Hall of Fame Robert Santelli invited me to be a panelist at the "Remembering Janis" symposium in Cleveland in 1999. There I first met Janis's siblings, Laura and Michael Joplin, and other luminaries who are no longer with us: Janis's beloved bandmate Sam Andrew, guitarist of Big Brother and the Holding Company; and Family Dog cofounder and Avalon impresario Chet Helms, who hitched with Janis from Texas to San Francisco in 1963. The wonderful weekend event honoring Janis and her music was the first of two such celebrations in Cleveland. In 2009, for the Hall of Fame's "American Music Masters" honoring Janis, Santelli's successor Dr. Lauren Onkey invited me to be keynote speaker along with fellow scribes Ann Powers and Lucy O'Brien. I got to spend time again with Laura Joplin, as well as hear from others close to Janis, including legendary songwriter-producer Jerry Ragovoy, who wrote some of Janis's favorite songs; John Cooke, Janis's road manager for three years; the great Bob Neuwirth, Janis's very close friend and coauthor of "Mercedes Benz"; Waller Creek Boy Powell St. John; Country Joe McDonald; and DJ Dusty Streets, among others. Again, another intriguing event that took me deeper down the rabbit hole in learning about Janis and her work.

In 2013 I discovered Janis's prowess as a producer while listening to Columbia Records's *Pearl* outtakes, after being asked to write liner notes for the two-CD set *The Pearl Sessions*. By that time, Sarah Lazin had brought me together with Laura Joplin and Jeff Jampol, founder of JAM, Inc., who represents Janis's music and legacy. I cannot express how much Laura's and Jeff's trust in me as Janis's biographer helped: Laura graciously and generously opened the doors to the Janis vaults and archives. She shared her own memories and her treasure trove of Janis's correspondence, memorabilia, artwork, scrapbooks, family photos, and even items such as Janis's school-days' slide rule, her fabulous boas and Nudie suits, and personal collection of books. Laura also provided transcriptions of the numerous interviews she'd conducted with family members, Janis's childhood pals, bandmates, and friends for her memoir, *Love, Janis*, originally published in 1992. All of this was shared without requiring any editorial approval over my manuscript. And she spent countless hours with me, answering my questions and being my tour guide to all things Janis. My gratitude to Laura, Jeff, and Michael Joplin is immeasurable, and to Sarah for bringing us together.

Janis's old friends gave me much of their time: thank you, Karleen Bennett, Herman Bennett, Arlene Elster, Jack Smith, Jim Langdon, Sam Monroe, Ray Solis and his wife, Angel (who accompanied me to Janis's childhood home), Henry "Wali" Stopher, Stephanie Chernikowski, Travis Rivers, Jae Whitaker, Peggy Caserta, and David Niehaus. In addition to her recording bands, several musicians who played with Janis—Larry Hanks, Jorma Kaukonen, and Stefan Grossman—shared their stories. I was also fortunate to spend time with Janis's "official" bandmates: Powell St. John of the Waller Creek Boys (and Powell's wonderful and helpful wife, Toby St. John); Big Brother's Dave Getz and Peter Albin;

Skip Prokop, Bill King, Snooky Flowers, and Terry Clements of the band that morphed into the Kozmic Blues Band; and Brad Campbell of Full Tilt Boogie (and Kozmic Blues), and John Cooke. Other essential interview subjects include legendary country music scholar Bill Malone, Johanna Hall, Richard Goldstein, Clive Davis, Herb Pedersen, Barbara Dane, Jesse Cahn, Marty Balin, Jack Casady, Grace Slick (via Stacie Huckeba), Mick Fleetwood, Eric Andersen, Lenny Kaye, Kris Kristofferson, Spooner Oldham, Bob Neuwirth, Elvin Bishop, Maria Muldaur, David Nelson, Jim Fouratt, Danny Fields, Cyndi Lauper, Michael Lydon, Ben Fong-Torres, Eddie Wilson, Rhoney Stanley, Yvonne Ruskin, Ian Kimmet, Lotti Golden, Pegi Young, Tony Foutz, Jeremy Wilber, Michael Lang, Elliott Landy, Baron Wolman, Bob Gruen, Sylvia Tyson, Johnny Winter's manager Paul Nelson, Fritz Kraai, Sally Grossman, Bill Ham, Bill Bentley, Bruce Botnick, Larry Litt, Karen Lyberger, and Robert Gordon (who took me to Janis's Larkspur home). I managed to grab quick conversations with and ask questions of John Simon and Ed Sanders. Likewise, I met D. A. Pennebaker at three different film screenings and seized the opportunity to interview him. During a brief conversation, Little Steven Van Zandt supplied a humorous account of his early band with Bruce Springsteen, Child, sharing an Asbury Park bill with Janis in 1969. I'm grateful to all the fans who described seeing Janis in performance from 1962 to 1970.

Many thanks to the very generous journalists who shared their interviews with me: Joel Selvin, author of several excellent books on San Francisco music, who lent not only numerous interviews but also a wealth of other material. Ben Fong-Torres, who taught me how to write biographies by hiring me as his assistant in 1989 while he researched and wrote the groundbreaking *Hickory Wind: The Life and Times of Gram Parsons*; Ben interviewed Janis in 1970 and covered San Francisco musicians for *Rolling Stone* and other publications and books; he generously shared his research materials and took me on a "Janis tour" of the city. John Glatt, who gave me interviews he conducted for his two thorough histories of Bill Graham's Fillmore venues. Jas Obrecht, who extensively interviewed James Gurley and Sam Andrew; Bob Sarles, of

Ravin' Films, who filmed conversations with members of Big Brother, Joe MacDonald, and other Haight-Ashbury fixtures. Dave Harmon, who interviewed Janis's high school friends for an excellent article in the *Austin American-Statesman*. Alice Echols's exhaustively researched *Scars of Sweet Paradise: The Life and Times of Janis Joplin* yielded a great deal of information, and books by the late Myra Friedman and John Byrne Cooke (who shared with me his transcribed interviews from the 1970s) also helped a great deal in this way. Journalist John Bowers expounded on the time he spent with Janis.

Julie Haas gave me a breathtaking tour of "Argentina" and provided a history of the property and her own Fillmore and Avalon days. Bruno Cerretti emailed from Italy his meticulously researched Joplin and Big Brother discographies. Rock & Roll Hall of Fame archivist Jennie Thomas and Sony Music archivist Tom Tierney each provided essential help, as did oral historian Dan Del Fiorentino at NAMM. Sarah Bellian, curator of the Gulf Coast Museum in Port Arthur, gave her perspective of Janis's hometown and provided essential materials. Michael Gray, at the Country Music Hall of Fame and Museum, aided my research as well. Dennis McNally gave me a private tour of the San Francisco Historical Society exhibition he curated for the city's fiftieth anniversary of the Summer of Love extravaganza, as did Peter Albin at the De Young Museum's fabulous exhibit *Summer of Love: Art, Fashion and Rock & Roll*. Exhibits at the San Francisco Public Library and the Castro's Gay Lesbian Bisexual Transgender History Museum were also helpful. Glenn Horowitz Bookseller supplied copies of Janis's correspondence with Peter de Blanc.

My gratitude to others who helped in various ways: photographer Franco Vogt, Cash Edwards, Peter Aaron, Tony Fletcher, David Dalton (the rock writer whom Janis adored), Austin filmmaker Tara Veneruso (*Janis Joplin Slept Here*), David Ritz, Suzanne Mowatt, David Kraai, Susan Brearey, Sparrow, Jann S. Wenner, Craig Inciardi, Andy Leach, Lucia Reale Vogt, Lisa Vianello, Petrine Mitchum, Rosanne Cash, Kate Pierson, Charles Cross, Holly Gleason, Bob Oermann, Parke Puterbaugh, Sylvie Simmons, Jean Caffeine, Brian Hassett, Roberta Bayley, Mary Lucchese, Mary Bassel, Mark Loete, Paula Batson, Fred Goodman, and

Doug Wygal. Very helpful were Amy Berg's documentary *Janis: Little Girl Blue* and the out-of-print *Janis: The Way She Was* (given to me by Sally Grossman), as well as *Festival Express*, D. A. Pennebaker's *Monterey Pop*, *Nine Hundred Nights*, *The Life and Times of the Red Dog Saloon*, and the fortieth-anniversary edition of Michael Wadleigh's *Woodstock* (with Janis footage)—all essential viewing. Numerous live recordings—legit and bootlegs, going back to 1962—helped me understand Janis's evolution as a singer and performer. Thanks to those who shared these priceless documents.

My deep appreciation to the photographers who captured Janis and those who enabled these indelible images to be part of my book: the late, great David Gahr, who told me so many Janis stories as did his friend and colleague Jim Marshall; Bob Seidemann, whose singular portrait graces this book's cover (thanks to Belinda Seidemann); Elliott Landy, Baron Wolman (thanks to Diane Duery), Herb Greene, Lisa Law (thanks to Geary Chansley), Amalie R. Rothschild, Marjorie Alette, Steve Banks, Jay Good (thanks to Frank While), Ivaan Kotulsky (thanks, Stephen Bulger and Paul Lamont), John Cooke (thanks to Susan and Charlotte), Terry Clements (who expertly documented his travels as a member of the Kozmic Blues Band), and Clark Pierson (Full Tilt Boogie drummer *and* band photographer). A special thanks to the keepers of David Gahr's flame, Joel Siegel and Bobby Ward (who let me explore David's extensive photo files), and Amelia Davis and Jay Blakesburg, who have done the same for Jim Marshall's legacy.

This book would not exist without the expertise and support of my brilliant editor, Priscilla Painton, whose patience and meticulous attention to detail took my manuscript to the place it needed to be. I am also very grateful to Simon & Schuster's Jonathan Karp, Richard Rhorer, Cary Goldstein, Jonathan Evans (thanks for choosing Phil Bashe!), Megan Hogan, Samantha O'Hara, Madeline Schmitz, Jackie Seow, Elisa M. Rivlin, and Elise Ringo. No biographer could ask for a more thorough and genius copy editor than Phil Bashe, who caught excruciating bloopers and entertained me with his copious comments, notes, and research. I'm grateful to the hardworking team at

JAM, Inc.: Kenny Nemes, Alicia Yaffe, John Logan, and Matt Abels. Thanks to my fantastic transcriber Judy Whitfield, as well as Margaret Schultz, Catharine Strong, Liz DeSiena, Dan Smith, the staff at both the Phoenicia Library and the Sojourner Truth Library at SUNY New Paltz, and my incredible writers group, Laura Claridge, John Milward, and particularly Richard Hoffman, who went above and beyond to help elevate my prose.

My supportive husband, Robert Burke Warren, unfailingly lent both hands via his excellent skills as writer, editor, music historian, collaborator, and sounding board: I am forever grateful that he is so generous with his many talents. This book would not be what it is without his help. And thanks to our very encouraging son, Jack Warren, who became a Janis Joplin fan—even after being forced to listen to numerous Big Brother and Janis bootlegs (instead of his own mixes) on several long road trips.

Most of all, I thank Janis Joplin, whose music changed my life by opening up a world of possibilities to a thirteen-year-old rock & roll fan living in small-town North Carolina. (If only I could have witnessed her 1968 gigs at my alma mater, the University of North Carolina at Chapel Hill, and my son's school, Wesleyan University. . . .) Between seeing her on *The Dick Cavett Show* and wearing out my copy of *Pearl*, my Janis journey began in 1970–71 and led me to this book.

NOTES

INTRODUCTION

xi   *"Don't compromise yourself"*: Laura Joplin, *Love, Janis* (New York: Harper, 2005), 8–9.

xii   *"the only sixties culture hero"*: Ellen Willis, "Janis Joplin," in *The Rolling Stone Illustrated History of Rock & Roll*, new ed., ed. Anthony DeCurtis and James Henke, with Holly George-Warren (New York: Random House, 1992), 383.

xii   *"her connection to the audience"*: Stevie Nicks, Rock & Roll Hall of Fame induction ceremony, Barclay's Center, Brooklyn, NY, March 29, 2019.

xii   *"What is this girl all about?"*: Lou Adler, audio commentary, *Monterey Pop* DVD set, Criterion Collection, 2017.

xiii   *"Three or four years ago"*: Chet Helms, audio commentary, *Monterey Pop* DVD set, Criterion Collection, 2017.

xiii   *"You are only as much"*: "Janis Joplin Talks About Rejection Four Days Before She Died in 1970," Janis Joplin, interview by Howard Smith, Dangerous Minds, last modified September 24, 2013, https://dangerousminds.net/comments/janis _joplin_talks_about_rejection_four_days_before_she_died_in_1970.

xv   *"When a soul can look"*: Holly George-Warren, ed., *The Rock and Roll Hall of Fame: The First 25 Years* (New York: Collins Design/HarperCollins, 2009), 97.

CHAPTER 1: PIONEER STOCK

1   *"Don't write"*: Joplin, *Love, Janis*, 25.

1   *"I'm from pioneer stock"*: Big Brother and the Holding Co. with Janis Joplin, *Nine Hundred Nights* DVD, Eagle Vision, 2001.

1   *"a tough pioneer woman"*: Joplin, *Love, Janis*, 15.

2   *"horrible verbal abuse"*: Dorothy Joplin, interview by Laura Joplin.

2   *"Dorothy East"*: "Operetta Is Well Played," *Amarillo (TX) Globe News*, n.d. (clipping in a framed collage given to Dorothy Joplin by her sister).

2   *"I always had the lead"*: Dorothy Joplin, interview by Laura Joplin.

3   *"judging from the applause"*: "Miss Dorothy East Can Sing," *Amarillo (TX) Globe News*, n.d.

3   *"a New York production man"*: Dorothy Joplin, interview by Laura Joplin.

3   *"business college"*: Ibid.

3   *"your kind of people"*: Ibid.

4   *"He once wrote"*: Ibid.

4   *"I can't figure"*: Joplin, *Love, Janis*, 24.

6 *"began with a roar"*: Lonn Taylor, "Oil on Canvas: The Fine Art of the Spindletop Gusher," *Texas Monthly*, June 2012.

6 *"hunches"*: Keith L. Bryant Jr., *Arthur Stilwell: Promoter with a Hunch* (Nashville: Vanderbilt University Press, 1971), 96.

7 *"had created the state's"*: Bryan Burrough, *The Big Rich: The Rise and Fall of the Greatest Texas Oil Fortunes* (New York: Penguin Press, 2008), 87.

7 *"the most brash"*: Adam Hochschild, *Spain in Our Hearts: Americans in the Spanish Civil War, 1936–1939* (Boston: Houghton Mifflin Harcourt, 2016), 168.

7 *"Let's do something"*: Joplin, *Love, Janis*, 28.

8 *"I wish to tender"*: Ibid., 29.

8 *"She never was cranky"*: Dorothy Joplin, interview by Laura Joplin.

8 *"a secret intellectual"*: David Dalton, *Janis* (New York: Simon & Schuster, 1971), 54.

9 *"If I'd had a choice"*: Dorothy Joplin, interview by Laura Joplin.

CHAPTER 2: TOMBOY

13 *"I nearly fell"*: Janis Joplin's scrapbook, 1956–1959 (Laura Joplin Collection).

13 *"was outgoing"*: Dorothy Joplin, interview by Laura Joplin.

13 *"She enjoyed"*: Roger Pryor, interview by Laura Joplin.

14 *"She played outside"*: Ibid.

14 *"I felt really ill"*: Ibid.

14 *"really liked me"*: Ibid.

14 *"We'd get those kids"*: Ibid.

15 *"a real pretty"*: Ibid.

15 *"the only other intellectual"*: Dalton, *Janis*, 54.

15 *"When we arrived at the Joplins' house"*: Kristin Bowen, written remembrance (Laura Joplin Collection).

15 *"You could hear"*: Pryor, interview by Laura Joplin.

16 *"I told her"*: Seth Joplin, interview by Laura Joplin.

16 *"Janis loved to draw"*: Pryor, interview by Laura Joplin.

16 *"Her coordination"*: Dorothy Joplin, interview by Laura Joplin.

17 *"Not a fierce"*: Kristin Bowen, interview by Laura Joplin.

17 *"When Mike came"*: Pryor, interview by Laura Joplin.

17 *"rest quietly"*: this and other teachers' comments from Tyrell Elementary School report cards for Janis Lyn Joplin, 1949–54 (Laura Joplin Collection).

19 *"the big best-seller"*: Grace Metalious, *Peyton Place* (New York: Dell, 1958), back cover.

20 *"the young housewife"*: Ibid.

21 she preferred that version: Karleen Bennett and Herman Bennett, interview by the author.

21 *"We got together"*: Jack Smith, interview by the author.

21 *"bright and cheerful"*: Ibid.

21 *"I didn't have the faintest"*: Ibid.

22 *"delightful and pretty"*: Jack Smith, interview by Laura Joplin.

22 *"If we ever get married"*: Jack Smith, interview by author.

22 *"I wore that dress"*: Janis Joplin's scrapbook, 1956–59 (Laura Joplin Collection).

22 *"a very capable student"*: Dorothy Robyn, comment from Woodrow Wilson Junior High School report card for Janis Lyn Joplin, 1956–57 (Laura Joplin Collection).

22 *"What a shock!"*: Janis Joplin's scrapbook, May 1957 (Laura Joplin Collection).

23 *"was named one"*: "Library Job Brings Out Teenager's Versatility," *Port Arthur (TX) News*, July 14, 1957.

23 *"because it gives me"*: Ibid.

23 *"Pop had always laughed loudly"*: Joplin, *Love, Janis*, 82.

23 *"used to talk and talk to me"*: Dalton, *Janis*, 54.

23 *"From about the age"*: Chet Flippo, "An Interview with Janis' Father," *Rolling Stone*, November 12, 1970.

CHAPTER 3: THRILL SEEKER

24 *"You shouldn't have to be"*: Janis Joplin to Peter de Blanc, 1965.

24 *"I found out"*: Janis Joplin, "Tell Mama" rap, Toronto, Canada, June 29, 1970.

24 *"I didn't have"*: John Bowers, "Janis: All She Needs Is Love," *The Golden Bowers* (New York: Tower Publications, 1971), 52.

24 *"What you wanted"*: Bowen, interview by Laura Joplin.

25 *"little pig eyes"*: Karleen Bennett, interview by author.

25 *"She didn't like"*: Ibid.

25 *"Janis's waist"*: Ibid.

26 *"an interest in the arts"*: Grant Lyons, interview by Laura Joplin.

26 *"naïve and shy"*: Jim Langdon, interview by author.

26 *"wanted to grow up"*: Ibid.

26 *"self-assured"*: Adrian Haston, interview by Laura Joplin.

26 *"One night Janis and I"*: Jim Langdon, interview by Laura Joplin.

26 *"lives in cars"*: Lyons, interview by Laura Joplin.

26 *"It wasn't your conventional"*: Randy Tennant, interview by Laura Joplin.

27 *"I think that summer"*: Jim Langdon, interview by author.

27 *"Everybody realized Janis"*: Dave Moriaty, interview by Dave Harmon.

27 *"She'd try to make people"*: Lyons, interview by Laura Joplin.

27 *"They read books"*: Bowers, "Janis," 52.

28 *"I remember going up"*: Karleen Bennett, interview by author.

28 *"Dear Mrs. S. W. Joplin"*: Janis Joplin to Dorothy Joplin, card, 1957 (Laura Joplin Collection).

28 *"Mrs. Joplin had"*: Karleen Bennett, interview by author.

29 *"when he got loose"*: Pryor, interview by Laura Joplin.

29 *"Nearly every boy"*: Herman Bennett, interview by author.

29 *"We always wondered"*: Karleen Bennett, interview by author.

29 *"We wanted to make sure"*: Ibid.

29 *"was eager and anxious"*: Ibid.

30 *"Janis and I"*: Ibid.

30 *"one of our favorite"*: Moriaty, interview by Harmon.

31 *"We took a chance"*: Jack Kerouac, *On the Road* (New York: Viking Press, 1957; Penguin Compass paperback ed.), 157–58.

31 *"sordid hipsters"*: Ibid., 54.

31 *"a revelation"*: Karleen Bennett, interview by author.

31 *"That was her first"*: Ibid.

32 *"Don't believe all the nice things"*: Janis Joplin's 1958 high school yearbook, *The Yellow Jacket* (Laura Joplin Collection).

32 *"To a good ole egg"*: Karleen Bennett's 1958 high school yearbook, *The Yellow Jacket*.

32 *"She'd ask, 'Is it annoying' "*: Karleen Bennett, interview by author.

33 *"I remember when she backed"*: Seth Joplin, interview by Laura Joplin.

33 *"She let them off"*: Bowen's diary pages (Laura Joplin Collection).

33 *"'How could you' "*: Joplin, *Love, Janis*, 60.

33 *"In a record store"*: David Dalton, *Piece of My Heart: The Life, Times, and Legend of Janis Joplin* (New York: St. Martin's Press, 1985), 151.

33 *"ox-driver songs"*: Ibid., 152.

33 *"I really dug it"*: Ibid.

34 *"From the very beginning"*: Jim Langdon, interview by author.

34 *"Grant Lyons"*: Ron Benton, "Janis Says Town Has Loosened Up," *Port Arthur (TX) News*, August 16, 1970.

35 *"a true chameleon's"*: Dave Harmon, "Rocker Joplin Sped Through 'Driven' Life," *Austin (TX) American-Statesman*, April 25, 1979.

35 *"It was an overwhelming"*: Lyons, interview by Laura Joplin.

CHAPTER 4: "BEAT WEEDS"

36 *"I would never be young"*: Janis Joplin to Peter de Blanc, 1965.

36 *"There wasn't anybody"*: "Rebirth of the Blues," *Newsweek*, May 26, 1969.

36 *"Everybody was against integration"*: Karleen Bennett, interview by author.

37 *"It just reached a thing"*: Tary Owens, interview by Laura Joplin.

37 *the Ku Klux Klan erected*: Herman Bennett, interview by author.

37 *assaulted African American pedestrians*: Janis, quoted in *Time*, August 9, 1968.

38 *"vistas of choppy water"*: Joplin, *Love, Janis*, 74.

38 *"had all these ideas"*: Dalton, *Piece of My Heart*, 162.

38 *"look at these"*: Ibid.

38 *"harlot"*: Karleen Bennett, interview by author.

38 *"smooch parties"*: Kristin Bennett diaries (Laura Joplin Collection).

38 *"didn't get asked to go"*: Karleen Bennett, interview by author.

38 *"I remember a couple"*: Jim Langdon, interview by author.

38 *"drinking and smoking"*: Karleen Bennett, interview by author.

39 *"It was the first drink"*: Ibid.

39 *"It started out"*: Tary Owens, interview by Dave Harmon.

40 *"a large, barnlike place"*: Jim Langdon, interview by author.

40 *"We opened the door"*: Michael Buffalo Smith, "Talkin' Trash with Jerry LaCroix: An Interview with the Former Lead Singer of Edgar Winter's White Trash," Swampland.com, last modified January 2000, http://swampland.com/articles/view/title:jerry_lacroix.

41 *"necking"*: Owens, interview by Laura Joplin.

41 *"We stayed out"*: Lyons, interview by Laura Joplin.

41 *"My friend and I"*: Ellis Amburn, *Pearl: The Obsessions and Passions of Janis Joplin* (New York: Warner Books, 1992), 19.

42 *"ass grabbing"*: Lyons, interview by Laura Joplin.

42 *"She wasn't sure"*: Karleen Bennett, interview by author.

42 *"she just seemed to want"*: Ibid.

42 *"She was hanging out"*: Pryor, interview by Laura Joplin.

43 *"That's what we talked about"*: Lyons, interview by Laura Joplin.

43 *"Dee Dee" wrote*: all inscriptions are from Janis Joplin's 1959 yearbook, *The Yellow Jacket* (Laura Joplin Collection).

44 *"We'd make a bonfire"*: Adrian Haston, interview by Laura Joplin.

44 *"'I'm drunk!'"*: Michael Joplin, interview by Laura Joplin.

45 *"He said that attending football games"*: Karleen Bennett, interview by Laura Joplin.

45 *"had much less respect"*: Joplin, *Love, Janis*, 82.

45 *"I didn't realize"*: Dorothy Joplin, interview by Laura Joplin.

45 *"the image of everything"*: Owens, interview by Dave Harmon.

45 *"We found a"*: Jimmy Johnson, as told to Ed Hinton, *Turning the Thing Around: My Life in Football* (New York: Hyperion, 1993), 62.

45 *"ran with the beatnik crowd"*: Ed Hinton, "Deep into the Job," *Sports Illustrated*, September 7, 1992.

46 *"Beat Weeds"*: Ibid.

46 *"People said she was loose"*: Patti Skaff, interview by Laura Joplin.

46 *"Am I dressed okay now?"*: Karleen Bennett, interview by author.

46 *"Janis said and did"*: Mrs. Roger Pryor, interview by Laura Joplin.

46 *"I didn't have anyone"*: Benton, "Janis Says."

47 *"They hated her"*: Flippo, "Interview with Janis' Father."

47 *"I remember fights"*: Michael Joplin, interview by Laura Joplin.

47 *"troubles at home"*: Dorothy Joplin, interview by Laura Joplin.

47 *"Mother would try"*: Nat Hentoff, "We Look at Our Parents and . . ." *New York Times*, April 21, 1968.

47 *"Some doctor told"*: Benton, "Janis Says."

48 *"Janis and another girl"*: Jim Langdon, interview by Dave Harmon.

49 *"We stopped"*: Clyde Wade, interview by Laura Joplin.

49 *"I don't know how long"*: Ibid.

49 *"Most of the girls"*: Owens, interview by Dave Harmon.

50 *"All I was looking for"*: Joplin, *Love, Janis*, 83.

CHAPTER 5: "18 AND FUCKED UP"

51 *"I'm one of those"*: Janis Joplin to Peter de Blanc, 1965.

51 *"You didn't escape"*: Alice Echols, *Scars of Sweet Paradise: The Life and Times of Janis Joplin* (New York: Metropolitan Books, 1999), 27.

52 *"I heard this awful"*: Gloria Lloreda Haston, interview by Laura Joplin.

52 *"She was so outspoken"*: Ibid.

52 *"There were a lot"*: Ibid.

52 *"One night"*: Ibid.

52 *"We spent"*: Skaff, interview by Laura Joplin.

53 *"When the monitor"*: Glorida Lloreda Haston, interview by Laura Joplin.

53 *"Janis liked"*: Ibid.

53 *"guy at the counter"*: Ibid.

53 *"I didn't even think"*: Ibid.

53 *"We sort of merged"*: Jim Langdon, interview by author.

54 *"lothario"*: Travis Rivers, interview by author.

54 *"Tommy was a brilliant man"*: Henry Stopher, interview by author.

54 *"With both of them"*: Ibid.

54 *"Wanna see the place"*: Karleen Bennett, interview by author.

54 *"If you're gonna damn"*: Skaff, interview by Laura Joplin.

54 *"We didn't ask"*: Ibid.

55 *"when you get"*: Janis Joplin, "Tell Mama" rap, Toronto, Canada, June 29, 1970.

55 *"not really a woman"*: Janis Joplin to Peter de Blanc, 1965.

55 *"clearly one of us"*; *"out-of-sight"*; *"I always thought"*: Echols, *Scars*, 29.

55 *"She was hurt"*: Skaff, interview by Laura Joplin.

56 *"Jim Langdon rummaged"*: Henry Stopher, interview by author.

56 *"cutting her heart open with a knife"*: Carl Van Vechten, "A Night with Bessie Smith" (originally published in *Vanity Fair*, 1926), in *Martin Scorsese Presents the Blues: A Musical Journey,* ed. Peter Guralnick et al. (New York: Amistad/HarperCollins, 2003), 112.

56 *"started reading books"*: Benton, "Janis Says."

56 *"The first ten years"*: Ibid.

56 *"No one ever hit"*: Chris Albertson, *Bessie* (New Haven, CT: Yale University Press, 2003), 278. Note: though Columbia Records sought publicity surrounding the ceremony presenting the Bessie Smith headstone on August 7, 1970, Janis did not attend because, according to Albertson, "she did not wish to be the center of attention at this event." Albertson recalled her saying, "I know the Columbia guys would want me to be there, but it wouldn't be cool, because people are just going to say that I wanted publicity, or some shit like that." Indeed, Myra Friedman implied as much in her biography *Buried Alive.*

57 *"We'd scrape up money"*: Skaff, interview by Laura Joplin.

58 *"When I was 17"*: Janis Joplin to Peter de Blanc, 1965.

58 *"cutting classes and her conscience"*: Friedman, *Buried Alive*, 27.

58 *"Phil's parents"*: Skaff, interview by Laura Joplin.

59 *"I wanna do what you do!"*: Echols, *Scars*, 30.

59 *"Singing makes you"*: Benton, "Janis Says."

59 *"We'd spend hours"*: Skaff, interview by Laura Joplin.

60 *"Be my white knight!"*: Jack Smith, interview by author.

60 *"Their seething hostility"*: Joplin, *Love, Janis*, 101.

60 *"a wonderful typist"*: Dorothy Joplin, interview by Laura Joplin.

60 *"Since I helped Mildred"*: Ibid.

61 *"smelly"*: Joplin, *Love, Janis*, 92.

61 *"perfect hands"*: Ibid., 93.

62 *"a great deal"*: Dorothy Joplin, interview by Laura Joplin.

62 *"bohemians [who] played new jazz"*: Lawrence Lipton, *The Holy Barbarians* (New York: Julian Messner, 1959), 40.

62 *"Beatsville"*: "Squaresville U.S.A. vs. Beatsville," *Life,* September 21, 1959.

62 *"known throughout the city"*: John Arthur Maynard, *Venice West: The Beat Generation in Southern California* (New Brunswick, NJ: Rutgers University Press, 1991), 147.

63 *"grasshead"*: Janis Joplin to Peter de Blanc, 1965.

63 *"You weren't raised"*: Joplin, *Love, Janis,* 96.

64 *"Barbara always wanted"*: Seth Joplin, interview by Laura Joplin.

64 *"I was hanging out"*: Janis Joplin to Peter de Blanc, 1965.

64 *"sangin'"*: Dave Archer, "Any Port Arthur in a Storm," Dave Archer Studios online, 2002, www.davearcher.com/Joplin.html, accessed August 20, 2017.

64 *"18 and fucked up"*: Janis Joplin to Peter de Blanc, 1965.

65 *"She had on her sheepskin"*: Rae Langdon, interview by Laura Joplin.

65 *"Jim was relentless"*: Stopher, interview by author.

65 *"I'll never forget"*: Seth Joplin, interview by Laura Joplin.

CHAPTER 6: HELL RAISER

66 *"I never seemed"*: Hentoff, "We Look at Our Parents and . . ."

66 *"They wanted a sweet"*: Jim Langdon, interview by author.

67 *"We put cornball"*: Ibid.

67 *"We were getting into"*: Owens, interview by Laura Joplin.

68 *"I'd sneak out"*: Skaff, interview by Laura Joplin.

68 *"Janis just ate them alive"*: Jack Smith, interview by author.

68 *"had no money"* . . . *"so that she could get some sleep"*: Skaff, interview by Laura Joplin.

69 *"Alcohol makes you do"* and *"Does this make me"*: Echols, *Scars*, 34.

69 *"very open about it"*: Jim Langdon, interview by Dave Harmon.

69 *"We were pretty wasted"*: Skaff, interview by Laura Joplin.

69 *"get drunk as a skunk"*: Gloria Haston, interview by Laura Joplin.

69 *"We followed her car"*: Adrian Haston, interview by Laura Joplin.

70 *"When Patti and Janis"*; *"hustled the guys"*; *"I finally drew the line"*: Jim Langdon, interview by author.

70 *"Janis could be adorable"*: Echols, *Scars*, 35.

71 *"We talked and joked"*: John Clay, interview by Dave Harmon.

71 *"We were playing"*: Powell St. John, interview by author.

71 *"command of style"*: Clay, interview by Harmon.

71 *"That night, she invited"*: Powell St. John, interview by author.

71 *"Jack, I think I'm going"*: Jack Smith, interview by author.

CHAPTER 7: WALLER CREEK BOY

72 *"When I sing"*: "The Queen Bees," *Newsweek*, January 15, 1968.

72 *"She told them"*: Jack Smith, interview by author.

72 *"I went to Austin"*: Janis Joplin to Peter de Blanc, 1965.

73 *"Virtually all who entered"*: Ted Klein, interview by Laura Joplin.

73 *"A sad, sad stream"*: Powell St. John, interview by author.

73 *"This nineteen-year-old"*: Powell St. John, Rock & Roll Hall of Fame "American Music Masters" (RRHOF AMM) symposium, November 2009.

74 *"With Janis involved"*: Powell St. John, interview by author.

74 *"I was in a hillbilly band"*: Dalton, *Piece of My Heart*, 95.

74 *"a paranoid personality"*: John Clay, interview by Laura Joplin.

74 *"to some kind of secrecy"*: Bill Killeen, interview by Laura Joplin.

74 *"made love in iambic"*: Stephanie Chernikowski, interview by author.

74 *"Janis's home away"*: Stopher, interview by author.

75 *"It was pretty spontaneous"*: Chernikowski, interview by author.

75 *"Other than her friends"*: Ibid.

75 *"She was so charismatic"*: Ibid.

75 *"Her vocals were just supersharp"*: Powell St. John, interview by author.

76 *"was unnerving"*: Ibid.

76 *"freshman majoring in art"*: Pat Sharpe, "She Dares to Be Different!," *Summer Texan*, July 27, 1962.

77 *"That's the only time"*: Clay, interview by Laura Joplin.

77 *"Janis said negative things"*: Killeen, interview by Laura Joplin.

77 *"She could sing"*: Powell St. John, interview by author.

77 *"I was fascinated"*: Jack Jackson, interview by Laura Joplin.

78 *"couldn't be with a boyfriend"*: Clay, interview by Dave Harmon.

78 *"Janis liked to fuck"*: Echols, *Scars*, 62.

78 *"Her next boyfriend"*: Clay, interview by Dave Harmon.

79 *"She was not like any"*: Killeen, interview by Laura Joplin.

79 *"We were together"*: Ibid.

79 *"she kept getting madder"*: Ibid.

79 *"I remember her"*: Ibid.

79 *"Janis was a pretty good"*: Ibid.

80 *"built like a fullback"*: Echols, *Scars*, 62.

80 *"It was a spontaneous"*: Bill Malone, interview by author.

81 *"a bluegrass band"*: Powell St. John, interview by author.

81 *"I remember the first time"*: Killeen, interview by Laura Joplin.

81 *"It was a very strange"*: Dalton, *Piece of My Heart*, 95.

82 *"in a high, shrill bluegrass"*: Dalton, *Janis*, 133.

82 *"Crowds got so big"*: Malone, interview by author.

83 *"I just took it upon"*: Jackson, interview by Laura Joplin.

83 *"wrote it one night"*: Joplin recorded live at Threadgill's, bootleg recording.

83 *"She exuded this energy"*: Jackson, interview by Laura Joplin.

83 *"because black people"*: Killeen, interview by Laura Joplin.

84 *"Once I went over"*: Powell St. John, interview by author

84 *"It was real hard"*: Killeen, interview by Laura Joplin.

84 *"It was my first joint"*: Powell St. John, interview by author.

85 *"Uppers and downers"*: Ibid.

85 *"I didn't put the make"*: Echols, *Scars*, 61.

85 *"took care of Janis"*: Ibid.

85 *"classic romantic"*: Powell St. John, interview by author.

85 *"I think Janis was priding herself"*: Jackson, interview by Laura Joplin.

86 *"went through men"*: Echols, *Scars*, 62.

86 *"Julie was built"*: John Clay, interview by Dave Harmon.

86 *"I was playing pool"*: Travis Rivers, interview by author.

86 *"She baited the swamp boys"*: Dave Moriaty, interview by Dave Harmon.

87 *"The poor bastard"*: Travis Rivers, interview by author.

87 *"In Lake Charles"*: Brad Buchholz, "Echoes of 1962: When the Threadgill's Faithful Gather for Reunions, the Music Is Familiar and the Memories Are Bittersweet," *Austin American-Statesman*, May 29, 2000.

87 *"I got a phone call"*: Travis Rivers, interview by author.

87 *"Normally, they would elect"*: Ibid.

88 *"She had already been profoundly"*: Powell St. John, in *Janis: Little Girl Blue*, dir. Amy Berg, 2015.

88 *"anguished letter"*: Myra Friedman, *Buried Alive*, 42.

88 *"Finally, I decided Texas"*: Janis Joplin to Peter de Blanc, 1965.

CHAPTER 8: BLUES SINGER

89 *"California . . . you can do"*: *Come Up the Years*, KQED-TV, April 25, 1967.

89 *"I rarely heard Janis"*: Chet Helms, Rock & Roll Hall of Fame "Remembering Janis" symposium (RRHOF RJ), March 7, 1999.

89 *"I couldn't stand Texas"*: Dalton, *Piece of My Heart*, 96.

89 *"beatnik on the road"*; *"knock 'em out"*: Helms, RRHOF RJ.

90 *"Janis started talking"*: Ibid.

91 *"a lot freer"*: *Come Up the Years*.

91 *"A lot of artists"*: Joplin, *Love, Janis*, 146.

91 *"a tough but likable New Yorker"*: Steve Martin, *Born Standing Up: A Comic's Life* (New York: Scribner, 2007), 5–6.

91 *"wilting flowers and chunks"*: John Gilmore, *Laid Bare: A Memoir of Wrecked Lives and the Hollywood Death Trip* (Los Angeles: Amok Books, 1997), 5.

91 *"Janis stood up"*: Helms, RRHOF RJ.

92 *"People later told me"*: Barbara Dane, interview by author.

92 *"looked more like"*: Gilmore, *Laid Bare*, 7.

92 *"sang with a mixture"*: Ibid., 6.

93 *"We were quite close"*: Helms, RRHOF RJ.

93 *"It was the break"*: Larry Hanks, interview by author.

94 *"Janis had heard us"*: Ibid.

94 *"I have to do"*: Ibid.

94 *"The songs are there"*: Gil Turner, "Bob Dylan: A New Voice Singing New Songs," *Sing Out!* 12, no. 4 (October/November 1962).

95 *"The three of us"*: Hanks, interview by author.

95 *"When singing"*: Ibid.

95 *"Nobody was booked"*: Ibid.

95 *"Janis wasn't wearing"*: Peter Albin, interview by author.

95 *"Billy's fingerpicking"*: Hanks, interview by author.

96 *"Afterward, she was either raring"*: Ibid.

96 *"She took a lot of pills"*: John Gilmore, "Janis" (unpublished manuscript, 1992).

96 *"she was up for"*: Hanks, interview by author.

96 *"She did a set"*: Herb Pedersen, interview by author.

96 *"saw her at the Coffee"*: Dalton, *Janis*, 141.

96 *"I had recently arrived"*: Jorma Kaukonen, interview by author.

97 *"Janis was [three years] younger"*: Gabe Meline, "Jorma Kaukonen on Janis Joplin and Recording the 1964 'Typewriter Tape,'" KQED Arts online, May 3, 2016.

97 *"She got up onstage"*: David Nelson, interview by author.

98 *"I never found out"*: Kaukonen, interview by author.

98 *"She wasn't using hard stuff"*: Gilmore, "Janis."

98 *"She could be tough"*: Ibid.

98 *"clicked right away"*: Linda Gottfried Waldron, interview by Laura Joplin.

99 *"a bisexual friend from Little Rock"*: Jae Whitaker, interview by author.

99 *"She thought we wouldn't"*: Ibid.

100 *"She felt that if she"*: Ibid.

100 *"I was Janis's picket fence"*: Ibid.

100 *"I told her, 'I can't support'"*: Ibid.

100 *"She absolutely loved Bessie"*: Ibid.

100 *"She used to thrill me"*: Christopher John Farley, "Bessie Smith: Who Killed the Empress?," *Martin Scorsese Presents the Blues*, 105.

100 *"charged them with joy"*: Chris Albertson, *Bessie*, 6.

101 *"I'd never heard of"*: Whitaker, interview by author.

101 *"speaking for me"*: Mac McDonald, "Times Have a-Changed Since Bob Dylan's '64 Show in Monterey Fairground," *Monterey (CA) Herald*, August 21, 2010.

101 *"Janis goes up"*: Whitaker, interview by author.

CHAPTER 9: METH FREAK AND THE SATURDAY NIGHT SWINDLE

102 *"'Kozmic blues' means"*: Dalton, *Janis*, 53.

102 *"I did really great"*: Janis Joplin to Peter de Blanc, 1965.

103 *"I'd see Janis"*: Jim Fouratt, interview by author.

104 *"She got up and"*: Bob Neuwirth, Country Music Hall of Fame Songwriter Sessions (CMHOF SS), 2016.

104 *"Record people"*: Helms, RRHOF RJ.

105 *"We just fit together"*: Kaukonen, interview by author.

107 *"a stocky, short-haired"*: Echols, *Scars*, 80.

107 *"announced they wanted"*: Ibid.

107 *"Anyone who lived"*: Ed Sanders, *Fug You: An Informal History of the Peace Eye Bookstore, the Fuck You Press, the Fugs and the Counterculture in the Lower East Side* (New York: Da Capo, 2012), 54.

107 *"stifling atmosphere"*: Janis Joplin to Peter de Blanc, 1965.

108 *"In the front bedroom"*: Joplin, *Love, Janis*, 142.

108 *"I love it!"*: Ibid., 141.

108 *"unfortunately the Nugget"*: Janis Joplin to the Joplin family, 1964.

108 *"Thur. 10:30 A.M. SIGH!"*: Ibid.

108 *"She soon lived"*: Archer, "Any Port Arthur in the Storm."

108 *"a tough-looking gal"*: Echols, *Scars*, 84.

109 *"I can't let her up"*: Ibid., 85.

110 *"We walked right into"*: Helms, RRHOF RJ.

110 *"I found Linda"*: Janis Joplin to Peter de Blanc, 1965.

110 *"we thought our creativity"*: Gottfried Waldron, interview by Laura Joplin.

110 *"Janis and Linda"*: Archer, "Any Port Arthur in a Storm."

110 *"how you guys always told"*: Dalton, *Janis*, 54.

110 *"The plan was"*: Archer, "Any Port Arthur in a Storm."

111 *"She was living"*: Seth Joplin, interview by Laura Joplin.

111 *"really intelligent"*: Gottfried Waldron, interview by Laura Joplin.

111 *"It's one of the few things"*: Dalton, *Janis*, 54.

111 *"It struck me like a fucking lightbulb"*: Ibid.

111 *"means no matter what you do"*: Ibid., 53.

112 *"I wanted to smoke dope"*: Ibid., 55.

112 *"twenty-four hours a day"*: Echols, *Scars*, 85.

112 *"Their relationship"*: Gottfried Waldron, interview by Laura Joplin.

112 *"a pretty messed up"*: Pat Nichols, interview by Laura Joplin.

112 *"Anyone caught giving Janis Joplin"*: Archer, "Any Port Arthur in a Storm."

113 *"Peter was this"*: Gottfried Waldron, interview by Laura Joplin.

113 *"He had advanced"*: Ibid.

CHAPTER 10: TEXAS COED

115 *"It's such a quiet"*: Janis Joplin to Peter de Blanc, 1965.

116 *"I hope you get to leave"*: Ibid.

116 *"I so want to be"*: Ibid.

117 *"You could be yourself"*: Echols, *Scars*, 88.

117 *"I've never read"*: Janis Joplin to Peter de Blanc, 1965.

117 *"My mother–Dorothy"*: Ibid.

118 *"She was waiting"*: Skaff, interview by Laura Joplin.

119 *"Strange, it's such"*: Janis Joplin to Peter de Blanc, 1965.

119 *"reading Sir Gawain"*: Ibid.

119 *"He was tall and"*: Joplin, *Love, Janis*, 154.

119 *"He looked at Janis"*: Seth Joplin, interview by Laura Joplin.

119 *"Soon Dad called us"*: Joplin, *Love, Janis*, 154.

120 *"grammer [sic] and sentence construction"*: Peter de Blanc to Seth and Dorothy Joplin, 1965.

120 *"If it's not too late"*: Janis Joplin to Peter de Blanc, 1965.

120 *"My mother was really"*: Ibid., August 21, 1965.

121 *"Mother has told me"*: Ibid.

121 *"Thought that since"*: Ibid.

121 *"Mother is getting worried"*: Ibid.

122 *"the most earnest recorder"*: Ibid.

122 *"Talking to you about"*: Ibid., August 24, 1965.

123 *"orbit . . . without its atmosphere"*: Ibid.

123 *"firms that are hiring"*: Ibid.

123 *"this was sort-of my last"*: Ibid.

124 *"I don't want to wait"*: Ibid.

124 *"taking the liberty"*: Peter de Blanc to Seth Joplin, September 11, 1965.

124 *"all the esoteric"*: Peter de Blanc to Seth Joplin, 1965.

124 *"I guess having depressing"*: Janis Joplin to Peter de Blanc, 1965.

124 *"I hope I look pretty"*: Ibid., September 28, 1965.

125 *"My guitar playing"*: Ibid., October 1965.

125 *"good old-fashioned"*: Ibid. Note: directed by Stanley Kramer and released in October 1965, *Ship of Fools* starred an ensemble cast, including Simone Signoret as a drug-addicted countess, and received several Academy Award nominations.

125 *"The people from the Halfway"*: Ibid.

126 *"been up there about 9 fucking hours"*: Ibid., October 10, 1965.

126 *"attempting to look"*: Ibid., October 14, 1965.

127 *"Sing it all you want"*: Joplin, *Love, Janis*, 163.

127 *"Turtle Blues"*: Copyright Janis Joplin, Strong Arm Music (ASCAP).

127 *"It was really nice"*: Janis Joplin to Peter de Blanc, October 1965.

128 *"Please have your"*: Ibid.

128 *"2 sheets & 2 pillowcases"*: Ibid., October 19, 1965.

128 *"'I want to be straight'"*: Echols, *Scars*, 94.

128 *"It's . . . getting hard"*: Janis Joplin to Peter de Blanc, November 11, 1965.

129 *"girls with pretty voices"*: Echols, *Scars*, 114.

130 *"the best blues singer"*: Jim Langdon, Jim Langdon's Nightbeat, *Austin (TX) Statesman*, November 1965.

130 *"she was very anxious"*: Echols, *Scars*, 114.

130 *"blew them away"*: Ibid.

131 *"encapsulates Janis's feminist"*: Powell St. John, RRHOF RJ.

131 *"She appeared in a very"*: Echols, *Scars*, 113.

132 *"a mixed crowd"*: Jim Langdon, interview by author.

132 *"stole the show"*: Ibid.

132 *"That was the electrifying"*: Powell St. John, interview by author.

133 *"She said she enjoyed"*: Friedman, *Buried Alive*, 60–61.

133 *"seriously contemplating"*: Ibid., 66.

133 *"He was bearing word"*: Ibid., 69.

134 *"I didn't trust Travis"*: Jim Langdon, interview by author.

134 *"Travis . . . is kind of a madman"*: Friedman, *Buried Alive*, 70.

134 *"she hadn't had a good"*: Ibid., 68.

134 *"to go be what I am"*: Echols, *Scars*, 128.

134 *"a really freaky methadrine"*: Friedman, *Buried Alive*, 70.

135 *"I really want to try"*: Ibid.

CHAPTER 11: BIG BROTHER'S CHICK SINGER

136 *"Playing is the 'mostest'"*: *Come Up the Years*.

136 *"The San Francisco music scene"*: Ibid.

137 *"Halfway through New Mexico"*: Dalton, *Piece of My Heart*, 98.

138 *"The big dances"*: Janis Joplin to the Joplin family, 1966.

138 *"[It] completely stoned"*: Ibid.

138 *"with a great deal"*: Ibid., June 6, 1966.

139 *"I just want to tell"*: Ibid.

139 *"It was an organic place"*: Sam Andrew, "Janis Joplin Remembered: Recollections of Janis Seen Through the Eyes of Big Brother's Sam Andrew," www.swampland.com, Summer 2000.

140 *"the strength and power"*: James Gurley, interview by Jas Obrecht.

140 *"When I first met Janis"*: Andrew, "Janis Joplin Remembered."

140 *"I met them all"*: Dalton, *Piece of My Heart*, 99.

140 *"It was as if she"*: Andrew, "Janis Joplin Remembered."

141 *"knocked us out"*: Dave Getz, interview by author.

141 *"At first, she sounded"*: Andrew, "Janis Joplin Remembered."

141 *"She seemed so scared"*: Bowers, "Janis," 64.

141 *"I'd heard it before"*: Dalton, *Piece of My Heart*, 99.

141 *"Janis changed the lyrics"*: Andrew, "Janis Joplin Remembered."

141 *"Still working"*: Janis Joplin to the Joplin family, June 1966.

142 *"a room in a rooming house"*: Ibid.

142 *"something of a recluse"*: Ibid.

143 *"She had a lot of misgivings"*: Dave Getz, interview by author.

143 *"We boys came out"*: Andrew, "Janis Joplin Remembered."

144 *"Nobody had ever heard"*: Dalton, *Piece of My Heart*, 99.

144 *"He played out there"*: Bill Ham, interview by author.

144 *"What a rush"*: Dalton, *Piece of My Heart*, 99.

144 *"was fabulous"*: Helms, RRHOF RJ.

144 *"We started trying to sing"*: Dave Getz, interview by author.

145 *"Suddenly this person"*: Helms, RRHOF RJ.

145 *"I couldn't stay still"*: Michael Lydon, "The Janis Joplin Philosophy—Every Moment She Is What She Feels," *New York Times Magazine*, February 23, 1969.

145 "What are you talking": Peter Albin, interview by author.

145 *"The whole environment"*: Helms, RRHOF RJ.

145 *"There was this sense"*: Dave Getz, interview by author.

145 *"When I sing"*: "Queen Bees," *Newsweek*, January 15, 1968.

145 *"The first time"*: Jack Casady, interview by author.

146 *"We made out"*: Dave Getz, interview by author.

146 *"sweethearts"*: Travis Rivers, interview by author.

146 *"She was very afraid"*: Dave Getz, interview by author.

146 *"She was easily"*: Travis Rivers, interview by author.

146 *"She said, 'I'm about'"*: Ibid.

146 *"two sides"*: Ibid.

147 *"She was a very cute"*: Dave Getz, interview by author.

147 *"really unfamiliar with"*: Ibid.

147 *"Are you really a go-go girl"*: Peter de Blanc to Janis Joplin, June 22, 1966.

147 *"the original earth mother"*: Albin, interview by author.

148 *"didn't dance much"*: Ibid.

148 *"were in love"*: James Gurley, interview by Laura Joplin.

149 *"took a hit and got very"*: Dave Getz, interview by author.

149 *"distrusted psychedelic"*: Sam Andrew, "Janis Joplin Remembered: Recollections of Janis Seen Through the Eyes of Big Brother," Swampland.com, last modified Summer 2000, http://swampland.com/articles/view/title:janis_joplin _remembered.

150 *"She pranced"*: Echols, *Scars*, 134.

150 *"Two of the bands"*: Janis Joplin to the Joplin family, 1966.

150 *"She was a tough woman"*: Andrew, "Janis Joplin Remembered."

151 *"Out in Marin"*: Albin, interview by author.

151 *"At last a tranquil day"*: Janis Joplin to the Joplin family, August 13, 1966.

152 *"A fashion note"*: Ibid.

153 *"I want to get"*: Ibid.

153 *"On many a night"*: Phil Lesh, *Searching for the Sound: My Life with the Grateful Dead* (New York: Little, Brown, 2005).

154 *"Isn't Pigpen cute?"*: Janis Joplin to the Joplin family, 1966.

154 *"Everybody just committed"*: Dave Getz, interview by author.

154 *"Everybody got a sort of high"*: Ibid.

154 *"We were all excited"*: Stefan Grossman, interview (via email) by author.

155 *"Rothchild feels that popular"*: Janis Joplin to the Joplin family, August 22, 1966.

155 *"It was a terrible"*: Albin, interview by author.

155 *"a band is like a"*: Dave Getz, interview by author.

156 *"I put it to her"*: Albin, interview by author.

156 *"I'm hoping . . . the Chicago job"*: Janis Joplin to the Joplin family, August 22, 1966.

156 *"We had to sit down"*: Albin, interview by author.

156 *"I wasn't into this"*: Helms, RRHOF RJ.

CHAPTER 12: "THE IDOL OF MY GENERATION"

157 *"Either we are all going to go"*: Greg Shaw, "Big Brother and the Holding Co.: An Interview with James Gurley, Peter Albin, David Getz, Sam Andrew, and Janis Joplin," *Mojo-Navigator* 1, no. 8 (October 5, 1966).

157 *"Chicago is Blues"*: Janis Joplin to the Joplin family, August 22, 1966.

158 *"We got lots of the 'Is it a boy'"*: Shaw, "Big Brother and the Holding Co."

158 *"They're really nice"*: Janis Joplin to the Joplin family, September 1966.

158 *"the teenagers wouldn't dance"*: Shaw, "Big Brother and the Holding Co."

158 *"They don't get"*: Ibid.

158 *"5 sets a night"*: Janis Joplin to the Joplin family, September 1966.

159 *"They didn't understand"*: Shaw, "Big Brother and the Holding Co."

159 *"As you have so"*: Seth Joplin to Janis Joplin, 1966.

159 *"Daddy brought up"*: Janis Joplin to the Joplin family, September 1966.

160 *"The record thing"*: Ibid.

160 *"She had a great sense"*: Dave Getz, interview by author.

160 *"which Janis sang"*: Ibid.

161 *"was very hip"*: Ibid.

161   *"I had a short haircut"*: Nick Gravenites, interview by Laura Joplin.

162   *"[shook] his head, saying"*: Ben Fong-Torres, "The Saddest Story in the World," *Rolling Stone*, October 29, 1970.

162   *"we're talking to ESP"*: Janis Joplin to the Joplin family, August 1966.

162   *"sort of an underground"*: Ibid.

163   *"They played about three"*: Helms, RRHOF RJ.

163   *"she could keep a commitment"*: Dave Getz, interview by author.

163   *"This real far-out cat"*: "Janis: 1943–1970," *Rolling Stone*, October 29, 1970. Note: Bob Shad's independent label Time recorded a 45, "Leave Her for Me" b/w "So Blue" with Lou Reed's high school band, the Shades, in 1957.

164   *"We were naïve kids"*: Ibid.

164   *"quite an experience"* and *"It took us 9 hrs."*: Janis Joplin to the Joplin family, September 1966.

164   *"The engineer"*: Andrew, "Janis Joplin Remembered."

164   *"First of all, you record"*: Janis Joplin to the Joplin family, September 20, 1966.

165   *"It was exciting"*: Dave Getz, interview by author.

165   *"entourage of very"*: Ibid.

165   *"One hit and you"*: Ibid.

165   *"I'm standing there"*: Shaw, "Big Brother and the Holding Co."

165   *"Lacking the finesse"*: untitled and unbylined newspaper clipping, *Chicago Sun-Times*, September 16, 1966, accessed November 5, 2016, from Sam Andrew's website, Sundays with Sam, http://samandrew.com/big-brother-and-the-holding-company -part-one-1965-1966.

166   *"But what about Sam?"*: Shaw, "Big Brother and the Holding Co."

166   *"They said we weren't"*: Ibid.

166   *"She said it was because"*: Peter Albin, interview by Laura Joplin.

166   *"It was a big sedan"*: Dave Getz, interview by author.

166   *"I almost drove"*: Janis Joplin to the Joplin family, September 20, 1966.

167   *"They warned us"*: Dave Getz, interview by author.

167   *"Wheeee! Now these"*: John Poppy, "Janis Joplin: Big Brother's White Soul," *Look*, September 3, 1968.

167   *"She worked with him"*: Dave Getz, interview by author.

167   *"She had a great time"*: Ibid.

168   *("So groovy!")*: Janis Joplin to the Joplin family, September 20, 1966.

168   *"Nancy Gurley kind of promoted"*: Pat Nichols, interview by Laura Joplin.

168   *"They all got"*: Dave Getz, interview by author.

168   *"It was a nice clean"*: Janis Joplin to the Joplin family, 1966.

169   *"Pretty soon we started"*: Nichols, interview by Laura Joplin.

169   *"an incredibly powerful singer"*: Greg Shaw, "Grateful Dead Exclusive Interview, Part Two," *Mojo-Navigator* 1, no. 5 (September 7, 1966).

170   *"tourists and drunken sailors"*: Shaw, "Big Brother and the Holding Co."

170   *"Everybody took acid"*: Nichols, interview by Laura Joplin.

170   *"thousands of high-loving heads"*: Tom Wolfe, *The Electric Kool-Aid Acid Test* (New York: Bantam, 1999).

170   *"Something's gonna happen"*: Shaw, "Big Brother and the Holding Co."

171   *"we're supposed to get 50"*: Janis Joplin to the Joplin family, October 1966.

171   *"why the 45"*: David Harris, "Blind Man/All Is Loneliness Mainstream 45," *Mojo-Navigator R&R News* 1, no. 10 (November 8, 1966): 13.

171   *"of me looking beautiful"*: Janis Joplin to the Joplin family, October 1966.

172   *"had this habit of throwing people"*: Nick Gravenites, interview by John Glatt.

172 *"Gawd, I feel so delinquent"*: Janis Joplin to the Joplin family, October 1966.

173 *"we all just stumble"*: Ibid.

173 *"radical anarchist group"*: Peter Coyote, *Sleeping Where I Fall* (New York: Counterpoint, 1988), 64.

173 *"Haight becoming a city"*: Sheila Weller, "Suddenly That Summer," *Vanity Fair*, June 14, 2012.

173 *"I was knocked out"*: Peggy Caserta, interview by author.

174 *"People had told me"*: Ed Denson, "The Folk Scene," *Berkeley Barb*, October 1966.

174 *"A white girl from Texas"*: Weller, "Suddenly That Summer."

174 *"She blew me away"*: Maria Muldaur, interview by author.

174 *"This business just isn't"*: Janis Joplin to the Joplin family, November 20, 1966.

CHAPTER 13: "HAIGHT-ASHBURY'S FIRST PINUP"

175 *"Haight-Ashbury's first pinup!"*: Janis Joplin to the Joplin family, April 1967. She also called herself this in a note accompanying the poster when she mailed it to Tary Owens.

175 *"The best of all"*: Rasa Gustaitis, "Janis Joplin," *Los Angeles Times West*, November 24, 1968.

175 *"I'm becoming quite"*: Janis Joplin to the Joplin family, November 20, 1966.

176 *"our crowning achievement"*: Ibid.

176 *"a complete madhouse"*: Ibid.

176 *"You thought you"*: Larry Litt, interview by author.

176 *"Who was that?"*: Peter Albin, interview by author.

176 *"There was a lot of drinking"*: Dave Getz, interview by author.

177 *"this huge noise"*: Ibid.

177 *"to feature me"*: Janis Joplin to the Joplin family, November 20, 1966.

177 *"heard a bit of"*: Ralph Gleason, "On the Town," *San Francisco Chronicle*, 1966 (clipping pasted into Janis's scrapbook, with the date missing).

177 *"People are getting"*: Hendrick Hertzberg, "The Nitty Gritty Sound," *Newsweek*, December 19, 1966.

178 *"all disorganized"*: Janis Joplin to the Joplin family, November 20, 1966.

178 *"So cute!"*: Ibid.

178 *"My car suffered"*: Ibid., December 1966.

178 *"had such a great"*: Jackie Mills, oral history interview by Dan Del Fiorentino, NAMM, 2010.

179 *"I'm a new-breed-swinger"*: Janis Joplin to Barbara Irwin, December 1966.

179 *"a scorecard from"*: Janis Joplin to the Joplin family, January 1967.

180 *"told me she invented her"*: Joe McDonald, RRHOF AMM.

180 *"the most harmonically complex"*: Jonathan Gould, *Otis Redding: An Unfinished Life* (New York: Crown Archetype, 2017), 365.

180 *"She wanted to be Otis"*: Ibid., 372.

180 *"started sighing like"*: Bill Graham and Robert Greenfield, *Bill Graham Presents: My Life Inside Rock and Out* (New York: Doubleday, 1992), 174.

180 *"heavily emotional"*: Gould, *Otis Redding*, 373.

181 *"It was more fascinating"*: Dusty Street, RRHOF AMM.

181 *"You can't get away"*: Hentoff, "We Look at Our Parents and . . ."

182 *"a communal feeling"*: Sam Andrew, RRHOF RJ.

182 *"The Angels pay"*: Coyote, *Sleeping Where I Fall*, 97.

182 *"a mind-boggling sight"*: Charles Perry, *The Haight-Ashbury: A History* (New York: Random House, 1985), 113.

182 *"Played a hippie party"*: Janis Joplin to the Joplin family, January 1967.

182 *"did a whole bunch"*: Ibid.

183 *"stunning country-western"*: Julius Karpen, interview by Laura Joplin.

183 *"Got ourselves a manager"*: Janis Joplin to the Joplin family, February 1967.

184 *"The more we argued"*: Julius Karpen, interview by Joel Selvin.

184 *"So far, moving"*: Janis Joplin to the Joplin family, March 1967.

184 *"I sit around"*: Ibid.

185 *"I was on acid"*: Felton and Glover, "Interview with Country Joe McDonald."

185 *"Things happened fast"*: Ibid.

185 *"I have a boyfriend"*: Janis Joplin to the Joplin family, April 1967.

186 *"fairly negative"*: Ibid.

187 *"Janis had a room"*: McDonald/Sarles interview.

187 *"The girl's voice"*: Scott Holtzman, "Now Sounds," *Houston Chronicle*, March 26, 1967.

187 *"the most dynamic"*: Phil Elwood, *San Francisco Examiner*, March 22, 1967 (clipping pasted into Janis's scrapbook, with the title missing).

188 *"James is quite a romantic"*: Janis Joplin to the Joplin family, March 1967.

188 *"I'm right across"*: Ibid., April 1967.

189 *"A simply amazing thing"*: Ibid.

190 *"playing [music] is the mostest"*: *Come Up the Years*, KQED, April 25, 1967.

190 *"Things are going"*: Janis Joplin to the Joplin family, April 1967.

191 *"they were on a mission"*: Karpen, interview by Laura Joplin.

191 *"They're bringing out"*: Janis Joplin to the Joplin family, April 1967.

192 *"'Summertime' was a"*: Andrew, "Janis Joplin Remembered."

192 *"I played the theme"*: Ibid.

192 *"It was as if molten metal"*: Ibid.

192 *"what Janis could do"*: Ibid.

193 *"could take a scream"*: Tracy McMullen, "Bring It On Home: Robert Plant, Janis Joplin, and the Myth of Origin," *Journal of Popular Music Studies* 26, nos. 2/3 (June–September 2014): 368–96.

193 *"That girl feels like"*: Willie Mae Thornton, interview by Chris Strachwitz.

193 *"When I do a song"*: Ibid.

193 *"seemed to get along"*: Felton and Glover, "Interview with Country Joe McDonald."

194 *"wasn't into political"*: Ibid.

194 *"our careers began to take"*: Ibid.

194 *"Joe dumped"*: Jack Jackson, interview by Laura Joplin.

194 *"She said, 'Before we'"*: Felton and Glover, "Interview with Country Joe McDonald."

195 *"We struck up"*: Mark Braunstein, interview by Joel Selvin.

195 *"She just couldn't"*: Ibid.

196 *"Richard Lester was"*: Dave Getz, interview by author.

196 *"hill country church"*: Andrew, "Janis Joplin Remembered."

197 *"It looked as if Hollywood"*: Ibid.

197 *"We all [got] the"*: Rock Scully and David Dalton, *Living with the Dead: Twenty Years on the Bus with Garcia and the Grateful Dead* (New York: Little, Brown, 1996), 99–100.

198 *"Those were real flower"*: Rasa Gustaitis, "Janis Joplin," *Los Angeles Times West*, November 24, 1968.

198 *"Janis was so nervous"*: John Phillips, *The Complete Monterey Pop Festival*, Criterion Collection DVD, special feature.

199 *"It was as if the earth"*: Joel Selvin, *Monterey Pop*, 37.

199 *"had everybody riveted"*: *The Complete Monterey Pop Festival* DVD, special feature.

199 *"When she came offstage"*: Ibid.

199 *"Do you think"*: Selvin, *Monterey Pop*, 39.

200 *"She came out and sang"*: D. A. Pennebaker, interview by author.

200 *"Wow! Did you"*: Dave Getz, interview by author.

200 *"Should we allow"*: Ibid.

201 *"All these meetings"*: Ibid.

201 *"I was in the front row"*: Richard Goldstein, interview by author.

201 *"The first big hit"*: Robert Christgau, "Monterey," *Esquire*, January 1968.

201 *"In the bright sun"*: Michael Lydon, "Monterey Pops! An International Pop Festival," unpublished; written for *Newsweek*, June 20, 1967.

202 *"Janis had no billing"*: Clive Davis, interview by author.

203 *"When you see"*: D. A. Pennebaker, interview by author.

203 *"Watching her perform"*: *Monterey International Pop Festival* CD box set booklet, Rhino, 1992.

203 *"We were making"*: Ibid.

203 *"I felt her energy"*: Ibid.

203 *"Otis Redding got"*: Ibid.

CHAPTER 14: WOMAN ON THE VERGE

204 *"I just may be a 'star'"*: Janis Joplin to the Joplin family, 1967.

204 *"the real queen"*: Phil Elwood, "Dreams Come True in Monterey," *San Francisco Examiner*, June 19, 1967.

204 *"Congratulations on being"*: Joplins, telegram, to Janis Joplin, June 1967.

205 *"she was serious"*: Robert Gordon, interview by author.

206 *"She was seven"*: Janis Ian, *Society's Child: My Autobiography* (New York: Jeremy P. Tarcher/Penguin, 2008), 67.

206 *"that mark a real"*: Janis Joplin to the Joplin family, 1967.

207 *"The audience went nuts"*: Peter Albin, interview by author.

207 *"neither principal"*: Charles Cross, *Room Full of Mirrors: A Biography of Jimi Hendrix* (New York: Hyperion, 2005), 196.

208 *"You'll just love"*: Janis Joplin to the Joplin family, 1967.

208 *"We were the only"*: Laura Joplin, in *Janis: Little Girl Blue*.

208 *"She was giddy"*: Joplin, *Love, Janis*, 244.

208 *"One minute there"*: Pattie Boyd with Penny Junor, *Wonderful Tonight: George Harrison, Eric Clapton, and Me* (New York: Three Rivers Press, 2008), 104–5.

209 *"George [and] . . . a new kitten"*: Janis Joplin to the Joplin family, 1967.

209 *"It hardly shows"*: Joplin, *Love, Janis*, 245.

209 *"slightly alter your"*: Janis Joplin to the Joplin family, 1967.

209 *"waived the admission"*: Joplin, *Love, Janis*, 245.

210 *"I couldn't imagine"*: Flippo, "Interview with Janis' Father."

210 *"no one would relent"*: Joplin, *Love, Janis*, 246.

210 *"I remember"*: Laura Joplin, in *Janis: Little Girl Blue*.

211 *"unapproachable"*: Linda Gravenites, interview by Laura Joplin.

211 *"She said, 'Oh'"*: Ibid.

211 *"was looking around"*: Ibid.

211 *"she knew exactly"*: Ibid.

212 *"The first thing"*: Peter Laufer, ed., *Highlights of a Lowlife: The Autobiography of Milan Melvin* (Portland, OR: Jorvik Press, 2016), 61.

212 *"Four Capricorn ladies"*: Linda Gravenites, interview by Laura Joplin.

213 *"liked me and S. Clay"*: R. Crumb, interview by Tony Baldwin, *Radio Eye*, ABC Radio National.

213 *"I even made out"*: Ibid.

213 *"jack . . . me around"*: Ibid.

213 *"I called them"*: Nick Gravenites, interview by Laura Joplin.

213 *"He said we needed"*: James Gurley, interview by Laura Joplin.

214 *"deserved to be"*: Peter Albin, interview by Laura Joplin.

214 *"backed out without"*: Pete Johnson, "S.F. Rock Groups in Bowl Show," *Los Angeles Times*, September 15, 1967. Note: fifteen thousand attended the concert, which earned a lukewarm review from Johnson, who primarily targeted faulty microphones and criticized the vocal abilities of both the Grateful Dead and Jefferson Airplane.

214 *"She was scared"*: Ralph Gleason, "Another Candle Blown Out," *Rolling Stone*, October 29, 1970.

214 *"There she was"*: Ibid.

215 *" 'Did you film' "*: Ibid.

215 *"the guts of Ma"*: Larry Kopp, "Janis Joplin, Too Full of Soul for Holding Company Partners," *Los Angeles Free Press*, September 29, 1967.

216 *"look terrible next"*: Julius Karpen, interview by Joel Selvin.

216 *"When I discovered"*: Ibid.

216 *"new world to"*: James Gurley, interview by Laura Joplin.

217 *shot heroin again*: Linda Gravenites, interview by Laura Joplin.

217 *"cute young boys"*: Ibid.

217 *"needed somebody to really lock"*: Graham and Greenfield, *Bill Graham Presents*, 205.

218 *"If you want"*: Linda Gravenites, interview by Laura Joplin.

218 *"no schmeeze"*: Dave Getz, interview by author.

218 *"He was a very"*: Ibid.

220 *"Don't carry their"*: John Byrne Cooke, *On the Road with Janis Joplin* (New York: Berkeley Books, 2014), 79.

220 *"connoisseur, a raconteur"*: Judy Collins, *Trust Your Heart: An Autobiography* (Boston: Houghton Mifflin, 1987), 123.

220 *"I don't care much"*: Cooke, *On the Road*, 99.

220 *"permanently alter"*: Ron Koslow, "Big Brother & the Holding Co.," *KYA Beat*, January 27, 1968.

221 *"flew into the"*: Gloria Haston, interview by Laura Joplin.

221 *"her hair long"*: Leonard Duckett, "Janis Joplin Drawing Acclaim, Blues Singer with Soul," *Port Arthur (TX) News*, December 1967.

222 *"everyone was wearing"*: Ian, *Society's Child*, 67.

222 *"John was totally"*: Dave Getz, interview by author.

222 *"seen much of the"*: Cooke, *On the Road*, 99.

223 *"Far out!"*: Ibid.

223 *"It wasn't the group"*: Dave Getz, interview by author.

CHAPTER 15: "ROCK STAR BORN ON SECOND AVENUE"

224 *"Rock Star Born"*: Robert Shelton, a later edition entitled this article "Janis Joplin Is Climbing Fast in the Heady Rock Firmament: Singer Makes her New York Debut with Big Brother and the Holding Company," *New York Times*, February 19, 1968. (The same article, written by Robert Shelton, was entitled "Rock Star Born on Second Avenue" and that clipping was pasted into Janis's scrapbook: perhaps it was from an earlier edition of the *New York Times*.)

224 *"What we've had"*: Nat Hentoff, "We Look at Our Parents and . . ."

225 *"Erma's an alto"*: Casady, interview by author.

225 *"We 'Big Brotherized' "*: Dave Getz, interview by author.

225 *"screaming tessitura"*: McMullen, "Bring It On Home."

225 *"that drummer"*: Linda Gravenites, interview by Laura Joplin.

225 *"lousy about it"*: Ibid.

226 *"difference in lifestyles"*: Cooke, *On the Road*, 108.

226 *"Columbia was putting"*: Clive Davis and Anthony DeCurtis, *The Soundtrack of My Life* (New York: Simon & Schuster, 2016), 69.

227 *"James suffered"*: Dave Getz, interview by author.

227 *"We're a band"*: Ibid.

227 *"Everybody tried"*: Ibid.

228 *"I couldn't believe it!"*: Echols, *Scars*, 182.

228 *"A quarter of a century!"*: Janis Joplin to the Joplin family, January 31, 1968.

229 *"she is by far"*: Ibid.

229 "Rolling Stone": Ibid.

229 *"honey, just congratulations"*: Ibid., July 1968.

230 *"famous literary type"*: Ibid., February 20, 1968.

230 *"a sloppy group of"*: Echols, *Scars*, 196.

230 *"uptight"*: Janis Joplin to Linda Gravenites, February 1968.

230 *"city . . . made us all"*: Ibid.

230 *"grand, raw, powerful"*: Friedman, *Buried Alive*, 106.

230 *"a somber room"*: Ibid., 101.

231 *"She tore the place"*: Echols, *Scars*, 196.

231 *"What a gorgeous lady"*: Elliott Landy, interview by author.

231 *"about the lack"*: Elliot Mazer, interview by Laura Joplin.

231 *"assaults a song"*: Richard Goldstein, "Pop Music: Ladies Day," *Vogue*, May 1, 1968.

232 *"As fine as the whole"*: Shelton, "Rock Star Born . . ." *New York Times* (from the clipping in Janis's scrapbook).

232 *"ball him"*: Davis and DeCurtis, *Soundtrack*, 70.

233 *"Janis saw how"*: Ibid.

233 *"Look! Our first"*: Janis Joplin to Linda Gravenites, February 20, 1968.

233 *"Too much, eh?"* Janis Joplin to the Joplin family, February 20, 1968.

234 *"When I'm singing"*: Michael Thomas, "Janis Joplin: Voodoo Lady of Rock," *Ramparts*, August 1968.

234 *"singing like"*: Echols, *Scars*, 203.

234 *"a big lecture"*: Joplin, *Love, Janis*, 267.

234 *"so far, at least"*: Janis Joplin to Linda Gravenites, March 6, 1968.

235 *"ragged but right"*: Lester Bangs, "In Concert," *Rolling Stone*, June 8, 1972.

235 *"So very busy"*: Janis Joplin to the Joplin family, March 5, 1968.

235 *"Lots of trouble"*: Janis Joplin to Linda Gravenites, March 6, 1968.

236 *"When Janis started"*: Bob Gruen, interview by author.

236 *"like a fishwife"*: Thomas, "Voodoo Lady."

236 *"a huge garage turned"*: Richard Goldstein, "Next Year in San Francisco," Richard Goldstein online, accessed May 15, 2015, www.richardgoldsteinonline.com /uploads/2/5/3/2/25321994/richardgoldstein-janis.pdf.

237 *"Every time"*: Fred Catero, interview by Dan Del Fiorentino, NAMM.

237 *"James was having the"*: Dave Getz, interview by author.

237 *"She was singing her"*: Echols, *Scars*, 204.

238 *"Janis was a very strong force"*: John Simon, interview by Peter Aaron.

238 *"Things still very"*: Janis Joplin to Linda Gravenites, March 1968.

238 *"Making this record"*: Hentoff, "We Look at Our Parents and . . ."

238 *"She was trying"*: Dave Getz, interview by author.

238 *"the minute we walked"*: Mark Wolf, "Janis Joplin: Queen of Rock, an Intimate Talk," *Downbeat*, November 1968.

239 *"her hair is unkempt"*: Ibid.

239 *"Music is just"*: Ibid.

239 *"Sometimes . . . you're with"*: Richard Avedon and Doon Arbus, *The Sixties* (New York: Random House, 1999).

240 *"Jim bellied his way"*: Danny Fields, interview by author.

240 *"the 3 tracks"*: Janis Joplin to the Joplin family, April 4, 1968.

241 *"I just can't tell"*: Ibid.

241 *"Just bought $115"*: Ibid.

241 *"B. B. King [sat]"*: Cooke, *On the Road*, 145.

242 *"She walked across"*: Andrew, "Janis Joplin Remembered."

242 *"Coming home triumphant"*: Dave Getz, interview by author.

242 *"I couldn't understand"*: Peggy Caserta with Maggie Falcon, *I Ran Into Some Trouble* (Deadwood, OR: Wyatt-McKenzie, 2018), 95.

242 the drug *"would bond"*: Ibid.

243 *"I don't feel quite free"*: Hentoff, "We Look at Our Parents and . . ."

243 *"She said, 'Hey'"*: John Simon, interview by author.

244 *"one of my two"*: Ibid.

245 *"The next day"*: James Riordan and Jerry Prochnicky, *Break on Through: The Life and Death of Jim Morrison* (New York: Quill/William Morrow, 1991), 229.

245 *"What if they find out"*: Linda Gravenites, interview by Laura Joplin.

245 *"I started noticing"*: Peter Albin, interview by author.

245 *"We were much amused"*: Andrew, "Janis Joplin Remembered."

246 *"just helping the band out"*: Al Aronowitz, "Janis Joplin: Singer with a Bordello Voice," *Life*, September 20, 1968.

246 wasn't his *"kind of music"*: Ibid.

246 *"means setting the balances"*: Janis Joplin to the Joplin family, 1968.

246 *"incredibly on top"*: Elliot Mazer, interview by Laura Joplin.

247 *"A lot of editing"*: Dave Getz, interview by author.

247 *"There was no"*: Dave Richards, interview by Joel Selvin.

247 *"resentment ran through"*: Dave Getz, interview by Laura Joplin.

247 *"Had to write"*: Janis Joplin to the Joplin family, July 1968.

249 *"It was a shock"*: Peter Albin, interview by author.

CHAPTER 16: KOZMIC BLUES

250 *"We were in our own"*: Dave Getz, interview by author.

251 *"She wanted our advice"*: Marty Balin, interview by author; Ben Marks, "From Folk to Acid Rock: How Marty Balin Launched the San Francisco Music Scene," *Collectors Weekly*, October 16, 2017.

251 *"Janis was the goddess"*: Mick Fleetwood, interview by author.

251 *"As musicians"*: Ibid.

251 *"It was after a night"*: Peggy Caserta, interview by author.

251 *"I was careful"*: Davis and DeCurtis, *Soundtrack*, 95.

252 *"I'll never be able"*: Friedman, *Buried Alive*, 133.

252 *"The Staple Singers"*: Andrew, "Janis Joplin Remembered."

252 *"He said it was"*: Dave Getz, interview by author.

252 *"We were relieved"*: James Gurley, interview by Jas Obrecht.

252 *"They're my family"*: Al Sorensen, "Janis," *Georgia Straight*, Vancouver, BC, December 6–12, 1968.

253 *"check out the scene"*: Coyote, *Sleeping Where I Fall*, 103.

253 *"Started seeing Emmett"*: Janis Joplin to Linda Gravenites, 1968.

253 *"Emmett and I"*: Coyote, *Sleeping Where I Fall*, 103.

254 *"I want a bigger band"*: Aronowitz, "Singer with a Bordello Voice."

254 *"There's a certain kind"*: interviews by author and Laura Joplin.

254 *"That was the biggest"*: Dave Getz, interview by author.

254 *"feeling a little malicious"*: Peter Albin, interview by author.

254 *"That great singer"*: Robert Shelton, "Rock Fete with Jimi Hendrix Draws 18,000 to Singer Bowl," *New York Times*, August 25, 1968.

255 *"a fair approximation"*: Jon Landau, "Cheap Thrills," *Rolling Stone*, September 14, 1968. (Sony Music released *Sex, Dope & Cheap Thrills*, comprised of the album's outtakes and alternate tracks, in 2018, which received a rave review from David Fricke in *Rolling Stone*.)

256 *"middle-class white"*: William Kloman, "The 50s Come Back," *New York Times*, September 1, 1968.

256 *"Janis Joplin had decided"*: Aronowitz, "Singer with a Bordello Voice."

256 *"my hardest task"*: Janis Joplin to the Joplin family, September 28, 1968.

256 *"Albert called me"*: Skip Prokop, interview by author.

257 *"We did stuff"*: Ibid.

257 *"I hereby tender"*: September 7, 1968 document (Laura Joplin collection).

257 *"A lot of pressure"*: Janis Joplin to the Joplin family, September 28, 1968.

257 *"They had just put"*: Robert Gordon, interview by author.

257 *"I'm already doing"*: Janis Joplin to the Joplin family, September 28, 1968.

258 *"The most fantastic"*: Ibid.

258 *"GOOD NEWS"*: Dorothy Joplin to Janis Joplin, 1968.

259 *"He comes right up"*: Skip Prokop, interview by author.

259 *"We were at"*: Ibid.

260 *"I was crushed"*: Al Sorensen, "Janis," *Georgia Straight*, n.d.

260 *"I'm making"*: Dave Getz, interview by author.

260 *"swearing, moaning, screeching"*: "Janis Rocks Festival," *Daily Pennsylvanian* (University of Pennsylvania, Philadelphia, n.d.).

261 *"something more subtle"*: Al Sorensen, "Janis," *Georgia Straight*, n.d.

261 *"Janis Joplin put"*: Ellen Willis, "Changes," *New Yorker*, March 15, 1969.

261 *"severely disjointed"*: Mike Jahn, "Big Brother and the Holding Company: Hunter College," *New York Times*, November 17,1968. (In the *New York Times* online version, this article is entitled "Janis Joplin and Big Brother Give a Concert at Hunter"; my source is a photocopy of the original article from a Columbia Records clipping file.)

261 *"I couldn't reach"*: Dave Getz, interview by author.

262 *"for her attitude"*: Friedman, *Buried Alive*, 317.

262 *"One went so far"*: Joplin, *Love, Janis*, 289.

263 *"We worried"*: Willis, "Changes."

263 *"posing like an imperious whore"*: Tony Glover, "Bands Dust to Dust," *Rolling Stone*, November 23, 1968.

263 *"I just want"*: Echols, *Scars*, 232.

263 *"I said to her"*: Skip Prokop, interview by author.

263 *"The three of us"*: Bill King, interview by author.

263 *"things started to"*: Ibid.

264 *"chaotic and unproductive"*: Terry Clements, interview by author.

264 *"There she was"*: Ralph Garcia, "Oh, Mama! Janis Joplin in Memphis," *Circus*, 1969.

264 *"all these great"*: Bill King, interview by author.

264 *"those shits at"*: Stanley Booth, "The Memphis Debut," *Rolling Stone*, February 1, 1969.

265 *"looked sort of like"*: Garcia, "Oh, Mama!"

265 *"At least they didn't"*: Booth, "Memphis Debut."

265 *"It was insanity"*: Andrew, "Janis Joplin Remembered."

265 *"might start over"*: Booth, "Memphis Debut."

266 *"She gave me respect"*: Etta James and David Ritz, *Rage to Survive* (New York: Villard Books, 1995), 192.

266 *"I'm scared"*: Lydon, "Janis Joplin Philosophy."

266 *"When I get"*: Ibid.

267 *"strangled the songs"*: Paul Nelson, "Janis: The Judy Garland of Rock & Roll?" *Rolling Stone*, March 15, 1969.

268 *"a brass burlesque"*: Ibid.

268 *"She is pale"*: Bowers, "Janis," 64.

268 *"scrap this band"*: Ralph J. Gleason, "No Opening Night Encores for Janis," *San Francisco Chronicle*, March 24, 1969.

269 *"I had never heard"*: Snooky Flowers, interview by author.

269 *"She opened her hotel"*: Ibid.

269 *"It freaked her"*: Ibid.

269 *"I wanted to look"*: Bowers, "Janis," 58.

270 *"She boasts a façade"*: Brian Connolly, "Janis Joplin," *Melody Maker*, 1969 (my source is a clipping in which the date is missing).

272 *"She was standing"*: Chuck Negron, *Three Dog Nightmare: The Chuck Negron Story*, 4th ed. (self-pub., 2017), 82.

272 *"Everybody was putting"*: Friedman, *Buried Alive*, 164; Brad Campbell, interview by author.

273 *"God! Did she ever"*: Friedman, *Buried Alive*, 169.

274 *"Your services are"*: Andrew, "Janis Joplin Remembered."

275 *"Janis came on"*: Ellen Sander, *Trips: Rock Life in the Sixties* (New York: Charles Scribner's Sons, 1973), 138.

275 *"the rentacops"*: Ibid.

276 *"a blow job"*: Country Joe's Place, accessed March 20, 2016, www.countryjoe.com.

276 *"Janis Joplin danced"*: Sander, *Trips*, 156.

277 *"He took out"*: Bob Neuwirth, RRHOF AMM.

278 *"Did you read"*: Janis Joplin to Linda Gravenites, 1968 (Friedman, *Buried Alive*, 174).

278 *"bent on becoming"*: Ralph J. Gleason, "No Opening Night Encores for Janis."

278 *"Writers rape her"*: Anwen Crawford, "The World Needs Female Rock Critics," *New Yorker*, May 26, 2015.

278 *"was singing stronger"*: Johanna Schier, "Riffs," *Village Voice*, October 2, 1969.

CHAPTER 17: PEARL

280 *"Onstage I make love"*: Dalton, *Janis*, 28.

280 *"I've been looking"*: Janis Joplin to the Joplin family, January 23, 1970.

281 *"real strong and"*: Janis Joplin to Linda Gravenites, 1969.

281 *"Y' know how we discussed"*: Ibid.

282 *"If you wear the mask"*: Bob Neuwirth, interview by Laura Joplin.

282 *"That just shows"*: Friedman, *Buried Alive*, 182.

282 *"a behavior pattern"*: Ibid.

283 *"doing . . . fantastic"*: Janis Joplin to the Joplin family, March and April 1970.

283 *"I managed to pass my"*: Ibid., January 23, 1970.

283 *"Ah, such a funny"*: Ibid.

283 *"I had the kozmic blues"*: Dalton, *Janis*.

284 *"lots of dogs"*: Janis Joplin to the Joplin family, March and April 1970.

284 *"Dogs are better"*: Julie Smith, "What Makes Janis Sing—Ol' Kozmic Blues?," *San Francisco Chronicle*, May 26, 1970.

284 *"felt like Brigitte Bardot"*: Janis Joplin telegram to Friedman.

284 *"because people seem nicer"*: Cooke, *On the Road*, 282.

285 *"she was smart"*: David Niehaus, interview by author.

285 *"We laughed"*: Ibid.

285 *"to put on the first"*: Ibid.

285 *"almost killed her"*: Ibid.

286 *"going into the jungle"*: "Janis Joplin 1943–1970," *Rolling Stone*, October 29, 1970.

286 *"We slept on a beach"*: David Niehaus, interview by author.

287 *"She treated me"*: Ibid.

287 *"They had guns"*: Ibid.

287 *"We'd go out"*: Ibid.

287 *"She said, 'I'll stop'"*: Ibid.

287 *"David really loved"*: Friedman, *Buried Alive*, 194.

288 *"'You meet me'"*: David Niehaus, interview by author.

288 *"difficult to direct"*: Paul Myers, *A Wizard, a True Story*, 40.

288 hot chocolate and tequila: Randy Nauert blog: www.nauert.com, accessed October 18, 2017.

288 *"We got in"*: David Niehaus, interview by author.

289 *"promise of love and family"*: David Niehaus journal as read to the author.

289 *"We were in love"*: David Niehaus, interview by author.

289 *"I met a really fine"*: Janis Joplin to the Joplin family, April 1970.

289 *"There's a man"*: Julie Smith, "What Makes Janis Sing."

290 *"was so much fun"*: Dalton, *Janis*, 50.

290 *"You can't go home"*: Ibid.

291 *"She was incredibly bright"*: Johanna Hall, interview by author.

291 *"pining about this"*: Ibid.

291 *"making faces"*: Ibid.

292 *"Really rushing through"*: Janis Joplin to the Joplin family, April 1970.

292 *"I never seemed"*: Nat Hentoff, "We Look at Our Parents and . . ."

293 *"Linda just got really"*: Johanna Hall, interview by author.

293 *"I'd get up, intending"*: Mikal Gilmore, "Kris Kristofferson: The Complete Monument & Album Collection" CD set booklet, Sony/Legacy, 2016.

294 *"I would always rather"*: Kris Kristofferson, interview by author.

294 *"expressed the double-edged"*: Mikal Gilmore, "Kris Kristofferson."

294 *"That put tattooing"*: Katie Vidan, "Janis Joplin: The First Tattooed Celebrity," Tattoodo online, last modified December 30, 2015, www.tattoodo.com/a/2015/12/janis-joplin-the-first-tattooed-celebrity.

295 *"the guy grabbed"*: Brad Campbell, interview by author.

295 *"started poking him"*: Ibid.

295 *"Last time I saw"*: John Cooke and Paul Rothchild, interview by Laura Joplin.

296 *"Man, I never had"*: Julie Smith, "What Makes Janis Sing."

296 *"She always presented"*: John Till, interviewed for *Final 24*, "Janis Joplin," season 2, episode 3, 2007.

296 *"The minute we went"*: Cooke, *On the Road*, 303.

296 *"The tangible affection"*: David Dalton, "Janis Joplin's Full Tilt Boogie Ride," *Rolling Stone*, August 6, 1970.

297 *"These guys are on"*: Ibid.

297 *"really big talent"*: Ibid.

297 *"was a great band"*: Johanna Hall, interview by author.

298 *"never been so happy"*: Roger Keene, "Janis Joplin's Full Tilt Boogie Band," *Circus*, October 1970.

298 *"she is pure energy"*: Ibid.

299 *"you could get shots"*: Eric Andersen, interview by author.

299 *"all of a sudden"*: Dalton, *Janis*, 81.

300 *"There were so many"*: Buddy Guy with David Ritz, *When I Left Home: My Story* (New York: Da Capo, 2012), 206.

300 *"Janis Joplin sings"*: Echols, *Scars*, 237.

300 *"She kind of picked me"*: Bill Bentley, interview by author.

301 *"Her eyes were bright"*: Paul Rothchild, interview by Laura Joplin.

301 *"Within the first ten"*: Ibid.

301 *"in the church-choir"*: Cooke, *On the Road*, 361.

301 *"What we want"*: Ibid.

302 *"Like the world's greatest"*: Paul Rothchild, interview by Laura Joplin.

302 *"I kicked!!!"* Janis Joplin to David Niehaus, July 24, 1970.

302 *"We want to do this right"*: Joplin, *Love, Janis*, 351.

302 *"All the players were"*: Brad Campbell, interview by author.

303 *"baroquely chromed"*: Seth Morgan, "Janis," *Berkeley Barb*, December 7–20, 1978.

303 *"not in love"*: Ibid.

303 *"an out-of-the-way"*: Ibid.

303 *"If the concert on"*: Mike Jahn, "Janis Joplin and Her New Group Give Rousing Forest Hills Show," *New York Times*, August 4, 1970.

304 *"like a sea shanty"*: Marc Myers, "The Story Behind Janis Joplin's 'Mercedes Benz,'" *Wall Street Journal*, July 7, 2015.

304 *"Janis stomped off"*: Ibid.

304 *"My music ain't supposed to make you"*: Friedman, *Buried Alive*, 318.

305 *"I couldn't convince"*: Echols, *Scars*, 287.

305 *"locals are surprised"*: "Janis Joplin Returns to Port Arthur," *Houston Chronicle*, August 14, 1970.

305 *"I just wanted them"*: Bowers, "Janis," 51.

305 *"My parents treated her pretty cold"*: Michael Joplin, interviewed for *Final 24*, "Janis Joplin," season 2, episode 3, 2007.

307 *"If you're gonna act"*: Friedman, *Buried Alive*, 300.

307 *"The reunion was really when"*: Seth Joplin, interview by Laura Joplin.

307 *"I was a real pessimist"*: Dalton, *Janis*, 24.

308 *"gruesomely schlocky sprawl"*: Morgan, "Janis."

308 *"Paul was very much"*: Bruce Botnick, interview by author.

309 *"being so goddamned drunk"*: Seth Morgan, "The Last Days of Janis Joplin," *Berkeley Barb*, December 21, 1978–January 3, 1979.

309 *"Fun was the underlying"*: Paul Rothchild, interview by Laura Joplin.

309 *"Paul said, 'You'"*: Spooner Oldham, interview by author.

309 *"I took the tape"*: Ibid.

310 *"There but for"*: Friedman, *Buried Alive*, 324.

310 *"She seemed so thrilled"*: Clive Davis, interview by author.

310 *"Janis was the best"*: Marty Balin, interview by author.

310 *"killed two bottles"*: Marks, "From Folk to Acid Rock."

311 *"I started off with"*: Bobby Womack with Robert Ashton, *Bobby Womack: My Story, 1944–2014* (London: John Blake, 2014), 157.

311 *"Jimi Hendrix had"*: Ibid., 158.

311 *"bury her thoughts"*: Ibid., 162.

312 *"wanted to be"*: John Till, interviewed for *Final 24*, "Janis Joplin," season 2, episode 3, 2007.

312 "You'll have to": Morgan, "Last Days of Janis Joplin."

313 *"Come on, Mama!"* David Niehaus to Janis Joplin, August 17, 1970.

314 *"We all believed"*: Brad Campbell, interview by author.

315 *"Janis's death"*: Paul Rothchild, interview by Laura Joplin.

315 *"My entire being"*: David Niehaus, journal entry, read to the author.

315 *"was so sensitive"*: David Niehaus, interview by author.

315 *"the first female superstar"*: "Rebirth of the Blues," *Newsweek*, May 26, 1969.

316 *"I use Janis Joplin"*: Greg Kot, "Old School Gets Some Pop," *Chicago Tribune*, February 28, 2010.

316 *"You give up every constant"*: Dalton, *Janis*, 80.

BIBLIOGRAPHY

Albertson, Chris. *Bessie*. New Haven: Yale University Press, 2003.

Amburn, Ellis. *Pearl: The Obsessions and Passions of Janis Joplin*. New York: Warner Books, 1992.

Avedon, Richard, and Doon Arbus. *The Sixties*. New York: Random House, 1999.

Banks, Steve. *Janis' Garden Party*. Los Angeles: Bugiganga Press, 1998.

Barger, Sonny, with Keith and Kent Zimmerman. *Hell's Angel: The Life and Times of Sonny Barger and the Hells Angels Motorcycle Club*. New York: William Morrow, 2000.

Bookstein, Ezra. *The Smith Tapes: Lost Interviews with Rock Stars & Icons, 1969–1972*. New York. Princeton Architectural Press, 2015.

Bowers, John. *The Golden Bowers*. New York: Tower Publications, 1971.

Boyd, Pattie, with Penny Junor. *Wonderful Tonight: George Harrison, Eric Clapton, and Me*. New York: Three Rivers Press, 2008.

Bragg, Rick. *Jerry Lee Lewis: His Own Story*. New York: HarperCollins, 2014.

Bryant, Keith L., Jr. *Arthur Stilwell: Promoter with a Hunch*. Nashville: Vanderbilt University Press, 1971.

Burrough, Bryan. *The Big Rich: The Rise and Fall of the Greatest Texas Oil Fortunes*. New York: Penguin Press, 2008.

Calhoun, Ada. *St. Marks Is Dead: The Many Lives of America's Hippest Street*. New York: W. W. Norton, 2016.

Caserta, Peggy, as told to Dan Knapp. *Going Down with Janis*. New York: Dell, 1980. First published 1973 by Lyle Stuart.

———, with Maggie Falcon. *I Ran Into Some Trouble*. Deadwood, OR: Wyatt-MacKenzie, 2018.

Christgau, Robert. *Going into the City: Portrait of a Critic as a Young Man*. New York: Dey Street Books, 2014.

Collins, Judy. *Trust Your Heart: An Autobiography*. Boston: Houghton Mifflin, 1987.

Cooke, John Byrne. *On the Road with Janis Joplin*. New York: Berkeley Books, 2014.

———. *Janis Joplin: A Performance Diary 1966–1970*. Petaluma, CA: Acid Test Productions, 1997.

Coolidge, Rita, with Michael Walker. *Delta Lady: A Memoir*. New York: HarperCollins, 2016.

Coyote, Peter. *Sleeping Where I Fall*. New York: Counterpoint, 1988.

Cross, Charles R. *Room Full of Mirrors: A Biography of Jimi Hendrix*. New York: Hyperion, 2005.

D'Allesandro, Jill, and Colleen Terry. *Summer of Love: Art, Fashion and Rock and Roll*. San Francisco: Fine Arts Museums of San Francisco, University of California Press, 2017.

Dalton, David. *Janis*. New York: Simon & Schuster, 1971.

———. *Piece of My Heart: The Life, Times, and Legend of Janis Joplin*. New York: St. Martin's Press, 1985.

Davis, Clive, and Anthony DeCurtis. *The Soundtrack of My Life*. New York: Simon & Schuster, 2016.

DeCurtis, Anthony. *Lou Reed*. New York: Little, Brown, 2017.

DeCurtis, Anthony, and James Henke, with Holly George-Warren, ed. *The Rolling Stone Illustrated History of Rock & Roll*, new ed. New York: Random House, 1992.

Diehl, Gaston. *Modigliani*. New York: Crown, 1969.

Douglas, Susan J. *Where the Girls Are: Growing Up Female with Mass Media*. New York: Three Rivers Press, 1994.

Downing, Michael. *Shoes Outside the Door: Desire, Devotion, and Excess at San Francisco Zen Center*, New York: Counterpoint, 2001.

Drummond, Paul. *Eye Mind: The Saga of Roky Erickson and the 13th Floor Elevators, the Pioneers of Psychedelic Sound*. Los Angeles: Process, 2007.

Echols, Alice. *Scars of Sweet Paradise: The Life and Times of Janis Joplin*. New York: Metropolitan Books, 1999.

Egan, Timothy. *The Worst Hard Time: The Untold Story of Those Who Survived the Great American Dust Bowl*. Boston: Houghton Mifflin, 2006.

Fleetwood, Mick, and Anthony Bozza. *Play On: Now, Then and Fleetwood Mac*. New York: Little, Brown, 2014.

Fong-Torres, Ben. *Becoming Almost Famous: My Back Pages in Music, Writing, and Life*. San Francisco: Backbeat Books, 2006.

———. *Not Fade Away: A Backstage Pass to 20 Years of Rock & Roll*. San Francisco: Miller Freedman Books, 1999.

Friedman, Myra. *Buried Alive: The Biography of Janis Joplin*. William Morrow, 1973.

George-Warren, Holly, ed. *The Rock and Roll Hall of Fame: The First 25 Years*. New York: Collins Design/HarperCollins, 2009.

Gilmore, John. *Laid Bare: A Memoir of Wrecked Lives and the Hollywood Death Trip*. Los Angeles: Amok Books, 1997.

Glatt, John. *Live at the Fillmore East & West: Getting Backstage and Personal with Rock's Greatest Legends*. Guilford, CT: Lyons Press, 2015.

———. *Rage & Roll: Bill Graham and the Selling of Rock*. New York: Carol, 1993.

Goldberg, Danny. *In Search of the Lost Chord: 1967 and the Hippie Idea*. Brooklyn: Akashic, 2017.

Goldstein, Richard. *Another Little Piece of My Heart: My Life of Rock and Revolution in the '60s*. New York: Bloomsbury, 2015.

Goodman, Fred. *Mansion on the Hill*. New York: Times Books, 1997.

Gould, Jonathan. *Otis Redding: An Unfinished Life*. New York: Crown Archetype, 2017.

Graham, Bill, and Robert Greenfield. *Bill Graham Presents: My Life Inside Rock and Out*. New York: Doubleday, 1992.

Greenfield, Robert. *Bear: The Life and Times of Augustus Owsley Stanley III*. New York: Thomas Dunn Books, 2016.

Guralnick, Peter, Robert Santelli, Holly George-Warren, and Christopher John Farley, eds. *Martin Scorsese Presents the Blues: A Musical Journey*. New York: Amistad/HarperCollins, 2003.

Guy, Buddy, with David Ritz. *When I Left Home: My Story*. New York: Da Capo, 2012.

Helm, Levon, with Stephen Davis. *This Wheel's on Fire: Levon Helm and the Story of the Band*. Chicago: Chicago Review Press, 2000. First published 1993 by William Morrow (New York).

Hochschild, Adam. *Spain in Our Hearts: Americans in the Spanish Civil War, 1936–1939*. Boston: Houghton Mifflin Harcourt, 2016.

Holiday, Billie, with William Duffy. *Lady Sings the Blues*. New York: Doubleday, 1956.

Hoskyns, Barney. *Small Town Talk: Bob Dylan, the Band, Van Morrison, Janis Joplin, Jimi Hendrix, and Friends in the Wild Years of Woodstock*. New York: Da Capo, 2016.

Hynde, Chrissie. *Reckless: My Life as a Pretender*. New York: Doubleday, 2015.

Ian, Janis. *Society's Child: My Autobiography*. New York: Jeremy P. Tarcher/Penguin, 2008.

James, Etta, and David Ritz. *Rage to Survive*. New York: Villard Books, 1995.

Johnson, Jimmy, as told to Ed Hinton. *Turning the Thing Around: My Life in Football*. New York: Hyperion, 1993.

Joplin, Laura. *Love, Janis*. New York: Harper, 2005. First published 1992 by Villard Books (New York).

Kaukonen, Jorma. *Been So Long: My Life and Music*. New York: St. Martin's Press, 2018.

Kerouac, Jack. *On the Road*. New York: Viking Press, 1957 (Penguin Compass paperback edition).

Knight, Tim. *Poor Hobo: The Tragic Life of Harry Choates, a Cajun Legend*. Port Arthur, TX: Port Arthur Historical Society, 2013.

———. *Chantilly Lace: The Life & Times of J. P. Richardson*. Port Arthur, TX: Port Arthur Historical Society, 1989.

Kruth, John: *To Live's to Fly: The Ballad of the Late, Great Townes Van Zandt*. New York: Da Capo, 2007.

Landau, Deborah. *Janis Joplin: Her Life and Times*. New York: Coronet Communications, 1971.

Laufer, Peter, ed. *Highlights of a Lowlife: The Autobiography of Milan Melvin*. Portland, OR: Jorvik Press, 2016.

Lesh, Phil. *Searching for the Sound: My Life with the Grateful Dead*. New York: Little, Brown, 2005.

Lipton, Lawrence. *The Holy Barbarians*. New York: Grove Press, 1959.

Lydon, Michael. *Rock Folk: Portraits from the Rock 'n' Roll Pantheon*. New York: Citadel Underground, 1990.

Martin, Steve. *Born Standing Up: A Comic's Life*. New York: Scribner, 2007.

Maynard, John Arthur. *Venice West: The Beat Generation in Southern California*. New Brunswick, NJ: Rutgers University Press, 1991.

McNally, Dennis. *A Long, Strange Trip: The Inside History of the Grateful Dead*. New York: Three Rivers Press, 2002.

Metalious, Grace. *Peyton Place*. New York: Dell, 1958.

Modigliani, Jeanne. *Modigliani: Man & Myth*. New York: Orion Press, 1958.

Modigliani: Paintings & Drawings. The Committee on Fine Arts Productions; Museum of Fine Arts, Boston; Los Angeles County Museum, 1961.

Modigliani: Paintings, Drawing, Sculpture. New York: Museum of Modern Art, 1951.

Mouton, Todd. *Way Down in Louisiana: Clifton Chenier, Cajun, Zydeco, and Swamp Pop Music*. Lafayette: University of Louisiana Press, 2015.

Myers, Paul. *A Wizard, a True Story: Todd Rundgren in the Studio*. London: Jawbone Press, 2010.

Negron, Chuck. *Three Dog Nightmare: The Chuck Negron Story*. 4th ed. Self-published, 2017.

Obrecht, Jas. *Talking Guitar*. Chapel Hill: University of North Carolina Press, 2017.

Perry, Charles. *The Haight-Ashbury: A History*. New York: Random House, 1985; Wenner Books, 2005 (paperback).

Porterfield, Nolan. *Last Cavalier: The Life & Times of John Lomax*. Urbana/Chicago: University of Illinois Press, 1996.

Powers, Ann. *Good Booty: Love and Sex, Black & White, Body and Soul in American Music.* New York: Dey Street, 2017.

Reid, Jan, with Shawn Sahm. *Texas Tornado: The Times and Music of Doug Sahm.* Austin: University of Texas Press, 2010.

Reynolds, Frank, and Michael McClure. *Freewheelin Frank: Secretary of the Angels as Told to Michael McClure.* New York: Grove Press, 1967.

Riordan, James, and Jerry Prochnicky. *Break on Through: The Life and Death of Jim Morrison.* New York: Quill/William Morrow, 1991.

Ritz, David. *Respect: The Life of Aretha Franklin.* New York: Little, Brown, 2014.

Rothschild, Amalie R., with Ruth Ellen Gruber. *Live at the Fillmore East: A Photographic Memoir.* New York: Thunder's Mouth Press, 1999.

Sander, Ellen. *Trips: Rock Life in the Sixties.* New York: Charles Scribner's Sons, 1973.

Sanders, Ed. *Fug You: An Informal History of the Peace Eye Bookstore, the Fuck You Press, the Fugs and the Counterculture in the Lower East Side.* New York: Da Capo, 2012.

Saviano, Tamara. *Without Getting Killed or Caught: The Life and Music of Guy Clark.* College Station: Texas A&M University Press, 2016.

Scully, Rock, with David Dalton. *Living with the Dead: Twenty Years on the Bus with Garcia and the Grateful Dead.* New York: Little, Brown, 1996.

Selvin, Joel. *Altamont: The Rolling Stones, the Hells Angels, and the Inside Story of Rock's Darkest Day.* New York: Dey St./HarperCollins, 2016.

———. *Monterey Pop.* San Francisco: Chronicle Books, 1992.

———. *San Francisco: The Musical History Tour.* San Francisco: Chronicle Books, 1996.

———. *The Summer of Love,* New York: Dutton, 1994.

Shaw, Suzy, and Mick Farren. *Bomp! Saving the World One Record at a Time.* San Francisco: AMMO Books, 2007.

Simmons, Sylvie. *I'm Your Man: The Life of Leonard Cohen.* New York: HarperCollins, 2015.

Slick, Grace, with Andrea Cagan. *Somebody to Love? A Rock-and-Roll Memoir.* New York: Warner Books, 1998.

Smith, Patti. *Just Kids.* New York: Ecco, 2014.

Sporke, Michael. *Big Brother and the Holding Company: Living with the Myth of Janis Joplin 1965–2005.* 1st ed., 2003. Norderstedt, Germany: Books on Demand GmbH, 2005.

Stanley, Rhoney Gissen, with Tom Davis. *Owsley and Me: My LSD Family.* Rhinebeck, NY: Monkfish Book, 2016.

Sullivan, Mary Lou. *Raisin' Cain: The Wild & Raucous Story of Johnny Winter.* New York: Backbeat Books, 2010.

Talbot, David. *Season of the Witch.* New York: Free Press, 2012.

Vorda, Allan. *Psychedelic Psounds: Interviews from A to Z with 60s Psychedelic Garage Bands.* Wolverhampton, UK: Borderline Productions, 1994.

Wilson, Eddie. *Threadgill's: The Cookbook, The Austin, Texas, Landmark of Southern Comfort Food.* Atlanta: Longstreet Press, 1996.

———, with Jesse Sublett. *Armadillo World Headquarters: A Memoir.* Austin, TX: TSSI, 2017.

Wolfe, Charles, and Kip Lornell. *The Life and Legend of Leadbelly.* HarperCollins, 1992.

Wolfe, Tom. *The Electric Kool-Aid Acid Test.* New York: Bantam, 1999.

Wolman, Baron. *Janis Joplin.* New York: Waverly Press, 2013.

Womack, Bobby, with Robert Ashton. *Bobby Womack: My Story, 1944–2014.* London: John Blake, 2014.

INDEX

LYRICS CREDITS